THE GREAT WESTERN RAILWAY
IN THE FIRST WORLD WAR

SANDRA GITTINS

The
History
Press

First published 2010

The History Press
The Mill, Brimscombe Port
Stroud, Gloucestershire, GL5 2QG
www.thehistorypress.co.uk

British Library Cataloguing in Publication Data.
A catalogue record for this book is available from the British Library.

ISBN 978 0 7524 5632 4

Typesetting and origination by The History Press
Printed in Great Britain
Manufacturing managed by Jellyfish Print Solutions Ltd

CONTENTS

INTRODUCTION

Not since Edwin Pratt's *War Record of the Great Western Railway*, published in 1922, has a history of the GWR been published that is completely dedicated to the work of the company and its employees during the First World War. But as interest in this war has never been higher, and as this year marks the 175th anniversary of the GWR, it seemed a fitting time to revisit the war years of 1914–18 and pay tribute to the GWR during this challenging period of its history.

It has been fascinating researching the GWR during those frantic years of activity under constant pressure to complete work for the Government, as well as deal with increased traffic, and expect to maintain its own infrastructure and stock with a lack of materials and manpower. With nearly a third of the manpower serving in the forces, including three GWR railway construction companies that were raised for the Royal Engineers, it would have been wrong not to include a short history of the military exploits of the GWR employees. Unfortunately, some of these men paid the ultimate price. For the first time a researched Roll of Honour of 2,543 GWR men is published. It has been compiled from names on the GWR Roll of Honour displayed at stations and entries from the *GWR Magazine* from 1914–21. Every conceivable database has been used to make this Roll as complete and precise as possible, but as mistakes were made when official records were drawn up, it is inevitable that some will appear here. Photos of around 80 per cent of the men are available, and were used to confirm rank, regiment etc. from badges shown, and anyone wishing to trace a name on the Roll of Honour can make a request for further information by email to: GWR1418@consultant.com

ACKNOWLEDGEMENTS

I would like to thank First Great Western for giving permission to reproduce photos from the *GWR Magazine*, also the National Archives and Commonwealth War Graves Commission for their first-rate online services. I would also like to thank Tim Bryan, John Ellis, Ken Surman (GWT), Pat Spearey, Mark Sutton, Keith Jones, John Pitman and all those who I have been in contact with, who have given information, help and encouragement which has been much appreciated. Lastly I would like to praise the excellent Railways Studies Collection at Newton Abbot Library. I have spent many a happy hour researching there, and I would like to thank Sherryl Healey, Librarian, for all her help.

CHAPTER ONE

Outbreak of War – Security of the Line – Departure of Austrian Ambassador – GWR Baths at Faringdon Street – Belgian Refugees – Horses – Enlistment of Men – Railway Service Badge – War Bonus Pay – Women and the GWR – Pensioners at Work – Safety

Outbreak of War

The First World War was one of the most important, and often overlooked, periods in the history of the Great Western Railway, and as the black clouds of war gathered in the summer of 1914 no one in the company had any idea how long the war would last, or what the consequences would be.

Before detailing the work of the GWR and its employees, a brief summary of the events and situation in Europe follows to give a better understanding as to why war broke out.

Gavrilo Princip, a student and Slav nationalist who was wrongly thought to be working for the Serbian government, assassinated the heir to the Austrian throne and his wife in Sarajevo on 28 June 1914; an act that was the catalyst which ended forty years of peace in Europe. The peace came about by the establishment of two blocs in Europe: the Triple Alliance of Germany, Austria-Hungary (the Central Powers) and Italy, and the Triple Entente of France, Russia and Britain. The two blocs maintained a balance of power, with each country within its bloc pledging to support the others in the event of war. There had been campaigns and crises, mostly in Africa and the Balkans, but nothing had happened to cause an outright war; so why did it happen? It was down to the state of the countries and the timing.

- Germany: militarily, commercially and industrially very strong; a major world power with a sense of destiny, but felt encircled.
- Austria-Hungary: this old empire had problems with pro-Russian factions within the empire. Had plans to dominate the Balkans but would have to crush the Slavs and Serbia, who wanted to acquire an Adriatic port.
- Italy: an ally of Germany and Austria-Hungary, but was deeply suspicious of the latter's designs on the Balkans as she was a rival for domination of the Adriatic. Had no desire for naval battles with France and Britain in the Mediterranean. Would eventually declare war on Germany.
- Turkey: although not a member of the Triple Alliance, was very pro-German, and with their help Turkey hoped to improve her influence in the Balkans, as well as gain territory in Russia.
- France: had tried to maintain a military counter-force to Germany, but knew that there was insufficient manpower in the country for a prolonged war, but possessed excellent artillery. France also knew she would be the target for her old enemy Germany and was determined not to lose land as she had done during the Franco-Prussian War of 1871; on the contrary, she wanted to find a way to win that land back.

- Russia: manpower was not a problem, but was weak in other military areas, and was expected to be slow to mobilise. Had lost to Japan in 1904 and crushed a revolution. Was wary of Austrian designs on the Balkans and supported the Slavs. Germany wanted to expand into Russia.
- Britain: although there was a treaty with Belgium to safeguard her neutrality, which Germany was convinced would not be honoured, the threat of the invasion of Belgium by Germany was not this country's main concern; the growth of the German navy was. The British Navy was still a dominant force, and if Germany was able to be a threat in the seas around Britain, this country's lifeline for food and materials would be severed. Britain's professional army was bolstered by the Territorials, with no conscription to enforce a growth in the forces. Germany considered this to be a weak point, especially as it was thought that the British Army was preoccupied with interests in India and the near civil war in Ireland.

Most did not want a war for they knew the devastation it would cause, but Germany had been making plans for some time. The Schlieffen Plan, drawn up in response to France and Russia's alliance (1892), was amended many times before the war, and was the blueprint for the rapid takeover of France as far west as Paris before concentrating on the Russians, as Germany knew it could not afford to fight a war on two fronts. Germany's railway infrastructure was also improved, in most cases beyond that needed for ordinary traffic, radiating out to the borders of Holland and Russia. Lines were also constructed through Luxembourg and Belgium, and ironically the Belgians helped in the construction; unfortunately they were unaware of the future use for these lines.

France had also embarked on a programme of railway modification, which included a designated army zone, where everything was available such as stations for mobilisation, hospitals, distribution depots, railheads etc., all designed to ensure that there was not a repeat performance of the disastrous Franco-German war. France was prepared for what she thought was inevitable.

The power in Europe appeared to be no longer in balance, and for Germany and Austria it was a case of now or never. Austria sent an ultimatum to Serbia, and requested that Germany guarantee their support, which they did. One by one the countries mobilised their troops, and although there had been attempts to mediate, there came a point when nothing could be done to stop it; the British fleet was put at a state of readiness. The German army invaded the neutral countries of Luxembourg and Belgium using the railways conveniently constructed before and, against German expectations, Britain declared war.

Troops at Swindon were mobilised by a pre-arranged signal of ten blasts of the Great Western Railway Works' hooter at 7.49 p.m. on 4 August 1914; the war had begun. On the following morning the Government took over the control of the railways under Clause 16 of the Regulations of the Forces Act 1871, whereby it was considered advantageous for them to do so for the welfare of the country in a state of emergency.

The efficient running of the railways was the main task of the Railway Executive Committee, originally formed in 1912, and comprised of general managers from all of the existing Railway Companies, with Frank Potter representing the Great Western Railway, and was to provide inter-company relationships under the guidance of the chairman, the President of the Board of Trade and the General Manager of the London and South Western Railway, who was appointed as acting chairman. To maintain elaborate accounts and exact running details of each company was, in itself, considered inefficient, time consuming and almost impossible. The committee put forward a proposal to the Government suggesting that compensation be allocated by aggregate, corresponding to the previous year's returns. Therefore those companies whose lines were used heavily for military and transportation traffic, as well as transference of rolling stock on a loan basis to other companies, would be compensated more greatly than those companies unable to

GREAT WESTERN RAILWAY.

GENERAL MANAGER'S OFFICE,

PADDINGTON STATION,

(CIRCULAR No. 2386.)

LONDON, W.

5th August, 1914.

The Government have, for the time being, taken over the control of the Railway in connection with the Mobilization of the Troops and General Movements in relation to Naval and Military requirements.

The Management of the Railway and the existing conditions of employment of the Staff will remain unaltered, and all instructions will be issued through the same channels as heretofore.

FRANK POTTER,

General Manager.

Message to GWR staff, September 1914. (*GWR Magazine*)

contribute to demands due to their size. The reason for this control was to ensure that the military had available the necessary resources for the transportation of troops, supplies and weapons whenever they were needed. The general public was informed of the necessity for the cancellation or amendments to the services on offer to them.

The importance of the railways at this time cannot be stressed enough. During the Second World War it was possible to use both railways and roads for military transportation on a grand scale, but the latter means of transport, although constantly improving, was still very much in its infancy, and at the outbreak of the First World War the railways were the most direct and efficient means available.

When war was threatened prior to 4 August all previously arranged plans, as laid down in the War Book of 1911, were put into action, and by 17 August 70,000 men of the British Expeditionary Force had been transported by rail. Not only were troops transported to the ports of embarkation, but thousands of personnel were sent to numerous training grounds around the country, especially the camps on Salisbury Plain.

Australians landed at Plymouth, December 1914. (*GWR Magazine*)

Mobilisation of naval Reservists at St Ives, August 1914. (*GWR Magazine*)

Throughout the day and night every conceivable item required by the fighting forces was transported by rail, which was complicated by the sheer bulk of delivering items such as motor vehicles, ambulances and thousands of horses, as well as the danger of conveying ammunition. Rolling stock was obviously in great demand and companies, including the GWR, assisted other companies by loaning any rolling stock required that was not already in use.

In order to carry out the efficient mobilisation of the troops on those first days of August it was necessary to cancel the transportation by rail of Territorials to their summer training camps. Instructions were sent out at 1.45 p.m. two days before war was declared to stop the movement of the Territorials, and to return them to their base stations which, for the GWR, involved the running of 186 special trains.

Contrary to expectations, disruptions in those early days were few and the public inconvenienced little, to such an extent that the *Daily Mail* was full of praise and admiration for the organisation, smooth running and patriotism of the Railway Companies and their employees. They stated that it was probably only those who lived near a railway that would be aware of the work of the 'sleepless organisation'.

During the first fifteen days of the war 632 special trains had run over the Great Western system, plus forty-one trains carrying coal for the Admiralty and 149 transporting petrol, oil and various stores. By 5 October the number of military and naval trains run by the company had risen to 2,470. Up until 30 September 10,227 officers, 366,560 men, 3,101 horses, 355 guns and limbers, as well as wagons, cycles, etc. had been dispatched from GWR stations. It must have been a formidable sight, one which is hard to imagine, especially when these figures do not include trains running over Great Western lines from other systems.

The day service from Paddington to Rosslare was cancelled on 8 August, but sailings to the Channel Islands on SS *Ibex* and *Roebuck* remained, and excursion trains were suspended, but on the whole services to the public were not affected except for where large numbers of troops were being moved from key areas such as Oxford, Basingstoke, Swindon, Bristol and Plymouth. Heavy military operations occurred on 17 August at Swindon which called for the diversion of some trains from Paddington to South Wales and the West Country.

It was a logistical nightmare running so many different trains, and prioritisation came to the fore. While military movements were carried out some goods trains had to be held back, except those carrying foodstuffs and perishables. It was found impossible for certain stations to cater for the increase in travellers and, at the expense of the War Office, temporary platforms and toilets were installed at key points such as Hereford, Reading and Park Royal. At Swindon the addition of platforms, toilets and available water cost £2,700. These were the first of many building works to be carried out by the GWR on behalf of the Government during the war.

The 'Golden Age' of the Great Western Railway was over, and a new period in the history of the company was beginning.

Security of the Line

The War Office instructed that as from 30 July 1914 the line from London to Avonmouth was to be patrolled by platelayers who had to pay special attention to bridges and tunnels, with the area under guard extended to include South Wales.

From 15 August this task was undertaken by the military, who were also to protect the Severn, Bincombe and Dorchester tunnels, and Saltash Bridge. The soldiers, unfamiliar with the workings of a railway, were instructed as to where to stand safely, but fourteen men were killed

The Antartic expedition, with Sir Ernest Shakleton, sailed into the GWR Docks at Plymouth on 5 August 1914. The *Endurance* berthed at the GWR Dock pontoon as there were no berths available at Devonport due to war activity. (*GWR Magazine*)

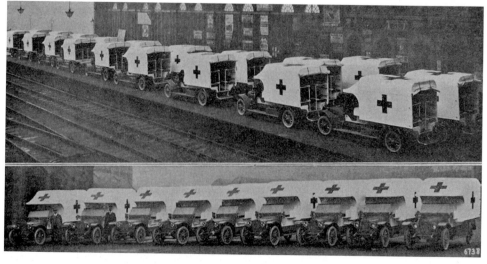

The King was presented with a Christmas gift of sixty vehicles from the Maharajah Scindia of Gwalior in 1914. Forty-five of the vehicles were built at the Sunbeam Motor Company at Wolverhampton, and were transported to London by three special trains. (*GWR Magazine*)

W.J. Nurden. (*GWR Magazine*)

by passing trains and two shot, it was recorded, 'inadvertently' by sentries. The Paddington to Bristol line was guarded by the 1/4th Battalion, the Loyal North Lancashire Regiment, who arrived at Swindon on 22 August and remained until November.

The security of the London to Avonmouth and the South Wales lines were put under the directorship of Brigadier-General Grove in October 1914, and he placed men of the National Reserve to guard the line rather than the Territorial Army, who were required elsewhere. Permanent waymen kept watch over important and vulnerable structures not being guarded by the military.

The guarding of the lines in Wiltshire was taken over by No.1 Company, Swindon Battalion, Wilts National Reserve. These men were mainly over the age for serving abroad but volunteered to carry out essential tasks at home. Unfortunately, on 11 December 1914, Lance Corporal Nurden, a striker in the Locomotive Department, was crossing the line at Newton Toney to relieve a sick comrade when he was killed by a passing train.

The Railway Executive Committee was to nominate a railway officer to be attached to the staff of the Brigadier-General to liaise between the railways and military authorities. The committee appointed GWR Chief Engineer W.W. Grierson, and he held this position until the end of the war.

The number of men guarding the railways reduced as the war progressed, as the men were needed elsewhere.

Departure of the Austrian Ambassador

The Foreign Office requisitioned a special train for returning the Ambassador of Austro-Hungary, Count Albert Mensdorff, to his home country. The train left Paddington at midnight on 16 August 1914 for Newton Abbot, and comprised:

Surgeon Major G. Rodway Swinhoe.
(*GWR Magazine*)

1 'Ocean' Van	|	
1 'Cunard' First	|	- First (Divided) portion from
3 Sleeping cars	|	- Newton Abbot
1 Brake First	|	
3 Firsts	|	
2 Thirds	|	- Second portion
1 Van Third	|	

Locomotive: *Princess Mary*

The first portion reached Falmouth at 6 a.m., and the second a quarter of an hour later to help ease the congestion at Falmouth due to the number of cars and buses needed to transport the passengers, numbering nearly sixty embassy staff and 200 Austrian refugees (together with luggage etc.), to the docks where they boarded the liner *Aaro*.

A letter from a member of the passengers was published in *The Times* on 9 September regretting the fact that they had to leave England, but praised the GWR for a safe and courteous passage.

GWR Baths, Faringdon Street

On 2 October 1914 the War Office made a request for a 100-bed hospital to be established in Swindon. The Red Cross supplied the staff and equipment, and rented the baths at Faringdon Street from the GWR Medical Fund at a cost of £12 per week, paid by the War Office. Major Swinhoe, chief of the company's medical staff, assisted in the organisation of the hospital, and the GWR helped by supplying pillows, blankets, springs for mattresses and much more. By the end of the month the hospital was overflowing, and during the period up to February 1915 some 815 patients had been admitted.

Unfortunately the baths were not as suitable as first thought as the glass roof made the interior unbearably hot, for both staff and patients, when the sun shone onto it. On 5 July 1915 the hospital closed and the patients were transferred to a new hospital at Draycott camp.

Belgian Refugees

In August 1914 the GWR was approached to render assistance to a large number of Belgian refugees who were seeking accommodation. Some houses in Eastbourne Terrace, Paddington, had just been purchased by the company and were made available to refugee employees of the Belgian State Railway.

The company found work for several Belgian refugees; one, who had sailed with his family to Lowestoft in his fishing boat, was employed on the Swansea Canal. Another, Mr. H. Caudell, was employed in the loco shed at Tondu, but he left in the autumn of 1917 to join the army. This much-liked man was given a wristwatch and money as a gift from his fellow staff. Miss H. van de Putte left Ostend in 1915 to seek refuge in England, and found employment in the hotels department, where she remained until returning to her home country in 1919.

Horses

An Army Horse Reserve Agreement was approved on 13 March 1913 whereby the Great Western was obliged to supply 221 horses at cost price plus 50 per cent. These horses were taken in early August 1914 together with an extra forty light draft horses and twelve 'commandeered' at Birmingham.

The railways were still very dependent on horses for the transportation of goods and parcels, especially in the outlying districts. At Bridport there were only two dray horses left to carry out all the carting from the station.

There were sufficient numbers of horses and keepers in some areas towards the end of the war to carry on the traditional condition competition, one of which was held between the staff of Hockley (Birmingham Moor Street) and Small Heath in 1918. Prizes were awarded to the winners of each class who had accumulated the most points in the year after being judged each month.

May Day prize winners, 1918. These horses were among the few lucky ones not to have been sent to the front. (*GWR Magazine*)

Enlistment of Men

As was found in all workplaces, to begin with the GWR men were eager and willing to answer the call to 'Join the Colours' and fight for their King and Country – a notion that today's generation would find hard to understand. Few of these men had ever ventured from these shores, let alone to fight, but during August 1914 some 4,048 men answered the call, this number being made up of volunteers and those in the Territorial Army and the Reserves. Many of those who left in the early days were experienced soldiers who had fought in South Africa and others thought it not an unnatural thing to do as members of their families had previously served in the forces; after all, the journey to the front was a short one, and it would be over by Christmas. They didn't want to miss out on a great adventure. Attitudes would change as it became obvious that this war would be a long and costly one.

Month by month the enlistment figures rose, reaching 8,466 by the end of October. At the beginning of December the first reports of casualties among GWR men were made public, which amounted to fifty-eight being killed, nine missing and 200 wounded or prisoners of war.

Frank Potter, General Manager, had announced at the outbreak of the war that the posts held by men who had joined the forces would be kept for their return wherever possible. If it was not found possible for the original posts to be made available, alternatives would be found, such was the optimism that the war would be one of short duration and the number of employees lost small, and there was great rivalry throughout the war between the Railway Companies as to the number of men who joined the forces.

The company promised to make contributions to the pension scheme on behalf of those serving in the forces for the duration of the time they were away from the company, as well as the continuing privileges such as cheap tickets, coal etc. They also supplemented the men's service pay and separation allowance, which was paid to wives and families of those who had joined up, though this was limited by the Government to 10s per week for each family, but it was also calculated that the men's service pay and separation allowance should be supplemented to amount to four-fifths of the men's regular weekly pay. Should the man be killed, this would continue to be paid for twenty-six months after the notification of death.

The end of 1914 found the GWR in the position of having a rapidly depleting workforce, with an increased expenditure due to overtime payments to staff covering absentees. New staff were taken on in a smaller ratio to those who had left and were employed on a temporary basis, and were also issued with armbands in place of uniforms. This was when the GWR began to look to women to fill some of the vacancies and later called on retired employees to return to their old posts.

In March 1915 Lord Kitchener made a request to the Executive Committee to compile a report to ascertain the minimum number of men required for the safe running of the railways due to the expectation of many more men being required to join the forces, and because of this never-ending demand for men the Executive Committee approached the War Office to ensure that men were not removed without the permission of the Railway Company. The War Office agreed that to deplete the railway staff to any great degree would jeopardise the running of the railways but insisted that the companies should assist in the recruitment of men in any way they could.

With this end in mind, from September the Railway Companies issued a card to those workers who wished to enlist, which was then handed to the recruiting officer. Once the men had attested they returned to work, only to be called up with others of their own age group and after informing the Railway Company that the man was employed with. These men were issued with an armband denoting their enlistment pending call-up.

Official notice to GWR staff. (Author's collection)

GREAT WESTERN RAILWAY.

NOTICE TO THE STAFF.

In connection with the raising of additional recruits for the Army, the Parliamentary Recruiting Committee are addressing to every householder a request for a return of male persons between 19 and 38 years of age who reside in his house and are willing to enlist for the period of the War.

In order to avoid misunderstanding, it is essential that any member of the Staff who intimates willingness to enlist should also state clearly on the form that he is in the Railway Service, as Recruiting Officers are under instructions not to enlist in such cases without a certificate from the Railway Company that permission has been given.

The opportunity is taken of explaining to the Staff that the reason for the caution which it has been felt necessary to exercise in this respect is that in the interest of the country it is of the utmost importance that the railway services should be maintained in a state of complete efficiency, not only to deal with the ordinary business, but also, and over and above that, to meet the special requirements of the military authorities.

FRANK POTTER,
General Manager.

Paddington Station,
23rd November, 1914.

At the end of 1915 those GWR men who wanted to enlist had to apply for permission by filling in this card and handing it to the recruiting officer. (*GWR Magazine*)

GREAT WESTERN RAILWAY.

............191

The Bearer.............employed at ....as a .... in the .... Department is authorised to enlist.

Signature of
Authorised Officer } ....

Railway Rank....................

Address ....

The GWR and Paddington Silver Band played outside local recruiting offices playing rousing and patriotic music said to 'greatly encourage recruiting' and to speed up the enlistment programme a temporary recruiting office was opened at Paddington Station on 17 November 1915. By January 1916, 23,564 GWR men had put themselves forward under Lord Derby's scheme for enlistment, with 20,809 being attested and 2,755 either rejected or deferred for re-examination. Within two months the number of men who were attested rose to 23,358 with 11,704 to be released for military service, but under an agreement with Lord Derby in March 1916 men could be retained if they were needed for railway work, and therefore the GWR were only able to release 2,222.

There was yet another problem for the GWR with regard to staffing levels as all unmarried men aged between 18 and 41 were liable for enlistment on 1 March 1916 under the Military Service Act, of which 1,008 of the GWR employees were eligible. By May all men within this age bracket who had not joined up, or classed as exempt, were automatically regarded as enlisted in the army.

As so many men had already joined the services there were few remaining within the company that fell into this category. The War Department authorised the issue of a card to retained railway employees which was used as proof that these men were not to be called up by recruiting officers without communicating with the Railway Company.

The year 1916 saw the appointment of the Manpower Distribution Board, whose main purpose was to investigate and report on the distribution of manpower between the army and essential services, and to ensure that the dilution of skilled labour was not to the detriment of the companies or country. But by October all the railways were obliged to release all single men under the age of 26, except shunters, firemen, signalmen and other skilled essential workers.

Although the company policy was to hold posts open for the duration and fill vacancies with temporary staff, it was during this period that the company found it necessary to appoint permanent staff in certain posts such as signalmen, guards and shunters. The GWR also thought that due to the inevitable slow return of its staff from the forces once hostilities had ended, it would be able to absorb its old members of staff into positions. In addition, one statistic was becoming clear: that staff who had been killed or those unable to return to work due to wounds would have to be replaced. It was also at this time that the Government separation allowance increased, and therefore the money paid by the company to the enlisted men's dependants was reduced.

On a lighter note, a consequence of men joining the services meant that the GWR Orchestra was short of musicians. Mr E. Burgess of Paddington Goods offices and secretary of the GWR Musical Society pleaded for those of a musical persuasion to come forward in February 1917.

In March the War Office requested that Railway Companies release 20 per cent of their staff of military age in reserved occupations, and of the 31,000 Great Western men who qualified, the company were only able to release 10 per cent; the principle of releasing single men before married men no longer applied. Staffing levels were getting desperate, necessitating the transfer of staff from other regions of the GWR system to cover in areas where there was a shortfall.

May 1917 saw the end of the trade card system of exemption of factory and workshop employees, whereby certain trades unions could issue members cards of exemption from military service. This system was replaced by a schedule of protected occupations and applied to railway shops, with a later additional schedule to cover other railway employees. This did not mean that enlistment faltered, but the order of enlistment did change from releasing all single men before those who were married to the following order:

1. Single men up to the age of 31
2. Married men up to the age of 31

Cigarettes for the Lancashire and Cheshire Troops. This load represents but a comparatively trifling part of the gifts provided by readers of the "Manchester Guardian," who have catered for nearly 70,000 men.

Those who enlisted were nor forgotten, and many gifts were sent abroad. (*GWR Magazine*)

   3. Single men up to the age of 41

   4. Married men up to the age of 41

This system was a success, but some companies insisted on all men undergoing a medical examination, which firemen and drivers resented when so few of them would eventually serve in the forces due to the lack of locomotive staff. There was also a growing resentment by a number of railway men who were only too willing to join up at the beginning of the war when they could not be spared from the railway, only to find that they were urged to do so in the latter years of the war when railway staffing levels were dangerously low.

The early months of 1918 were important as more men were needed to push back the over-stretched German army after the offensives of March and April, even though the fighting ranks were swollen with the addition of American forces. The push at the front had to continue at all costs and a call was made in May to release as many men as possible, and between then and the end of June the GWR had released 1,055 men – 335 more than had been promised. Although this was of great benefit to the war effort, it left not only the GWR but all companies dangerously short of workers. The director of National Service gave the Railway Companies permission to retain men over the age of 43 and to employ men over that age who were eligible for military service. It was also recognised that younger men holding posts of essential workers such as firemen and shunters had to be retained.

An order issued by the War Cabinet in the latter part of June 1918 stipulated that all young men born between 1898 and 1899 who were employed on munitions work were to be called up immediately. It was also stated that this order was to be extended to include men who were

Telegraphic Address
"POTTER, PADDINGTON STATION."

Great Western Railway

General Managers Office.

Paddington Station,

London. W.

IN YOUR REPLY
PLEASE QUOTE
THIS REFERENCE.

R.

13th April 1918.

Private.

My dear Sir,

              In view of the anticipated immediate passing into effect of

the new Man Power Bill and the probability that in any event the

Railway Companies will be called upon to make an increased contri-

bution of men for service with the Colours, it becomes necessary

to review the position in regard to staff and I shall probably be

asking you to confer with me in the course of the next day or two

in respect of the matter.

         Meanwhile, I should be glad if you would call for

the minutes of the Chief Officers' Conference held on October 16th,

1916 and of a preliminary meeting of the Staff Committee held on

March 10th,1916.   I am aware that the circumstances in connection

with the working of the railway and the amount of traffic passing

have changed since those meetings took place and that although there

has been an appreciably reduced passenger train service, there has

been a greater volume of traffic than was the case 18 months or two

Official GWR letter underlining the difficulties experienced by the company in April 1918. (Author's collection)

years ago, while there has also been a great expansion of
freight traffic.   There can, moreover, be no doubt that the
Company are, and have been for some time past, carrying on under
very pronounced difficulties, but it will not be necessary for
me to remind you that the grave national crisis with which the
country is to-day confronted leaves us no alternative but to see
what further steps can be taken in the direction of releasing men
and the object of this letter is to ask you to turn over the whole
subject in your mind with the view of submitting suggestions as to
the directions in which it might be possible, with, of course,
added inconvenience, to release more men.

As you will have gathered from the debates in
Parliament and the various statements that have obtained currency
in the press, the proposals divide themselves into two parts.   One
refers to the raising of the military age limit generally and the
other to what is known as the 'clean cut' of men up to 25 years of
age and, subject to any conclusions that may be arrived at when the
question is discussed between us, it seems to me that so far as the
railways are concerned we shall have to ask for consideration under
each head.   It may also be necessary to ask for consideration in
regard to specific grades and this is one of the directions in
which I should like preliminary consideration to be given to the
matter.   There are, of course, some grades in respect of which we
may have to say that the whole of the men of military age will be
released, subject to some of them being utilised for the purposes

of substitution.

Yours faithfully,

employed in railway workshops, even though the Railway Companies were doing their utmost to release as many men as they could, which lead to 484 men leaving the GWR in June with a further 631 by the end of October.

It is worth adding at this point that towards the latter part of the war more men were joining the Royal Flying Corps, or, as from April 1918, the Royal Air Force. The pay was good, and if the man had entered the force voluntarily he could not be transferred to the army or navy without his consent. Some applied for a transfer from their active unit to pursue a service career in the air, but although it was thought to be glamorous, many an inexperienced flyer found, to his cost, that danger followed his every move.

The final figures released by the GWR in June 1922 stated that 32.6 per cent of the total male staff in 1914 had joined the colours, of those 2,500 had been killed or died of wounds.

Although the war had ended it would be some time before those who were able would return to work with the GWR, as their services were still required by the military, and there were some members of staff that had been wounded and would never work on the railway again. The number of those killed would continue to rise into 1920 as records of the men's military actions were confirmed, or due to some of the wounded men losing their fight for life.

Railway Service Badge

Introduced in 1915, this badge was worn only by employees who had every intention to enlist but were not given permission as they were needed to work on the railway. The blue and white enamel badge with gold lettering, denoting the Railway Company the employee was working for, and crown went some way to ensure that the wearer would not be presented with a white feather by enthusiastic and often ill-informed people who thought such members of the work-force were shirking their responsibilities or, at worse, cowards. However, those without a badge were seen as fair game to the white feather brigade.

These badges are relatively scarce as they were given to a select group of railway workers, unlike the Railway Service badge of the Second World War that denoted the wearer was in a reserved occupation and could be called upon in an emergency.

GWR Railway Service badge. (*GWR Magazine*)

War Bonus Pay

A war bonus was first introduced in February 1915 to ease the financial pressures due to the rising cost of living. Originally this bonus was not altogether fair, paying 3s per week to men earning less than 30s, and 2s to men on a higher weekly wage, but this only applied to men engaged in the manipulation of transport. Amendments made a couple of months later awarded 1s 6d per week to male employees under the age of 18, and a further amendment in October awarded 5s a week for men and 2s 6d those under 18 on the proviso that no strike action was taken nor demands made for an increase in wages or bonus.

In 1916 shop men in the locomotive works were dissatisfied with a bonus awarded to them as their piecework pay percentage rise did not put them in line with other company employees. The men went to arbitration and an acceptable deal was struck.

As the war progressed and the cost of living continued to rise, the GWR were obliged to double the bonus in April 1917, at the same time awarding 3s a week to females over the age of 18, and half that amount to those who were younger.

The war bonuses were borne by the Government as part of the working expenses of the railway, and by the beginning of 1918 the bonus had risen to 21s per week, proportionately less for female employees and juniors. The annual wages bill, including bonuses, was £3.5 million, which did not include overtime and Sunday duty pay.

Women and the GWR

By early 1915 nearly 13 per cent of the total staff of the GWR had enlisted which caused a worrying shortfall of available railway workers. All companies turned their attentions to women to help fill suitable posts, even though it was quoted that 'under normal circumstances women would be regarded as unsuitable for most railway posts'. The choice of work became more varied as time progressed and companies found themselves more dependent on the female worker.

Women had already made inroads into the railway workplace, and at the beginning of the war the GWR employed 1,371 women, with two thirds of that number holding domestic posts such as charwomen, washerwomen, hotel staff etc., while the remaining were of clerical grades as typists, telephonists and the like.

During the war women were eager to make themselves available for work to release men for active service, and a special register of 'Women for War Service' was set up by the Board of Trade. Such was the eagerness of some women that they approached companies directly stating their willingness and availability, as is shown in a letter written by Vera George to the GWR:

BOSBURY LODGE

MALVERN LINK

Sir – If you would care to engage me as a ticket collector here, or at any of the smaller stations on the line, and so release a man for more important work, I should be very willing to undertake the duty.

I have earned my own living for 10 years, but am now 'unemployed' owing to the war.

It struck me that a woman could be a 'ticket collector' just as well as a man.

Believe me, yours faithfully

(Miss) Vera George

Miss George, the first female ticket collector.
(*GWR Magazine*)

This letter was successful in convincing the GWR that women could indeed perform the tasks of ticket collector, and Miss George was employed as the first in the company.

This was an exciting time for women as they were able to find employment opportunities outside of the vacancies usually open to them, and for women brought up in families where the male members were railway employees they found the railway environment familiar.

Women were obviously restricted as to the position they could hold within the company due either to the lack of experience or physical capabilities, but in those positions they were allowed to take the women did well and excelled in some such as clerical work. Plus, in the case of carriage cleaners such was the quality of their work they won the praises of travellers – although they did take longer over their tasks than the men did!

The women were employed on a temporary basis as the positions originally held by men were to be kept available for them on their return from active service. Many women left the railways partly because of the uncertainty of future work and the lack of any career structure, but mostly because of the low wages as they could earn considerably more in the munitions factories. However, sufficient numbers remained with the GWR – by August 1918 there were a total of 6,345 of which 2,900 were engaged in clerical work. The company was quick to agree that there should be equal pay for equal work, but doubted whether all the women's work was equal to the men's. They also argued that war wages were, in fact, a special allowance based on the rising cost of living and domestic responsibilities, and it was greatly agreed that the majority of women had no responsibilities. An interesting idea, given the situation at the time, with many women having to look after the home and family while their male relatives were away serving in the forces. The

Photos by]   [*A. L. P. Reavil.*

Above Female refreshment
department workers at Paddington.
(*GWR Magazine*)

Right A female wartime booking
clerk. (*GWR Magazine*)

Below Women ticket collectors and
the men they replaced at Truro. (*GWR
Magazine*)

Various female GWR employees. (*GWR Magazine*)

GWR pensioners who returned to work at Didcot. (*GWR Magazine*)

GWR did admit to this anomaly, especially when single men or men with no responsibilities were being paid the same war wage as those who had responsibilities.

The following figures give the numbers of women compared to men who were employed with the GWR in various grades in August 1918:

Porters: 346 women – 1,346 men
Goods Porters: 616 women – 777 men
Carriage Cleaners: 594 women – 153 men
Ticket Collectors: 323 women – 155 men
Messengers: 111 women – 495 men
A number of women were also employed to drive company motor vehicles.

An interesting position to be held by a woman was that of Police Constable. In March 1917, under the GWR Act of Parliament, Mrs A.E. Martin was given the powers of a Special Constable and assigned to the Special Police Department at Paddington. Having completed some months of work experience she was found to be more than satisfactory, especially when investigations required a female approach. At the time it was thought that Mrs Martin was the first, if not only, female detective employed on the railways. The magistrate, upon signing her warrant card, hoped that she would not find her duties unpleasant or too onerous.

The total number of women employed by British Railway Companies during the war was 55,797, but by 30 July 1919 the figure had fallen to 34,545 with men returning from the war to resume their positions.

The women who temporarily worked for the GWR enjoyed their work and the financial independence that went with it. They knew the day would come when they would have to give up this work but they had 'done their bit' for the country, and their fellow workers were appreciative, presenting them with gifts on their leaving. The following is a list of a few of the temporary women workers:

Miss V. Nott – Parcel Porter Minety Station
Mrs Edith Taylor (*née* Smith) – Paddington Goods Station
Miss N. Lang – Ticket Collector Landore Station
Miss Gladys Lewis – Landore
Miss E. Jones and Ms N.L. Gresham – Clerk Loco. Dept Croes Newydd
Miss M. Wheeler – The first Ticket Collector at Newport and the last woman to leave in 1920
Mabel Bull – Carriage Cleaner Cardiff

Miss F. Pillar was employed as a rail motor conductress at Plymouth (Millbay) where she took the place of a Mr Pillar, who was called up for military service and it is very possible that they were from the same family. Miss Pillar remained in this post until she left to marry in January 1918.

Pensioners at Work

Many retired railwaymen offered their services to the GWR to work in place of those who had enlisted for military service, the obvious advantage of these men being their experience. In the photo opposite we can see three such stalwart gents who volunteered to work at Didcot station as platform porters.

In the centre of the photo is the oldest of the pensioners, 73-year-old David Ireland who originally joined the GWR in 1862 and moved to Didcot in 1864, where he remained as a ticket collector until his retirement in 1910. He returned for service in December 1914.

To the left is 68-year-old James Stock who first joined the company in 1871, and was a special travelling ticket examiner for thirty-six years until he retired in November 1911; he returned in May 1915.

The youngest of the trio is George Wilks, aged 66, and like James Stock joined the GWR in 1871, firstly as a porter at Paddington Goods Station, then as a brakesman, goods guard and lastly passenger guard, until his retirement in February 1912. He rejoined the company exactly three years later.

Safety

The GWR introduced the 'Safety' movement which, at the time of its inception just prior to the war, was a groundbreaking idea to encourage employees to be always aware of the dangers around them. Statistics showed that it worked, but much against expectations statistics also showed a steady decline in accidents during the war years, which was strange as traffic was heavier, with less staff to ensure that all duties were carried out as per schedule, coupled with the fact that there were a large number of workers employed with little or no experience of the environment.

CHAPTER TWO

*GWR Ambulance Trains – GWR Ambulance and VAD Work
– GWR Ships – The Men at the Helm*

GWR Ambulance Trains

The importance of ambulance trains was first noted during the American Civil War, but Britain's first experience of these trains came about in the Boer War with the 'Princess Christian Hospital Train' working in South Africa, with an additional five-coach train, specifically designed by the London and South Western Railway and used in England for the transportation of wounded soldiers. During the inter-war period plans were drawn up for the construction of ambulance trains in the event of another war.

At the beginning of August 1914 the Government ordered twelve ambulance trains to be constructed by the various Railway Companies for use in the home country; two of the trains were constructed by the GWR at Swindon, each of which consisted of nine eight-wheeled vehicles:

Saloon with eight beds for orderlies plus a stores area

Restaurant car

Two ward coaches each containing eighteen beds for men

Pharmacy coach – divided by partitions to form a dispensary, linen store, and an operating theatre (the
    floor of which was covered with zinc and a central drain fitted for ease of cleaning). The coach was
    fitted with an 8ft sliding door to enable stretchers to be taken in sideways. A special boiler was
    installed to provide hot water for sterilisation etc.

Two ward coaches each containing beds for eighteen men

Ward coach with beds for eight officer patients plus accommodation for two doctors and two nurses

Alterations were made to eight-wheeled passenger brake vans for use as the ward coaches which were already fitted with Westinghouse brakes, as well as vacuum brakes, to enable the trains to run over any railway in the country. Except for the restaurant and pharmacy cars, lavatories were provided, together with a 90-gallon water storage tank. The interiors of the ward and pharmacy cars were painted white and each was equipped with a special steam heating system, with lighting supplied by oil gas lamps which could be screened when necessary. The gangways were wide enough to accommodate the transfer of the wounded by stretcher from the ward coaches to the operating theatre while the train was in motion, should the need arise. The familiar Red Cross on a white background was painted on each side of every coach, together with one on the roof so that the trains could be instantly recognised.

The ward car of a GWR ambulance train. One of a series of postcards produced to raise funds. (Author's collection)

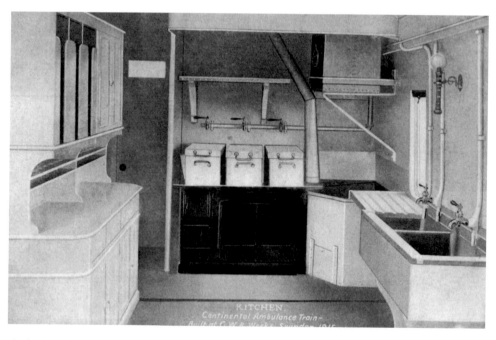

The kitchen of a GWR ambulance train for use on the Continent. (Author's collection)

All the alterations required to enable the trains to enter active service were completed by 14 August, then the equipment supplied by the War Office was installed. The first GWR ambulance train (official No.4) left Swindon on 24 August, with the second (No.5) leaving the following day. Both trains travelled to Southampton to begin their work of conveying the sick and wounded from the docks to hospitals in the Midlands and the north. The GWR was also required by the War Office to supply two cooks for each train.

Throughout the war around 6,000 loaded ambulance trains passed over the GWR system en route to various destinations in Britain, but of that number 2,828 were destined for GWR stations as follows:

Bristol Temple Meads	395	Portland	36
Paddington	351	Stratford-on-Avon	33
Plymouth North Road	239	Warminster	18
Cardiff	207	Hereford	13
Birmingham	200	Newbury	9
Oxford	154	Oswestry	9
Reading	136	Wrexham	8
Birkenhead	134	Newton Abbot	7
Taplow	116	Denham	7
Paignton	99	Buildwas	6
Stourbridge	75	Devizes	6
Berrington	69	Bridgnorth	5
Chester	62	Windsor	4
Cheltenham	57	Ironbridge	4
Newport	51	Codford	3
Avonmouth Docks	49	Whitchurch	2
Torquay	49	Aylesbury	2
Truro	46	Baschurch	2
Shrewsbury	42	Burghclere	2
Gloucester	39	Much Wenlock	2
Torre	39	Exeter St Davids	1
Winchester	38	High Clere	1
		Southall	1

In March 1915 work was carried out to strengthen the lines of Portland dockyard as it was proposed to divert one of the hospital ships to Portland which would result in three ambulance trains a week using these lines. The work was paid for by the Admiralty but no details have been found to confirm if this arrangement continued for any length of time.

Many praised the GWR for their work in transporting the wounded, including a Major-General Sir W.G. MacPherson, Headquarters Southern Command, who had observed work done at Reading, and he wrote commending the arrangements there and the efficiency with which the work was carried out.

A letter was received from the commissioner of the American Red Cross (GB) thanking the GWR for all their help, despite the company's reduction in the labour force, and for the special rates charged to the organisation.

There were no British ambulance trains available in France at the outbreak of the war, and casualties were transported by French trains made up of goods trucks, with brake vans for stores,

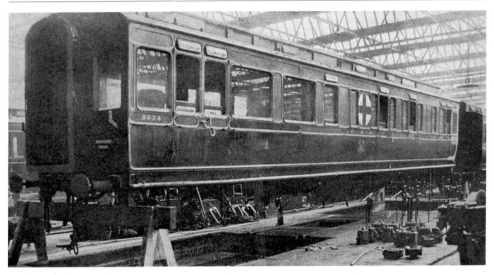

An ambulance train carriage body in the workshops at Swindon in 1915. (*GWR Magazine*)

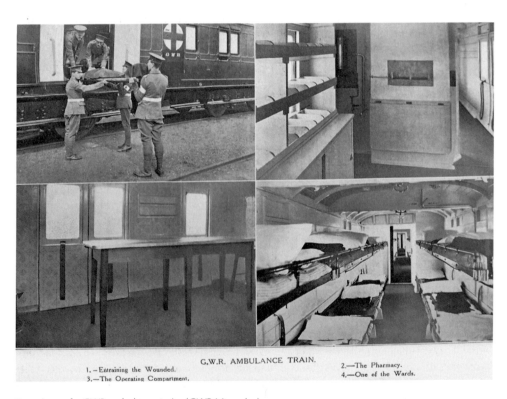

G.W.R. AMBULANCE TRAIN.

1. – Entraining the Wounded.
3. – The Operating Compartment.

2. – The Pharmacy.
4. – One of the Wards.

Four views of a GWR ambulance train. (*GWR Magazine*)

office and dispensary, a restaurant car for the kitchen, and first and second-class coaches for personnel. Each truck was fitted with upside down 'U'-shape frames bolted to the floor at a distance of 6ft between each frame. Metal poles were strung between these frames to facilitate the holding of three stretchers per frame. Four of these complete frames, known as 'Brechet Apparatus', were installed in each truck which could then hold twelve lying patients. The greatest disadvantage at the time to these first French ambulance trains was the lack of connecting passages between the coaches and trucks.

As time progressed a desperate shortage of trucks in France led to the use of straw-lined cattle trucks being used for the transportation of casualties. Sometimes, on good days, mattresses were placed on the floors of the trucks. The shortage of available trucks in France was due to the transportation of their own casualties and the loss of rolling stock by capture or destruction by the Germans, although those who experienced railway conditions during the war in France commented, with some anger, that many coaches suitable for ambulance train use lay idle, such as dining and sleeping cars, as well as corridor coaches of the Nord Railway. It was this shortage that brought about the call for ambulance trains to be supplied by companies at home for the transportation of British troops at the front. French ambulance trains were numbered one to eleven, with British ones being numbered twelve to forty-four; there was no ambulance train numbered thirteen that served abroad.

A new ambulance train (No.16) for use in France was built by the GWR works during February and March 1915 from new vehicles at a cost of £12,500, which was paid for through the War Office by the United Kingdom Flour Millers Association. Also in March, the Government ordered four new ambulance trains for use at home, of which the GWR built one at a cost of £11,540 (paid for by the War Office) and consisted of six ward coaches, one staff car, one dining car, one stores and ward car and a pharmacy car.

In April 1915 arrangements were made for a GWR inspector and eight men to accompany the UK Flour Millers train and supervise its transportation to France. These men performed the same duty for the Birmingham Carriage and Wagon Co. *Princess Christian* train (No.15). Five cross-Channel voyages were undertaken to deliver the trains to France, and the GWR had to take out special insurance to cover the men in their work at a cost of £75, which was added to the final costs of the trains.

An order for eight additional corridor coaches was placed in May 1915 for the Flour Millers' train to be paid for by the War Office, together with a requisition to all the Railway Companies to provide eight additional ambulance trains for use on the Continent with four trains required immediately; the GWR constructed one of these, No.18. In July 1915 a further request was made for another ambulance train for use in France (No.19) at a cost of £29,000, which meant that three trains for use at home and three for continental use had been made at Swindon by September 1915.

Once the construction of these last two trains was completed transportation was to be by ship from Tilbury to France. The first consignment of four coaches of No.19 train left Tilbury and, according to the July report of the GWR General Manager to the Board, the ship SS *Africa* was either mined or torpedoed off the Kent coast near Deal. Two of the crew were killed in the explosion, but Mr C. Godsell of the carriage and wagon department, who was supervising the transportation, and the GWR loading gang together with the rest of the crew, escaped in lifeboats. Although the ship beached it was impossible to salvage any of the coaches due to unsuitable lifting gear and the inaccessible position of where the ship was lying, although the General Managers' report for January 1916 stated that work in hand at Swindon included the 'renovation of salvaged material from S.S. *Africa*'! The War Office paid £6,400 for four replacement coaches.

A GWR ambulance train. (*GWR Magazine*)

The Mayor and Mayoress with officials attend the exhibition of a GWR ambulance train at Millbay docks, Plymouth, on 1-3 May 1916. (*GWR Magazine*)

G.W.R. Ambulance Train constructed at the Swindon Works for U.S.A. Troops on the Continent.

The exterior of an ambulance train carriage constructed at Swindon for American troops. (*GWR Magazine*)

During May 1916 two ambulance trains (Nos 26 and 27) were exhibited to the public at Birmingham, Bristol, Cardiff, Exeter, Oxford, Paddington, Plymouth, Reading, Shrewsbury, Swindon, Truro, Westbury, Weston-super-Mare, Weymouth and Windsor, prior to their transportation to the Continent. A charge was made to visitors of 1s for the public and 3d for GWR staff; some 34,555 people paid the fees and, together with the sale of postcards etc., £1,710 was raised. Most of the money was divided between various hospitals, the St John's Ambulance service, the Railway Benevolent Institution and the Railway Troops Comfort Committee, with the balance of £635 held in trust. In March 1917 £100 was sent to France for comforts to railway troops who did not receive any comforts from monies raised for fighting troops, and as there were some 2,000 GWR men serving with the railway troops further amounts of money were sent out at later dates from the money raised at ambulance train exhibitions.

By the end of the war four ambulance trains had been constructed at Swindon for use at home, and eight for use on the Continent, with the last two (Nos 39 and 43) of standard type requested by the War Office for use by American troops. Train No.43 was exhibited the week prior to shipment at Paddington, Bristol and Birmingham, raising £152 which was distributed as before.

In addition to the ambulance trains listed, an order was placed by the American government for two ambulance trains for use by their own army on the Western Front. Made at Swindon during the winter of 1917–18, these trains were the most modern available, complete with the

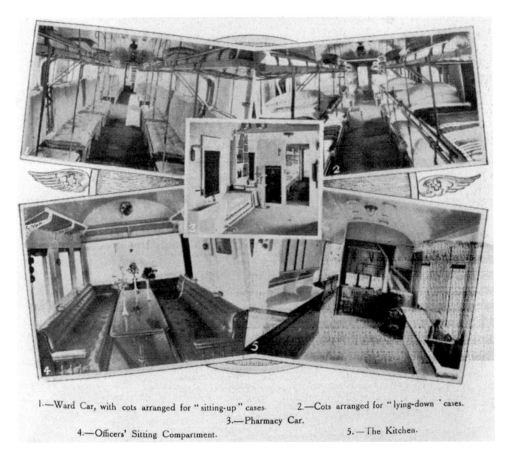

1.—Ward Car, with cots arranged for "sitting-up" cases.   2.—Cots arranged for "lying-down" cases.

3.—Pharmacy Car.

4.—Officers' Sitting Compartment.   5.—The Kitchen.

The interior of a GWR ambulance train constructed for American troops on the Continent.

now standard electric lights; they also had electric fans. These sixteen eight-wheeled coach trains were 960ft in length and weighed 441 tons, with a capacity for 360 cots and an extra 33 patients in the personnel car. They also contained almost everything that was needed for the transportation and treatment of the wounded, including an enormous range in the kitchen car, large storage facilities for food in the brake van and a battery of accumulators charged by dynamos on each coach to power the lights and fans while the train was stationary. Comforts for the patients were also built in, as on the side of each cot were fixed a paper rack, ash tray and a cup holder. Yes, the ubiquitous cup holder is not such a modern innovation as was first thought!

The outside of the trains were painted khaki and at the end was painted 'U.S. 54' and 'U.S. 55' respectively, with two red crosses added towards the ends of each coach, and in the middle was a large 'U.S.' painted in red and white. One record states that US ambulance train No.53 was also built by the GWR.

A train was converted to War Office requirements at Dundalk. This train, No.13, was made up from GWR (Ireland) stock and distributed patients around the Dublin area from ships that arrived up the River Liffey.

A model of a Pharmacy Ambulance Coach was made at the Swindon Works immediately after the war and presented to the Australian government, and was built to a scale of 1½in to 1ft. Enquiries made at the Imperial War Museum confirm, via a contact in Australia, that the model is held by the Australian War Memorial (exhibit number RELAWM04318), although at the time of writing the model was in storage.

It is worth stating here that British locomotives were used to pull the ambulance trains abroad as drivers had difficulty in starting, braking and stopping the trains gently enough so as not to cause discomfort to the patients when French locomotives were used!

GWR AMBULANCE TRAINS ABROAD

TRAIN	COUNTRY	DATE OF ENTRY	PATIENT CAPACITY:	
No	Sent To	Into Service	Sitting	Lying
16	France	24 Apr. 1915	162	320
18	France/Italy	27 Sep. 1915	162	320
19	France	8 Feb. 1916	192	266
26	Italy	14 May 1916	306	64
27	France	24 Jun. 1916	306	64
33	France	28 Aug. 1917	306	80
39	France/Italy	28 Jan. 1918	356	39
43	Italy	3 Jun. 1918	356	39

At the end of the war nineteen of the British ambulance trains had their roles changed to that of leave trains, with their routes being from the Rhine to Calais and Boulogne. The trains were also given names as follows:

GWR AMBULANCE TRAIN NO	NAME	ROUTE
18	Carina	Calais
19	Yvonne	Calais
26	Elizabeth	Calais
27	Arctic	Boulogne

| 33 | Gabrielle | Calais |
| 39 | Oceanic | Boulogne |

The service to Boulogne carried officers, while the Cologne to Calais trains carried officers and other ranks.

GWR ambulance trains 39 and 43 were at Didcot in 1921 and were thought to be for sale; they possibly ended up at the Military Railway at Longmoor. Most other ambulance train coaches were converted back and returned to normal service after the war, such as 3639 Toplight Corridor Third, which was built in Swindon in 1905 and converted for ambulance train use during the war, returning to regular service in 1921, later converted to camping coach No.9887, and is now undergoing restoration at Williston (West Somerset Railway Trust).

During the war there was an Ambulance Trains for the Continent Sub-committee which comprised of notables from various Railway Companies. One of those was GWR Carriage Manager, Mr F.W. Marillier, and, as well as carrying out his works for the company and the committee, his main claim to fame was that he designed the ambulance train three-tier cot system for use overseas. This versatile system allowed the cots to be folded flush against the wall of the coach for ease of cleaning, but by folding the middle cot only against the wall allowed the bottom cot to be used as a seat for the less seriously wounded, while the upper cot could still be used for patients needing to lie down. The cots themselves could, if needed, be used as stretchers.

GWR Ambulance and VAD Work

The number of sick and wounded transported from hospital ships to stations around the country by ambulance trains is quite unimaginable today, and the work carried out by the GWR ambulance men in helping with the transportation of these patients should not go unrecorded. The GWR Ambulance Service, a voluntary organisation, was distributed throughout the system and during peacetime men were encouraged to train in first aid, which served them well when helping on the ambulance trains and at the stations where the patients were detrained before being sent on to hospitals. As the war progressed a great number of women trained as first aid personnel in the GWR Ambulance Service.

Employees also practiced this in the London area during air raids, and as members of the St John Ambulance Brigade of No.37 Division or the GWR Ambulance Corps, reported to either Paddington or St Johns Gate police stations, where they were called on to perform their duties on some eighty occasions, and twice over forty GWR men and women reported for duty. During a raid in early 1918 members of the GWR ambulance personnel were praised for their work when rescuing casualties from collapsed buildings in Warrington Crescent, Maida Vale, near Paddington Station. This raid accounted for twenty people killed and forty-five injured, which was quite high for the First World War.

Many members were awarded war badges for their excellent work during dangerous and difficult situations.

Some forty GWR employees, who were qualified ambulance men through the GWR courses, worked at the military hospital at Southall. When the hospital was being made ready for the first patients these men helped by cleaning windows and floors, putting beds together etc., and once the hospital was opened the men acted as orderlies and stretcher-bearers. They were part of the Voluntary Aid Detachment (VAD), attached to the Territorial branch of the Royal Army Medical

Corps, and wore regulation khaki uniforms with a VAD badge on the sleeve. Many of the men attended a course to become nurses, as did female GWR employees, working in their spare time in local hospitals, and some from Paddington attended St Dunstan's Hospital for Blinded Soldiers.

GWR men in Cheshire 9a and b VAD from Birkenhead dealt with 114 ambulance trains between August 1914 and June 1918, which amounted to 21,126 wounded servicemen. During this time a record was made when an amazing 340 sitting cases were taken off a train, and the station completely cleared within eighteen minutes. Another train containing 180 stretcher cases was completely unloaded at Birmingham in only seventy minutes.

All the first aid and ambulance work was carried out in addition to their routine railway work, and many members of the GWR Ambulance Service joined the forces during the war where their training was put to good use.

On 12 May 1915 Mr W.H. Maunder of the Audit Office, Paddington, was appointed sergeant major in the Royal Army Medical Corps, and from August he was working at the 1,154-bed Royal Herbert Hospital, Woolwich, as Chief Ward Master. He had been a prominent member of the GWR and St John Ambulance movements, but he unfortunately died of double pneumonia in December 1916. His son, who was in the forces, died of wounds shortly before this.

GWR Ships

GWR shipping status prior to August 1914:

Turbines	**Route**
St David	Fishguard–Rosslare
St Andrew	"
St Patrick	"
Steamships	
Great Western	Fishguard–Waterford
Great Southern	"
Waterford	"
Ibex	Channel Islands
Reindeer	"
Roebuck	"
Lynx	"
Gazelle	"
Tenders	
Pembroke	Based at Fishguard
Sir Walter Raleigh	Based at Plymouth
Sir Francis Drake	"
Sir Richard Grenville	"
Smeaton	"
Atlanta	"

Fishguard to Rosslare Service

The three ships, *St David*, *St Andrew* and *St Patrick*, made up five ships that were requisitioned by the Government in the first month of the war, and the GWR ships were the first to be put into service as hospital ships. These ships had to be adapted for their wartime use which was carried

GWR ship *Roebuck*. (*GWR Magazine*)

out by the Marine Department staff at Fishguard. The conversions included accommodation for 200 cots on each ship and the installation of lifts for the transportation of the wounded in cots to each deck. The speed with which these conversions were carried out was quite amazing, enabling the ships to be sent to Le Havre on 24 August, with the first shipment of wounded being made by *St Andrew*, which carried sixty-three lying and 147 sitting casualties from Rouen to Southampton.

So quickly had these ships been commissioned they were painted slate grey before they could be painted in the usual colour scheme of all over white with a green band around the hull. This also meant the omission of red crosses on all sides which were to protect ships against enemy attack as laid down in the Geneva Convention. This was immaterial as in 1917 the Central Powers opted to disregard the Geneva Convention, making hospital ships targets for enemy attacks.

During the war the Fishguard to Rosslare service ran with SS *Great Western* and SS *Great Southern*, with assistance from SS *Rathmore* which had been borrowed from the London and North Western Railway. This arrangement was short-lived as the *Rathmore* had to be returned to its owners, but was replaced by SS *Duke of Connaught* from the London and North Western and Lancashire and Yorkshire Railway Companies. The route was bolstered for a short while when SS *Reindeer* was transferred from Weymouth on 18 August.

From 10 to 24 August 1914 only one sailing was possible in each direction per day but a near-normal service resumed after 24 August with a rescheduling of the service due to the slower speeds of the replacement ships. The vessels on this route were further supplemented by the Great Central Railway SS *Dewsbury* and the Lancashire and Yorkshire Railway SS *Mersey*.

Fishguard to Waterford Service

Government demands led to a suspension of this service between 5 and 17 August 1914, but as SS *Waterford* had not been called upon to perform Government work it was possible to run a limited service.

Channel Islands Service

Except for the three days of 7 to 9 August 1914 when the ships were engaged in the transportation of troops, the Channel Island service continued uninterrupted. However, it was considered

2811. 50. G.W.R. STEAMER, S.S. "REINDEER."

GWR ship *Reindeer*. (Author's collection)

unjustifiable to continue daily sailings from Weymouth and Southampton, so the winter timetable of three sailings per week was brought into operation on 24 August 1914.

On 30 September 1914 the Admiralty requisitioned SS *Roebuck* (which they renamed *Roedean*) and SS *Reindeer*, and later SS *Lynx* (renamed *Lynn*) and SS *Gazelle*, which were equipped for minesweeping. SS *Ibex* was left to continue the mail and passenger service, a situation that the GWR strongly objected to, but the Admiralty insisted that the ships were urgently needed and were suitable for the tasks they had in store for them.

Maintaining the Channel Island service with only one ship led the GWR to search for ships that could be loaned from other companies to safeguard the delivery of mail to the Islands. SS *Vera* was loaned from the London and South Western Company in October 1914, but was returned in December. Another ship, SS *Bertha* from the same company, carried cargo on the Weymouth to Guernsey route from 24 October 1914 for a short period. *Ibex* continued the service on a reduced schedule of three times a week, alternating with Southampton, but with only one vessel to rely on it was difficult to maintain the service when annual checks and boiler cleaning were due, and if another vessel was unavailable for loan the service had to be suspended.

The GWR tender SS *Pembroke* had been employed to work the Cunard liners off Fishguard but was transferred, after modifications, to Weymouth in March 1916 to work cargo to and from the Channel Islands. SS *Ibex* left the service for a short time in March 1918 to act as a troopship prior to the Spring Offensive on the Western Front, and again in 1919 when she transported troops for twelve days from Le Havre to Weymouth.

Plymouth Tenders

Requisitioned by the Admiralty, these tenders remained in Plymouth where they were employed in the embarkation and landing of troops to and from ships in the Plymouth Sound, as well as examining ships approaching. SS *Atlanta* was equipped for salvage work and was used extensively during the German submarine campaign. SS *Smeaton* was loaned to the American forces on their entry into the war.

War Service

The GWR ships sailing on the regular services were in constant danger of attack by the enemy, and the insurance for *Ibex*, *Great Western* and *Great Southern* was increased at considerable expense against war risks. The staff of the GWR ships had their wages increased because of the risks and increased workloads.

SS *Pembroke* was attacked by gunfire from a German U-boat on 24 September 1916, with the result that the Admiralty suggested that the Channel Island vessels be armed. *Ibex* was fitted with a stern-mounted 12-pounder gun in October at Plymouth and *Pembroke* received her armament in January 1917 at Portland.

Ibex had two encounters with submarines: the first in May 1917, when she narrowly missed being torpedoed, and the second on 18 April 1918 when she opened fire with her gun, sinking a submarine; for this act the Admiralty awarded £500, which was shared between the officers and crew. A brass tablet praising her war efforts was fixed to the saloon staircase after the war, and stated that she had three encounters with submarines in total.

There were heavy loses to shipping in the Irish Sea but the GWR escaped any loss, although SS *Waterford* encountered a German submarine during bad weather and altered course in an attempt to ram it, but the submarine submerged in the nick of time.

Reindeer delivering mail to the fleet at Constantinople. (*GWR Magazine*)

St Andrew as a hospital ship. (*GWR Magazine*)

Captain A.E. Davies. (*GWR Magazine*)

It is interesting to note that even though all shipping had to make their way with no lights show-ing, and without the benefit of modern navigation equipment, there were only two instances of collision recorded on the Channel Island service – remarkable considering that the route con-stantly crossed the shipping lanes. SS *David* unfortunately sunk a destroyer, luckily without loss of life. SS *Roebuck* was lost in January 1915 when it impaled itself on the French battleship *Imperieuse*, after dragging its anchor during bad weather at Scapa Flow. *Roebuck* was more than a little accident prone, having spectacularly run aground on rocks off Jersey in July 1911, being totally out of the water at low tide. Earlier, in January 1905, she caught fire at Milford and suf-fered the embarrassment of sinking due to the weight of water used to extinguish the fire. She was re-floated nine days later after the water had been pumped out, and it was hoped that the same could be done at Scapa Flow, but the Admiralty declared she was finally lost.

The navy sent SS *Reindeer*, *Lynx* and *Gazelle* to the Mediterranean where their tasks included chasing submarines, minesweeping (in the Dardanelles), patrol work, together with delivering supplies and mail. SS *Lynx* is recorded to have rammed and sunk a submarine and, together with SS *Gazelle*, arrested former sister ship SS *Antelope* in the Aegean Sea. *Antelope* had been sold to a Greek company and during the war it had been proven that she was running contraband. Whilst in the Dardanelles SS *Reindeer* was unfortunate in sinking a similar vessel belonging to another Railway Company.

Most of the GWR ships were engaged in the demobilisation of troops once hostilities had ceased, and after an overhaul and checks, returned to the GWR during 1919 and early 1920.

The Men at the Helm

Captain Richard Sharp was the company's Harbourmaster and Assistant Superintendent at Fishguard. As well as his normal duties it has been quoted that he 'rendered noble service in connection with torpedoed vessels and the landing of shipwrecked crews'.

Captain John Humphreys was the Marine Superintendent at Fishguard and, again, in addition to his usual duties, acted as senior officer at Fishguard under the admirals at Milford Haven and Queenstown. He was also responsible for the running of the hospital ships *St Andrew*, *St Patrick* and *St David* between this country and France, which included appointing captains, officers, engineers and crew, and the carrying out of all repairs. As if his working day was not full enough he was also responsible for the catering of the crew, medical staff and the wounded passengers.

Alonzo Ernest Davies was the captain of SS *St Patrick* and the commodore captain in the GWR service; he remained the captain of *St Patrick* while it was under Government control as a hospital ship. His vessel made 758 passages across the Channel and carried over 125,000 sick and wounded troops, as well as having many narrow escapes with the Germans throughout the war. The ship returned to the GWR in April 1919 and Captain Davies resumed his duties with the company.

On the night of 30 April 1920 Captain Davies sailed his ship from Rosslare to Fishguard, but the following day, at midday, he complained of feeling unwell and died a few hours later. At the age of 60, although a strong and normally healthy man, the stress he experienced through the war years had left its mark. His qualities were recognised by the navy and by his country, which awarded him the MBE.

CHAPTER THREE

War Manufacture – Munitions and Ordnance – Military Camp Railways – Tank Wagons – Armoured Train – 'Monster' Wagons – Seaplane Station – Chepstow Shipyard – Motor Car Department – Coal Gas

War Manufacture

At the outbreak of the war British Railway Companies were obliged to carry out work for various Government concerns, namely the War Office, Ministry of Munitions, the Woolwich Arsenal, the Admiralty and companies with Government contracts, as well as maintain their own schedules of work to enable the railways to run efficiently. By their very nature Railway Companies, especially the larger ones with their wealth of industrial expertise, skilled labour, machinery, means of storage and transportation, made them ideal candidates for the task. This extra work coupled with a reduced skilled labour force, lack of materials, unrest in the labour force due to temporary workers having to be used and the varying rates of pay would, in the latter years of the war, be a cause of great concern.

The first order received by the GWR, recorded on 9 October 1914, was to alter sixty pair-horse vans to meet War Office requirements; construct 500 wagons for the Artillery and 200 for transport; and supply 1,600 stretchers, an item for which there would be a great demand for. By the middle of December 1914 the GWR had made fifty water tank carts, 30,000 spokes for military wheels, 1,850 picketing posts and 18,000 picketing pegs. It was at this time that the Railway War Manufacture Sub-committee of the Executive Committee was formed, and all Government requests for work were made through this body. The final arrangements for payment for these works were also settled, being that all work carried out would be paid at replacement cost with no profit to the participating companies.

The items produced by the GWR varied greatly in type, material used, end product use and quantities manufactured, which had called upon the diverse skills of the manufacturing departments of the company. It is difficult to list exactly what was manufactured and the quantities involved, but the following will give an insight into the unusual work undertaken during the war years:

Military Wagons and Carriages:

Artillery x 500; Transport x 200; General Service Wagons x 1,160; straps for GS Wagons x 1,800; water tank carts x 50 (plus 300 wheels for same); oak spokes for artillery wheels x 40,000; repair of same x 585; ammunition wagons and limbers, sets for the construction of carriages and limbers for various size guns (over 200,000 parts made up the total number of sets)

War work in the GWR shops, Swindon. (*GWR Magazine*)

Ordinary Wagons transformed for Military Traffic.

Ordinary wagons transformed for military traffic 1914. Fig.1 wagons with raised sides for horse transport; fig.2 twin timber trucks (bolsters removed) with ramps at ends for loading guns and carriages; figs 3 & 4 eight-wheeled bogie rail trucks capable of 30 tons in weight carried ramps fitted to load guns and carriages; figs 5 & 6 improvised from partly constructed open wagons for carts and guns. (*GWR Magazine*)

Sets for 4.5in howitzers:
Gun carriage x 338 (27,662 parts); ammunition wagons x 1,078 (126,004 parts); limber x 1,078 (53,854 parts); carriage limber x 338 (17,249 parts); carriages for 6in naval guns converted to land use x 40 (8in howitzer carriages converted likewise)

Guns:
6lb Hotchkiss guns supplied to the GWR for completion x 327; the same but rifled only x 327 (later also the repair and retube); howitzer 4.5in and 8in guns; 6in Field guns, 18lb gun parts, 60lb bomb guns; Nordenfeldt guns (including conversions, adding mountings and provision of shoulder pieces)

Munitions:
16, 65 and 100lb high-explosive bombs for Woolwich; 103,127 6in H.E. shells from 265,652 tons of forgings (an output of 2,500 per week); 10 tons of mild steel bars made into forgings for 3in H.E. shells for the Admiralty each week; 9.2in bars rolled to 3in diameter for 18lb shells; 18lb cartridge cases reformed x 5,329,000; 18lb cartridge cases reformed brazed x 43,328; shell nose forgings – 8.25in x 6,500, 2.75in (shrapnel) x 42,276; copper bands for various shell sizes x 1,863,000 (1,000 per week for 18lb shells); gaines x 428,248; stampings: nose x 144,665, fuse body x 83,437, base plate x 76,484; fuse adapters x 74,493; base adapter forgings x 5,572; fuses – with adapters x 240,000,

without adapters x 11,210, cast iron x 45,108; mines – hemispherical pressings x 17,825, anchor flukes x 30,000+; 8.25in shell noses for the Italian government

Misc.:

Stretchers x 2,950; picket posts x 3,850; picket pegs x 38,000; scantlings for rifles (butts) x 5,000 sets; leather work for Royal Arsenal x 105,000 pieces; cable drums x 103,000; mobilisation store boxes x 2,950; perambulators for carrying shells at various munitions stores x 100; 15in cartridge cases x 500; wood blocks for Bovington Camp x 12,000; mattresses x 168; pillows x 336; wooden saddle trees x 1,000; hooks for tackle x 1,000; leather work for saddler; stable for sick horses at County Road Swindon

Airforce (RFC & RAF):

Machined loops for aeroplane bombs x 8,000; mild steel stampings for aeroplane bombs x 1,100+; ash timber cuts artificially kiln dried for the Air Board x 10,000 cubic feet

As was stated earlier, this is not a complete list as one has to draw the line somewhere especially as the records available are vague and contradictory, but as much as possible has been included, though it must be remembered that along with the above, the construction and supply of engines, ambulance trains, rolling stock etc., as well as repairs, replacements and spare parts, was still classed as Government work and expected to be carried out alongside the work needed to ensure the healthy running of the company. The company still found time to carry out work for outside parties, such as 500 spokes for artillery wagons for Armstrong Whitworth, 4,000 machine loops for aeroplane bombs for Still & Co., forgings for Callandars Motor Co., as well as forgings for G.S. Wagons for a number of other Railway Companies.

Some of the varied work carried out at Swindon for the War Office called for specialist machinery and during October 1917 difficulties had arisen, even though the company had covered every angle, in the form of breaking steel billets. The men who worked the machines were unskilled (due to falling labour numbers in the works) and were paid 'piece rates', which were fixed by the Ministry of Munitions, and was the cause of great unrest as these unskilled workers were taking home more money than the skilled workers. Such was the unrest that the GWR felt it would be unable to continue such work, especially as munitions factories were, by then, fairly commonplace. But discussions had been opened with the Aircraft Department of the Ministry of Munitions to construct aeroplane parts at Swindon, parts which were in great demand as the war approached the end of 1917. Other Railway Companies had also been asked to take part in this plan, but as the railway workers who were to make the parts felt that they should be paid an equal sum to those employed in the aircraft factories, problems as far as worker dissatisfaction caused the Railway Executive Committee to request that Railway Companies not be involved in this manufacture if at all possible, to which the Department of Aeronautical Supplies agreed.

One aspect of munitions work that the Great Western pioneered was the repairing of splits in cartridge cases. Some 18lb cases were returned to England after firing to be reformed and used again – astonishingly up to six times. Splits sometimes occurred during the reforming process as well as cartridges arriving from the front with their mouths split. Instead of repairing the splits over a fire, the GWR boffins at Swindon devised a system of brazing the splits with an oxyacetylene blow pipe prior to repair. The Great Eastern Railway Company spent £500 installing machinery for brazing cases this way. In November 1916 a large quantity of used cases with splits arrived in the country, and the GWR agreed to do 300 per week, the Great Central 200 per week

EIGHT-INCH HOWITZERS.

1.—An array of trails in the Boiler Shop at Swindon.
2. Elevating gear, cradles, and finished carriages.

3. A finished carriage—one of the first batch made at Swindon.—
ready for dispatch.

8in howitzer construction at Swindon. (*GWR Magazine*)

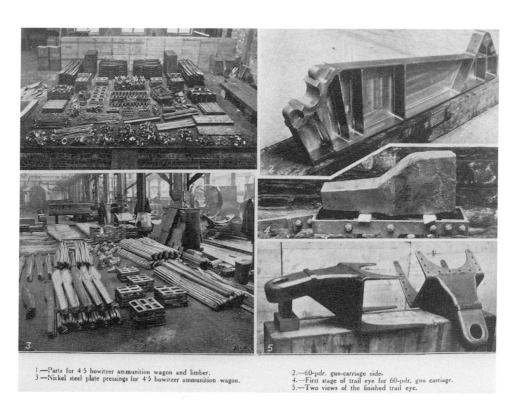

1.—Parts for 4.5 howitzer ammunition wagon and limber.
3.—Nickel steel plate pressings for 4.5 howitzer ammunition wagon.

2.—60-pdr. gun-carriage side.
4.—First stage of trail eye for 60-pdr. gun carriage.
5.—Two views of the finished trail eye.

Wagon and limber parts constructed at Swindon. (*GWR Magazine*)

Howitzer gun work at Swindon. (*GWR Magazine*)

and the Great Eastern 20,000 per week. So successful was this method that it was applied to other cases requiring repair.

War work for the Ministry of Munitions was to finish at the end of December 1917, once a revised programme for the repair of 18lb cartridge cases was over. The GWR was not exactly sad to see the end of their munitions work, with the labour shortage, and the commitment to the work until more munitions factories were constructed made the company reluctant to take on such work in the event of another war.

Munitions and Ordnance

Forty-seven Government storage depots, aeroplane depots and munitions factories, together with 230 private facilities where Government work was carried out, were located on the GWR system, all with siding accommodation provided. The main munitions factories in the Great Western area were Hayes, Pembrey in South Wales and Rotherwas near Hereford.

The GWR was called upon to co-operate in the building of an explosives factory at Stratton, near Swindon, and Henbury near Avonmouth. Henbury was planned to be the second largest factory of its type in the country, and involved a great deal of work for the GWR; the first phase, at a cost of £186,761, consisted of:

Temporary workmen's platforms and five sidings at Cittening (Pilning)
Holding accommodation at Stoke Gifford
Loops between Henbury and Pilning lines and junctions to the factory
Doubling of Henbury line between Filton West Junction and Hallen Marsh, and additional accommoda-
    tion at Hembury
Double line junction between Pilning line and main line and additional sidings at Pilning Low Level

Loop line connecting Avonmouth and South Wales line at Patchway
Up and down line at Filton
Double junctions with Factory, Hallen Halt. Workmen's platforms at Hallen Halt
Holding accommodation for workers trains at Dr Day's Sidings, Marsh Junction, Bristol
Telephone installments in all areas concerned with the works

All work carried out was paid for by the Government on the understanding that the GWR would take over a large part of these works at a depreciated value at the end of the war, as was the agreement for most of the works carried out by the company for the Government. It was estimated that some 20,000 workers would travel to and from Henbury, and the Ministry of Munitions asked for twenty-five trains to run each morning and evening.

The work of the GWR at Henbury began in February 1917 and was on a major scale, work which was to help the war effort and eventually benefit the company, but no one, let alone the GWR, could foresee the consequences of America entering the war, and at the end of May 1917 the plans for the factory were abandoned by the Government. So much work had been undertaken by the GWR at Henbury that a great deal of disappointment was felt by those concerned at its premature abandonment, although the company was reimbursed for costs incurred.

Amended plans were introduced due to other factories within the Avonmouth area, one producing picric acid for use in explosives. With the increase in dock traffic, negotiations took place for the GWR to retain some of the lines laid and some of the works to relieve any congestion in the Avonmouth District, although it was financially difficult for the company.

The increased production at the factories called for an increase in labour, but as the nearby towns were unable to accommodate large numbers of workers they had to be drawn upon from further afield, thus increasing the train services. A good example of this was a large munitions factory at Lando, near Pembrey in South Wales. Originally seven trains a day transported the workers to this sparsely populated area from Carmarthen and Swansea, but this was increased to twelve trains a day. In total 4,057,000 workers were carried by the GWR to and from Pembrey during the war. Production at Pembrey and other factories was seven days a week, calling for arrangements to be made to relax the suspension of cheap tickets at weekends to allow some of the workers to return home.

Cordite paste was manufactured at Pembrey and great care had to be taken when transporting this dangerous material, which was done by using special dust-proof vans which were steam-fitted to maintain an even temperature. Trains of around seven vans in length travelled east out of Wales to Faversham and Chilworth, via Reading and the South Eastern and Chatham Railway.

The shell-filling factory at Hayes accounted for an average of 3,800 wagons being dealt with each month, and daily trains ran from Hayes to Southampton and Richborough. It is recorded that during the war an astonishing 25 million passengers travelled in connection with the work at this factory.

An average of three trains of ammunition a day, and on occasions up to seven trains, ran from the large shell-filling factory at Rotherwas to the south and east ports. As well as the workers being transported to and from the factory, there was heavy inwards traffic from the north and Midlands of shell cases and explosives.

In 1917 the GWR was requested to carry out sidings work at the motor manufacturing works of Morris Cowley, who produced items for the Government during the war, such as hand grenades, howitzer bomb cases and mine sinkers. The plans for the sidings were hatched on 7 May 1917 and were sufficiently laid to allow traffic to use them by 30 May. So impressive was this work that a letter of praise was sent on behalf of the Director General of Trench Warfare Supply, stating that '… the line was essential, and there was no doubt that the prompt action taken by the GWR has materially assisted the Ministry in its operations in connection with the supply of the particular class of munitions concerned'.

Last, but by no means least, was the Royal Ordnance Depot at Didcot. This important depot originally had twenty-four sheds, which increased to ninety, with store dumps by the end of the war. The railway track within the depot stretched to 32 miles, with an additional 7 miles connecting Didcot Depot with the Royal Air Force Milton Aircraft Stores Depot.

Much of the ordnance requirements for the armies on all fronts originated from Didcot, as being centrally located meant that little difficulty was encountered, with special through trains to London docks, Swansea, Barry, Cardiff, Avonmouth, Liverpool, Littlehampton, Newhaven and Richborough, and then to the various ordnance depots overseas. An average of 884 trucks ran in and out of Didcot Depot per month, the heaviest month being April 1918 with 11,103 loaded and unloaded trucks; additional trucks were also being worked within the confines of the depot.

In the very early days shipment of items less than 1 ton were sent via the GWR at Didcot, but as traffic increased all shipments were handled by the depot.

Other munitions depots and factories within the GWR area were Swindon, Laira Bridge, Rowley Regis (small arms ammunition) factory, Park Royal, Shepherds Bush, Speech House Road (Acetone factory), Small Heath (rifle testing factory), Milton and Brockworth Aircraft Depots.

Munitions Storage

In the winter of 1915 the Ministry of Munitions reported that although they had new stores in fourteen centres and gaining others, they requested that the GWR make available to them any vacant sheds or covered areas. Such was the increased munitions manufacture at this time that a consignment of shells, way in excess of the storage facilities at Plymouth, had to be put into temporary storage at Swindon.

Military Camp Railways

In the spring of 1918 the War Office made a request that the Railway Companies oversee the maintenance and working of the railways serving the military camps, which amounted to around fourteen camps throughout Britain, the expenditure of which was to be charged as 'work done for the Government'.

The GWR was responsible for two camp railways constructed by the War Department, the first being the camp at Codford which had a track mileage of 4 miles and 212 yards (2¾ miles of which was main line), and the line at Sutton Veny near Warminster, with a track length of 4 miles 1,739 yards (3 miles 1,170 yards of main line). 'Special staff' were employed at Codford who dealt only with the military.

At that time, the War Office were constructing lines to serve other camps within the Winchester area, one of which was an American camp that was to utilise the Didcot–Newbury and Southampton Railway for the transportation of large numbers of troops from the disembarkation port of Liverpool, and upon completion the GWR was expected to take on the task of maintenance and the working of these lines as well.

Tank Wagons

All new innovations have teething troubles and the development of the new war machine, known by its secret code name of 'Tank', was no exception, as was the means by which they were to be

A " War " Crowd at Codford Station.

Workers waiting at Codford to go to the military camps in the area. (*GWR Magazine*)

transported. To understand the development of the tank wagon it is necessary to take a brief look at the history of the tank on the Western Front.

Tanks began to arrive in France in August 1916 in small numbers, and were first used on 15 September at Flers. Manufacture rose to 280 tanks per month by September 1917, increasing still further to two and a half times that amount by 1918. During the tank's development many alterations were introduced changing the weights and dimensions.

At a width of 13ft 9in, the earliest tanks were too wide for loading gauges at home and abroad, but with the sponsons (gun mountings) removed, which weighed 3–4 tons, the weight of this 28-ton tank was reduced, and had an overall width of 8ft 6in, but by 1918 design changes meant that tanks varied in weight from 14 tons, for the Whippet Tank, to 40 tons.

The movement and storage of the tanks was carried out with the utmost secrecy. Tarpaulins covered them while in transit in an attempt to disguise these new weapons, and secluded areas were chosen for storage and detrainment, with most of the movements carried out under the cover of darkness. It was necessary to transport tanks by rail as their reliability and speed discouraged using their own power, as did their thirst for fuel.

There was great difficulty in finding suitable wagons in France for the transportation of tanks. The Nord Railway possessed a truck with a capacity of 20 tons, which was fine for lightweight models, and the load height was just within the Nord capacity. These trucks were used for the first tanks weighing up to 26 tons, with the predictable damage being caused by over-loading. The Nord trucks, when loaded with tanks, were too high for the Etat System, but the Etat Railways had fifty wagons with a capacity of 25 tons and could just clear the loading gauge with a tank weighing 28 tons. This type of wagon was used extensively during November 1917, but of forty-three wagons used, twenty-eight were so badly damaged they could not be used again.

Wagons built for carrying rails would have been suitable for the task but were in heavy demand for the rebuilding of damaged lines on the Western Front, and therefore could not be spared. British wagons sent to France for this purpose were capable of bearing 45 tons, but the overhangs on the bodies would not take the weight of a tank loaded on to the wagon. End loading and unloading of the tanks under their own power was less conspicuous and more convenient than loading by crane, but the overhangs on these wagons were incapable of bearing the weight of a tank being driven on, and without the modifications needed to support the overhangs it is easy to visualise the damage that would occur. Specially adapted wagons to overcome these problems were requested to be supplied by British companies, and the GWR is credited with supplying the first of these fifty special tank wagons capable of carrying a load of 25 tons. These were by no means perfect, but later consignments of wagons were modified to make end loading of tanks more efficient. Twenty-six modified Macaw B wagons were produced in the summer of 1917 and were given the War Department numbers 39201 to 39226. These wagons, with a capacity of 30 tons, were ready and used to transport tanks immediately prior to the Battle of Cambrai in the November. End loading was not always used, as special earthworks were built alongside railway lines, such as at the Tank Corps Central Workshops at Teneur, where tanks could be driven up to the same height as the wagon and manoeuvred into place.

Large orders were placed at home for the building of 'RECTANKS' (Railway Executive Committee Tank Trucks) which were capable of carrying up to 40 tons. In the Annual Report for works carried out by the Wagon and Carriage Works at Swindon during 1918, it is stated that a large number of these were produced. Nearly 400 Rectanks, manufactured by British companies, were working in France by the end of the war.

Armoured Train

Two armoured trains were constructed with the co-operation of various Railway Companies for the defence of the east coast in the event of an invasion. On one of the trains the infantry vans were converted from 40-ton GWR coal wagons, numbers 53989 and 53996. The whole train was armour plated, including the GNR locomotive No.1587, which was sandwiched between the two converted GWR wagons. Although the wagons were of different patterns, they were changed out of all recognition as the body panels were replaced with half-inch plating. The sides of the wagons retained their original height, but the central roof height was increased to 6ft 9in by adding sheet plating at either ends designed to facilitate a curved roof.

The wagons were installed with drinking water tanks, tables, a cooking stove and rifle racks. The sides of the wagons had rifle loop holes and sliding doors incorporated into them.

'Monster' Wagons

The year 1918 saw the introduction of 'Monster' vans, specifically designed for the transportation of dismantled aeroplanes. Built at Swindon, these 50ft-long vans were 8ft 6in wide and 8ft 5in high, with good ventilation and light. Although doors were fitted to the sides of the van, doors opening to the full height and width of the van were to be found at each end to allow the loading of aeroplane wings. After the war these vans were used for transporting motor cars and bulky items requiring loading through the ends of the van.

Armoured wagon constructed by the GWR. (*GWR Magazine*)

GWR 'monster' wagon. (*GWR Magazine*)

Chassis erecting shop, Slough. (*GWR Magazine*)

Seaplane Station

In the spring of 1917 the Admiralty approached the GWR with a plan for establishing a seaplane station at Fishguard, and a collapsible hangar was installed near the marine factory on the company's land. These planes, flown by 245 Squadron, were needed for the war against the ever increasing submarine attacks on shipping. A larger structure for accommodating an airship was planned for later.

Chepstow Shipyard

November 1917 saw increasing difficulties in dealing with traffic at Portbury and, especially, Chepstow shipyards. Shipyard work at Chepstow had been started by the Standard Shipbuilding Company and an agreement was proposed whereby the costs involved in the reconstruction of the station and yard would be refunded by the rebates from the additional traffic the yard might bring to the GWR. However, the Standard Shipbuilding Company was taken over by the Government who authorised additional accommodation at the yard. The work consisted of siding accommodation on the down side amounting to £12,866. This cost was borne by the Admiralty and Munitions Department.

August 1918:
Siding accommodation for RAF stores at Ruslip   £18,971
Sidings for tank testing at Newbury   £7, 004
Extend siding at POW camp at Dorchester   £329

Motor Car Department

As with other company departments, the Motor Car Department undertook work for the Government, including work on engines for the Ministry of Munitions and the repair of lorries for the Army Service Corps. Mechanised road transportation was still in its infancy but the GWR fleet of road vehicles was increasing, so the facilities at the Slough Depot were improved by converting the open shed into a four-bay chassis erecting shop, complete with all the modern amenities such as roller doors, gas lighting overhead and electric lamps lower down. This helped while the depot was involved in the extra war work, but over 50 per cent of the depot staff had left to enlist in the forces.

There were some twenty-nine road motor depots scattered throughout the system, and their pre-war work consisted of running repairs to the vehicles in their area, but during the war they took on the overhaul of vehicles to take the pressure off the Slough Depot. They were kept busy as vehicles were used to transport soldiers to remote areas away from the GWR system, and extra motor cartage rounds had to be added due to horses being taken by the Government. Orders were placed for more vehicles but manufacturers were unable to fill them due to war work.

Many makes of chassis were handled at Slough such as Pagefield, Maudslay, Berna and Kelly, as well as the light chassis Sunbeam which were used by the Ministry of Munitions for transporting officials around London. Ten Berna 5-ton chassis were overhauled at Slough prior to being sent to Swindon, where charabanc bodies were fitted before being handed over to 606 Company, Army Service Corps, predominantly made up of members of the Women's Legion, who used the vehicles to transport munitions workers in various areas of the country. The Sunbeams used by officials in London were also driven by women.

The depot found time to diversify by working on the preliminary design of a marine paraffin engine, which was fully developed and built by an engineering company in the Midlands.

Coal Gas

Owing to the shortage of petrol, alternative fuels were sought, and in the autumn of 1917 there was a great deal of excitement at the prospect of coal gas being used as a substitute for that rare commodity. It was recognised that engines designed to run on petrol would readily accept coal gas as fuel with little alteration, and it was calculated that around 250 cubic feet of coal gas would give the equivalent power of one gallon of petrol.

The problem of designing a suitable container for the storage of such a large quantity of gas on a vehicle was overcome by manufacturing rubber and balloon fabric, with the original container being of a cylindrical shape which was anchored to the roof of the vehicle. Unfortunately this shape of container had the tendency to roll from side to side with the movement of the vehicle and in windy conditions. When the gas level dropped the deflated container would flop over the sides of the roof obscuring the passengers' view from the windows as well as, said the GWR, giving the vehicle an 'untidy appearance'.

It was considered that a rectangular container anchored by soft rubber cords, with smooth wooden fingers hinged at the base, was the most aesthetically pleasing and suitable design, with the largest being of 700 cubic feet; as the container deflated the pressure of the wood fingers allowed the container to fold into itself. As gas companies charged for refills of cylinders at their full capacity, drivers were advised to allow the gas to completely run out and drive to the gas company using the minimum amount of petrol as possible.

The original enthusiasm for the alternative fuel was dampened by problems that arose in obtaining suitable cylinders. The need for modifications came with experience and the standard container was made like a double football, with the inner casing being a red rubber gas-tight bag and the outer being rubber-treated canvas which prevented wear on the gas-tight bag and eliminated the tiresome problem of melting the seams of the rubber bag during hot weather. The containers were carried on trays which had webbing straps at the bottom to allow drainage of water and ventilate the bottom of the container to stop damp rot. The original rubber anchor

Various Great Western road vehicles converted to run on coal gas. (*GWR Magazine*)

belts caused great problems as they were apt to snap in high winds, necessitating the driver to hot foot it up the road or across fields to recover the escaping container! One unforeseen technical hiccough was that the forward motion of the vehicle drove the gas to the rear of the cylinder, which was rectified by the gas being piped by engine suction from the rear of the cylinder.

As an average, a 3-ton passenger vehicle consumed 30–40 cubic feet of gas per mile, which was dependent on the quality of the local gas supply. Except for the cylinder, all the fittings were designed by the GWR Motor Car Department and were manufactured in the various shops.

From the inception of this alternative fuel to the spring of 1919, vehicles adapted to run on gas were found on the following road motor services:

Neath to Pontardawe; Penzance to St Just; Penzance to Pendeen; Saltash to Callington; St Austell to Bugle; St Austell to St Dennis; Redruth to Falmouth; Redruth to Portreath; St Day to Carharrack; Paignton to Totnes; Slough to Farnham; Uxbridge to Denham; Windsor to Ascot; Weymouth to Wyke; Wolverhampton to Bridgnorth; Wrexham to Farndon

Parcels services: in the areas of Cardiff, Manchester and Penzance

It is worth adding that improvements were made to the Great Western road vehicles in June 1916 when adjustable seats were fitted for the driver and, for added comfort, a weather screen, though it did not afford much protection against the elements – but was better than nothing!

CHAPTER FOUR

Traffic – Ports – Coal – Air Raids – Travel and Passengers – Royal Journeys

Traffic

As with all companies, the volume of traffic on the GWR system increased dramatically with the introduction of Government traffic at the outbreak of the war. By early 1915 routes were very congested, not only because of Government demands with regards to military traffic, but the increase of ordinary merchandise traffic normally sent by sea, shortage of staff, and if that was not enough, very bad weather in January of that year resulted in landslips and flooding of the lines. This bad weather returned with an unexpected blizzard in March 1916 when 1,500 telegraph poles on the GWR were broken.

There are reasons why the company experienced a great increase in traffic during the war. Geographically, the area covered by the Great Western included access to the South Wales coal-fields and many ports, such as the major South Wales ports, Avonmouth, Plymouth, Weymouth and Portland, all having a steady flow of troops, munitions and stores inwards and outwards, and the fact that the company served Salisbury Plain with one of its lines, accounting for much traffic from the large collection of military camps there.

In June 1916 the GWR ran eighty-eight special trains to transport the 60th (London) Division, who were destined for France, from Warminster and Codford. The transportation went so smoothly that a letter was sent by Lieutenant Colonel Malcolm thanking the GWR for their assistance, especially the stationmasters at Warminster, Codford, Heytesbury and Westbury.

Up to 31 August 1915 84,024 officers and 1,799,770 men, 340,501 horses, 1,114 guns and limbers, and 18,130 wagons, bicycles etc. had been transported from Great Western stations. By February 1917 the number of military personnel that had left company stations had risen to 261,045 officers and 5,005,051 men.

August Bank Holiday was postponed in 1916, but traffic was as busy as ever even though cheap tickets had been suspended. To try to deter unnecessary travel, the increase in fares introduced in 1917 brought about a 29 per cent reduction in passenger traffic, which eased the demands made upon the company, but the transportation of workers increased by 32 per cent, augmenting revenue even though there were less trains running.

The increase in munitions factories, the workers, transportation of raw materials inwards and finished goods outwards, coupled with Admiralty coal trains, military and ambulance trains etc. gave rise to the volume of traffic running over Great Western lines, greatly exceeding that which would have normally been anticipated.

By December 1917 the GWR were facing major problems, brought about by the shortage of engines and men, certain traffic (especially coal which had to be hauled over greater distances) and the 'unsettled feeling of the men', as it was put by the directors. It was hoped that an increase in war wages would help ease the men's situation, but they were doubtful if this would reduce the feeling of discontent and the stress of being overstretched.

Congestion on the lines, especially at Severn Tunnel Junction and Rogerstone, which were affected the greatest by the alteration in flow of traffic, was worsening. Providing additional accommodation at these trouble spots went a long way to easing the congestion, which is what the GWR preferred to do rather than take the drastic steps of refusing traffic.

A greater amount of freight had to be transported by rail that would otherwise have been taken by sea owing to the submarine threat, and because shipping was being used for other purposes, so there was an increase in traffic both in and out of the Great Western area. China clay from Cornwall was sent north to Staffordshire at the rate of 3,500 tons a month, 900 tons of gas coal sent south from Yorkshire to Plymouth each week; the list is long and varied with goods travelling north to south and east to west continuously.

Another consequence of the submarine activity was food. Britain was not self-sufficient, relying greatly on imports, which were landed at many ports within the GWR area, and had to be transported to various destinations. However, they found that because of the large agricultural industry within its region the transportation of home-grown foodstuffs was of equal importance, not only for a needy country but also for the army abroad. It wasn't only troops that needed feeding; the phenomenal number of horses and mules employed by the army required vast quantities of fodder which was transported to various Government depots, such as the remount depot at Avonmouth and the concentration point set up at Newbury Racecourse where fodder was held prior to distribution. The GWR allocated 2,500 trucks for the carriage of fodder per week, together with the necessary sheets and ropes. It has been calculated that almost a quarter of all shipping to the Western Front was animal fodder.

Owing to the scale of munitions and military equipment manufacture in the north and Midlands, a great deal of traffic was travelling south to the channel ports, and as the loads carried by these trains restricted their passage on the congested London routes, connecting links using what were obscure lines became extremely important, especially the Great Western Bushbury and Basingstoke route.

Goods from Scotland and the north of England were brought south by the London and North Western Railway to Bushbury Junction, where the GWR connects north of Wolverhampton. The goods were forwarded to Basingstoke and handed over to the London and South Western, and taken to the ports of Southampton and Portsmouth. On this route the GWR also connected with the Great Central Railway at Banbury, whereby goods from the north-east could be conveyed to the southern ports. Later large consignments from the north using the Bushbury or Banbury route made their way to Reading where they were handed over from the GWR to the South East and Chatham Railway for the final destination of the Channel port at Richborough.

Nearly all the shell traffic from the north of England destined for Southampton used the Bushbury–Basingstoke route, and so busy was the traffic here that seven special trains of fifty wagons in length were frequently seen in a day. As well as this traffic all kinds of war equipment was carried over these lines such as tanks, heavy guns on their own carriages, locomotives and rolling stock etc., all destined for the Western Front via the Channel ports.

One of the most important items of freight that the GWR was involved with was that of Admiralty coal. At the beginning of the war the Admiralty was dependent on colliers shipping steam coal from South Wales to fuel the fleet at Scapa Flow, and although arrangements had been made previously to send some of the coal by rail it was not foreseen, at this point, the effect German submarines would have on the colliers while on their voyage from South Wales, into the Irish Sea then round Scotland. Many of the colliers were sunk, increasing the Admiralty's dependence on the railways to supply the fleet with coal.

The wagons, most of which were supplied to the Admiralty by a hire company, when loaded with coal from the Aberdare and Rhondda districts, were made up into the Admiralty coal trains, or Jellico Specials as they were known, at Pontypool Road. Their destination was Grangemouth, a 375-mile journey which took around forty-eight hours. The trains were dealt with by the GWR as far as Warrington, and from there onwards the responsibility was shared by Railway Companies en route. Labels were affixed to the trains denoting their importance, and were specially signalled for the whole journey. So great was the Admiralty coal traffic to Scotland that nearly all of the Great Western 2-8-0 locomotives were engaged on this work throughout the war.

Because of the congestion at Pontypool Road two alternative routes were planned: Cardiff to Gloucester and Gobowen, via Talyllyn, to Chester for Warrington. The coal was also sent to other ports where it was required by the navy, such as Glasgow, Tyneside and Devonport. From 27 August 1914, when the first Admiralty coal train left Pontypool Road, to the end of the war, 13,631 coal specials were run from South Wales, accounting for an estimated 5,425,400 tons of coal.

Much has been said of the increase in mileage of trains run over the various British railways, but in March 1918 figures were produced for 1917 comparing services with 1913, and the GWR goods mileage had increased by 23 per cent compared with 3 per cent for the London and North Western, and 2 per cent for Midland. These figures only confirmed what the company already knew; they were stretched to the limit but owing to the superior power of the Great Western engines much of the increase was worked without the need for double heading, which was not the case for other companies.

From 1 September 1918 single and outward halves of ordinary return tickets were available on the day of issue only, exceptions being where the journey was a long one or complicated, such as travel to Scotland or the Channel Islands.

By the end of the war 63,349 special Government freight trains of stores, ammunition, tanks and Admiralty coal had run on the Great Western system, and the number of naval and military trains, ambulance trains, either GWR or running on the system, amounted to 37,283. These figures do not include trains run for workers, ordinary freight and passengers.

Praise Indeed

In 1916 a series of articles appeared in the *Morning Post* entitled 'The Front revisited', in which the transport arrangements at the front were said to be 'a miracle performed every day with apparent ease', and the writer went on to state that 'everything goes a smoothly as a Great Western Railway timetable'.

Ports

South coast ports may feature as the most important during the war, but Avonmouth certainly did more than its fair share, with more than 200,000 troops dealt with, both inward and outward. The troops were destined for the Eastern Front, and the wounded from this front were landed at the port for transportation to hospitals in Bristol, London and Manchester by ambulance trains which, in total, carried 1,600 officers and 23,500 other ranks. In all sixty-five hospital ships and 250 ambulance trains were dealt with at the port.

1859

Carriage Free.

From NATIONAL FUND FOR WELSH TROOPS,
11, Downing Street, London, S.W.

To the Officer Commanding

_____*Unit*

_____*Regiment*

c/o MILITARY FORWARDING OFFICER,

AVONMOUTH.

*Date*_____ Per G. W. RAILWAY.

Carriage free parcel label for items to be sent to Welsh troops serving abroad – the parcels were carried by the GWR to Avonmouth. (Author's collection)

Avonmouth was busy, with many sailors passing through on leave, and prisoners of war laded at the port. Between 7 and 11 February 1915 a division of 17,973 men and 5,061 horses, plus equipment, arrived at Avonmouth in ninety-two trains. They were sent overseas in nineteen ships.

As well as men, there was a large flow of vehicles to the port to be shipped out, in particular tanks and London omnibuses destined for the Western Front, together with over 130,000 trucks of ammunition, guns, naval stores, mail and aeroplanes to be sent to various fronts, and materials for munitions manufacture were landed at the port for distribution around the country.

The port received over 339,000 mules and horses from South America and other countries, and a remount depot was built at Shirehampton to deal with these, which required the GWR to convey 14,000 tons of building material and fodder. A large number of the horses and mules were trained to Wiveliscombe and Minehead, where they were rested in the district before returning to the depot and then on to the fronts. During the war it was estimated that the Great Western dealt with over 3.5 million tons of goods traffic at Avonmouth.

With the south and east coast ports attracting the attention of the Germans, Avonmouth was not the only port in the area to be considered important, so was its neighbour across the Bristol Channel, Newport. Only three weeks before the outbreak of the war a new sea lock and dock extension had been ceremoniously opened by Prince Arthur, and it was claimed the new lock was the largest in the world, with the docks capable of dealing with the largest ships afloat. Newport was known for the distribution of South Wales coal, but became increasingly important for the import of iron ore, which was distributed to iron works mainly by the GWR. Nitrate of soda was also dealt with in vast quantities.

The Government established a large factory at the docks for rectifying 18-pounder and 4.5in brass cartridge cases. The salvaged shells from the battlefields of Flanders were stored in a warehouse covering 13 acres. Once the shells were ready, they were transported to the filling factories again mostly by the GWR.

Cardiff was another busy port, with Admiralty colliers leaving with all kinds of military stores and items, mostly to the Mediterranean, and it has been recorded that up to 500 truckloads of stores were, on occasions, waiting for shipment, all of which was railed to Cardiff by the GWR.

In July 1917 the Controller of Shipping visited the west of England with a view to using the ports in the region for handling foodstuffs and wheat. It was proposed that some 6,000 tons of grain a day would be offloaded, needing twenty trains of fifty wagons in size to deal with such quantities. This would require provision of empty stock and the working of loaded traffic to its distribution points – a situation that the Great Western thought was an extra strain on resources, especially as the unloaded ships would have to be refilled with cargo brought to the docks by rail. The ports that were highlighted for this cargo were Plymouth, Devonport, Avonmouth, Newport, Cardiff, Barry and Swansea.

Originally all cargo of this type, with the exception of a small amount transported by rail to London, was handled by waterborne transport to granaries and mills in the area of the Port of London, but neither the mills nor the Port of London itself had the facilities to handle freight from the railways. The waterside premises used by the Railway Companies were, at that time, being used for Government stores and munitions traffic, which it was felt would have to cease if this proposal went ahead, although the GWR embarked on work to provide additional sidings in the area.

The situation did not improve, and a Traffic Diversion Committee came into being with Colonel Pringle of the Board of Trade as chairman, with representatives from Government departments and the Railway Executive Committee, which by March 1918 had completed investigations to finally divert sea traffic from east to west coast ports for the transportation of foodstuffs to London and other cities. Avonmouth and Southampton docks were already at full capacity and the suitability of the South Wales ports was, as far as possible, discouraged by the GWR as this would have meant using the Gloucester line and Severn Tunnel Junction, which was already straining under the weight of the increased coal traffic. However, the company was fully aware that if the eastern ports, especially London, were closed because of enemy action then drastic action on behalf of the GWR would have to be taken to keep essential supplies reaching London, but this would only be possible if there was a reduction in munitions and Government traffic.

A report was submitted to the Board of Trade in early April 1918, and although a complete diversion to western ports was considered to be detrimental to the efficient running of traffic and trade, it was thought that a partial diversion would cause little inconvenience, depending on the storage facilities at the ports and at London.

This partial diversion was calculated to be 12,000 tons of supplies a week, and with this in mind works were carried out to provide additional accommodation between Hanwell and West Ealing, and at Iver, as well as extensive extensions to the waterside buildings at Brentford. A report was also called for planned action should the diversion be on a large scale, which suggested the following number of trains would have to be run each day to London: Cardiff 5, Avonmouth 8, Liverpool 12, Birkenhead 2 and Manchester 9.

Improvement works were also called for on the Great Eastern Railway, and minor work at Liverpool and Manchester, as well as extensive works at the Port of London as the final destination. The GWR also put forward that if such numbers of trains had to run then a corresponding number of Government trains would have to be cancelled due to insufficient numbers of trains, rolling stock and men.

Coal

The subject of the availability of coal during the war years might not seem that interesting, but what will become clear is that this otherwise taken for granted pre-war commodity was suddenly in great demand, so much so that it was outstripping supply to a dangerous degree.

By the early months of 1915 the GWR was beginning to experience difficulties in obtaining coal from its contractors due to demands by the War Office and Admiralty, lack of productivity from the collieries, congested lines and orders for coal from neutral countries, which was permitted under licence. The stock of coal in August 1914 was 223,000 tons and by May 1915 this reserve stock was down to 122,000 tons. The situation improved temporarily after May 1915 due to an enterprising arrangement made with the South Wales district collieries, whereby each morning empty GWR wagons were placed in such a position in the colliery sidings that they passed under the screens first, thereby filling the GWR wagons before any from other companies. This system of 'first come, first served' was ensured by keeping loco and traffic inspectors in the area to monitor wagon workings. This system was also incorporated into the Wolverhampton and Wrexham areas and was the only way the company could ensure adequate supplies. There were also anxious moments for the company in respect of the Park Royal generating stations, as the coal for these were supplied from collieries in the Midlands, and London and North Western Railway sectors where considerable troop train movements hampered deliveries.

Another aspect that put a strain on supplies was that during the Whitsuntide holiday of May 1915 the collieries contracted to supply the Great Western were closed for two days, and on short time for the rest of the week, and in July 200,000 Welsh miners went on strike over pay. It must be stated that the miners were not the only workers engaged on essential work that went on strike during the war.

By the autumn regular supplies of coal were being received, but there was still a deficit compared to the beginning of the war, which would not have caused much of a problem under normal circumstances but the Great Western were now running more trains over longer distances causing higher consumption and, coupled with the increase in the price of coal, they felt they were under a strain of which they had no control. Diversion of coal from North Wales mines in February 1916 meant a serious shortfall for the GWR, with the supplies being one-third short of the contracted amount.

It wasn't only industry that was having trouble with coal. Rises in domestic prices in 1915 found those with little income struggling to buy coal at the increased prices; a situation that would not improve.

In August 1917 a proposal was made by the Controller of Coal Mines of a scheme calling for consumers to take coal from their nearest possible producer in an attempt to cut down excessive, unnecessary transportation, and coal companies would not be allowed to sell coal outside of their areas. The GWR foresaw problems with this scheme as their consumption of coal in North Wales was greater than the area's output, plus the fact that this coal could not be supplemented with coal from South Wales. This meant that the GWR Northern and Midland districts would have to draw on supplies from Lancashire, Yorkshire, Derby and Northampton, which would entail coal wagons passing through very congested areas. Great Western locos were designed to run on Welsh coal, and a change to the lower-grade coal of other areas would have incurred an increase of coal usage, as well as the increase in train mileage for the company if it had to supply London with coal from South Wales.

With all the foreseeable problems and anxiety from the Railway Companies, the scheme became operational on 10 September, but in November the Coal Controller made special arrangements to supply London with gas coal from Durham, which was to be carried in wagons belonging to the Admiralty. This new concession did not help the GWR as the Admiralty coal from South Wales had to be transported to the north, then the locos and wagons worked a triangular route from the north picking up the gas coal at Durham, conveying it to London, then returning the wagons back to South Wales to be reloaded with Admiralty coal for the north. Not only did this increase the traffic on the already congested route from London to South Wales, but it tied up the company's locos to such an extent that it was requested that other companies assist with locos to run some of the distance.

The price of coal increased in October, under the Coal Prices (Limitation) Act, by 2s 6d per ton, raising the price of South Wales, Monmouthshire and Forest of Dean coal to 9s per ton, with coal from the rest of the country priced at 6s 6d.

The start of 1918 saw the GWR having to run twenty-two additional trains for coal, involving seventeen extra trains, together with seven more engines working the Admiralty 'triangular route'. Congestion was created where sidings were unable to cope with the extra traffic, especially at Rogerstone where the sidings were originally planned for the transportation of coal from the collieries to ports, whereas during the war the bulk of the coal was for mainland destinations with almost every wagon destined for a different place, calling for an increase in shunting to such an extent that additional sidings had to be laid. Of the twenty-two additional trains put on to cope, fourteen ran through Severn Tunnel Junction, increasing freight train traffic by 2,396 in the first few months of 1917 compared to a corresponding period in 1913, causing the exchange accommodation at Severn Tunnel Junction to be stretched to breaking point.

The Great Western also experienced difficulties in the working of their regular Admiralty trains to the north and south-west. In 1915 1,784 loaded trains ran from South Wales but by 1917 this number had increased to 3,417. There were developments to move coal from South Wales to Birkenhead for bunkering, for which the Admiralty had authorised additional accommodation at Pontypool Road which, as time went by, became totally inadequate. The Admiralty coal was exchanged at Quakers Yard from the Taff Valley Railway, and the accommodation there was designed to cope with 289 wagons, but during thirteen days in November 1917 some 11,054 wagons were exchanged (an average of 850 per day), and running lines were used to store wagons causing more congestion.

These were not the only places with difficulties, nor were the GWR the only company to experience problems. The North Eastern Railway was in the same position, whereas the other companies found the scheme of benefit to themselves. The Executive Committee and the Controller of Coal Mines discussed the matter with the GWR, and the Controller, although agreeing to do as much as possible to help with the loan of engines from other companies and ensuring that materials were available for engine repairs etc., thought the main problem was the increase of traffic due to the diversion of freight from the canals to rail.

In the first months of 1918 much-needed work on additional sidings, accommodation etc. to ease the difficulties experienced with Admiralty coal at Nelson and Llancaiac, Pontypool Road, Quakers Yard, Bishton, Rogerstone and Severn Tunnel Junction amounted to £81,075, with £39,420 being spent on Severn Tunnel Junction alone, and included accommodation for 258 wagons.

A crisis occurred in the early part of May when collieries at Markham and Oakdale (Tredegar Colliery Company) went on strike over a dispute about deductions made to the pay of some men who had attended a funeral. The dispute spread, and this industrial action meant that the branch lines of Ebbw Vale, Nantyglo, Nine Mile Point and Penar were silent. The pits involved supplied locomotive coal for the district and left a shortfall of 37,390 tons (over a week's supply for the whole system). A settlement for the strikers did not come about until 31 May, but the GWR was anxious knowing that the extra supplies of coal would be slow in materialising owing to the shortage of manpower at the collieries.

On 1 June a scheme became operational whereby coal from South Wales was transported by ship across the Bristol Channel to the south-west, which did a lot to relieve the congestion at Severn Tunnel Junction, as well as releasing much-needed wagons. It was now finally realised that the Admiralty coal trains could be better utilised by transporting iron ore to South Wales on the return empty runs.

In July the Controller of Mines advised the Railway Companies to economise on their coal consumption to the tune of 7 per cent, or a million tons of coal over a twelve-month period, as the output from mines was declining. All other concerns such as munitions works were also requested to economise.

Although essential, it was difficult for the Railway Companies to cut back on consumption – especially the GWR as their goods train mileage was far in excess of the other companies, due mostly to the demands of Government departments together with the longer routes in operation, which meant it was difficult for the company to find any way of economising without affecting Government traffic. GWR goods train mileage had increased by 4,781,635 miles, from 20,169,166 in 1913 to 24,950,801 in 1917, an increase of 23.7 per cent.

Air Raids

Air raids affecting the civilian population during the First World War were nothing compared to the raids experienced during the Second World War, but nonetheless this new form of enemy destruction aimed at the Home Front must have been frightening for those who were on the receiving end of these attacks. Chronicled below are details of raids that directly affected the GWR.

Early in the war the Admiralty and police issued instructions that lighting be reduced in Paddington goods and passenger stations and between Paddington and Acton because of the possibility of air attack. Trains approaching or leaving London after dark were requested to have blinds drawn.

GREAT WESTERN RAILWAY.

Defence of the Realm (Consolidation) Regulations, 1914.

OBLIGATION ON PASSENGERS TO KEEP BLINDS OF COMPARTMENTS LOWERED AFTER SUNSET.

Extract from Clause II of Order of Secretary of State, dated December 15th, 1915:—

"Passengers in railway carriages which are provided with blinds MUST keep the blinds lowered so as to cover the windows. The blinds may be lifted in case of necessity when the train is at a standstill at a station, but if lifted they must be lowered again before the train starts."

Carriage window poster, December 1915. (Author's collection)

Shrapnel damage to parcel van, 1917. (*GWR Magazine*)

31 January 1916 – there was an extensive attack by German aircraft. The Executive Committee was informed of the impending attack at 5.13 p.m., and by 6.25 p.m. it was apparent that the Midlands was the target area. The train service was suspended and a blackout was imposed from 8.15 p.m. to 10.40 p.m. There was damage but the only property belonging to the GWR to suffer was the Dudley goods shed which was hit by a bomb causing a fire that was quickly extinguished. Enemy aircraft were spotted over the Wolverhampton area where the trains were stopped, and a blackout ensued between 11.30 p.m. and 2.25 a.m. Although no aircraft were sighted over London, precautions were put into action in the Paddington to Hayes area.

28 February 1916 – instructions were issued by the Plymouth Garrison Commander to extinguish lights at Plymouth docks and all stations, and halts between Saltash and Plympton between 8 p.m. and 9.15 p.m. All work in this area was suspended, although the reasons for the instructions were not known to the GWR as they were of a secret nature, but it has been recorded that it was due to a telegraph sent by the Dartmouth Coastguard to Devonport Command warning of Zeppelins being sighted, but it was in fact a British airship.

31 March 1916 – an air attack took place and although it did not happen within the GWR district, great disruption was caused bringing about the cancellation of eight passenger trains from Paddington with many delayed, but the up trains suffered even greater disruption with two ocean specials from Falmouth being held up for four and a half hours each.

26 April 1916 – new instructions were received from the Home Defence Headquarters stating that trains would no longer be stopped during an air raid but would run at a speed not exceeding 15mph.

13 June 1917 – slight damage to the company's premises at Victoria and Albert Docks and the Minories. Three horses were injured, one of which later died, and several employees were injured by flying glass. This air raid carried on for another two days but there was no further damage to company property.

Incendiary bomb photographed by Mr Bayliss.
(*GWR Magazine*)

7 July 1917 – enemy squadron raided at 9.35 a.m. Passengers sought shelter in the subways at Paddington, with trains delayed in leaving. Shrapnel caused some damage to Paddington, Westbourne Park, Royal Oak and Acton stations, and one delivery van, although no employees were injured. An emergency telephone exchange was set up at a low level in the General Office building as its original position on the top floor was considered too vulnerable.

August–October 1917 – there were many moonlight raids, with shrapnel falling on the Paddington area, amounting to £34 worth of damage. On 24, 29, 30 September and 1 October all working was stopped due to anti-aircraft gun firing, resulting in shrapnel falling on the premises. Raids during this time resulted in the delay of 195 passenger trains and 252 down goods from London. Precautions were extended to a radius outside London as far as Maidenhead. One consequence of the increasing air raids at this time was a rise in passenger traffic escaping the raids in London to the safety of the suburban and country districts.

January 1918 – on 28 January air-raid precautions were extended as far north as Brill and Lugershall, and west to Twyford, lasting five hours in the city and three and three-quarter hours in the suburbs. The roof of the top corridor at Paddington was damaged by shrapnel, and damage also occurred at Poplar and Smithfield (where a policeman and injured in the wrist by shrapnel).

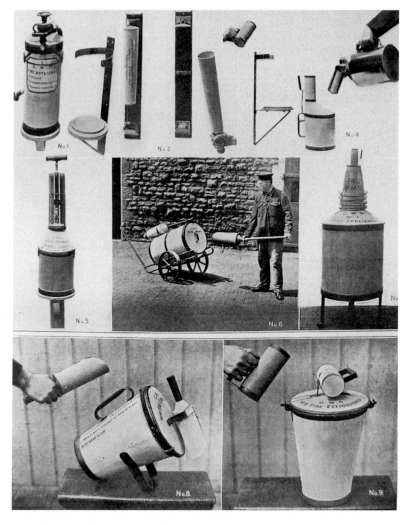

GWR fire extinguishing appliances. (*GWR Magazine*)

An unexploded bomb crashed through the lavatory roof at Brompton Road Receiving Office and embedded itself in the floor. It was removed by the Royal Engineers. The following day the same area was affected by an air raid, but only slight damage was caused by shrapnel to Victoria and Albert Docks.

February and March 1918 – air raids occurred on 16, 17, 18 February and 7 March and although precautions stretched as far as Solihull, the raids were concentrated on the London area with damage, mostly from broken glass, amounting to £61. However, on 17 February a bomb fell on the departure road of Paddington station, embedding itself in the wood paving, and the Royal Engineers were called in once again to make the area safe. Later in March more glass was broken at Paddington passenger and goods stations, and Old Oak Common carriage and engine sheds amounting to a cost of £30.

May 1918 – an air raid on 10 May caused considerable damage to the glass at the Paddington stations, Old Oak Common sheds, West London carriage shed and Clapham Junction No.12 platform, with repair costs of £80. The GWR receiving office at 11 Red Cross Street was also damaged.

1.—Swindon G.W.R. Fire Brigade on Motor and Steam fire engines.
3.—Interior of Fire Station.

2.—Dressing and Instruction room at the Fire Station.
4.—Another view of the Interior of the Fire Station.

Swindon Works fire station. (*GWR Magazine*)

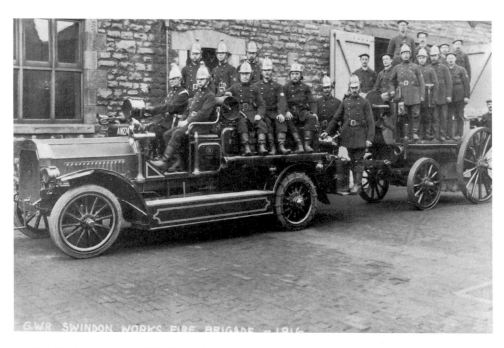

Swindon Works fire engine, 1916. (Author's collection)

The last air raid reported to the Board of Directors was on 5 August, and although it caused some disruption, no damage was recorded.

Paddington

Because of the vulnerability of the telephone exchange on the top floor of the General Office building at Paddington, a room on a lower floor was fitted out with duplicate communication equipment. Two emergency exits were also added to the building.

Glass was used extensively in the roof at Paddington to let in light, but it could be dangerous during an air raid if damaged by shrapnel, with shards of glass falling on workers and passengers. It was at this time that the usefulness of the tubes in the vicinity as shelters came into being, with everyone in the station being encouraged to use them during a raid.

It was important that lights inside the station or its surrounds were not visible to any aircraft, and it was the responsibility of a member of the electrical department to turn out all the lights during a raid and place oil and emergency glow lamps on the station platforms.

The air raids were frightening to a population unfamiliar with such warfare, but they were still looked upon as something of a novelty, and because of this it was possible to make some good of a bad situation. Mr Bayliss of Dudley Station removed an incendiary bomb after a local raid which he had photographed, with copies produced in postcard form and sold for charity. The bomb was also put on display in local shops, again to attract charitable donations; a total of £90 was collected.

Fire-fighting and Emergency Training

The company had a full range of fire-fighting equipment installed throughout the system, but in August 1915 the *GWR Magazine* contained an article on this equipment and how to use it once

Dated March 1918 and posted in Brixham, this card makes a light-hearted joke of the problem of the shortage of trains and increased ticket prices. (Author's collection)

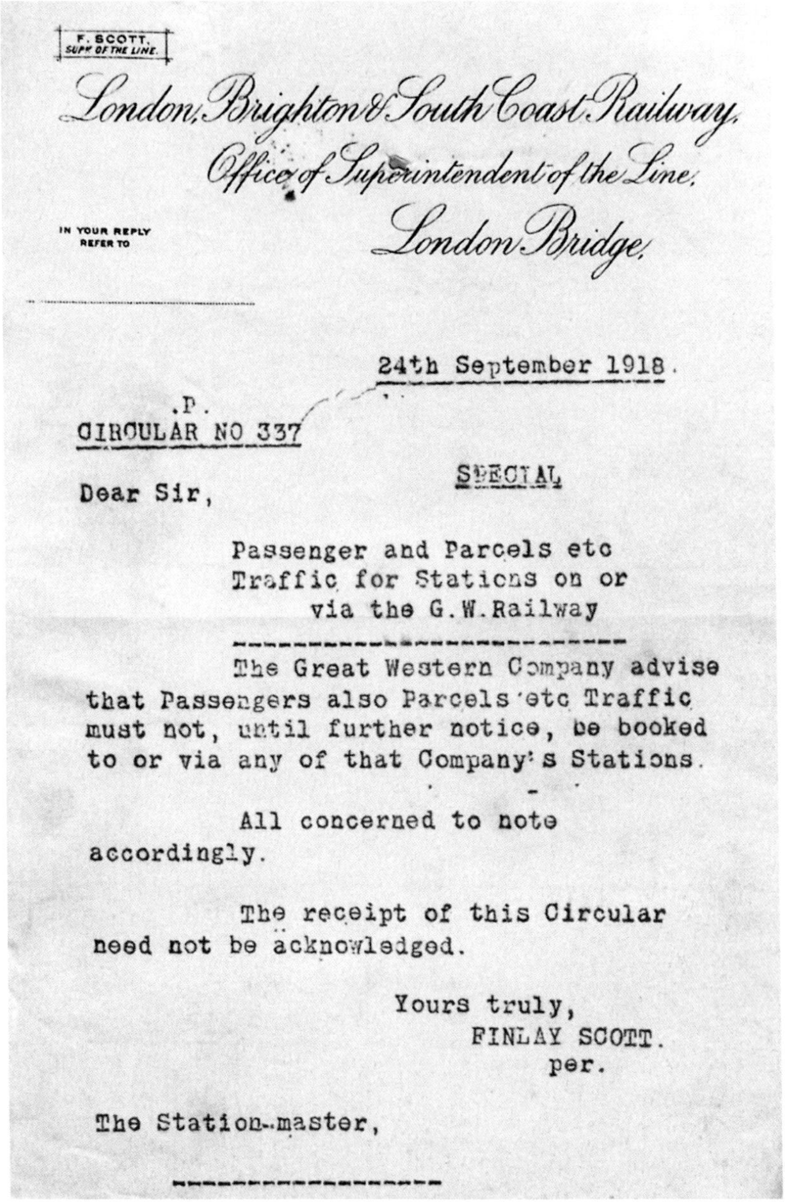

F. SCOTT.
SUPT OF THE LINE.

London, Brighton & South Coast Railway,
Office of Superintendent of the Line,
London Bridge.

IN YOUR REPLY
REFER TO

24th September 1918.

.P.
CIRCULAR NO 337

SPECIAL

Dear Sir,

Passenger and Parcels etc
Traffic for Stations on or
via the G.W.Railway

The Great Western Company advise
that Passengers also Parcels etc Traffic
must not, until further notice, be booked
to or via any of that Company's Stations.

All concerned to note
accordingly.

The receipt of this Circular
need not be acknowledged.

Yours truly,
FINLAY SCOTT.
per.

The Station-master,

London, Brighton & South Eastern Railway letter about no through bookings to any GWR station, September 1918. (Author's collection)

GREAT WESTERN RAILWAY.

OFFICE OF SUPERINTENDENT OF THE LINE,
(Circular No. 3698.)   PADDINGTON STATION, LONDON, W. 2,
26th August, 1918.

AVAILABILITY OF TICKETS.

Ordinary single and return tickets issued on and after September 1st, 1918, will be available as shewn below :—

SINGLE TICKETS AND OUTWARD HALVES.

Single tickets and outward halves of return tickets } Day of issue only.

    (with following exceptions) :—

Between Stations in England and Wales and
  (1) Stations in Ireland
  (2) Stations north of Berwick, Carlisle and Hexham
  (3) the Channel Islands.
  (4) the Isle of Man.

Between Stations on Northern Companies' lines (including G.W. Stations north of the direct line from Bristol to Maidenhead inclusive, excluding the suburbs of London) and
  (5) G.W. Stations between Maidenhead and Penzance inclusive and branches

} Three days including day of issue.

A ticket issued for a train by which the passenger cannot complete the through journey by the same or connecting train on the day of issue will be available the following day for the completion of the journey.

RETURN TICKETS.

Between any G.W. Stations (with a few exceptions) where the third class single fare charged does not exceed 1/6 } Two days or from Saturday to Monday.

Between any G.W. Stations where the third class single fare charged exceeds 1/6 } Two months.

Between any G.W. Station and any Station on another Company's line where the distance does not exceed 12 miles } Two days or from Saturday to Monday.

Between any G.W. Station and any Station on another Company's line where the distance exceeds 12 miles } Two months.

C. ALDINGTON,
Superintendent of the Line.

GWR official notice on availability of tickets. (Author's collection)

Company, ... (Service) Battⁿ. Royal Fusiliers.

RAILWAY WARRANT.

Fare to be paid at time of booking.

To the Booking Clerk at _____

(any Railway Station in Great Britain)

Please issue to bearer, in uniform, a Third-Class Return Ticket to any Station he may name, to which through fares are in operation, on payment of the Single Fare for the Return journey, and on surrender of this Voucher.

_____
Signature of Officer Commanding.

To be filled in by Booking Clerk.

No. of Ticket Issued.   Fare Paid.   Initials of Booking Clerk.

Early railway warrant.
(Author's collection)

Wt.W7447—P1792. 30m. Bks. 11-18. C. & Co., Grange Mills, S.W. E4182.

Army Form W. 3950.
(IN PADS OF 50).

'VOUCHERS MUST BE OBTAINED FROM THE MAN'S UNIT.

To be handed to Booking Clerk, and Fare to be paid at the time of Booking.

No. 5 20

Stamp of
Issuing Office.

APPLICATION for issue of Third Class Railway Ticket at reduced Fare to **MEN** of His Majesty's Forces, Naval and Military, and of Ambulance Corps engaged with the Forces, travelling on leave **IN UNIFORM.**

To the Railway Company at _____ Station.

Please issue to (No.) _133814_ (Rank) _Spr_

(Name) _____ (Regt.) _RE_

* One Third Class Single Ticket at half the ordinary single fare ⎫ Minimum charge
* One Third Class Return Ticket at the ordinary single fare ⎭ One Shilling (1/-).
(* The words which are not applicable must be struck out as necessary.)

to _____ (Railway Station).

for Staff Captain
H.Q., Abbeville Area.

Signature of Officer Commanding.

This voucher is not valid after _22 . 4 . 15_
(This date to correspond with the date of the termination of the man's leave.)

To be filled in by Booking Clerk.

No. of Ticket Issued.   Fare Paid.   Initials of Booking Clerk.

Unless this Voucher is surrendered at the time of booking, the ordinary fare will be chargeable, and no refund will be made in respect of the extra fare or fares paid.
* If the Booking Clerk cannot issue a Ticket through to destination, he will book to furthest point and issue a re-booking Voucher.

Voucher for travelling
servicemen in uniform.
(Author's collection)

H.M. FORCES OVERSEAS (IN UNIFORM).

COMBINED LEAVE AND RAILWAY TICKET.

Available for an authorised journey on the Railways in Great Britain and Ireland (including the Metropolitan and Metropolitan District Railways) and on the Steamers running to and from the Ports.

NOT available on the London Tube Railways.

No. B **859148** *Third Class.*

FOR ONE PERSON ONLY.

From **FRANCE**

To _____ *Station.*

(Insert Destination Station. Any alteration will render the Ticket useless, unless made and signed by a Railway Transport Officer.)

Leave granted from _____ *to* _____

Through Tickets in cases where the journey is not continuous do not include the cost of transfer between Railway Termini in Towns or between Railway Stations and Steamboats.
This Ticket is issued subject to the Regulations of the respective Companies over whose Lines it is available, and to the Conditions stated in their Time Tables. It must be shown and given up when required.

Half of a combined leave and railway ticket. (Author's collection)

a fire had been found, speed and efficiency being the most valuable assets when dealing with fires. With the increased danger of fires due to air raids, fire wardens were placed at Paddington, and a demonstration of fire-fighting took place at Swindon. Swindon Works had a good fire brigade before the war, but with the possibility of bombing and the ever increasing danger of accidents occurring due to heavy workloads and the reduction of staff, a new motor fire engine was bought: a gleaming Dennis engine capable of delivering 400 gallons of water per minute. The old steam-driven fire engines formed the stand-by equipment.

Training in rescuing passengers from a railway accident was carried out at Paddington in October 1916, and the 'patients' had to be treated for various injuries including the effects of gas from bombs dropped by aeroplanes. A motor van was used to evacuate the patients to a designated hospital.

Domesday Book and the Crown Jewels

Owing to the increased threat of air raids the Domesday Book and other valuable records were sent to Bodmin Jail in the early months of 1918; the Domesday Book was escorted by an official custodian. Later, other items were taken to the Post Office underground railway at Newgate Street. Some references have stated that the Crown Jewels were also sent to Bodmin for safe storage but there are no records confirming this at the Tower of London.

Season Ticket Holders

An unacceptable rise in attempts to defraud Railway Companies occurred in 1916, with passengers posing as season ticket holders. The blame was put on the genuine holders of season tickets as they thought it unnecessary to show or be questioned about their tickets, and many a heated moment resulted between passenger and railway staff.

Railway staff had a tendency to climb down and accept that the ticket holder was right. This led to some passengers chancing their arm, using the same indignant attitude when questioned, which resulted in many being let through virtually unchallenged. Company attitudes changed and ticket inspectors were ordered to be more vigilant, resulting in a number of travellers being charged.

This situation prompted a gentleman to write to a railway journal stating that genuine season ticket holders would welcome any check, and the inconvenience of showing the ticket on each journey was a petty complaint. He went further in saying 'it is the inconsiderate or foolish person who renders it necessary for the companies to employ an army of inspectors and collectors who might otherwise be released for a more useful form of national service'.

Railway warrant for travel pending commission, 24 August 1917. (Author's collection)

(80)   **GREAT WESTERN RAILWAY.**
LOCAL TICKET,
For MILITARY, NAVAL, and POLICE ON DUTY.   THEATRICAL PARTIES
and MUSIC HALL ARTISTES.

This Ticket is issued subject to the Conditions and Regulations set out in the
Company's Time Tables, Bills and Notices.

No. 79   *Date* April 10   191 7

From PILL

To   Bristol   *on G. W. Rly.*

Via

| Description. | Class. | No. of Passengers Conveyed at | | | Ordy. Single Fare. | Amount Payable. | | |
		¾ of Single Fare.	⅔ of Single Fare.	½ of Single Fare.		£	s.	d.
Officers	1st							
Sailors	3rd							
Police, &c.	3rd							
Soldiers	3rd	One						
„ Wives	3rd							
„ Childn. above 12 years	3rd							
„ „ under 12 years	3rd							
Professionals { Theatrical Parties or Music Hall Artistes. }	1st							
	3rd							
					TOTAL...£			

No. of Warrant

Booking Clerk.

N.B.—This Ticket must be shown or given up when required.

GWR local ticket for
military men, police
and theatrical parties.
(Author's collection)

Restrictions on Travel

During the spring of 1918 there was a great move of people from London to the Thames Valley in a bid to escape the air raids, despite there having been a 50 per cent price increase in standard tickets, which lead to customers buying season tickets. With a view to limiting the issue of these season tickets, the GWR ruled that any new issues were to be for a period of not less than six months to try and discourage their short-term usage.

Still, the move out of London continued on an overstretched region of the GWR, and the company found that the cost of travel was not enough to deter passengers. As such they were forced to bring about measures to reduce the numbers travelling, which included the restriction or prohibition of passenger or other traffic from any station, restriction or refusal to renew traders' season tickets, and to discontinue the issue of return tickets and through bookings.

Paper Restriction Order

An order banning the putting up of advertising material was made by the Board of Trade in early 1917. The order was made with holiday advertisements in mind, but the GWR had already decided not to publish the edition of *Holiday Haunts* for 1917 because of the cost of paper and the fact that they were trying to discourage travelling for relaxation purposes by an increase in fares. It was hoped that the restriction would not affect the issue of timetables and important announcements.

The restriction order did affect the company in an unexpected way because they had a contract with Wyman & Sons, who provided newspapers etc. for the GWR bookstalls, and they too were banned from using any advertising material. The lost revenue from the bookstalls was felt, even though the amount was small in comparison to most of the company's income.

The reduction in production of paper resulted in less fuel being used as well as labour, and British Railway Companies economised be re-using paper, with letters being written on the reverse of old ones, but there was much condemnation of the Government for wasting paper with their never-ending stream of circulars.

The *GWR Magazine* was not exempt from the restrictions, but there were calls in 1917 for men to place orders for the magazine to reduce the overage each month, and the 1918 issues are extremely thin with no index produced for that year. There could have been greater savings had the editor been a little more economical with the wording in the magazines.

The shortage of paper resulted in the suspension of passenger timetables and travellers were urged to use publications such as *Bradshaws* and take notice of announcements made at stations. Public timetables did not reappear until July 1920.

Guides

Throughout the war volunteers, amounting to some twenty-five gentlemen under the leadership of a Mr Lort Phillips, acted as guides at Paddington Station to help members of the armed forces to catch the right train or give directions as to the best way to a destination.

Parlez Vous?

Due to the large numbers of French and Belgians travelling on the GWR system an interest arose in learning to speak French. A French class opened at Paddington in 1916 for members of the staff who would, in their normal work, encounter non-English speaking Europeans. The classes were interrupted in the summer of 1918 when the lecturer, Professor Despretz, was recalled to France for a short while to be employed on special war work.

The *GWR Magazine* printed a section in French each month to encourage the learning of the language.

Passports

On 30 November 1915, under the Defence of the Realm Regulations, strict rules were laid down as to travel in and out of Britain. A passport issued not more than two years previously or other official document confirming nationality together with a photograph had to be produced. The regulation did not apply to British subjects travelling to and from Ireland or the Isle of Man but did apply to all persons travelling to and from the Channel Islands. The exceptions to this regulation were members of His Majesty's armed forces, provided they were in uniform.

An additional restriction was that 'alien passengers', except with the permission of the Secretary of State, were not allowed to travel in either direction on the steamer services from Fishguard to Rosslare, Waterford and Cork, Bristol to Cork, or Weymouth to the Channel Islands.

Station booking staff had to question travellers wishing to go to Ireland and the Channel Islands as to their nationality and assess if they were 'friendly aliens'; if they were, they were directed to the approved ports: London, Bristol, Folkstone, Holyhead, Liverpool and Southampton.

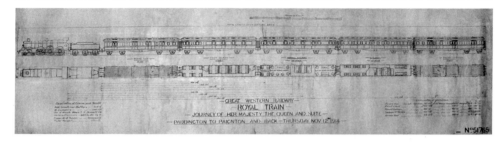

Official GWR plan for the Royal Train of November 1914. (Author's collection)

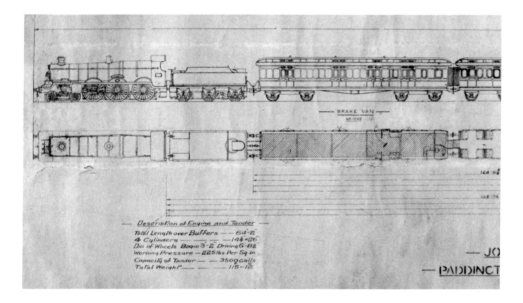

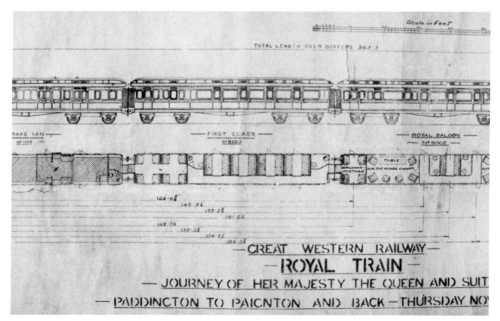

Travelling Servicemen

Service personnel in uniform were issued with railway warrants which were presented to a station booking clerk in return for the required ticket; a procedure that was extremely time consuming for the station staff. There were great improvements later with regard to members of the forces serving abroad with the introduction of the Combined Leave and Railway Ticket. This ticket of two halves: one for the forward journey and the other for the return was completed by the Railway Transport Officer and enabled the uniformed personnel to travel from their base abroad on to a ship, then train to the stated destination without the need to have tickets issued en route. It was only when military personnel were returning after the war in late 1919 and 1920 that these tickets had to be exchanged for standard tickets at stations.

Royal Journeys

The Royal Family was eager to travel round the country during the war to visit the wounded in hospitals, workers at factories and suchlike, to show their support and boost morale. Possibly the first use of the Royal Train during the war was on the occasion of the Queen's visit to Paignton on 12 November 1914, returning the same day, after she had visited Oldway Mansion, which had been converted into a war hospital.

The Royal Train was in use again on 8 September 1915, when the King and Queen visited Plymouth, where they inspected troops, awarded medals and visited military hospitals. The train collected the royal visitors at Devonport and travelled to Horrabridge; the train was put into the siding and the occupants spent the night there. Two days later, on the return journey, the royals made a surprise visit to Exeter.

Many trips were made by the Royal Family throughout the war period, and in November 1917 the King and Queen toured the Bristol area visiting hospitals and factories. The train, which on this occasion was the London and North Western Royal Train, left Paddington at 9.30 a.m. on

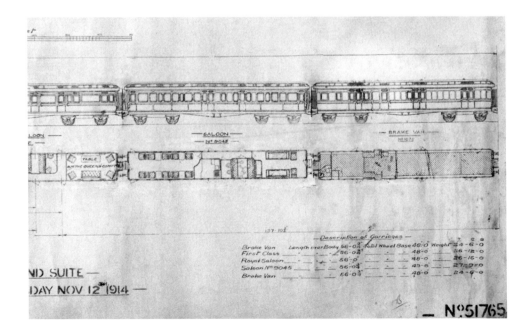

The Prince of Wales' visit to Exeter, February 1918. (*GWR Magazine*)

8 November, arriving at Bristol Temple Meads at 11.45 a.m. The royal party lunched on the train while it was in the station. Later in the day the train travelled to Hembury and stayed there overnight and they slept on the train. The following morning the train travelled to Bath Station where the King and Queen left to motor to Trowbridge, and then to Melksham and the waiting train, which returned the party to Paddington at 3.55 p.m.

On 20 February 1918 the Prince of Wales travelled through South Wales and the West Country visiting collieries, steel works and on to his estates, while on the 25th the King and Queen, on the GWR Royal Train, made the short journey to Reading and visited Huntley and Palmers, and Suttons Seeds, as well as local hospitals. The Royal Train left Paddington at 9.45 a.m., arriving at Reading at 10.30, with the return leaving Reading at 4.30 p.m. and arriving at Paddington at 5.15 p.m.

Not all of the royal journeys were connected with the war. On 6 May 1915 a special train was run from Paddington at 11.00 a.m. to Windsor and Eaton, taking the King and Queen, and other members of the Royal Family and guests, to a memorial service for the late King Edward VII in St George's chapel.

Happy Holiday-makers
at Paddington Station,

Sent by the Children's
Country Holiday Fund.

A children's country holiday fund, of which the Queen was patron, provided a change of environment for ailing poor children of London. Despite the war some 20,000 children made the trip in 1915, with the GWR taking the largest number to their destinations, and some of the eager children can be seen here waiting to leave Paddington. (*GWR Magazine*)

It wasn't only the British Royal Family that used the GWR for visits, for on 10 March 1916 her Royal Highness, Princess Napoleon, daughter of the late King Leopold, stopped at Birmingham (Snow Hill) as she was opening an exhibition of Belgian art nearby, and met exiled Belgians.

In October free travel was allowed to visiting representatives of the Dominion Republics to inspect organisations dealing with war issues throughout the country.

Arthur Balfour wrote to the GWR thanking them for making the travel arrangements 'pleasant and interesting', and owing to the political climate the courtesies afforded the visitors did much to ease the visit.

CHAPTER FIVE

Sir Eric Geddes Report and its Consequences – Locomotives and Rolling Stock –
Train Services – Common User Wagons

Sir Eric Geddes' Report and its Consequences

While Lloyd George was Minister of Munitions he brought about a programme whereby supply could meet demand, which it had been struggling to do, but by June 1916, when he became Minister of War, the munitions situation had improved to some degree. Lloyd George knew that there would be an increase in demand for munitions in the near future, and as the French ports were already congested to a dangerous point, he called upon Sir Eric Geddes, Deputy General Manager of the North Eastern Railway, to compile a report as to the condition of the transport facilities available and what could be done to improve the situation. Geddes was appointed on 7 August to carry out investigations into transportation arrangements for the British Expeditionary Force both at home and on the Western Front; the task was immense and time was of the essence.

Having investigated the transport conditions at home, he left for France at the end of August, accompanied by two other civilian experts, where they would experience the transport conditions and converse with Sir Douglas Haig, who had already expressed the need for the improvement of the railways with the increase of locomotives, rolling stock, track and personnel. Improvements in France had taken place but with no real system, and they only came about by adapting when the situation called for it within the limited resources available. Geddes was to have a fresh professional approach to the problem and, it was hoped, a solution. However, he must have been surprised and shocked while he was on the Somme carrying out his investigations, when the commander-in-chief commented to him that warfare was about men, munitions and movement – and although they had the men and munitions, they seem to have forgotten about the movement.

Geddes was appointed Director General of Transportation in France, with a temporary commission of major general, overseeing the transportation of the BEF on the Western Front and other theatres. He was also Director General of Military Railways at home, being responsible for the provision of personnel, material for railways, canals, dock and roads (but not vehicles), with the right of direct access to the Secretary of State for War. Sir Guy Garnet of the Midland Railway was deputy to Geddes and acted as his representative in his absence.

The Report's Findings

In November 1916 the Geddes Report stated that it was necessary for 300 to 350 locomotives, of as similar type as possible, be sent to France immediately, together with 20,000 trucks and the personnel required for maintenance and repair, and 1,000 miles of track. He also suggested that the United Kingdom was the only possible source of these urgent requirements.

The report was put forward to the Railway Executive Committee for consideration as to how the requests were to be met, either in part or full. The committee reported to the Board of Trade that demands would be met without affecting the transportation of troops and munitions provided that:

a. There was a reduction of train services

b. Drastic reduction of passenger travel

c. General pooling of all railway-owned wagons of certain classes

d. Arrangements were made for the indiscriminate use of wagons in private hands

In addition to the above were suggestions to lessen the impact of the demands made upon the Railway Companies:

1. Increase the fares by 50 per cent (which was not a popular suggestion with the Board of Trade)
2. The end of special trains connected with shows, sporting events etc.
3. The end of Sunday services and Post Office collections in rural areas
4. Substantial increase in demurrage charges
5. Where possible prohibiting certain railway traffic
6. Closing of branch lines that were little used or where alternative transport was available
7. Modify regulations of running mixed trains
8. Where more than one route was available, allocation and restriction of traffic
9. Restriction of passenger luggage
10. Restriction in weight of single parcels carried by passenger trains
11. Reduction of leave to the Home Forces
12. End of private saloons, slip and through coaches, dining and sleeping cars
13. No longer accept motor vehicles, carriages etc. for transportation by passenger trains

The committee suggested that the Government make any changes statutory and commence on 1 January 1917.

The Effect on the GWR

The GWR had to close Box Tunnel in January to carry out work. They also had to print new timetables to make allowances for this, which they found difficult to do being unsure, at that time, as to the exact nature of the alterations involved.

It was expected that the GWR would have to reduce passenger train mileage by 8,784 miles per day, withdraw all dining and sleeping cars, slow down express services and possibly exclude some services altogether to enable the company to make available forty engines to be sent to France. With so many engines being withdrawn there was a worry that there would be insufficient numbers of engines to stand in for those that needed essential repairs.

The GWR had already considered measures for closing down selected stations and the reduction of some passenger trains before the report because of the need to release men for the military services, but the proposed new measures went much further than the company initially thought. As recommended these measures came into force on 1 January resulting in a reduction of train services, increase of passenger fares (except season tickets) and revised regulations regarding passenger luggage, as well as other minor changes.

All these changes, including the general pooling of railway-owned open goods wagons on 2 January, had legal sanctions under the Defence of the Realm Act.

The increase in passenger fares was met with a great deal of public criticism and although ticket sales were slightly in excess of those in 1916, the sale of season tickets at Paddington Station increased from £562 in 1916 to £1,248 in 1917. The GWR had to carry the equivalent of two-thirds of the pre-price increase of passengers to maintain sufficient revenue. At a time of trying to reduce passenger traffic the GWR found itself in the situation of having to carry more passengers than it would have liked under the circumstances, a problem that would have been easier had the Government slightly increased the cost of season tickets.

The GWR was requested to supply two lengths of 28 miles each of permanent way for use overseas, but the condition was that the track had to be of the same type, which was difficult to comply with. The company was able to supply for shipment two lengths of same type track, one of 28 miles and one of 12 miles.

The need for track, rolling stock, locomotives, men and the reduction of traffic led to the closure of some halts, stations and branch lines especially where there was a lack of use or there were alternative forms of transport were available. Where the volume of traffic allowed, double track was reduced to single.

The demand for track was not only from overseas, but new track, which was impossible to purchase, was required elsewhere on the system where munitions works and depots were being developed, as well as at military establishments. These new works were gaining in numbers and importance, and the measures taken by the GWR were little understood by the civilian population who protested strongly about the drastic cuts taken. Nevertheless, the GWR had sent by the end of the war, in total, 49 miles of complete permanent way, plus an extra 500 sleepers and spares etc.

Locomotives and Rolling Stock

To comply with the request for locomotives the GWR provided seventy-two of the 0-6-0 class for use overseas. Those companies who were not sending locos overseas were obliged to make engines available for loan to those companies who felt their stock of engines was low because of this measure. The GWR received twelve engines taking the net reduction in their stock to sixty, of which thirty-six were ready for immediate shipment in February 1917.

By early summer 1917 the position with regard to locomotives was at a serious level with most companies. Materials for repairs and construction were nonexistent, and had been for some time, to such an extent that it was estimated that 3,000 engines were awaiting repair at depots throughout the country. Although passenger traffic had decreased, holiday traffic was still a problem as few were aware of the strain they were inflicting on the railways, let alone giving a thought to if their journey was necessary. Traffic was increasing due to munitions transport and the use of West Coast ports for the importation of foodstuffs, which meant that many locomotives were working when they were due for an overhaul.

So desperate was the situation by July that representations were made to the Government to secure supplies of materials and spare parts necessary for the repair of locomotives in this country as well as the building of new ones. It was also requested that men be released from the army to work in the railway shops, for it was felt that without these actions there would be an irretrievable breakdown in the working of the Railway Companies. The War Office temporarily reduced its original number of locomotives to be supplied for overseas use, but was adamant that high-powered locomotives should be supplied, and it was put to the War Office that if their demands were met replacement locomotives would have to be built before any existing engines were sent overseas, otherwise the number of useable engines available in this country would be dangerously low.

The Ministry of Munitions was instructed to ensure the supply of steel, copper and brass (or as much as they could find), although Lord Derby would not promise that any men would be released from the forces.

British companies were requested to supply a further 160 engines, preferably of the 0-8-0 class, of which the GWR had none (and their 2-8-0 class locomotives were heavily employed on Admiralty coal work), but the company was quick to point out that their 2-6-0 engines were as reliable and nearly as powerful as the 0-8-0's of other companies. The GWR arranged to supply twenty of the 2-6-0 class and twenty-two of the 0-6-0 class, although the stock of these engines was only seventeen, with the remainder being made up of engines loaned from other companies.

Provided that the GWR were supplied with materials, it was proposed to build five new engines each month to meet Government demands; but materials were not the company's only production problems. War work at Swindon, of which much was overdue owing to excessive strains on the workers and lack of supplies, culminated in a strike in October 1917 which resulted in the company being unable to fulfil its target of engine production per month – a situation that the GWR found difficult to catch up with later.

A meeting took place on 1 November with the Minister of Munitions, his staff and the President of the Board of Trade, where the question of supplies was discussed. The demand for steel in shipbuilding and munitions was very high and was at the forefront with regard to the Government, but the seriousness of the situation due to lack of supplies of the Railway Companies was pointed out too. However, although he agreed that there was an urgent need, he urged the companies to restrict their supply requests as far as they could and suggested that a conference be held a week later with the departments responsible for supplies so that questions could be aired, but the Government bodies calculated that sufficient supplies had been requisitioned to ensure the efficient running of the railways for the first half of 1918. As always, these people assumed they knew best.

A total of 20,000 trucks were needed overseas of which the GWR supplied 4,000, and the first shipment in early 1917 consisted of 132 open 10-ton trucks and thirty-five Macaw-B wagons, with the balance being prepared at Swindon. Again, the large concentration of munitions factories on the GWR system and the consequent transportation of raw materials and finished goods made the withdrawal of such a large number of trucks more than a minor problem for the company. The general pooling of wagons was to aid the companies experiencing problems, but the GWR disliked privately owned wagons. As well as the ordinary trucks, the GWR were to supply twenty-five rail and timber trucks of which, for once, they had a considerable number.

An urgent demand for 1,000 ordinary open goods wagons for use overseas was received in 1918, in addition to those previously sent. The amount each company was to supply was in proportion to that of the original 20,000, which required the GWR to send a further 200 wagons that were taken from stock and made available for shipment by the end of July 1918. This seriously depleted the stock available, and the men and materials were not available to build replacements. Companies were encouraged to hire private wagons, of which 20,000 were available and were to be distributed in agreed proportions, with 923 allotted to the GWR at the following costs:

8-ton wagon at 6s 6d per week
10-ton wagon at 7s 3d per week
12-ton wagon at 8s 3d per week

The GWR had hired some wagons prior to this in early 1917, and to give some idea of how difficult it was to keep track of where rolling stock was at this busy time an announcement was made by the Chief Goods Manager offering a reward to anyone who knew of the whereabouts of five hired wagons; despite extensive searching they could not be found.

Unfortunately the GWR experienced considerable difficulties with regard to the shortage of rolling stock by the autumn of 1918 as the expected influx of hired wagons was not making its presence felt.

Under the Act of 1871, the Government had the power to requisition any of the companies' stock subject to the payment of compensation. Permanent way material was paid for in full (together with the cost of removal) as it would not be returned to its original owner. All rolling stock and engines were subject to compensation payments plus making right any repairs or damage and, where necessary, replacement after the war.

The end of the war did not mean that requests for rolling stock finished and the GWR sent two carriages to France to make up trains to repatriate prisoners of war (at the end of the war the carriages were temporarily in Switzerland) and a train for demobilisation (No.20). Nor did the Armistice mean that stock was quick to return to its owners for at the end of 1919 over 17,000 wagons belonging to British Railway Companies were still in France under the control of the War Department.

War Department Wagons Owned by the GWR

Series	Type	Capacity (Tons)
5301–5350	Bogie (Macaws)	30
19001–22350	Open	10
22721–22820	Covered	10
31548–31554	Compo. & brake vans	
35601–35900	Box	10
35901–36300	Pill	10
38994	Unspecified coach	
96001–98500	Open	10

The numbering system related to the date the wagons arrived in France, 1–50 being refrigerated wagons sent at the beginning of the war by the London and South Western Railway. Nos 35901–36300 were specially fitted to carry concrete sections for the construction of pillboxes. All the GWR wagons were oil lubricated; grease-box wagons were not permitted on the Nord main lines.

GWR Engine Records

The following is a record of the GWR engines loaned or sold to the Government and sent abroad during the war:

Dean Goods

These engines worked in an area of the Western Front, mostly as ammunition trains from Boulogne to Audruicq and Zeneghem, with one loco hauling from the front with another banking from the rear:

2303, 2306, 2309, 2311, 2313, 2316, 2317, 2330, 2332, 2338, 2339, 2348, 2349, 2355, 2357, 2383, 2403, 2415, 2430, 2446, 2452, 2457, 2458, 2461, 2463, 2469, 2470, 2473, 2476, 2480, 2484, 2489,

2531 (*GWR Magazine*)

2514, 2517, 2518, 2519, 2520, 2522, 2528, 2531, 2535, 2549, 2566, 2577, 2578, 2580, 2308, 2318, 2322, 2327, 2329, 2334, 2336, 2387, 2420, 2453, 2454, 2488, 2533, 2542, 2557, 2563

The last eleven Dean Goods were sent to Salonika from France at the beginning of 1918 and renumbered ROD 71–84. Two of the engines, 2308 (ROD 73) and 2542 (ROD 84), were sold to the Ottoman Railway in October 1919.

Because of work carried out near the front line where water supplies were very limited, records show that auxiliary pannier tanks were fitted to 2578, as well as condensing gear.

No.2531, together with a Caledonian locomotive, were the first engines from Britain to cross the Rhine when they took a staff train to Cologne. No.2531 was called up again for war service in 1940.

43XX CLASS 2-6-0s
5319, 5320, 5321, 5322, 5323, 5324, 5325, 5326, 5328, 5329, 5330

These engines were sent to Audruicq, France (locomotive headquarters of the Railway Operating Division, Royal Engineers) in September 1917, and although allocated to the ROD, they retained their original numbers. They worked supply trains, which could weigh up to 1,000 tons, for the Second Army between Les Fontinettes (Calais) marshalling yard, Riviere Neuve and the railheads around Hazebrouck. They were returned in April and May 1919.

The tender of 5325 was damaged by a shell at Tachincourt on 25 March 1918; the crew plugged the holes with wood and she remained that way until returning to England. No.5322 was involved in a 'mishap' in France in April 1918 (details unknown), but is now preserved at Didcot and has been restored, thankfully, by a dedicated team.

Armstrong Goods
In November 1915 Nos 27, 434, 508, 794, 1100, 1186 were sold to the Government, but were returned to stock in March 1916.

5322 during restoration at Didcot. (Author)

5322 during the last years of its working life. (Author's collection)

In August 1916 Nos 447, 508, 794, 1091, 1100, 1198 were sold to the Railway Operating Division (ROD) and shipped to Serbia. Nos 794 and 1091 returned in 1921.

In May 1917 Nos 24, 438, 716, 781, 784, 1107, 1189, 1191 were sold to the ROD and were on their way to Salonika when the transport ship was sunk.

In September 1917 Nos 39, 427, 451, 495, 674, 796, 878, 1084 were shipped to Salonika and renumbered in ROD series; the only exact recorded numbers were: 427 (ROD 32), 495 (34), 878 (36), 1084 (37), 39 (39) and 508 (40).

After the war Nos 427, 495, 1084 and 508 worked on the Ottoman Railway. Nos 39, 451, 674, 878, 794 and 1091 were returned to the GWR in April 1921 in place of six Dean Goods that were on loan to the ROD and not returned.

Locomotives at Home

During 1916 engines of the 2-8-0T and 2-6-0 types were put into traffic, with the 2-6-0 class (4300s) proving themselves very capable for all types of goods, troop trains and express services, especially below Newton Abbot. 4-2-0, 0-6-0, 2-4-0 and 2-4-2T type engines were condemned and broken up.

With the exception of renaming loco No.4017 *Knight of the Eagle* to *Knight of Liege* in the autumn of 1914, the naming of locomotives was suspended during the war, and unlike other companies the GWR did not name locomotives with place names and battles associated with the war.

Late in 1915, due to the shortage of skilled labour, locomotives and tenders (except express passenger engines) were painted khaki and although a number of locos were painted so, the colour was quickly discontinued. Even with the shortage of labour and materials locomotive production remained fairly healthy, and between 1914 and 1919 the following were built:

Mogul 2-6-0s Nos 4300, 4361–4399 and 5300–5369
Small Prairie 2-6-2Ts Nos 4540–4554
42xx 2-8-0Ts Nos 4242–4261
28xx 2-8-0s Nos 2856–2883
During 1914 Star class 4-6-0s Nos 4046–4060, and 42xx class 2-8-0Ts Nos 4232–4241 were built.

Train Services

Many alterations and restrictions were imposed after the findings of the Geddes Report were made available at the close of 1916, and the new timetable, effective from January 1917, saw great changes. Many services were withdrawn such as the 10.30 Cornish Riviera Express from Paddington, the final run of which was on 30 December 1916 (engine number 4051). Other withdrawn services were:

West of England	12 noon Paddington to Torquay
	1.30 and 3.30 p.m. Paddington to Penzance
	1.10 p.m. Penzance to Paddington
South Wales	8.30 p.m. Paddington to Fishguard (Irish Mail)
	5.25 a.m. Fishguard to Paddington
	8.45 a.m. Paddington to Cardiff, Swansea & Carmarthen
Northern Services	9.10 a.m. and 4 p.m. Paddington to Birmingham, Chester & Birkenhead
	11.55 a.m. Birkenhead to Paddington

West Midland	1.40 p.m. Paddington to Worcester, Malvern & Hereford
	12.50 p.m. Hereford to Paddington
Cross Country	All of the following between:
	Birkenhead, Birmingham & Bournemouth via Basingstoke
	Birkenhead, Birmingham & Folkstone via Reading
	Barry, Cardiff & Newcastle via Banbury
	Birmingham & Bristol via Stratford-on-Avon

Later alterations to the timetable that year included the suspension of the following trains on a Sunday:

11.10 a.m.	Paddington to Birmingham
10.45 a.m.	Cardiff to Birmingham
12.25 p.m.	Birmingham to Cardiff

The summer of 1918 saw further reductions in passenger services, but some trains were made longer to cope with the traffic. It was not unusual to see trains of fourteen to eighteen coaches in length. The coaches were normally the 70ft type, and the locomotives were 4-6-0, 40XX and 29XX classes which proved more than adequate to pull such heavy loads.

Slip carriages and restaurant cars ceased to run, and the amount of luggage that could be carried by a passenger for free was restricted to a maximum of 100lb in weight. From 2 April the sender of all parcels to be transported by passenger trains had to pay the charge to the forwarding officer or at the station prior to loading onto the train, although this did not apply to parcels from the Continent.

STATIONS CLOSED

STATION	LINE	REASON	DATE
Park Royal	Acton–Wycombe	Free lines for military and other traffic	01/02/1915
Brentford	Brentford	Release staff – goods traffic only, no passengers	22/03/1915
Henbury	Filton and Avonmouth Docks	Release staff – closed to passengers	
Camerton	Camerton and Limpley Stoke	Release staff – closed to passengers	22/03/1915
Dunkerton			
Monkton Combe			
Stourbridge Town	Stourbridge	Release staff and due to decrease in passengers	29/03/1915
Great Bridge	Great Bridge	Rail motor car withdrawn to release staff	01/01/1916
Bridport East St	Bridport branch	Closed to passengers and release staff	01/01/1916
Bridport West Bay			
Stretton-on-fosse	Shipton-on-Stour	Release staff	01/01/1917
Dunstall Park	Northern main	Release staff	01/01/1917
Daisy Bank	West Midland	Release staff	01/01/1917
Harts Hill and Woodside			
Linley	Severn Valley	Release staff (open for goods – reopened 02/04/1917)	01/01/1917
Teigngrace	Moretonhampstead	Release staff	01/01/1917
Bampford Speke	Exe Valley	Release staff	01/01/1917
Dawlish Warren	South Devon main line	Release staff	01/01/1917

Ide	Exeter railway	Release staff	01/01/1917
Bradley & Moxley	Northern main	Station pulled down to make way for loop between Wednesbury and Bilston	01/01/1917
Cheltenham (Malvern Road)	Kingham and Cheltenham	Release staff	01/01/1917
Saltney	Northern main	Release staff	01/01/1917
Bassaleg (GWR)	Monmouthshire valleys	Release staff	01/01/1917
Llangeinor	Garw Valley	Release staff	01/01/1917
Llangonoyd	Llynvi Valley	Release staff	01/01/1917
Pontnewydd (lower)	Nowport–Pontypool Road	Release staff	01/01/1917
Tidenham	Wye Valley	Release staff (open for goods)	01/01/1917
Tidenham		reopened February 1918 due to new shipbuilding yard at Beachley	
Pontrhydyrum	Eastern Valleys	Release staff	
Burnham Beeches			02/04/1917
Golant	Lostwithiel–Fowey		02/04/1917
Roath			02/04/1917
Manod			02/04/1917
Exeter St Thomas			02/04/1917
Twerton-on-Avon			02/04/1917
Cheltenham High St			02/04/1917

HALTS CLOSED

LINE	HALT	REASON	DATE
Pembroke and Temby	Beavers Hill, Lydstep	Release staff/summer motor service withdrawn	22/09/1914
Acton and Wycombe	Old Oak Lane, Brentham, Perivale	Line closed to rail motor car; traffic to free lines for military and other trains	01/02/1915
Brentford Bridge	Trumpers Crossing	Bridge closed to passenger traffic	22/03/1915
Oxford District	Hinksey, Abbingdon Road, Horsepath, Iffley, Garsington Bridge, Wolvercote	To release staff – rail motor car service withdrawn	22/03/1915
Filton and Avonmouth	Filton, Charlton, Hallen	Line closed to passengers (except workers) to release staff	22/03/1915
Camerton and Limpley Stoke	Paulton, Radford and Timsbury, Dunkerton Colliery, Combe Hay, Midford	Closed to passengers to release staff	22/03/1915
Wrexham and Minerva	Brook Street, Pant, Wynn Hall	Rail motor car withdrawn to release staff	22/03/1915
Legacy Branch	Fennant Road, Aberderfyn, Ponkey Crossing	To release staff	22/03/1915
Oxford, Wolvercote platform		Rail motor car withdrawn to release staff	01/01/1916
Stafford-on-Avon Branch	Broad Marston, Chambers Crossing, Evesham Road Crossing	Save expense of keeping halts open	14/07/1916
Torquay Branch	Preston	Save expense	01/07/1917
Bodmin Branch	St Lawrence	Save expense	Rhos lines

Rhos lines	Vicarage Crossing, Berwig	Rail motor car withdrawn to release staff	01/07/1917
Much Wenlock	Lightmoor Platform	To release staff	01/07/1917
Pontypool and Neath	Penar Junction	Rail motor car withdrawn to release staff	01/07/1917
	Duffrryn Crossing		02/04/1917
Garnant to Gwaun -Cae-Gurwen	Gors-Garnant, Red Lion Crossing		02/04/1917
Newnham–Cinderford	Ruddle Road		02/04/1917
Pontypool to Abersychan	Wainfelin		29/04/1917
Bath	Hampton Row		29/04/1917

LINES CLOSED

FROM	TO	STATIONS CLOSED	REASON	DATE
Langley Green	Oldbury	Oldbury	C	03/03/1915
Madeley Junction	Lightmoor Jct	Madeley (Salop)	B	22/03/1915
Rowington Juntion	Henley-in-Arden		A	01/01/1916
Moorswater	Caradon	Mineral Line	A	01/01/1917
St Denis Branch		Mineral Line	A	01/01/1917
Titley	Eardisley	Lyonshall, Almeley, Eardisley	A & B	01/01/1917
Bearley	Alcester	Great Alne Alcester	A & B	01/01/1917
East Usk Branch (Part)		Goods Line	A	01/01/1917
Wyesham Junction	Coleford	Newland, Coleford (G.W.)	B	01/01/1917
Clynderwern	Letterston	Llanycefn, Maenclonchog, Rosebush, Puncheston	A	08/01/1917

DOUBLE LINES CONVERTED TO SINGLE TRACK

CClarbeston Road	Neyland		A	01/01/1917
Dymock	Ledbury		A	01/01/1917
Uxbridge (High Street)	Denham	Uxbridge High Street closed for passenger traffic	A & B	01/01/1917
Tregoss Moor	St Dennis Jct		A	01/01/1917

Reason key:

A To recover permanent way

B To release men for enlistment

C For Government reasons

Passenger Road Motor Services

The shortage of petrol necessitated the suspension of the following services:

Suspended Altogether:

Helston and Porthleven

Suspended Three Days a Week:

Abergavenny and Crickhowell

St Austell and St Dennis

Haverfordwest and St Davids
Wrexham and Farndon
Moretonhampstead and Chagford
Llandyssul and Aberayron

Suspended Two Days a Week:
Wolverhampton and Bridgnorth
Penzance and Lands End
Kingsbridge and Salcombe
Yealmpton and Modbury
Llanelly and Cross Hands
Corwen and Cerrig
Weymouth and Wyke Regis
Saltash and Callington
Carmarthen and Llandebie

Suspended One Day a Week:
Stroud and Cheltenham
St Austell and Bugle

It was necessary in August 1918 to remove materials from little used or closed lines for relaying elsewhere.

	MILES	CHAINS
GWR Coleford Branch, Wyeshaw Jct.–Whitecliff Siding	4	2
Aynho Up and Down Loops (Excluding Junctions)	54	
Ashendon Up and Down Loops	65	1/2
Brill Down Loop	25	1/2
Barnstaple East Loop	16	1/2
Pentrefelin Sidings Nos 3 & 4 (Excluding Junctions)	19	1/2
Carneddwen Summit Crossing Loop	12	
Wheatsheaf Sidings (Part of – including one junction)	30	
Kidderminster Sand Siding Loop	10	
Deeside Passenger Siding Loop	19	1/2

The Government paid the expenses for the removal of the above and payment for the eventual relaying once hostilities had ended.

Not all permanent way material was destined to be used at home as much was needed to repair damaged track on the Western Front and it was also needed for the laying down of new track to meet ever-changing demands. Many of the above were reinstated after the war.

Common User Wagons

For some time prior to March 1916 the Coal Mining Organisation Committee and the Port and Transit Executive Committee had been calling for the pooling of railway wagons to reduce the congestion at ports and large railway centres; a proposal that was strongly opposed to by smaller private companies. The GWR could see no benefit in pooling wagons as it sent many more loaded wagons to other companies than it received, plus they were protective of their own stock of first-class wagons and did not relish the thought of having to use wagons of an inferior standard; but the Government insisted that something had to be done.

After a meeting at Paddington on 3 March 1916, with representatives from other Railway Companies attending, it was agreed that a system of common user (which they all agreed was preferable to the general pooling of wagons) between companies in regions with running lines beneficial to each other would be run for an experimental period. Machinery was set up at certain junctions to adjust any inequalities between wagons, which was inevitable when using stock from various companies.

The experimental system began on 3 April 1916 and proved to be successful, with the shunting in yards and positioning of wagons improved. However, there was a certain amount of mileage incurred of empty wagons due to the balance of stock over the systems, and that traffic flow had been affected by air raids and an unexpected blizzard.

Although the GWR was not enthusiastic about the idea of pooling privately owned wagons, they could see the benefit in the South Wales Coal Fields where they would not have to take up valuable time shunting wagons belonging to specific companies, but an order issued on 16 March 1917 brought the South Wales Colliery wagons under Government control. This order gave the Railway Companies the power to take possession of privately owned wagons which could be used for backward-loading return journeys, thus reducing empty haulage.

On 1 April 1917 a Board of Trade order came into force whereby a revision of the demurrage regulations meant that wagons had to be loaded and unloaded by the trader within a specific period or the Railway Company would perform the task at a cost. It was also an offence to keep any wagons beyond their allotted time, and companies were given the right to take possession of privately owned wagons that would otherwise be sent on a homeward journey empty.

By August the common user arrangements had extended to include sheets and ropes, although there continued to be a shortage. The end of the war did not stop the Government amending the arrangements, for on 3 June 1919 all covered goods vans not fitted with brakes came under the arrangement. The exceptions to the common user scheme were open and covered goods wagons constructed for specific purposes such as carrying fish, or insulated vans.

CHAPTER SIX

*Refreshments for the Troops – Care for Wounded Soldiers – Canals –
Cultivating Land – Crime – Prisoners of War – Daylight Saving Act –
Public Outcry – Use Of Old Plans – Poetry*

Refreshments for the Troops

Banbury

The Banbury Rest Station and canteen was opened on 14 September 1914 and was thought to be the first of its type in England; a rest station had opened in Perth, Scotland, the week before. Four days before that a Miss Freda Day (Quartermaster of a Red Cross detachment) read in a local paper that troops passing through Banbury were so desperate for refreshment that they drank the water from the station fire buckets. Miss Day decided to act, and with the co-operation of the Oxfordshire Red Cross and Banbury Stationmaster Mr Short, nurses were ready to distribute lemonade to two trains containing 1,000 troops that afternoon. Within a few days fruit and cigarettes gifted by supporters in the district were available for the troops.

The rest station was attended daily by nurses working shifts from 7 a.m. to 10 p.m., with provisions for cover during the night hours. The War Office made Banbury an official rest station for ambulance trains, and an advance warning of one and a half hours was given to allow extra nurses to be summoned. Each patient was given a small cardboard tray containing a sandwich, bread and butter, cake, fruit, chocolate, cigarettes or tobacco, a newspaper and postcards upon which the troops could write messages home, which were collected before the train left, stamped and posted.

All the provisions were free to the troops, with funds raised by public donations. The whole business was overseen by Miss Day, who presided over a committee which in turn managed an enthusiastic volunteer force. Some four years and nine months passed before the rest station was closed in June 1919, during which time the nurses attended to over 3 million troops.

Chester

The Chester Station Coffee Tavern was a popular refreshment stop, and during 1918 a quarter of a million cups of tea and coffee were served, as well as 400,000 cakes and pies to an average of 500 soldiers per day who passed through the station.

Birmingham

During the war 2,390 ambulance trains containing 38,000 wounded men called at Snow Hill for refreshments, and because of this and the efficient unloading of ambulance trains, Platform Inspector Harris was awarded a silver cup from the St John Ambulance Brigade after the war.

Red Cross nurses at Banbury, 1915. (*GWR Magazine*)

The Banbury Stationmaster gives details of train times to the nurses. (*GWR Magazine*)

Nurses giving drinks to soldiers on a train at Banbury. (*GWR Magazine*)

Nurses at Banbury Station. (*GWR Magazine*)

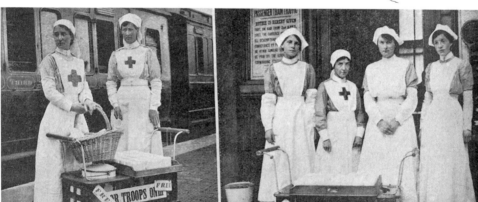

Paddington

The 'Paddington Station Club' was opened in December 1914 at 19 Eastbourne Terrace, next to the station, where there was free admission to reading and recreation rooms, and refreshments were available at low prices. It became obvious that more convenient facilities were needed and a vacant space at the eastern end of the station was made available for this purpose by the GWR.

In April 1915 a Soldiers' and Sailors' Free Buffet was opened at Paddington Station, but unlike Banbury the Paddington buffet was run under military supervision. Mrs J.J. Runge was superintendent in charge with a staff consisting of a secretary, treasurer, caterer and eighty ladies each working a rota of shifts covering a twenty-four-hour period. The women wore uniforms of dark blue overalls and black caps with official badges.

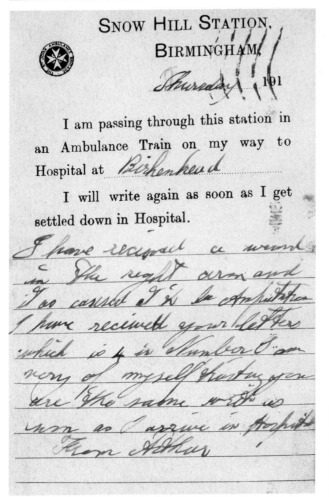

Postcard dated 18 May 1917 from a wounded soldier on an ambulance train which stopped at Snow Hill. Arthur says in his card that he had been wounded in his right arm, which had to be amputated. (Author's collection)

The workers were all volunteers and the refreshments were funded by donations, subscriptions and collections, with the expenses amounting to between £30 and £40 per week. The banners at the buffet declaring 'Soldiers and Sailors Welcome' and 'Free Buffet for Soldiers and Sailors' ensured that there was always a steady flow of men needing refreshments, and the buffet could be very crowded at times. A trolley was also available to dispense food and drink from the platform to the military on trains. It was estimated that some 3 million men passed through the refreshment room during the war years.

Mrs Runge also received gifts of vegetables, eggs, cakes and alike, which enabled the staff to prepare more substantial meals, especially to troops who were travelling during the night or to those who were extremely fatigued after returning from the front. Although the buffet was under military supervision, the GWR willingly responded to any requests for aid made by the volunteer workers.

The Soldiers' and Sailors' Buffet was closed on 28 June 1919.

Without the valuable work carried out by the volunteers at Paddington, Banbury, Birmingham and many other stations, travel would have been less comfortable – something that the men very much appreciated.

The last men to take refreshments at the Soldiers' and Sailors' Free Buffet at Paddington. (*GWR Magazine*)

Mrs J.J. Runge OBE. (*GWR Magazine*)

Care for Wounded Soldiers

Many a GWR worker helped in their spare time to entertain and arrange visits for wounded soldiers. The stationmaster at Reading, Mr Noble, collected money from the Traffic Department staff in the summer of 1917 for two boat trips on the River Thames. Nearly 120 recuperating soldiers were taken on each trip, and a meal was enjoyed while listening to a string band.

In other areas staff entertained soldiers hospitalised in their local area, with music, sketches, competitions, raffles and alike keenly performed. Money for these events was raised by individuals or sponsorship.

Southall Goods clerical staff entertained 200 wounded soldiers and friends on 8 December 1917 with a whist drive and games, music, singing and dancing. Sergeant G. Harris was present who, it was quoted, had been rendered dumb through shell-shock.

River trip provided by the Traffic Department, Reading, for wounded soldiers. (*GWR Magazine*)

Wounded soldiers' outing on the Monmouthshire Canal provided by the Loco & Carriage Department staff at Pontypool Road. (*GWR Magazine*)

Canals

During February 1917 many canals that were not owned by Railway Companies, and therefore not under Government control, were taken over by the Board of Trade under an amendment of the Defence of the Realm Act. The canals in question were suitable in their length and location to carry goods which would otherwise be sent by rail, with the sole purpose of reducing the traffic on the over-burdened railways of the country.

Unfortunately there were not enough trained staff to work on the canals, as many of the original canal workers had joined the forces, many of whom found work with the Royal Engineers on the canals of France and Belgium where their expertise was in great demand. But the committee in charge of the British canals devised a scheme whereby men from the transport workers' battalions could be trained. A training school for boatmen was opened at Devizes, on the GWR-

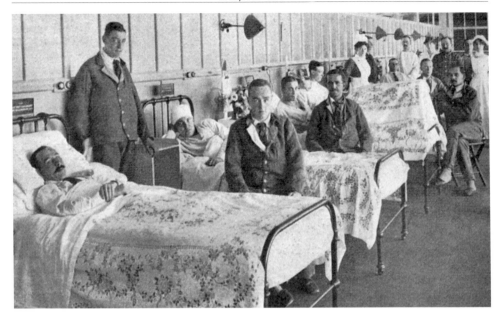

Beds in King George Hospital, London, donated by staff at Shrewsbury. (*GWR Magazine*)

owned Kenet & Avon Canal, which was little used for ordinary traffic and therefore ideal for training purposes.

Boats and horses were purchased for training the men, who attended the course in batches of thirty. The course covered instruction in loading and unloading of boats and the art of navigating the boats along the canal and through locks. After their three weeks of training, and sometimes longer, men considered proficient enough were sent to canals where their services were needed. During the relatively short life of the Devizes school over 200 men had trained there.

Cultivating Land

During the war there was a national call for the cultivation of unused land for the growing of foodstuffs, and at the end of 1916 the GWR made available for rent any available line-side land for this purpose, with the first two years being rent free. Where the land by the side of the line was unsuitable for cultivation other land owned by the company, beyond the fence along the line, was offered. By January 1917 some 660 tenancies had been arranged amounting to an area of 32 acres, and it was said that the growing of foodstuffs was helping the nation to take control of one of the most threatening crises in the history of this land, although the amateur gardeners found it difficult to make the most of their crops this year due to the shortage of chemical fertilisers. There were exceptions, as the staff at Bridgend had a bumper crop of potatoes in 1917 having taken the advice of the Board of Agriculture after their crop of the previous year had been ruined by 'black scab'.

Subtle incentive schemes came about to encourage the cultivation of waste ground, such as at Wolverhampton where the GWR let 1½ acres to seventeen employees in an area where the local council were awarding prizes for the best kept allotments; eight of the GWR men were prizewinners.

As time progressed guides on how to plan and maintain allotments came into being, presumably as the more enthusiastic gardeners would have been the first to take up the offer of land for food production, whereas the 'allotment novices' would have been among the last to secure a plot. Offers from companies producing fertiliser and seeds from Suttons were available to ensure the continuous growth of all things edible; 730lb of onions were grown from 1¾oz of Suttons onions seeds by the stationmaster at Neyland, Mr J.W. Berry – a man who certainly knew his onions!

The allotments were a great success. Some 7,653 men had allotments on company land before the war, and by the end this figure had increased to 13,059.

Many stations had beautifully kept gardens before the war and regularly entered competitions, but these were suspended during the war as the gardens were turned over to food production, although they were resumed in 1919.

Crime

During the war there was, surprisingly, a reduction in adult crime to such an extent as to allow the closure of some prisons. The decline in convictions was largely due to so many men serving in the forces and the demand for workers, which included the employment of women, but there was a price to pay during this period of shortage of labour – that of the children.

One lad who was caught stealing at Paddington said that his mother was away all day, not returning until 11.30 p.m., and during this time he and his younger brother were left to fend for

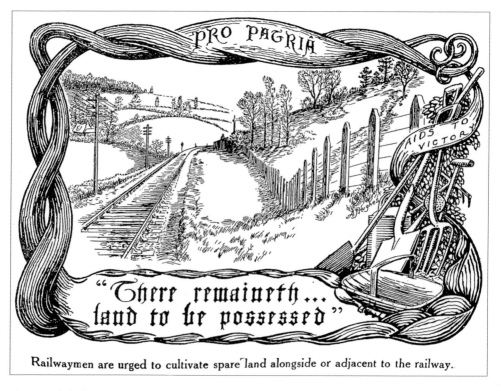

The original 'dig for victory' – an advert to encourage the cultivation of waste land by the side of railways. (*GWR Magazine*)

GWR men in their lineside allotments near Bridgend. (*GWR Magazine*)

themselves. This was by no means an isolated case; such were the circumstances of the Home Front during the war. A shortage of teachers and leaders of Scouts and other clubs added to the lack of supervision, which would have helped the younger ones from straying from the straight and narrow.

There were some youngsters that found work, and for the first time they had money which sometimes led to gambling, and restricted lighting in stations and on trains gave rise to opportunities to exploit the situation for those willing to take the risk.

By 1916 juvenile convictions in London had risen by 50 per cent, with similar percentage increases noted in other cities. The GWR experienced an increase in juvenile crime of some 54 per cent during the first year of the war, and around 400 juvenile cases had been handled by the GWR police department by the spring of 1916. The offences included wilful damage, gambling, endangering the safety of passengers, larceny and trespassing.

One form of trespassing came about from acting out the 'adventures' of the boys' heroes, and was described in the *GWR Magazine* as follows:

> The 'storming' of a railway embankment and the 'bombarding' of telegraph poles serve to emulate the brave deeds of our soldiers at Hill 60 and the Battle of Ypres. But the lives of the youngsters are imperilled during the 'charge' up the embankment and across the line, while passing trains are in danger of being struck by stones which are used as 'bombs'. The telegraph service is also liable to be impaired if the insulators are dislodged by the 'snipers'.

It was inevitable that there would be crime due to rationing and general hardships in war time, and in the autumn of 1916 three car men from Paddington Station and a foreman from a flour company were charged by the Metropolitan Police with stealing and receiving flour. The GWR men were dismissed immediately, to be reinstated should their names be cleared by the court. Their fellow GWR workers felt this was an unjust action as the men had not been found guilty, and many of the workers at Paddington Goods went on what would be termed as a 'work to rule'. Due to the exceptionally high amount of goods traffic travelling through the station, as the war conditions would dictate, congestion was inevitable; so bad was this congestion that traffic was limited and sometimes stopped. The noble act of supporting their fellow workers caused considerable disruption but normal service was resumed when the men were convicted at the court hearing.

Prisoners of War

Prisoners of war were kept at various places around the GWR, such as the old Abbey Carriage Works at Shrewsbury, and most were set work tasks.

Twenty-three German prisoners were building a road round an orchard at Pencoed on 26 September 1917 when, in the afternoon, two escaped unnoticed. Although having a head start on their guards, once the alarm was raised news quickly spread of their escape, and at 8 p.m. two men were sighted going over the crossing at Llanwern. The alert signalman there, suspecting they were the escapees, informed the stationmaster, Mr W. Evans, who gave chase on his bicycle. He was quick enough to overtake the prisoners who, by that time, were exhausted and wet through. When challenged the Germans surrendered at once and a triumphant Mr Evans handed them over to the police.

Not all prisoners were from opposing forces. Large numbers with strong political or religious beliefs felt they could not fight because of their convictions and were imprisoned or sent to the military if it was considered that their case was not convincing enough. The GWR ran several special trains for the transportation of these men to prisons within their area, such as Portland and Dartmoor Prison at Princetown.

Daylight Saving Act

Summertime, as it is now known, or the Daylight Saving Act came into force at 2 p.m. on Sunday 21 March 1916, when all clocks were advanced an hour, and ceased at 3 p.m. on1 October, when Greenwich Mean Time was resumed. It is something that is very much taken for granted these days, but was a great change for those experiencing it for the first time and, surprisingly, the changes went very smoothly.

The purpose of the Act was to maximise the number of daylight hours during a working day, which reduced the amount of fuel used due to less lighting etc. The greatest bonus was that the making up of the night goods trains, usually done in the twilight, was able to be completed in daylight.

The altering of the clocks was, to some extent, a war-time experiment, but by 1918 it was clear that the advantages brought about by this 'experiment' were too good to ignore in the future.

The idea of altering the clocks to maximise daylight hours was thought to have been conceived by Benjamin Franklin, but it was an Englishman, William Willet, who published a pamphlet in 1907 explaining the benefits of such a change. So convincing was his argument that Germany adopted the system before Britain, and fearing that Germany would have an industrial production advantage, the British Government decided to adopt the system as well.

As of midnight on 30 September 1918 the times of all military trains had to be quoted using what was known as the 'Continental System', or 24-hour clock – arrangement for which had been made between the War Office and the Railway Companies. It would be another two years before the 24-hour clock would be considered for universal adoption.

Public Outcry

The general public were more than willing to criticise that which they knew little or nothing about, and caused the GWR, unusually, to make a retaliatory comment in June 1917 after a letter was printed in a weekly London paper which read as follows:

HOW MUCH LONGER? – We are asked under date April 12, how much longer the train of Cornish broccoli or cauliflower is to remain at Newton Abbot Railway siding. About fifteen truck loads had been dumped there since the 3rd. By this time, let us hope, the railway traffic manager has found an engine strong enough to pull them to their destination without bursting its boiler, or has got the cargo absorbed into the local markets instead of allowing it to rot on the line and monopolise railway trucks. We take it he knows vegetables are good to eat?

The following week another comment appeared in the paper by yet another over vigilant member of the public who, while travelling out of London, noticed a passing goods train containing vegetables. On close examination the gent noticed the wagons were labelled from Newton Abbot and naively assumed that the previous week's letter had had the desired effect of giving the GWR the shake-up they needed to get the vegetables on the move.

Justifiably the company were incensed by the comments and decided that these gents would benefit from a little educating, explaining that on each morning of the period covered by the comments new wagons with vegetables arrived at Newton Abbot from Cornwall and were in the sidings awaiting a through train to Paddington, adding that the wagons seen were successive consignments, and not, as was imagined, the same ones day after day!

If this was not enough, a West Country daily newspaper blamed the GWR for the increase in the price of pilchards. The company were quick to point out that everyone concerned, such as fishermen, curers and retailers, had greatly increased their prices, but not so the railway, explaining that as far as questions of overcharging of rates of transportation of foodstuffs, it was worth noting that for hauling a loaded churn of milk and returning the empty on a 90-mile round trip was at the rate of 1*d* per gallon, the retail price of which was just under 2*s* per gallon. Broccoli from Cornwall was transported over 300 miles to London at a rate of 1*d* for 2½lb in weight; mackerel, also from Cornwall, was 1*d* for 4lb in weight – nowhere near the price of the goods in the shops.

Use of Old Plans

In November 1917 Sir Francis Fox made a request to Railway Companies and alike for old linen-backed plans. The plans were sent to a specialist company where they were prepared and the linen cleaned. The linen was used in military hospitals as dressings etc., and some 53,000 yards were obtained this way. The GWR sent a substantial number of plans away for this purpose.

Poetry

Like it or not, no First World War history would be complete without poetry, and a GWR employee, Henry Lang Chappell, was quick to show his literary prowess to all in the first months of the war with the rousing poem 'The Day'. When it appeared in the *GWR Magazine* it was hailed as a 'poem of outstanding merit', and the press announced that it was 'lifting the author to the rank of National Poet'. The poem was originally printed in the *Daily Express* and copies of the poem were sold by the paper at the price of two copies for 1*d*, with larger quantities available of up to 1,000 for £1 10*s*; the proceeds from sales went to the Prince of Wales National Relief Fund. The poem was also printed in postcard form as shown.

H. Chappell, GWR poet. (*GWR Magazine*)

At the time of writing 'The Day', Henry Chappell was a luggage labeller at Bath. Born in London in 1872 and educated at Craven Street School and City of London Middle Class School, he joined the GWR in May 1891 as a lad ticket collector and thence to Chippenham and Clifton Bridge Stations before returning to Bath in 1893. This was not his first foray into writing, for he had penned some fifty to sixty lyrics before the war, and in 1903 wrote a poem 'A Record Run to the West', which was followed by 'Queen Bath', 'A Crown of Love' and others.

'The Day' made Chappell famous and within a very short time he followed with another patriotic poem, 'Britain'. He also published a book at the end of 1917 entitled *The Day and Other Poems* which had an introduction by Sir Herbert Women, who had been Professor of Poetry at Oxford.

Chappell was not the only GWR employee to put pen to paper. E.H. Hiorns, a ganger at Llanelly Dock, wrote an eleven-verse poem, quoted as being 'of much merit', entitled 'The Call'; two verses follow:

The call has come – To arms! To arms!
To all you Britain's sons;
The foes are striking swift and strong-
Hark! Listen to their guns.

They say they mean to crush us all,
And lay old England low;
Then up to arms, and show them lads,
That your not out for show.

Patriotic writing did not stop at poetry, and Jenkin Hopkins, a goods checker at Bridgend, composed a recruiting song, copies of which were sold locally with the proceeds going to the Belgian Relief Fund.

THE DAY.

By HENRY CHAPPELL.

[The author of this magnificent poem is Mr. Henry Chappell, a railway porter at Bath Mr. Chappell is known to his comrades as the " Bath Railway Poet." A poem such as this lifts him to the rank of a national poet.]

You boasted the Day, and you toasted the Day,
    And now the Day has come.
Blasphemer, braggart and coward all,
Little you reck of the numbing ball,
The blasting sheil, or the " white arm's " fall,
    As they speed poor humans h..me.

You spied for the Day, you lied for the Day,
    And woke the Day's red spleen.
Monster, who asked God's aid Divine,
Then strewed His seas with the ghastly mine ;
Not all the waters of all the Rhine
    Can wash thy foul hands clean.

You dreamed for the Day, you schemed for the Day ;
    Watch how the Day will go.
Slayer of age and youth and prime
(Defenceless slain for never a crime)
Thou art steeped in blood as a hog in slime,
    False friend and cowardly foe.

You have sown for the Day, you have grown for the Day ;
    Yours is the harvest red.
Can you hear the groans and the awful cries?
Can you see the heap of slain that lies,
And sightless turned to the flame-split skies
    The glassy eyes of the dead ?

You have wronged for the Day, you have longed for the Day ;
    That lit the awful flame.
'Tis nothing to you that hill and plain
Yield sheaves of dead men amid the grain ;
That widows mourn for their loved ones slain,
    And mothers curse thy name.

But after the Day there's a price to pay
    For the sleepers under the sod,
And Him you have mocked for many a day—
Listen, and hear what He has to say :
" Vengeance is mine, I will repay,"
    What can you say to God?

Reprinted from the London " Daily Express " (Copyright).

'The Day' poem on a postcard.
(Author's collection)

Poetry remained the greatest fundraiser and R.W.E. Griffiths, a goods car man at Bristol, sold 53,000 copies of various poems to raise funds for patriotic and charitable institutions. His poem 'Somebody's Boy' sold 12,500 copies and 'Our Blinded Heroes' sold 11,000. The sale of poems raised much needed funds at a time when money was required for the care of the wounded and dependents of those who had been killed. One of Griffiths' poems raised over £40 for the St Dunstan's Hostel for Blinded Soldiers.

Alfred Williams was a steam hammer driver and later a hammerman at Swindon, and studied as a correspondence student to become a scholar in Latin, Greek, French and English literature, and established himself as a poet. Although he resigned from the GWR in September 1914 due to ill health, he continued writing poetry which was well received during the war, especially his 'Crossing the Marne', although he is best known for his classic book *Life in a Railway Factory*, published in May 1915.

Chapter Seven

GWR Men at War – 116th, 275th and 262nd (GWR) Railway Companies Royal Engineers – Signal Company RE – GWR Civilian Railway Company – GWR Volunteer Company – 565th (Wilts) Army Troops Company RE – Notes on some GWR Military Men – Young Recruits – Tales from the Front – Channel Ferry

GWR Men at War

During the first months of the war some 4,000 GWR men, who were army and naval Reservists as well as members of the Territorial Force, were called upon for immediate military service.

In August 1914 almost half of the regular British Army was serving abroad in the various corners of the Empire. It was impossible for the overseas battalions to reach the front line quickly, especially those in India, even though they were mobilised on the first day of the war. The battalions based at home, with their shorter travelling distance, were of immediate use, and the place of those battalions sent to the front was taken by the Territorials and Reservists. This military reserve which contained many experienced men was thought to be sufficient in numbers in the event of a war, but until 1914 there had not been a war that would stretch the nations forces in such a way, so greedy was it for men's lives, and as the war progressed the losses of the original army had to be replaced.

The GWR men went in that first month of the war to do the duty for which they had been trained, confident in the knowledge that it would be over before Christmas and comforted by the fact that their jobs would be there for them upon their return. What must have eased the anxious minds of those who were called to the military were the GWR's arrangements to supplement their service pay and separation allowance to ensure that those of the family left at home did not suffer any financial hardship.

Many of the GWR men joined the county regiments local to where they worked or lived, such as the Berkshire and Devonshire regiments, and owing to the large number of employees at Swindon the Wiltshire Regiment contained many GWR men; a look at the Roll of Honour confirms this. There was a great deal of pride in serving with the local regiment, and a steady stream of Swindon men joined Wiltshire's and an equal number of men were required to replace those who were lost. To illustrate this it is worth looking at the 1st Battalion at the beginning of the war. They sailed for France on 13 August and by October they were fighting at Neuve Chapelle. Between 23 and 27 October the battalion's estimated casualties (killed, wounded and missing) were fourteen officers and 350 men. One-third of the battalion strength lost in one encounter, and only two months into the war. Similar losses occurred when the battalion was at Thiepval during the first week of the Battle of the Somme in 1916. This was why

From top

Taunton GWR men in Burma in A Company 2/5th Somerset Light Infantry. (*GWR Magazine*)

5th Devonshire Regiment in India, 1915. Fifty of the battalion's strength was made up of GWR men from Plymouth and Newton Abbot. (*GWR Magazine*)

GWR men serving with the Royal Flying Corps. (*GWR Magazine*)

Birmingham GWR men serving in the Royal Navy. (*GWR Magazine*)

Swindon lads with the Wiltshire Regiment in India. (*GWR Magazine*)

so many recruits were called for during the war, and as time progressed experienced battalions had their numbers diluted with inexperienced recruits as drafts attempted to bring the army up to strength. Inexperienced Territorial battalions were put into the front line and paid dearly, especially on the Somme in 1916, but it must be remembered that the world had not seen a war such as this and every month and year was a period of learning, costly as it was, but by 1918 the lessons had been learned.

The 1st Wiltshire Regiment 'cheering during the great advance' – Thiepval, Somme, 1916. (Author's collection)

116th, 275th and 262nd (GWR) Railway Companies Royal Engineers

The corps of Royal Engineers was perhaps the most natural choice for many railway employees as skills learned in the workplace were easily adapted into the various units.

Not only was the Home Front dependant on the railways, but as time progressed it was increasingly so on the war fronts. Troops, supplies, horses, artillery and tanks, after arriving at the French ports, were transported by train to the railheads or designated areas such as stores for the supplies, holding areas for horses and depots for the tanks. Marching, horses, road and canal transport bridged the gap between detraining and the front line, as did the ever increasing narrow-gauge lines. Any distance travelled was a slow progress with congestion playing a major role due either to damage, weather or just sheer numbers.

At the beginning of the war only one Railway Company of the Royal Engineers was stationed in France which was due to sufficient numbers of French engineers being available at that time to carry out any maintenance required, coupled with the fact that the French Railway Companies wished to remain in control of the railways in their own country, as laid down in a pre-war agreement, which General Joffre denounced in November 1916. As time progressed and it became obvious that the war would not be a short one, situations arose whereby the British forces made it clear that they wished to control sections of the lines, especially in the Pas de Calais area and Belgium. This control extended as far south as Amiens by 1918, with British trains and crews regularly working connecting lines.

With this control came the need to recruit men for railway operating and construction, to work as crews for the trains and carry out improvements and repairs to the lines, as the French railways and military establishments found themselves to be overstretched. The obvious recruiting ground was the British Railway Companies as the men, apart from military training, were already experienced in railway work. Although civilian railwaymen from the South Eastern and Chatham Railway, together with their own shunting engines, had successfully taken over the working of the port of Boulogne, the running of military railways were not the same as civilian ones, which

GWR Swindon Works men with the Railway Operating Division Royal Engineers. (*GWR Magazine*)

GWR men with the 111th Railway Company Royal Engineers. (*GWR Magazine*)

is why there were Railway Companies and the Railway Operating Division, to combine railway expertise with that of military knowledge. The numbers of men recruited for this work were in addition to the numbers already eligible to serve in the forces, which put an even greater strain on the workforce at home.

During the war the GWR were able to raise three Railway Companies (all attached to the Royal Engineers), one volunteer company and one civilian company. Accounts of their time and duties make for interesting reading, as does the comparison of where they were stationed, as many only think of the Western Front in connection with the First World War, but the first company raised by the GWR were destined for warmer climes.

116th (GWR) Railway Company (RE)

The GWR was requested to find sufficient employees to form a Railway Construction Company to serve overseas and was to consist of:

6 officers (3 of which were to be chosen by the War Office)

220 permanent way men

12 carpenters

6 blacksmiths

116th (GWR) Railway Company - first draft of fifty men leaving Paddington on 18 June 1915. (*GWR Magazine*)

NCOs and officers of the 116th Railway Company. (*GWR Magazine*)

Anti-clockwise from above

Lieutenant E. Lake. (*GWR Magazine*)

Captain R.C. Kirkpatrick. (*GWR Magazine*)

Lieutenant A.S. Quartermaine. (*GWR Magazine*)

2 cooks

1 clerk (shorthand typist)

1 draughtsman

The three officers from the GWR were: Officer Commanding R.C. Kirkpatrick, Chief Assistant to the Divisional Engineer at Wolverhampton, E. Lake of the Divisional Engineers (Office Plymouth) and Alan S. Quartermaine of the Chief Engineers (Office Paddington).

There was no difficulty in finding volunteers, and it was only a few days before the full strength of men were enlisted and sent to the British Railway Troops Depot at Longmoor in June 1915.

After an initial training period, a detachment was sent to Portsmouth to lay additional sidings for ammunition traffic, and after completion moved to Blaydon, near Newcastle-upon-Tyne, where new sidings were needed for a number of munitions works.

In December 1915 the lives of the men were to be changed for the next three years as orders were sent out that the company was to return to Longmoor to pick up their technical equipment (amounting to some 50 tons) and report to Devonport. The company left Devonport on 14 December on HMT *Minniapolis*, sailing to their final destination of Port Said, Egypt.

First the company was sent to El Ferdan on the Suez Canal, where they laid a 5-mile long, 2ft 6in narrow-gauge railway in the desert in an easterly direction. The railway was finished in February 1916, during which time the men had to reinforce the local garrison as the area was poorly defended.

The men sent reports of their exploits to the *GWR Magazine* and said they were very busy in the summer of 1916, and it was very hot, averaging over 100 degrees; to avoid working in the heat of the day the men often started before daybreak. Helmets and dark glasses were issued to the men to help shade them from the sun, but a great deal of satisfaction was felt when the work they had done contributed to the successes of the army during that summer.

It wasn't all hard work, and despite the heat football and cricket was very popular; a cricket pitch was improvised by laying grass matting on the sand.

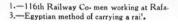

1.—116th Railway Co. men working at Rafa.
3.—Egyptian method of carrying a rail.

2.—Egyptians carrying sleepers, one per man.
4.—Earthwork done with baskets.

116th Company at work. (*GWR Magazine*)

Being based so far away from home the company was very dependent on ships for supplies and mail, but the loss of a number of ships meant that they did not always receive their mail. The loss of one ship in particular shook them: HMT *Minniapolis*.

Natives were employed to help with the unskilled tasks, and the men of the 116th started to pick up a little of the language. Although very basic, it was enough to make themselves understood. The natives were excellent at digging and carrying and were used to the high temperatures, but it was their strength that most surprised the men as it was usual to see one of these industrious workers carrying a sleeper on his back, running with it!

A detachment of the company was sent back to Port Said to lay a narrow-gauge railway along the coast, while the rest of them were sent to Kantara to lay a standard-gauge line from the Suez Canal to Katia, an oasis in the Sinai Desert, a length of some 30 miles. This length was later extended to an incredible 600 miles to Haifa, with branches to Jerusalem and Beersheba, together with eighty-six stations along the whole route.

The terrain upon which the track was laid was certainly nothing like the men had ever encountered before, with the first 120 miles being sandy desert; and although no bridge building was required, the desert was not flat, and 20ft cuttings were not unusual. They used sand as ballast, which worked quite well except during sandstorms or when it was wet. Stone was used where possible near Palestine, although the urgency for the completion of the line forced them to lay the track on the earth, which was fine as a short-term measure but full-time maintenance was in question due to the lack of suitable ballast. The type of track laid was a flat-bottomed rail spiked to wood sleepers, with a maximum gradient of 1 in 100.

During the time the 116th worked on this line they worked alongside the 115th Company, made up of platelayers from the London and North Western Railway. The two companies worked in shifts and remained together for over two years. Unskilled Egyptian labourers carried out all the earthwork and the average day's construction by the combined force was 1¼ miles, although on one occasion this was exceeded to 2 miles.

The Railway Operating Division oversaw the running of the railway, with the rolling stock being mostly supplied by the Egyptian State Railway, although it was possible to point out wagons from various British railways, including the GWR.

The conditions experienced by the men were in total contrast to those who worked on the Western Front, as the terrain was totally alien to them, with sand and dust making life very uncomfortable, together with the flies and high temperatures. Although the company only experienced one bomb attack on their camp (with no injury), almost every man visited the hospital during their time abroad due to malaria, dysentery and septic sores and also suffered losses this way.

NON-COMMISSIONED OFFICERS AS AT DECEMBER 1915

Sergeants

G. Bass, Paddington	G.E. Knight, Bearley
A.E. Easty, Battersea	J. Price, Llanvihangel (died 3/11/1918)
W. Jones, Stourbridge	A.J. Squires, Gwinear Road
A. Kitchen, Brill & Ludgershall	E.C. Stone, Paddington

Corporals

A.E. Blick, West Ealing	A.S. Nicholls, Plymouth
H. Bowden, Manheniot	J. Norris, Denham
G. Curtis, Bristol	G. Reynolds, Greenford

W.J. Edge, Shrewsbury

W.C. Geach, Plymouth

J. Hawkins, Bath

J. Holton, Bilston

E.J. Smith, Maidenhead (later Sergeant)

E. Staple, Taunton

W. Waring, Wolverhampton

2nd Corporals

W. Anderson, Reading

T. Bridges, West Ealing

G.J. Down, St. Dennis Junction

F. Huxtable, Taunton

F. Hamley, Millbay Docks

G. Jeavons, Dunstall Park

W. Round, Worcester

J. Sims, Hanwell

Lance Corporals

W. Andrews, Reading

A.M. Alexander, Maidenhead

A.G. Birch, Hereford

E.C.H. Cumbes, Hereford

H. Dryden, Lostwithiel

F. Gill Norton, Fitzwarren

J. Hartland, Bilston

J. Hollick, Wednesbury

J. Kirtland, Banbury

W. Meadows, Cheltenham

C.H. Mumford, Devonport

W. Smith, Gloucester

War Diary

The 116th Company war diary (WO 95/4410), covering February 1916 to February 1918, is held at the National Archives.

275th (GWR) Railway Company (RE)

The 275th (GWR) Railway Company was raised on 3 May 1916, with the first draft of men reaching the training camp on 1 June and the rest following over the next few days. Training completed, the company left for France on 21 August 1916.

The company comprised: 200 platelayers, 18 carpenters, 12 blacksmiths, 2 fitters, 2 engine drivers, 2 firemen, 1 clerk, 1 draughtsman, 2 cooks and an interpreter.

The officers from various GWR engineering departments were: Capt. H.S.Whitley (Neath), Capt. V.W. Beckley (Shrewsbury), Lt F. Garthwaite (Paddington), Lt E. Perfect (Newport).

This company was the only one not reported on in the *GWR Magazine*, except for when the wife of Capt. Whitley appealed for books, cigarettes etc. for the troops of the 275th, to be sent to her in Newquay in 1916. Perhaps it was thought that their war record was not sufficiently exciting enough, but it fills a gap as much is written on the exploits of units at the front so it is interesting to record what was happening at the rear. The following is largely taken from the company's war diary, and starts on 1 August 1917, a whole year after they arrived in France; by then Capt. Whitley had been promoted to major and left to join the Railway Survey Section, RE, as the Officer Commanding.

We pick up the story with the company divided into three main detachments, each concerned with work within their allotted geographical area as follows:

Dieppe Area:

British lines maintenance

Martin Eglise chalk quarry

Serqueux sand mine

Rouxmesnil – line work including extensions and alterations for the ordnance depot

Clockwise from above

Captain H.S. Whitley, 1916. (*GWR Magazine*)

Lieutenant E. Perfect. (*GWR Magazine*)

Lieutenant F. Garthwaite. (*GWR Magazine*)

Railway laying by engineers on captured ground. (Author's collection)

Basse Foret D'Eu – metre gauge siding

Mers (Le Treport) – new tank sidings

Rouen Area:

British lines maintenance

Dismantling of track at old ordnance depot

Quevilly – loading dock and coal dump, new ROD camp with new offices and huts, sidings for petrol depot

Grand Quevilly hydrogen plant – sidings for electrolytic plant

St Etienne – constructed inspection pit and wheel dropping pit at the large locomotive works, and lowering of siding

Oissel – new transportation depot

Foret De Lyon – survey and construction of transhipment siding

Le Havre Area:

British lines maintenance

Camp and locomotive accommodation at the ROD base park

Shunting spur and sidings for ordnance sheds

Siding for Royal Flying Corps Park

Canal Depot siding

Excavation of site of new bridge for metre gauge line

Much work was done by the company in a large area, which involved a great deal of travelling by the men to and from the work places and the exchange of men, probably due to individual expertise, from one work base to another. Officers also had to journey around to inspect the work being carried out and considering the congestion on the railways and roads, even in the rearward areas, it is amazing that they managed to move around the locality relatively quickly.

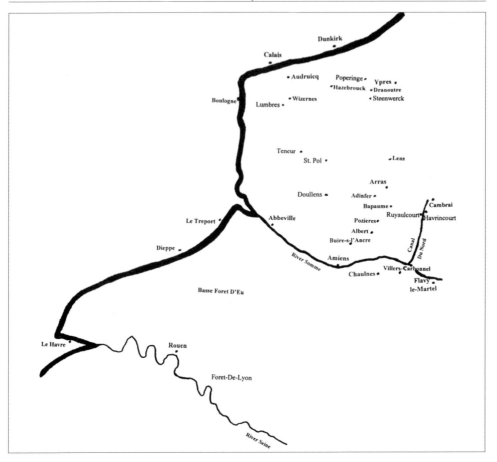

Map of the Western Front. (Author)

Meetings were held to discuss future engineering works at the major ROD establishments, and it was while returning from such a meeting at St Omer on 4 January 1918 that Captain Beckley sustained slight facial injuries when, it is recorded, box car No.9819 was 'badly damaged', although it is not known how this happened. Captain Beckley was admitted to the No.1 South African Hospital at Abbeville, together with Private Snell, who had a severe scalp wound.

Encounters with the 'enemy' were rare in this area, just the odd air raid, so many of the entries in the diary for men requiring hospital treatment must have been due to illness or what could be classed as industrial injuries, and might have been the reason that Sapper A.W. Powell was admitted to hospital after being injured by explosives at Le Havre on 27 September 1917.

Illness could be extremely dangerous, especially in 1918, and it is interesting to note that the first cases of influenza were recorded on 4 July; within five days thirty-six men had been admitted to hospital.

Training was carried out while in this area with many of the men attending the gas school at Rouen; Sapper Goldring was sent to the cookery school at Havre.

With one detachment remaining at Havre, the rest of the company moved to Oissel (Rouen) on 12 May 1918 to set up a new HQ where land was available to build a new transportation depot. Work at St Etienne locomotive works continued. In July Captain Beckley was promoted to major.

All through this period men were transferred to and from the company, and in September two sappers and a number of labourers were sent to the 200th Signal and Interlocking Company at Auxi-le-Chateau near Abbeville.

There came a major relocation of the company on 6 September 1918, and Major Beckley and Lieutenants Chester and Hill, with 146 other ranks, two horses, huts, stores and tools, left Oissel for Buire-sur-L'Ancre, south-east of Albert, taking a day to arrive. They were followed the next day by Captain Strangeways-Jones, Second Lieutenant Manning and seventy-one other ranks, complete with stores etc. The whole company was in place by 7.30 a.m. on 8 September, but unfortunately fifteen minutes later Sapper G. Farmer was fatally wounded by a bomb explosion; the circumstances of this were not explained.

The work of the company consisted of line maintenance between Albert, north to Beaucourt (Nord main line), and the salvaging of materials and reconstruction of Meault Dump (metre gauge) and Pozieres Line (30cm), as well as repairing the water tank at Buire Station. The section of worked line was handed over to the French on 21 October.

Orders were received on 31 October to move the whole company to Gouzeaucourt, south of Cambrai, and they carried out line maintenance work taken over from various Canadian Railway Troops as follows:

Marcoing Juction to Cambrai from the 7th Battalion
Cambrai to Bouchain from the 4th Battalion
Cambrai to Busigny from the 1st Battalion

Much of the work was handed over to the 263rd and 119th Railway Companies, Royal Engineers after a few days. The occurrence of 11 November and the end of the war appears to have been just another working day.

On 17 November, Major Beckley and half of the company moved to Cattenieres (south-east of Cambrai) to concentrate on working the lines radiating out of Cambrai, mostly to the north-west, carrying out bridge and culvert reconstruction as well as maintenance and salvage work.

From February 1919 men began to be released from the company, although there was much work still to be done, and a detachment worked at Le Cateau on deviation and salvage of track.

Authorisation was received on 19 June to break up the company, and Captain L.V. Grimes and Lieutenant Perfect were transferred to the 10th Railway Company, Royal Engineers, at Cologne, while Lieutenants Hill and Manning, with the remaining ninety-three other ranks, moved to Audruicq.

Lieutenant Hill, three other ranks and four Army Service Corps personnel dismantled the living train, and the twelve wagons, which consisted of the company office, drawing office, stores and tools vans and CQMS office, were handed over between 13 and 21 July to officials at Audruicq.

The remaining company motor vehicles (two Albion lorries, one Ford box car and one Douglas motorcycle), together with all the company records were taken to the Railway Cadre Camp at Terlincthun, on the northern outskirts of Boulogne, and handed over between 21 and 31 July.

War Diary

The 275th Company war diary (WO 95/4055), covering August 1917 to July 1919, is held at the National Archives.

262nd (GWR) Railway Company

On 5 February 1917 over 250 employees of the engineering department from various parts of the GWR arrived at Longmoor camp. This construction company comprised:

6 officers (2 appointed by the War Office)

200 platelayers	5 fitters
20 carpenters	2 cooks
10 blacksmiths	2 clerks
7 masons and bricklayers	1 draughtsman
5 strikers	

The Officer Commanding was Captain G.S. Hasell, who, together with Second Lieutenant S.J. Askham, was appointed by the War Office. Those from the GWR who were given commissions were: Captain O.T. Wood (second in command), Chief Assistant to the Divisional Engineer at Paddington; Second Lieutenants: A. Boxall (Divisional Engineers Office Shrewsbury), F.G. Price (Divisional Engineers Office Paddington), R. Gibb (Divisional Engineers Office Plymouth).

The company was billeted near to Longmoor and completed three weeks' intensive training before leaving on 26 February for Southampton, with the final destination of Le Havre.

After arriving at Le Havre, the company was billeted in a rest camp until 3 March, after which they travelled by train to Bailleul, and on to billets at Dranouter. They then moved their headquarters, under canvas, by the side of Clapham Junction, where they constructed a line from this point to Brulooze, near Kemmel. Although the line no longer exists, evidence of the

Ypres Railway Station. (Author's collection)

work of the GWR remains on maps with the naming of three junctions on the line: Paddington, Swindon and Penzance.

Good progress was made laying the 4½ miles of track (including a portion of GWR 86A section, double-head 'overseas' material), considering the intense cold and heavy snow falls and the interruptions by shelling (fortunately with no casualties) and the line was completed by 30 April.

During this time No.3 platoon, under Second Lieutenant Boxall, moved to Poperinge to work on the lines in the Ypres Salient, and were joined by the majority of the company on 5 May, leaving No.1 platoon at Clapham Junction for maintenance.

The company was housed in a living train of twenty-seven trucks at Brandhoek, on the Ypres to Poperinge line, and worked in the area for the next six months – before and until the end of the Third Battle of Ypres. The work ranged from the construction of stations, platforms, branches, howitzer spurs, laying of sidings, such as that laid to serve the Casualty Clearing Stations at Remy (Lijssenthoek), locomotive water supply points, Royal Engineer parks and the repair of shelled lines.

Some of the areas they worked were relatively quiet, but the company war diary records places where work was carried out that are synonymous with the Ypres Salient: Hellfire and Shrapnel Corners, Railway Wood, Zillebeke Lake, including the draining of the railway cutting at Hill 60. Consequently, working conditions were hazardous not only for the men of the company, but also those of the labour units attached to the company from time to time, sometimes amounting to over 1,000 men, who carried out the unskilled work. The first casualties occurred on 12 May when two men were wounded by shrapnel near Ypres Asylum.

All work was carried out by continuous shifts, with much done under the cover of darkness, especially when they were called upon to transport ammunition and stores handed over by the

A. Boxall. (*GWR Magazine*)

Grave of A. Boxall at Bedford House Cemetery. (Author)

Men of the 262nd who were awarded medals at Paddington, February 1918. (*GWR Magazine*)

Railway Operating Division at Ypres and, with an officer in charge, worked up to gun crews in various areas.

While constructing a howitzer spur at Ypres Station men, under Second Lieutenant Boxall, experienced heavy shelling with casualties but completed the spur in six days. Boxall was awarded the Military Cross and Sergeant Greening (later wounded) the Military Medal for work carried out under dangerous conditions.

There was no rest from the shelling and aerial bombardment when the men were in camp. While at Brandhoek their living train was attacked on three occasions. The first caused only material damage but on the second occurrence four of the trucks were destroyed, though luckily they were unoccupied at the time. The third attack resulted in one man being killed and several others injured.

The German flying ace Richthofen and his fellow pilots paid much attention to the work in the area causing casualties including, on 18 October, Captain Hatch, who had replaced Captain Wood. Wood was admitted to hospital on 2 July 1917 and did not return to the unit.

The men were transported by train to the various work places and on 19 October their train was in collision with a runaway ammunition train at Vlamertinge; seven men of the company and seventy of the attached labour unit were injured.

On 12 October earthwork was begun on No Mans Land Station, which was not at that time actually in 'no man's land', but it attracted as much attention from the enemy artillery as if it was. Originally there were to be eight sidings there, but owing to the number of casualties only one siding of 1,000ft in length was completed; it was ready for traffic on 15 November.

The company left the Ypres sector at the end of November 1917, and the total casualties for the company and the attached labour units amounted to 232, including Second Lieutenant Boxall who died of wounds on 25 October; he was working in an advanced position that was shelled. It was recorded that Boxall was a very able and fearless officer who had won the hearts of his men.

Just before the company left Ypres, the Railway Construction Officer (Royal Engineers) addressed the men, thanking them for the work they had done and stating that 'their work and courage had

Destruction at Ham Station. (Author's collection)

been second to none'. A very proud moment for the men and the GWR. On 24 November Brigadier General Sydney D'A. Crookshank, Royal Engineers, decorated the NCOs with the immediate awards at Ypres; a more formal ceremony was attended by the men at Paddington on 23 February 1918.

Decorations awarded while working in the Ypres area:
Military Cross: Second Lieutenant Boxall
Distinguished Conduct Medal: Sergeant Whitehead
Military Medal: Sergeant Duke
    Sergeant Greening
    Corporal Brush
    Corporal Joint
    Lance Corporal Birch (plus Bar)
    Lance Corporal Reeves
    Second Corporal Blood
    Second Corporal Betteridge

The company train steamed its weary way towards the coast for a rest period at Bergues, near Dunkirk, which in reality involved maintenance and siding accommodation work. However, this was interrupted in the middle of January 1918 by emergency bridge work on the Yser Canal due to serious flooding.

On 28 January the company was at Wizernes, outside of St Omer on the Boulogne line, where a 7-mile section of the line was doubled and a lattice girder bridge over the River Aa at Lumbres was constructed. The work was slow as no labour units were available to help until 26 February, when Chinese labour joined the company as well as prisoners of war.

A great deal was accomplished during the time in the area with only one casualty, Lieutenant F.G. Price, who was sent to England on 29 April with a broken leg. Captain Hassell was mentioned in despatches.

GWR signal and telegraph department men in France. (*GWR Magazine*)

One half of a platoon left for Tenur on 13 June to work on two additional sidings at the Tank Corps Central Workshops and Depot, and a large metre-gauge transhipment yard at nearby Anvin.

After the completion of these works the headquarters and three platoons travelled in their train, which by that time consisted of fifty-three trucks and two engines, and headed for Amiens on 31 August to construct a double line avoiding the town, which entailed the laying of 20 miles of track and heavy earthworks.

On 18 September orders were received to stop the track-laying owing to the success of the British advance, as the materials would be of greater use elsewhere. Two days later, with the work at Amiens halted, the company moved to Chaulnes to assist a French company in reconstructing a double line behind the French advance. The work took the company and its French comrades from Chaulnes, through Nesle, Ham, Flavy-le-Martel, St Quentin, Bohaim, Busigny and on to Wassigny.

The country up to St Quentin was totally devastated, with practically every rail broken and bridges blown up. The Germans had placed explosive charges on alternate joints on all four rails but a few lengths were undamaged due to the charges failing to explode. Air raids were frequent but progress was rapid, keeping up with the advancing artillery behind the front line.

It is interesting to note that the majority of the track used to reconstruct a long section of line east of Ham was taken from, the war diary states, the 'Big Bertha' spur at Flavy-le-Martel. This spur was one of the firing positions for the 'Paris Gun', which had an 80-mile range.

A new danger was awaiting the men when they reached Fresnoy-Le-Grand (south of Bohain) in the form of delay mines. These were placed at strategic points along the railway, such as bridges, level crossings, high embankments and main junctions. This was an extremely hazardous time for the men, not knowing where or when a mine might explode, and there were many narrow escapes. To give an example of the damage that could be caused by a delay mine, two had been set in a 30ft embankment at Bohain. Their combined explosion caused two craters measuring 109ft x 30ft, removing some 4,000 cubic yards of earth each (800 truck loads). Such was the intensity and urgency of the work in this area that Armistice Day passed with no celebration for the men; in fact the last mine to explode did so on 14 November 1918.

The work finally done, the company's train left for Aulnoye on 19 December, then the men were taken a few days later by road to Soire-Sur-Sambre (south-east of Mons), where they were to erect three trestle wooden bridges at Soir, Hantes and one a little further on.

The company left Belgium on 20 March 1919 under the command of Captain Hatch, with Lieutenants Cambel and Grant and Second Lieutenant Bowler, to the destination of Audricq, a little way along the main line out of Calais, where they were in charge of unloading of stores and materials for the railway with the help of prisoners of war and Chinese labourers.

The company finally returned home late in 1919.

Two men of the 262nd who appear on the Roll of Honour could possibly have been members of the GWR Civilian Company (see later). This company was in contact with the 262nd while working in the same area, and Sappers Bakehouse and Wyatt both enlisted at Brandhoek, which was unusual and could have meant they enlisted with the 262nd rather than return home. Why else would two GWR men enlist in Belgium?

War Diary

The 262nd Company war diary (WO 95/4054), covering from February 1917 to February 1919, is held at the National Archives.

Trench Map References

Swindon Junction: Kemmel 28SW1-3b M36b and Penzance Jct N19a
Paddington Junction: Bailleul 28SW3-2b S6d

Signal Company RE

A small party from the Signal and Telegraph Department was gathered together in the summer of 1915 to join 'L' Signal Company of the Royal Engineers in order to work on the lines of communication in France, which they began in October. Their commanding officer was Maurice George Tweedie of the Signal Engineers Office at Reading, who held the rank of second lieutenant and was acting captain by 1918. Work consisted of assisting other units in the building of permanent telegraph lines, which they did until January 1916. Later work involved providing and maintaining telephone communication between artillery and railway construction companies, telephone and bock and bell circuits on new railways, the establishment of signal offices to deal with railway construction traffic, and the installation of circuits and instruments on living trains, as well as a great deal of repair work due to shelling and bombing.

GWR Civilian Railway Company

In early 1917 the Railway Executive Committee, prompted by a letter from Sir Eric Geddes, made an urgent request for 3,000 civilian platelayers to form companies for work overseas, and they were to be selected with care for their suitability and fitness. This was not an unusual request as the same had happened in Crimea in 1855 and Egypt in 1882. The British railways supplied enough men to form eight companies, with five companies joining them from the railways in Ireland, all of which were contracted for three months' work overseas. The reason for these volunteers was simply that there was so much work to be done, and though there were many more Royal Engineers on the Western Front they were fully engaged, plus there had been an increase in the number of labour corps and although they were very adept at the heavy manual work, they lacked the skills and experience to carry out the urgent engineering tasks. It is generally thought that the call went out for volunteers in 1917, but it was on Sunday 20 February 1916 that suitable candidates for work in France were first sought.

The GWR company was known as the 3rd Civilian Railway Company and was some 261 men strong:

GWR Civilian Railway Company in France. (*GWR Magazine*)

Detachment of B Company. (*GWR Magazine*)

1 Senior Engineer	198 Platelayers
2 Junior Engineers	6 Blacksmiths
1 Draughtsman	10 Carpenters
1 Surveyor	2 Storekeepers
1 Cashier	1 Timekeeper
1 Clerk	4 Timbermen
1 Permanent Way Inspector	2 Signal Locking Fitters
13 Gangers	2 Motor-Cyclists
13 Sub-Gangers	2 Cooks

Raymond Carpmael, Chief Assistant to the Divisional Engineer at Gloucester, was in charge of the company with F.T. Bowle of Reading and S. Deans of Neath being allocated the positions of Junior Engineers.

The company assembled at Paddington on 15 March 1917 and spent the night at Holborn Stadium, with their food provided by the YAMC. The following day the men marched to a War Office depot where they were issued with army kits comprising canteens, water bottles, blankets etc., after which they were transported by train to an awaiting ship.

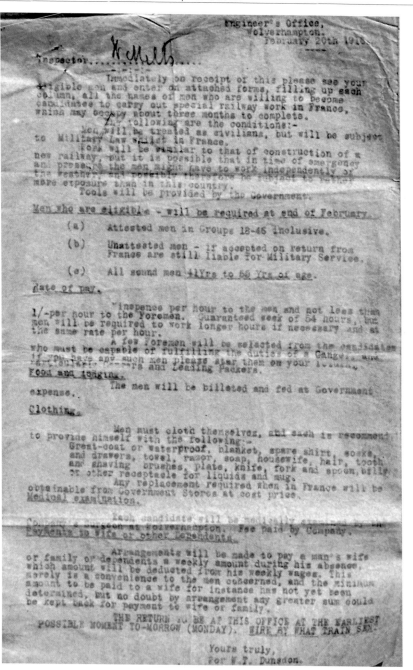

Engineer's Office,
Wolverhampton.
February 20th 1916.

Inspector......*H.Mills*......

Immediately on receipt of this please see your eligible men and enter on attached forms, filling up each column, all the names of men who are willing to become candidates to carry out special railway work in France, which may occupy about three months to complete.

The following are the conditions:-

Men will be treated as civilians, but will be subject to Military Law whilst in France.

Work will be similar to that of construction of a new railway, but it is possible that in time of emergency and pressure the men might have to work independently or the weather, and possibly therefore be subject to more exposure than in this country.

Tools will be provided by the Government.

Men who are eligible - will be required at end of February.

(a)   Attested men in Groups 18-46 inclusive.

(b)   Unattested men - if accepted on return from France are still liable for Military Service.

(c)   All sound men 41Yrs to 56 Yrs of age.

Rate of pay.

9inspence per hour to the men and not less than 1/-per hour to the Foremen. Guaranteed week of 54 hours, but men will be required to work longer hours if necessary and at the same rate per hour.

A few Foremen will be selected from the candidates who must be capable of fulfilling the duties of a Ganger, and if you have any such men please star them on your lists, and particular.......rs and Leading Packers.

Food and lodging.

The men will be billeted and fed at Government expense.

Clothing.

Men must cloth themselves, and each is recommend to provide himself with the following:-

Great-coat or waterproof, blanket, spare shirt, socks, and drawers, towel, razor, soap, housewife, hair, tooth and shaving brushes, plate, knife, fork and spoon, billy or other receptacle for liquids and mug.

Any replacement required when in France will be obtainable from Government Stores at cost price.

Medical examination.

Each candidate will be medically examined by the Company's surgeon at Wolverhampton. Fee paid by Company.

Payments to Wife or other Dependents.

Arrangements will be made to pay a man's wife or family or dependents a weekly amount during his absence, which amount will be deducted from his weekly wages. This merely is a convenience to the men concerned, and the minimum amount to be paid to a wife for instance has not yet been determined, but no doubt by arrangement any greater sum could be kept back for payment to wife or family.

THE RETURN TO BE AT THIS OFFICE AT THE EARLIEST POSSIBLE MOMENT TO-MORROW (MONDAY). SIRE AT WHAT TRAIN SAY.

Yours truly,
For W.T. Dunsdon.

Original letter calling for civilian platelayers, 1916. (Author's collection)

Candidates for Civilian Force for

GREAT WESTERN RAILWAY,

Railway Construction work in France

Envelope of original letter calling for civilian platelayers. (Author's collection)

Steenwerck Station looking towards Nieppe and Armentieres. (Author)

Their first week in France was spent in a camp waiting to be transported to their allotted destinations. This was a frustrating time for the men as they could see that much work needed to be carried out at a railway yard adjoining the camp. Finally at the end of the week the men were moved some 200 miles by train, a journey taking forty-two hours which, they were told, was good under the circumstances.

On arrival at their destination near the front, the company was split into two sections, 'A' and 'B', and each section was divided into detachments and allotted areas where they were to work which entailed emergency repairs, doubling of lines and construction of new lines, as well as routine maintenance. It was agreed that the civilians would work from the bases to the railheads, while the Royal Engineers would work the lines from the railheads to the front line.

While the men were at their place of work, food and sleeping accommodation was supplied by the War Office to the same standards as experienced by the troops, with billets comprising of anything from a tent to an old barn.

One detachment of 'A' section were carrying out emergency repairs to the lines at Steenwerck (between Bailleul and Armentieres), which involved working for eleven and a half hours a day for ten consecutive days. At the time the men were only 4½ miles from the front line, which was the closest of any of the civilian companies to the front, and must have felt even closer when a shell exploded in their camp.

On 13 May GWR Chairman Viscount Churchill and Chief Engineer Mr W.W. Grierson toured the section of the Western Front where the GWR Civilian Company was working; they praised the men for their hard work under such difficult conditions.

'B' section had been working on the laying-in and maintenance at a large goods yard at Dunkirk, and were joined by 'A' section. They then both took over the maintenance of the Arques-Berguette widening, and extensive alterations at Arques Station.

The company returned to England at the end of their three-month contract, and on arrival in London were given a 'welcome home' tea at a YMCA building before being taken by bus to Paddington to make their journeys home.

Judging by the account of the experiences of the men in the August 1917 edition of the *GWR Magazine*, they thought themselves privileged to have taken part and 'done their bit', and even described it as 'one of the finest experiences in their lives'.

Although the work of the civilian companies was a success, the War Office declined to accept an offer of more civilians to carry out work. This was because as civilians they could only be sent to areas of relative safety and special arrangements had to be made for housing and feeding. Also, the price of pay to the civilian men was higher than that given to those who had enlisted and would have caused resentment if the civilians had worked alongside enlisted men in construction companies. All these facts led to the belief that the cost and trouble involved outweighed the benefits. The War Office turned to Australia, South Africa and Canada to form additional companies, which were urgently needed.

GWR Volunteer Company

In June 1917 the staff of the GWR London offices put forward a proposal to the General Manager to raise a volunteer company from within its staff members. Up to 130 members of staff had already made it known that they wished to join this new company, and it was thought there would be no difficulty in increasing the number to 250 men, which was the requirement to form one company.

This company would be part of the Paddington Battalion, West London Volunteer Regiment, and would have the use of the local drill hall and the facilities at the regimental headquarters at Porchester Road. The rifle range provided by the GWR at the beginning of the war for the use of Paddington staff was to be made available for the volunteer company.

The uniforms for the volunteers had to be paid for, so to encourage an increase of numbers of volunteers the directors paid for each of the uniforms for the first 250 men to join (each uniform cost 30s), and £1 was refunded by the Government when each volunteer was passed as being 'suitable material and efficient'. Each of the Government pounds was put into a fund for meeting expenses, such as repairs or new uniforms for the men. The initial funds required for kitting out the men were found from the monies raised from the exhibitions of ambulance trains, of which £375 was made available at the start of the recruiting campaign.

On 15 September 1917 the GWR Volunteer Company was 'sworn in' at the Paddington Battalion HQ (2/19th County of London Volunteer Regiment), with the Mayor of Paddington administering the oath. The General Manager, Frank Potter, was unable to attend but sent a message of congratulations and hope for the future, which was read out to the men.

The commander of the Volunteer Company was Lieutenant F.T. Barrington Ward, who was a barrister and has been associated with the GWR on legal matters. The company was divided into four platoons, with the following as commanders:

No.1 Platoon P. Frampton (Office of Superintendent of the Line)
No.2 Platoon H.D. Anderson (Assistant Divisional Superintendent)
No.3 Platoon S. Witherington (Solicitor)
No.4 Platoon T.E. Tavener (Goods Office)

Mr. C. Aldington, who witnessed the " swearing-in " ceremony of the G.W.R. Volunteer Company, with the Company Officers.

GWR Volunteer Company. (*GWR Magazine*)

Each had held positions in the regular army or volunteer battalions, as had many of the men in the company who had been wounded and invalided out of the forces, such as: Company Sergeant Major J.E. Peart, who was with the 29th Division at Suvla Bay and in November 1915 was invalided home after suffering from frostbite due to floods and blizzards there; Sergeant W.J. Reynolds, who worked in the Special Police Department at Paddington, was with the Irish Guards at the retreat from Mons and fought in the Battle of the Marne and the Aisne, and was wounded at Ypres; Lance Corporal J.H.H. Nightingale was a member of the Chief Accountants Office and during his time with the Duke of Cornwall's Light Infantry he fought at Armentieres, Ypres, Hooge and was wounded at Arras; Sapper J. Greenleaf and Private James F. Britton were both discharged from the regular army on physical grounds.

On 9 December the company took part in manoeuvres at Epsom Racecourse and was inspected by Field Marshall, Commander-in-Chief Home Forces, Lord French. The company acted out a mock attack, and the men and officers were pleased to see that their training had progressed well.

Battle conditions of a different type were encountered when the company helped out at Paddington Station with the Christmas rush of increased passengers, mail and parcels from 20 to 23 December.

In the summer of 1918 the company was entrusted with the manning of an anti-aircraft gun station on two nights each week, but by now their numbers were declining due to men from its

G.W.R. VOLUNTEER COMPANY

1.—With the Battalion at Headquarters.
2.—On the march to Hyde Park.
3.—The Mayor of Paddington administering the oath.

GWR Volunteer Company. (*GWR Magazine*)

Major F.G. Wright. (*GWR Magazine*)

Major F. G. Wright, Wilts Fortress R.E. (T.), at Weymouth, watching the departure of his first company for the Front.

Sketch of Major Wright. (*GWR Magazine*)

Wilts Fortress, 1915. (*GWR Magazine*)

ranks being enlisted for active service overseas, and therefore the company, in its own right, never saw active service.

565th (Wilts) Army Troops Company RE

The 1st Wilts Fortress, Royal Engineers (Swindon), was a Territorial company made up almost entirely of Great Western Railway men. GWR men that were serving as officers were Major F.G. Wright, Captain C.S. Wilson, Lieutenants J. Dawson, S.E. Tyrwhitt, D. Williams and G.E. Knapp, with H.C. Rodda as company sergeant major.

As with other Territorial units, they were away at the summer training grounds when war was declared, and were immediately recalled from Fort Purbrook, Portsmouth, to their base at Swindon. They were then ordered to Weymouth to work on the defences around Portland and, with the aid of a large number of infantry, the work was completed by the end of November. This was followed by a month of strenuous training which included heavy bridge building and trench digging by night, as well as the usual route marches, before the company set off on a sixteen-hour sailing for France on 20 January 1915, aboard SS *Blackwell*.

From Le Havre they travelled by train in horse boxes to St Omer, where they worked on part of a large defensive scheme before marching to Ypres in April. Their work was at St Eloi, south of Ypres, uncomfortably close to the front line, where they worked hip deep in water and under constant rifle fire, which accounted for the company's first casualties. The company constructed a trench along the bank of the Comines Canal and bore tunnels into the other bank to serve as hidden approaches; while doing so the men had to cross an exposed bridge and pass a machine gun. Consequently the men were counted on their way out and back.

Lieutenant Dawson (1914). (*GWR Magazine*)

Lieutenant Knapp. (*GWR Magazine*)

Ramp into the dry Canal du Nord at Ruyaulcourt, built by the 565th Wilts. September 1918. (*GWR Magazine*)

Ruyaulcourt Cemetery. (Author)

After this first taste of battle the company were encamped at Brielen, and called upon to erect some huts by the Yser Canal for arriving divisions. Unfortunately, shortly after completion the area attracted the attention of German artillery, and the huts were reduced to matchwood. While this work was in progress some of the company surveyed the roads north of Ypres together with the canal, over which a heavy timber bridge was planned. Floating bridges were also in use on the canal and the company was entrusted with their repair, which was a very dangerous occupation. Roads, railway lines and canals that were existing and mapped before the war meant that their exact location was known to the Germans, and the accuracy of their shelling bore testimony to that fact, but temporary structures, such as floating bridges, caused the Germans some problems, and as it was imperative that they destroyed these routes across the canal – the only way to locate them was to shell as much of the area as possible. The company was inundated with repair work, the danger being all too obvious, and not a day passed without the returning work party being one or two men short. It was while carrying out the bridging work on the canal that GWR man Sergeant O. Davis, together with Sapper Perry, made emergency repairs to a shelled bridge so that wounded French soldiers could be brought back to a dressing station as quickly as possible. They were both awarded the Distinguished Conduct Medal.

The company had great difficulty in completing their tasks as their workforce was eventually down by 50 per cent, and as if this was not enough they had been ordered to move their camp to the outskirts of Ypres where they found themselves the target for a battery of 8in guns, but fortunately they were ordered to hand over their work and proceed to Dranoutre where they had a well-earned rest.

Dranoutre, near Kemmel, was a quiet sector at that time, and during June half of the company worked here on defences with three companies of Belgian infantry, while the other half, which consisted of mechanics, was engaged in work at an engineering shop and sawmill at Bailleul. Here many items were designed, manufactured and supplied, such as observation towers, gun platforms, thousands of huts and miles of wooden railway track. The company won the praises of the War Council after they sent an inspector to the sawmill and he found that the engine and saws were run by steam generated entirely from the refuse of the mill.

As the organisation and scope of the work at Bailleul progressed additions were made to the civilian staff, which in turn released the Swindon men to perform other tasks such as work on concrete dugouts, machine gun posts at Nieppe, as well as giving them time to attend a course in heavy steel bridge construction at Armentieres.

September 1915 saw the biggest change to the company when its name was changed from the 1/1st Wilts Fortress RE (T) to the 565th Wilts Army Troops Company, Royal Engineers, with the number of men increasing from 105 to 149.

The building of a new mill at Steenwerck and a hospital at nearby Trois Ambres occupied the company for some time, as did work on emergency roads, light railways and water supplies. In July 1916 all this work came to an abrupt halt and was handed over for completion while the 565th travelled to Carnoy Valley on the Somme where they worked on water supplies in the area while being encamped at Bronfay Farm. It was recorded that 'from now onwards an exciting time was experienced', an expression that seems strange today but was often used when recalling events after the war.

The Battle of the Somme had opened, and transportation and supplies were struggling to keep pace with demand. Water was of great importance to the men and horses, and as more of both were transferred to the battlefield, the greater that demand became. The main job of the 565th at this time was to construct watering points, reservoirs, pumping stations and lay miles of pipes to convey the water. To say that their work was carried out in inhospitable surroundings would be a gross understatement. They laid the water pipes across infamous, shell-riddled ground from Bray to Suzanne on the north bank of the Somme, and through Meaulte to Fricourt, Carnoy, Mametz and Montauban.

There was fine summer weather on the opening day of the battle but by its end in November winter had made itself felt, and the company were busy mending bursts and trying to bury pipes to protect them from the frost; the bitterly cold weather dropped to a low of -17.5°C on 4 February 1917. Unfortunately the burying of the water pipes in the early winter was not completed owing to more urgent work, such as making good the pumps at Suzanne because of the collapse of the dugouts in which they were housed.

Another phenomenal piece of engineering work was begun at this time at Fargny Mill, with the installation of a pumping mill designed to deliver up to 22,500 gallons of water per hour from the River Somme, pumped through a 6in pipeline to Trones Wood and beyond.

Enemy activity was greatly reduced during the winter so that work continued at a pace, but the weather made the going very tough, and at the end of winter the 565th handed over their work to another company and moved on to Foucaucourt to erect a Corps HQ Camp, which they did in two days in very wet weather. They then moved to work on an Army HQ Camp to accommodate 2,000 at Villers Carbonnel, which lay just beyond the old German front line and was littered with the dead of battle.

The 565th were aided by some infantry companies, and later by field companies of the Royal Engineers, and the building was nearing completion by April 1917. However, they were moved, yet again, to La Chapelette to construct five heavy steel bridges, varying in spans from 20–60ft, over the Somme at Peronne. The work was to be completed in twelve days, but orders were received on the seventh to move to Dunkirk. Only three of the bridges were in place with the fourth, and most difficult, ready to launch; 160 men worked on these bridges, with the materials being transported by a train of twenty-six vehicles, the contents of which had to be unloaded by hand and carried three-quarters of a mile. The speed at which this work was carried out constituted a record and won the praise of the corps commander and chief engineer.

The company's work at Dunkirk was in stark contrast to that on the Somme. They were detailed to fit out the Terminus Hotel at Leffrinckoucke, between Dunkirk and Bray Dunes, by laying carpets, fitting window blinds, installing electric and water, and building outhouses etc. Working by the sea was a welcome change for the company after their experiences on the Somme, but it was not long before enemy shells were landing in the vicinity, making life unpleasant.

A detachment of the men were sent to the docks to construct water tanks and install pumps in some Thames lighters, and when this was finished a large detachment was sent to Pont Remy, near Abbeville, to construct a musketry school. When all the work was finished the rest of the men were sent to the school at the beginning of November, but at the end of the month they were all suddenly transported by special lorries to the Cambrai front. Here they were employed in filling in mine craters where the Hindenburg Line crossed the Bapaume–Cambrai road, between the Canal du Nord and Graincourt. They were under sporadic machine-gun fire at night, and to make life more uncomfortable rations went very short for several days owing to large troop movements and lack of communication with the authorities.

Over a week passed before they were provided with a camp at Bihucourt, and the men were placed at several watering points and casualty clearing stations. A little later a detachment with a substantial labour party was sent to Vaulx-Vraucourt to construct a new line of defence to St Leger.

After the German counter-attack in December the company headquarters was moved to a more central position at Ervillers, where they worked in the forward area, installed water supplies

Row of graves at Ruyaulcourt Cemetery of those killed on 18 September 1918, five of which belong to GWR men. (Author)

Canal du Nord bridge linking Hermies and Havrincourt, September 1918. (*GWR Magazine*)

and camps in the middle area, as well as, rather optimistically, searching for and cleaning wells in the back area for returning civilians.

All through the beginning of 1918 the defences in the area improved to formidable proportions, complete with hidden machine-gun positions. Unfortunately the defences were not fearsome enough to halt the German offensive (Operation Michael), which began on 21 March and saw the 565th, and the rest of the army, on the retreat. This was a very strenuous time for all, and the men of the company were working at night, then shifting camp and marching through the day. One night they had to march 4 miles to take charge of 900 labour personnel constructing a trench, and then find their way back again.

Operation Michael was called off by the Germans on 5 April, their army overstretched, to then concentrate on the next offensive in the north; although a large number of British troops had to be transferred north, this gave the chance for those left in the south to organise and reconstruct defences, and the 565th worked on a defensive line between Foncquevillers and Adinfer Wood. This was not an easy task as the area was full of guns of all descriptions and other war detritus, as well as being constantly harassed by enemy fire. The company repaired a section of the old British and a German front line, and constructed a maze of connecting trenches between and surrounding the old front lines. One of the connecting trenches was named 'Swindon Trench' by the general Officer Commanding.

Throughout the summer the 565th worked in this area, and in August two companies of American engineers were attached for instructional purposes.

As August progressed so did the Allied advance, and the company were called upon to construct a watering point at Douchy; several of the men worked non-stop for thirty-six hours, so important was this task, especially as there had been a breakdown of several of the neighbouring water systems; hundreds of horses had to be watered there and water carts filled.

The company followed the advance, opening up watering points along the way until they reached Ruyualcourt on 12 September, when they were given orders to build a 300ft-long ramp down the face of a retaining wall to carry all traffic up to 6in guns into the dry Canal du Nord. This important job had a fixed time schedule but the work was hampered by being constantly observed by Germans in a balloon, who could look right down on the site; there was no way of screening the work from prying eyes and because of this there was constant heavy shelling of the site. Fortunately the balloon was dispatched by an accurate 6in gun, which lessened the tension and allowed them to carry on unhindered. At 4 p.m. on 18 September, two days before the ramp was completed, the enemy attacked. The barrage was severe, resulting in the wounding of twenty-two and the death of six men (two of the wounded died the following day). The six men that were killed on the 18th are buried together at Ruyaulcourt Cemetery, five of whom are GWR men. One of the two to die the following day was also a GWR man.

The men of the 565th took these losses badly. Theirs was a small company and they all knew each other well and had been together for some years in some of the most dangerous areas, but had been lucky until then. On 22 September the company was sent to Boyelles to rest for a week.

On 27 September the company was joined by the New Zealand Tunnelling Company, Royal Engineers, for the construction of the largest heavy steel bridge erected on the Western Front, bridging the Canal du Nord between Hermies and Havrincourt. The Hopkins-type steel girder bridge had a span of 180ft over a 100ft depth of gap. Its launching length was 240ft, which allowed it to be manoeuvred into place by the use of rollers.

The material was carried in eighty 3-ton lorry loads, and the time allotted for unloading and erecting the bridge was 104 hours. A combined force of fourteen officers and 310 men worked on the construction, and so interesting and important was this bridge that Sir Douglas Haig twice inspected the work. Traffic was allowed across the bridge on 2 October, and three days later all work had finished and stores removed.

A short rest followed before moving to Raches for work in the Douai area to repair heavy bridges, but lack of materials made progress painfully slow, and one day before the Armistice was signed six men were working on the railway bridge at Douai when a delayed German mine exploded only 15ft away; each of the men sustained injuries. Lieutenant Rodda wrote 'Armistice Day found the company, who after being in the thick of it so long, feeling sadly misplaced'.

The company remained in Raches until 8 January 1919 when they were moved to Andenne, situated on the River Meuse, which was untouched by the war except for the total absence of metal door handles! Their final move came at the end of January when they travelled to Troisdorf, Germany, where they remained until the company was disbanded on 19 November 1919.

C.S. Wilson

Cyril Spencer Wilson was born on 12 July 1883 and entered Swindon Works as an engineering pupil in July 1902. He completed his training and became a member of the salaried staff by 1905, and was promoted to Assistant Works Manager of the Carriage and Wagon Works on 22 July 1907.

In the pre-war days he was an enthusiastic member of the Wilts Fortress, Royal Engineers, and at the outbreak of war he was captain of the unit, remaining so until September 1917 when he was appointed Officer Commanding No.4 Royal Engineers Workshop Company; his place with the Wilts Fortress was taken by Lieutenant J. Dawson, who was promoted to captain.

Wilson was promoted to major, awarded the Military Cross in the summer of 1917, twice mentioned in despatches and wounded at Amiens.

He was sent back to England suffering from dysentery and died from pneumonia brought about by influenza on 27 October 1918. He is buried in Charlcombe Churchyard near Bath.

Major C.S. Wilson. (*GWR Magazine*)

H.C. Rodda. (*GWR Magazine*)

The bridges over the Canal du Nord today showing two different designs, neither of which are the same as the 1918 bridge. Note the plinth visible in the bushes which could have been for the 1918 bridge. (Author)

Henry Colenso Rodda

Joining the GWR in 1892 at Weymouth, Rodda was transferred to Swindon in 1895 where he completed his training and entered the Drawing Office three years later. He had served with the Medical Corps as a stretcher bearer in the South African war.

He was mobilised with the Wilts Fortress at the outbreak of war, holding the rank of company sergeant major, and was granted a commission in November 1916 in his own company, which was unusual as most new officers were transferred to other units. He was awarded the Medaille Militaire on 6 November 1915 for valuable work carried out on a survey round brigade headquarters near Verbranden-Molen, and the Military Cross in June 1919, and mentioned in despatches in 1915.

When he returned after the war he was appointed Assistant Divisional Locomotive Superintendent at Newport. Fortunately it was Rodda who had the foresight to photograph the work at the Canal du Nord, which is now an important historical record.

The Canal Du Nord Bridge Today

If a visit to the Western Front is planned, and you find yourself in the vicinity, it is well worth taking a look at the crossing over the canal. Today two bridges span the canal cutting taking each half of the D5 road, which splits just before the canal on either side. The canal cutting that the bridges span is very deep and one can appreciate the importance of building the bridge in 1918, and what a great feat of engineering it was.

It has to be said at this point that almost every source of information on the building of the bridge attributes the work solely to the New Zealand Tunnelling Company. One well-known battlefield tour guide even calls it 'The New Zealand Bridge'! A web site goes as far as to say that the south bridge, carrying the carriageway to Havrincourt, is the original one, and yes, built by the New Zealanders.

Now is the time to put a few things right. It appears that neither of the bridges that cross the canal today are the original one (see photographs), also the two bridges are supported on elaborate brick plinths – the original wasn't. It is quite possible that the 1918 bridge was replaced, and the new one sited in the original position, except for one thing: plinths can be found on each side of the canal, between the bridges, which could have been the supports for the original bridge.

War Diary

The war diary of the 565th (Wilts) Army Troops Company (WO 95/400), covering from May 1915 to September 1918, is held at the National Archives.

Trench Map Reference

Swindon Trench: Fonquevillers (corrected 1918) 57d NE 1&2 (parts of) E11c-d
Canal du Nord: Hermies 57c NE3-5a K26

Notes on some GWR Military Men

Trevor Carus-Wilson

After leaving Shrewsbury school Trevor Carus-Wilson began his working life with the GWR at Swindon Works. A short time in Mexico followed before settling in England where he joined the engineering staff in 1899, and at the outbreak of war he was employed as an assistant on the staff of the New Works Engineer at Paddington.

Carus-Wilson in pre-war uniform with the Queen's medal with five clasps. (*GWR Magazine*)

Lieutenant-Colonel Trevor Carus-Wilson 5th Duke of Cornwall's Light Infantry. (*GWR Magazine*)

As with many men of his era he was very much a soldier, having served with the Composite Cyclist Corps in the Boer War, and awarded the Queen's Medal with five clasps. As a Territorial he was called to his regiment, the Duke of Cornwall's Light Infantry, in August 1914. Serving with the 4th Battalion, with its headquarters in his parents' home city of Truro, he was first engaged guarding the wireless station at Poldhu, after which he left Cornwall with his battalion on 9 October and set sail for India, where he spent his time training and serving on the Viceroy's Guard of Honour. His time in India was short, for he left the country and his battalion in November 1915, returning to Cornwall to join the 5th Battalion, at which time he was promoted from captain to major.

The 5th Battalion set sail for France in May 1916, serving in the Neuve Chappelle area before moving to the Somme in October, when Carus-Wilson took command of the battalion, which moved to Arras in 1917, where he was promoted to lieutenant-colonel, then on to Ypres, Cambrai and St Quentin in 1918, before returning to the Somme in that fateful March of the German spring offensive.

Carus-Wilson was on a much-needed short leave when on 25 March he returned with all haste to the battalion, having left orders that he was to be recalled should the situation suggest that the offensive was imminent. After a meal at midday, Carus-Wilson took 'B' Company out to find others of the battalion who had been caught up in some heavy fighting. He led the company into positions along the canal bank in front of Moyencourt, but heavy attacks caused the company to withdraw, during which time, while sighting battle positions, Carus-Wilson was fatally wounded. He was taken to a casualty clearing station where he turned to his servant, Private Stacey, and said 'Give my love to the Battalion'. His last journey was on an ambulance train destined for the hospital at Rouen.

He believed in leading from the front and was greatly missed by his battalion. It was written that no battalion had a finer commanding officer, and his memory was cherished for his unselfish bravery, kindly disposition and interest in the welfare of his men.

Carus-Wilson was awarded the Territorial Decoration, the Distinguished Service Order and was mentioned in despatches three times. He is buried in St Sever Cemetery, Rouen.

GWR Director

Colonel, the Hon. Charles E. Edgcumbe died on 14 September 1915, and his place as Company Director was taken by another man with West Country connections, Mr Francis Bingham Mildmay MP, in December 1915. While being elected to the board, Mr Mildmay was serving as a lieutenant-colonel in the West Kent Imperial Yeomanry as an interpreter.

On Loan

Many senior employees left the GWR temporarily to be 'loaned' to the Government. M.H. Campfield of the Chief Engineers Office at Paddington was engaged on Ministry of Munitions work and was eventually in charge of the depot at Crew Works, and J.W. Shackell from the Office of the Superintendent of the Line was loaned to the National Filling Factory (No.14) at Rotherwas.

Both men were much liked by their fellow workers, and presented with gifts on their leaving.

G.T. Smith-Clarke of the Motor Car Department, Slough, was unable to join the forces due to ill health, but found his way into the Aeronautical Inspection Directorate, and sent to Daimler's Works, where he was in charge of testing and inspecting aircraft engines for the Royal Flying Corps. He was promoted to Chief Engineer in charge of the Midland District in August 1916, and was promoted again, to Assistant Inspector, being given the rank of lieutenant in charge of the

F.B. Mildmay MP, GWR Director. (*GWR Magazine*)   Captain G.T. Smith-Clarke. (*GWR Magazine*)

On Active Service

THE following extracts from letters received at home from Mr. H. T. Rendell, of the Office of the Superintendent of the Line (Motor Car department) will be interesting to our readers. Lieutenant Rendell was a Reserve Officer in the Army Service Corps prior to the war, and since its commencement has been attached to the 1st Cavalry Division Supply Column of the Expeditionary Force. It must be borne in mind that all letters are strictly censored so far as military operations are concerned.

August 6th. AVONMOUTH.—Arrived here by catching special train . . . Hundreds of lorries here. Much bustle.

August 10th.—Have charge of 69 lorries. Just returned from Upavon, having delivered six lorries to Royal Flying Corps who are sending them to Montrose with aeroplanes. Have been sleeping in a Maple's furniture van on two sacks of oats, which make a comfortable bed. Finally examined all lorries; scrapped several. My job has been to select suitable machines and types, also men, and you may rely I have selected the best.

August 13th.—Nearly all our lorries are loaded up on two steamers. I am in charge of the *Whateley Hall.* Our drivers are most excellent and willing. The cars are Leyland, Thorneycroft, Halley, London Daimler, Milnes Daimler, and Maudslay, in approximately equal numbers . . . It is rather surprising how fit we all are considering that for over a week we have had 5 hours sleep per night, and that on the floor.

August . . . —Just sailing with confidential orders. This ship is a 6,000 tons turret collier from Cardiff, very steady—s.s. *Whateley Hall.* I am subaltern of the No. 2 Section of the 1st Division Cavalry Supply Column. My " boss " is Captain Hayter, who is on another ship with another lot of men. He is an engineer and a most delightful man to work with. It was he who, after some hours' discussion, entrusted me with the selection of 74 lorries from amongst the thousand or so at Avonmouth. Two men per car had to be appointed, placed on suitable machines, clothed, fed, instructed in rifle drill, cars loaded on board and all arrangements made for feeding, sleeping, and washing them —and all this on a turret collier! I find every man is on board who should be. Quite a lot of the drivers are G.W.R. Motor Car Dept. men. There are Page from Wolverhampton, Averies from Birmingham, W. Thomas, formerly at Wolverhampton, and Adams from the Stroud service. We have had a rough time of it, but one gets used to anything. The great secret seems to be to keep very cheerful, eat a lot, and keep fit. The outstanding features are the enthusiasm of the men and the admirable way in which independent movements join up at some predetermined place.

ST. QUENTIN.—Have passed through Amiens, everything O.K. Flowers thrown at us everywhere, car full of them, also bottles of wine; enormous enthusiasm.

August 19th. MAUBEUGE.—All well. Glorious weather. Many hardships and rough experience. Am now speaking French and German easily.

August 22nd. VALENCIENNES.—Everything all right. Great hospitality. Food, wine and flowers. The people apparently cannot do too much for us.

August 24th. LE CATEAU.—Just returned here. Let me know results of Naval engagements. We have only inaccurate local papers.

August 28th. CHANNY . . . TOURNAM, *August 30th.*—All well. There are many things I should like to mention, but must not.

August. PLACE UNKNOWN.—The Mayor of Melun gave me a very nice revolver, which is just small enough to carry in the pocket.

Recently during our advance I have been going for two continuous days and a night, then having a huge meal and a sleep, then repeating, and so on. The other day I witnessed immediately overhead a fight between a British and a German aeroplane. The English plane was twice as fast as the German, and the way in which it dived over and under was amazing. . . . I have just been dashing off about 80 miles with a locomotive and 38 large trucks for more rations and oats for the Cavalry. I have not washed for three days, and not been out of my clothes for two weeks.

September 21st.—We are now very close to the German big guns, and as I am writing the noise is deafening. One, nicknamed " Sighing Sarah," makes an extraordinary noise, the shell sighing or wheezing until it drops and explodes with a " plonk." This sort of experience has been our lot ever since we arrived over here. Every other day, in going out to the firing line to deliver foodstuff, we have to cross ricketty bridges, pontoons, and awful roads, sometimes digging out and towing lorries, at the same time keeping them in repair. The general scheme is this : Our Section (No. 2) leaves the railhead, or the place where the lorries are loaded, proceeds to the preliminary rendezvous and waits instructions. After these have been received we proceed to the final rendezvous, unloading the lorries as nearly as possible to the fighting line. To get the provisions to the men is sometimes most exciting. The other night I had to pass along a road shelled by the Germans. Before proceeding I noticed that every quarter of an hour they dropped shells, and then waited a quarter of an hour, and so on ; I thought it would be a good idea to run my lorries through during one of the quiet quarters of an hour. This worked excellently, but unfortunately a shell burst 130 yards behind the rear lorry and killed seven horses.

October 3rd.—We are now well on the move again after being at —— for some days. Of course, every other day and night we are at the front chasing cavalry and warming our hands on German shells which won't explode. You should see us sprint when the shells come close by us ! Our naval guns are playing havoc with the Germans, who are being killed in great numbers.

October 12th.—A German aeroplane has just interrupted the writing of this letter, so I had to stop and, with the sight set at 1,800 yards, let off at him with my rifle, and some others did the same. The German rocked ominously, quickly turned, and disappeared, and I am sorry to say we did not bring him down.

October 15th (Card).—I am quite well.

Extracts of letters from H.T. Rendell. (*GWR Magazine*)

AID Coventry District (engines). He was made Inspector of Engines in April 1917, and promoted to captain, being responsible for material inspection and testing of some 12,500 engines of different types, ranging from 80–700hp.

He installed laboratories and designed his own apparatus, and even had the GWR system of jet calibration and measuring flow-meters accepted by the Government. He also carried out experiments with carburetion, and was responsible for the inspection of over half the magnetos manufactured in the country.

H.T. Rendell

Beginning his GWR career as a pupil of the Chief Mechanical Engineer at Swindon Works, Rendell spent a year in Pennsylvania, USA, then returned to the company in 1911 and joined the Motor Car Department at Slough.

In 1912 he accepted a commission as a Special Reserve Officer in the Mechanical Transport Branch of the Army Service Corps. On the outbreak of war he was called to Aldershot and immediately sent to the Western Front, and took part in the Battle of Mons. In January 1915 he was in charge of an advance base workshop, and in May 1916 was transferred to General Headquarters and appointed Inspector of Mechanical Transport of the Army in the Field. In June he was mentioned in despatches for gallant and distinguished conduct, and was promoted to major in the October.

Old Timers

William Bond, a retired GWR signalman, was very likely the oldest man to enlist in the army, being nearly 68 years of age at the time.

Born in July 1847, he joined the GWR in 1866 and was a signalman at Portobello Junction when he retired in April 1915. A long-serving GWR man, he also possessed the Long Service Medal for being in the Paddington Volunteer Regiment (36 & 18th Middlesex Regiment) for twenty-three years before retiring in 1897. He joined the newly formed National Reserve in January 1912, which was open to men who had previously served in the forces.

William Bond. (*GWR Magazine*)

Immediately Bond retired from the GWR he went to enlist in the regular army, giving his age as 50, and was accepted! He was put through three months of rigorous training before being sent to the 10th County of London Regiment, then to the Royal Defence Corps at Alexandra Palace guarding German prisoners. At the end of 1917 he and his company were transferred to Abbey Wood, where he carried out sentry duty, often on 24-hour guards, but at Christmas he was appointed Camp Post Orderly. He remained in this post until he was demobilised in April 1919, having served three years and eleven months in the army, and having reached the age of 72. Throughout this time Bond was fit and healthy.

Bala Station staff not only accounted for one of the youngest employees to enlist, but one of the oldest. Stationmaster Slack left Bala on 30 December 1915 to join the School of Musketry at Bisley and Hythe. He held the rank of Staff Sergeant Instructor of Musketry, and it was said that he was 'considerably over military age'.

Mr Hearnden

Mr H.R. Hearnden, a member of the General Manager's staff, was engaged as a confidential secretary to General Mance (Director of Railways and Roads) of the War Office, at the peace conference in 1919.

George Arberry

George Arberry, a striker in the Signal Department at Teignmouth, was a driver with the 216th Company, Army Service Corps. He took part in a heroic act on 8 January 1916 when he saved a Mr Fletcher and Miss Cox from the YMCA workers' hut at Larkhill Camp which had caught fire, killing two others.

Norman Family

Lance Corporal Frank P. Norman, a clerk in the GWR Live Stock Department at Paddington, was discharged from the army suffering from shell-shock, but died later after being run over by a lorry. He was one of six brothers; two were killed in action, one was reported as being 'missing', another was killed in a car accident and the remaining brother was serving in the army at the time of Frank's death in 1918. The father of these unfortunate men was James Norman, who worked for the GWR at Southall.

Private Henry James Conway Eades

The regimental history of the Devonshire Regiment records that the first VC awarded to a man of the 1st Battalion in the war 'had hardly ever been earned by a stranger incident', and another reference refers to the event as 'bizarre'; but it was a GWR man that played a major part in this 'incident'.

On 22 August 1918 the 1st Battalion was holding a line in the Achiet-Le-Petit area, and prior to withdrawing Private Eades, a GWR policeman at Plymouth, and Lance Corporal George Onions were sent out as scouts to investigate the situation at the front following a heavy bombardment. It was a foggy morning but the two scouts managed to proceed, and reached an unoccupied old trench. One assumes that they were relieved to find the trench empty and were probably about to leave and progress across more open ground, when suddenly a group of Germans appeared and jumped into the trench. Instinctively, Eades and Onions opened rapid fire, with satisfactory results. Without attempting to reply, the Germans, of which there were nearly 250, put up their hands and surrendered, and they did not complain when the two Devonshire men encouraged them to be lined up in fours and marched off to the company commander, who promptly sent the

H.J.C. Eades. (*GWR Magazine*)

Grave of Private Eades at Varennes Cemetery. (Author)

group to the commanding officer. With Onions leading at the front, strolling with rifle slung, and Eades at the rear acting as 'whipper-in', the column of prisoners approached battalion headquarters, passing the East Surreys as they went who, unaware of what was happening, enquired as to why the Devons had taken to practising ceremonial drill while on the battlefield!

After investigation it transpired that the Germans were to counter-attack a New Zealand division nearby and had got hopelessly lost.

For this action Onions was awarded the Victoria Cross, and Eades the Distinguished Conduct Medal. Enquiries have been made as to why there was only one VC awarded. It could have been thought that the action only warranted the awarding of one VC and it was naturally bestowed on the man of higher rank. Another reason was that Onions was well educated and, in pre-war years, had his own business making him a natural leader; obviously many were unaware that Eades was a policeman.

Whatever the reason, it cannot detract from the fact that they were both the right men for the job, and having to face nearly 250 men of the German army must have been a heart-stopping moment for both – they must have thought they had little or no chance of getting out of the situation alive.

Onions survived the war but Eades' glory was short-lived; he was wounded shortly after and died on 1 September, and is buried in Varennes Military Cemetery.

Mr. C. Blunsdon and his eight sons, each of whom has served, or is serving, with the Colours.

Mr Blunsdon of the locomotive works at Swindon had eight sons, all of whom had worked for the GWR at some time, and all enlisted, the youngest being sixteen. Mr Blunsdon, having served in the Royal Engineers before the war, tried to enlist but was turned down. (*GWR Magazine*)

Corporal Ward

The *GWR Magazine* reported in June 1915 that Corporal G.R. Ward, signalman at Blaenavon serving in the Devonshire Regiment, had been awarded the Distinguished Conduct Medal for bravery in the field on 24 October 1914, when after a bayonet charge he left his trench, ran 250 yards and brought back a wounded officer to safety while under a heavy downpour of rain, and murderous rifle and shell fire. Unfortunately another report in the May 1916 issue stated that there had been a military investigation and it transpired Ward had not been awarded the DCM; he had forged a letter purporting to have been from the War Office.

Ward, who had been wounded in France and discharged from the army, appeared at Blaenavon Court on 4 April 1916 and was charged with falsification and imprisoned for one month.

Why would a man do this? It is strange, but on 23 October 1914 an almost identical incident occurred while the Devonshire Regiment was under heavy attack at Givenchy, only it was a lieutenant that left the trench to rescue a wounded corporal. Was it this that inspired Ward's story; had he taken part in the rescue or carried out a similar heroic action prior to this that he thought warranted an award? No one will ever know, but this illustrates the fact that the war affected people in different ways, and it was rare that those at home understood the reasons why.

Others

Private Bundy, a fireman from Gloucester, was wounded and lost his sight while serving with the Gloucestershire Regiment on the Somme. He was cared for at St Dunstan's Hostel for Blinded Soldiers where he was taught Braille, typing and boot repairing, all of which he became very proficient in. His ability to master these skills may well have been down to his young age, as he was described as being 'quite a boy' when he joined up.

Corporal G.R. Ward. (*GWR Magazine*)

Private Charles Brooks, a signalman at Bedlinog, was captured unwounded by the Germans on 31 July 1917, and was set to work unloading barges on a canal. But on the night of 19 September 1917 he slipped into the canal, and although every effort was made to save him, unfortunately he died. He was aged 27.

Private A. Frost, a porter at Cardiff, died when the *Transylvania* was torpedoed on 4 May 1917. His body was washed ashore at Hyeres, France. One of the only English people in the area, Mrs Annie Kennedy, kept watch over the body until arrangements could be made for a proper burial, which took place with full honours and was conducted by an English chaplain. Soldiers and sailors of many nations from local hospitals attended the funeral at Hyeres New Communal Cemetery, France.

George Josiah Cooke, a lad messenger at Paddington Goods Station, enlisted in September 1914 at the age of 17. He went through the Gallipoli campaign before serving in France. In February 1917 he was granted a commission with the London Regiment, and after a short time requested to be attached to the Royal Flying Corps. His military record came to an abrupt end when, as it could be said, his luck ran out during aerial combat on 23 November 1917.

The *GWR Magazine* reported the circumstances of many of the men's deaths, and the frankness was quite astonishing, but none more so than that of Second Lieutenant George E. Brown, Honourable Artillery Company (Deeds Office, Paddington), who volunteered for active service as a private in August 1914. The magazine states that on 20 April 1917, while going into action in

France, he met his untimely demise by drowning in a shell hole. This must have sent a chill down the spines of his colleagues, especially those who were about to experience the horrors of the war for themselves, let alone members of the Brown family who, conjuring up visions of how their loved one had died in such a slow and agonising way, would have found the exactness of the report upsetting.

Another sad report was that of Second Lieutenant Frank S. Hart of the Divisional Superintendent's Office, who had made his way up through the ranks before his commission in the Somerset Light Infantry. He had been sent home early in 1916 suffering from shell-shock, but returned only to be killed in September on the Somme.

GWR men were represented in all the services: army, Royal Flying Corps and air force, Royal Marines and of course the navy. Some of the early GWR casualties were serving in the navy, and 22 September 1914 was a particularly bad day when 1,459 sailors lost their lives, some of them GWR men, when the *Aboukir*, *Hogue* and Cressy were sunk by the German U-boat *U9* in the North Sea. There was one sailor aboard HMS *Aboukir*, Thomas H. Spragg, a wireman on the Electrical Engineers' staff at Paddington, who had a lucky escape – twice!

At 6.20 a.m. there was a loud explosion which was thought at first to be a mine and the ship listed heavily to port. The wounded were put into the only surviving lifeboat, but Spragg was unhurt, and he took the opportunity to put extra clothing on because of the cold. The captain bid all hands 'good luck' as they entered the water. Spragg had seen the *Hogue* and *Cressy* steaming towards the stricken *Aboukir*, and he took a bearing of *Hogue* and swam towards it as fast as he could to be far enough away from *Aboukir* so as not to be affected by the suction of the ship as she went down. Spragg was picked up by *Hogue*'s cutter. Soon two more explosions were heard

T.H. Spragg.
(*GWR Magazine*)

and it was then clear that a submarine was attacking. At first the cutter headed towards the stricken *Hogue*, but Spragg's commander took charge of the boat and gave orders to head for *Cressy*. All the survivors were put aboard *Cressy* and given cocoa and a blanket. *Cressy* steamed ahead, firing at the submarine some 500 yards off, then a torpedo hit *Cressy*, and Spragg said to a man standing by him 'this is no place for us now, we are in the way' and jumped overboard. Spragg caught hold of a floating mess stool and drifted away. Another man grabbed hold of the stool, but he could not swim, and after a while Spragg felt the stool go light as the other sailor was lost to the sea.

Spragg was picked up by a destroyer and transferred to a fishing smack, *Coriander of Lowestoft*, before being taken by the Legion destroyer to Harwich. This was a very lucky sailor.

Another lucky sailor was Frederick Henry King, Office Porter, Goods Department, South Lambeth, who was also on the *Aboukir*, and after swimming in the sea for two and a half hours, was picked up by another vessel. These were not the only GWR men serving on the *Aboukir*, and some were not so fortunate.

Spare a thought for Fred J. Lovejoy who had been a fireman at the Loco Department at Pontypool Road before joining the Royal Field Artillery, then the Royal Engineers. Whilst serving in France he was a fireman on an ammunition train, and when taking a load to the front the train was attacked by a German plane, which dropped a bomb, killing the driver and resulting in the loss of Lovejoy's fingers. He was subsequently discharged from military service, and on 2 March 1917 resumed his duties with the GWR, but on 20 April, while walking from the signal box at Llangollen Junction to his engine, he was knocked down and killed by a passing train.

F.J. Lovejoy. (*GWR Magazine*)

Young Recruits

Much has been written over the years on the subject of underage recruits into the armed forces, and many lads from the GWR workforce decided that they would go and do their bit. They, unlike many of their older colleagues, had no experience of war or idea of the consequences of going off to fight. Why did they do it? That is difficult to answer. They were young, impulsive and seeking adventure, and after all they were deemed old enough to work in a man's world, so why not volunteer for the forces? Whatever the reason, and no one will really know, they went and, unfortunately, many did not return.

Using the GWR Roll of Honour it can be seen that nearly fifty of those who died or were killed in action were 18 years of age, and almost three times this number were 19, but some were even younger.

The following were 17 years of age at the time of their demise:

William George Barson	Arthur Charles Kinnerley
William Walter Bishop	Alfred Henry Lambourne
Edward John Chipp	Albert George Povey
Francis Victor Davies	William Luke Saloway
William Davies	Alfred Harry Waldron

Another is Ernest Clifford Plane who is recorded in the *GWR Magazine* as being 17, but the Commonwealth War Graves Commission recorded his age as 16. Two others, Frank Vincent Paine and Roland Voden Hill, were also 16 years of age.

Many anomalies have been found while compiling the Roll of Honour, one of which is that of Isaac Jones of Bala. When his death was first announced in the *GWR Magazine* in March 1916 his

Ernest C. Plane. (*GWR Magazine*)

Grave of Ernest Plane at Dud Corner Cemetery, Loos. (Author)

John or Isaac Jones. (*GWR Magazine*)

Sydney G. Brookman - killed aged fifteen. (*GWR Magazine*)

name appeared as I. Jones, but two months later, when his picture appeared in the magazine, his name had changed to John Jones, stating his age as 15. The only match on the official records is that of Isaac Jones of Bala, aged 19, who was a lance corporal in the Royal Welsh Fusiliers, which is confirmed by the cap badge shown in the magazine photo. Which age is right for this chap is unsure, but what is sure is the age of Sydney George Brookman, who was definitely 15 years of age when he was killed.

Brookman joined Hood Battalion, Royal Naval Division, on 4 January 1915, and on 29 April Hood Battalion landed on 'V' Beach, Gallipoli. On 6 May the battalion headed up Achi Baba Nullah in an attempt to drive the Turks off the heights, sustaining large casualties; but Brookman was still with them.

The 4 June saw British and French forces stretched out right across the peninsula, and after two artillery barrages, the whole front advanced at 12 noon. Hood Battalion was towards the middle, flanked on the right by the French who, unfortunately, lagged behind, making Hood vulnerable to the Turkish. Hood Battalion casualties were so great that orders were given to retire, and sometime during the day Brookman died, exactly six months after joining.

This was a bloody encounter for all the men in that advance, but Brookman was only 15. His photo shows a boy who looked as if he could easily fool a recruitment officer, but one cannot help thinking that during his short time at Gallipoli he wished he was just a lad back home.

There is an entry for him in de Ruvigny's Roll of Honour stating that he was born in Swansea on 22 December 1899, and had successfully enlisted twice before but was 'claimed out' as under-age by his parents. The entry also states that he is buried in an unmarked grave at Sedd-el-Bahr, but the Commonwealth War Graves Commission only have him as being commemorated on the Helles Memorial.

Not all of the young recruits were so unlucky. Alfred Dixon, who was employed at Swindon, was also 15 when he enlisted and continued serving in the army after the war in Northern Ireland.

Tales from the Front

On 6 November 1918 the New Zealand forces captured the town of Le Quesnay, and upon doing so used some of the buildings for billeting, one having been used as a German officers' club. A Major Reeve occupied one of the rooms in which a coat had been nailed to part of the door to hide a damaged panel. Upon close inspection Reeve was surprised to see that the buttons of the coat were clearly marked GWR. Le Quesnay had been in German hands for four years, leading to the conclusion that the original owner of the coat must have been a GWR man captured back in 1914.

The buttons were cut off and sent to the GWR as a curio, and it was the intention to send the coat back eventually as it might have contained evidence as to the original owner.

Private R.R. Smith, one-time clerk at Evesham Goods Station, while in the desert in Mesopotamia with the 9th Worcesters, saw half buried in the sand what looked like tickets. On inspection he found them to be GWR omnibus tickets; possibly a soldier's keepsake which was unfortunately lost.

Writing in the magazine towards the end of 1917, Second Lieutenant C G. Scarfe, a member of the staff of the Chief Accountant's Office, related the following:

> Whilst moving from one part of France to another a short time ago, I was amazed to find that the authorities had thoughtfully provided us with a GWR engine and crew. The train was one usually seen in this part of the world, composed of French cattle trucks for the men and about a dozen ballast trucks, which I discovered to be also marked 'GWR'. On arriving at our destination the first thing I saw was a hose cap stamped 'GWR', and just lately I have been attached to a battery of the Royal Field Artillery whose shells were mostly turned out by the company. Such a sequence of events was remarkable. I thought that readers, civilian and others, might like to learn that the work of the railway is much appreciated on this side of the Channel.

A letter appeared in the *GWR Magazine* in January 1919:

> Dear Sir; As an old employee of the GWR and a constant reader of this magazine prior to joining the Army, I thought it might be of interest to some of its present readers in quoting the following narrative bearing on the utility of the Company's locomotives out here.
>
> A short time ago, whilst trudging along a rather lonely road 'Somewhere in France', I happened to fall in with a comrade who was displaying the badge of the RE and whose destination was a large locomotive yard in the neighbourhood, wherein was stabled a number of engines of various types that had been sent overseas from English and Canadian Railways for the purpose of transporting and feeding our gallant and now victorious Army.
>
> My friend turned out to be an engineman of the Railway Operating Division, in which corps he had served in France during the past three years. Prior to enlisting he was an engineman on one of the railways in the north of Scotland.
>
> Our conversation was mainly confined to railway work, in the course of which I incidentally questioned him as to his opinion of the best locomotive out here. His reply was that he had manipulated in turn the various types which included the War Department engine (a special design), and found that the GWR engine was by far superior to any of them in power, speed and durability.
>
> Such an expression of opinion emanating from a man of practical experience and who had no connection with the GWR, and to whom I had not disclosed my identity with the Company, I consider is a fine tribute to the mechanical genius of the chief of our works at Swindon.

I remain, Sir, yours faithfully

J.W. MORGAN Det. L/C/ p 10805

M.F. Police B.E.F. France

A soldier on leave, who was travelling on the GWR ship *Ibex*, was sitting on the deck when the ship was in Weymouth. Resting his feet on the rail while he slept, his feet slipped through the rails and his body was torpedoed into the water. A kind sailor swam to his aid.

On a cold January day in 1917 at Paddington, a soldier bound for France was alarmed to find that he had left his false teeth in the waiting room at Taunton. He asked the stationmaster if he could send a telegram to Taunton to see if the teeth could be put on the next available train to Paddington. This was done but the soldier had to continue his journey before the arrival of the Taunton train, so the GWR made arrangements to send the teeth to France to be reunited with their owner.

Shortly after the war, a Maltese gentleman was apprehended and accused of not paying his fare. In court the GWR ticket collector explained that he was able to converse with the gent, who could not speak English, by using Arabic, which the collector had learned while serving with the army in Egypt.

Blood

It was during the war that it was possible for the first time to store blood owing to breakthroughs by medical personnel, but the donation of blood was still newsworthy enough to warrant inclusion in the *GWR Magazine*.

In 1918 D.W. Foster, a clerk in the Goods Department at Cheltenham, donated blood to a wounded comrade, and a pint of blood from Edward Edwards, signal porter at Arenig, was transfused into an officer who had lost both his legs.

Donors remained in hospital after their ordeal to recover from the 'sacrifice' they had made, as it was put then.

Great Western Railway Magazine

The *GWR Magazine* was much sought after by the company's men at the front, with scarce copies being eagerly passed around. Such was the demand for the magazine that a plea appeared early in 1915 for those at home to forward copies to the front, and the call did not go unnoticed for at many stations and offices colleagues contributed a 'copper' each a month to meet the costs of sending them.

The year 1916 saw what was thought to be the first agency to be set up for an English railway journal in France. The agent was Company Quartermaster Sergeant W. Whiddington, who was attached to 275th (GWR) Railway Company, Royal Engineers, who distributed between 100 and 200 copies each month.

Reading of the magazine was not restricted to the Western Front, for a Private W.G. Hudson, who prior to enlistment was working in the Loco Department at Tyseley, was with the Royal Army Medical Corps (Mediterranean Expeditionary Force), and reported that copies of the magazine had been received at the hospital where he was based, and on one occasion was read by a fireman from Paddington, a checker from Hereford, a signalman from Small Heath and one from Acocks Green.

Not all of the readers were attracted solely to the pages of the magazine by company news, as the following letter written by three lonely soldiers 'Somewhere in France', and published in the magazine in June 1916, illustrates:

Donated gifts for the troops. (*GWR Magazine*)

Clerks in the Cardiff District Goods Manager's Office.

The 'lonely soldiers' wrote to the magazine having seen this photo. (*GWR Magazine*)

Dear young lady friends,

I daresay you will consider this as taking a great liberty, but still we will risk it, we have to risk greater things than that out here.

I was just behind the firing line when I went into a dugout and found one of the *GWR Magazine*s on the floor, and on glancing through it I happened to see your photos, and showed it to my chums. They were delighted with the idea of writing to you, so I took up the job. But we do hope you will not be offended.

Pte. ... ... B.E.F. France

We should be so pleased if you would oblige us with a line from you all as we are rather lonely and you could do ever so much in that way to cheer us up.

One wonders if the ladies did reply to the 'three lonely soldiers' – we will never know.

Channel Ferry

One of the transport improvements that came about during the war was that of the train ferry. Three such ships were in service from the beginning of 1918, running from Richborough in Kent to Calais, Dieppe and Dunkirk, the longest of the trips to Dieppe taking eight hours.

The ferries, powered by oil-fired boilers, were fitted with four sets of rails, with a carrying capacity of fifty-two loaded 10-ton trucks, or eight 2-8-0 locomotives and twenty-four 10-ton trucks; the load was secured by means of chains attached to ring bolts on the deck. A load of fifty-two trucks could be drawn off the ferry in twenty-five minutes by an engine, which was much more efficient than using lifting gear. Chinese labour was employed from March 1918.

All Railway Companies immediately recognised the commercial potential of the train ferry in peacetime, as perishable goods transported from Europe to London could, conceivably, make the whole journey with no need for transferring goods from one wagon to another. However, their preference was for a Channel tunnel, of which there was much discussion.

The efficiency of the ferries at Richborough can, in some part, be attributed to a Great Western man: Mr G.G. Morris. He was employed in the GWR Receiving Office in King William Street, London, prior to the war, and enlisted in the Honourable Artillery Company in October 1915. In June 1917 he left the HAC for a commission in the Royal Engineers and was appointed Railway Traffic Officer at Richborough, being in control of the loading and unloading of the cross-Channel ferries, and was promoted to captain in 1918.

He was temporarily loaned to the Chatham and South East Railway, where he acted as Assistant Traffic Superintendent.

CHAPTER EIGHT

The Armistice – Influenza – Frank Potter – Remembrance and Memorials

The Armistice

At 11 a.m. on 11 November 1918 the war ended; the guns fell silent. As far as the Railway Companies were concerned they could all breathe a collective sigh of relief, for had hostilities continued into 1919 it would have been difficult for them to continue in anything like the efficient way that they had prior to the Armistice.

On that day the number of Government trains being run by the GWR reduced immediately, releasing rolling stock and engines. From 11–14 November some 700 freight trains were cancelled, as were a number of shunting engines, although it must be added that some of these were due to factories being closed during Armistice celebrations.

Traffic continued to be high due to materials from the war fronts being shipped back home, and the demobilisation of the men. By December 1918 some 20,000 employees were still with the forces, with many remaining so until late spring of 1919; of 5,143 men of the Traffic Department who had originally enlisted, 993 were still to return in December 1919. Civilian traffic took on a pre-war normality because of travel and season ticket restrictions being lifted, but the war-time restriction of 100lb of luggage per travelling passenger was not withdrawn until June 1920.

Due to an inevitable decrease in demand for coal by the Admiralty, stocks were replenished at the rate of 20,000 tons per week to be distributed between all the Railway Companies, with the GWR receiving 1,000 tons per week. This amount was increased by the Coal Controller when an additional 3,050 tons was released from the North Wales collieries, which was prepared in time

Peace treaty signed – decorated GWR vans in celebration. (*GWR Magazine*)

Train ferry at Dieppe returning after the war with four GWR locomotives on board. (*GWR Magazine*)

for the Christmas and New Year's leave granted by the War Office to enable servicemen to return home for the festive season.

The whole railway scene was looking brighter, especially after the lighting restrictions were lifted, and February 1919 saw the introduction of the eight-hour working day. For some the pleasure of relaxation returned, and this showed when 300,000 people visited the motor show at Olympia, and more importantly for the staff at Swindon the summer 'trip' was reinstated in July, with the works being closed for eight days.

Although life was more settled, the workforce was not, and industrial unrest culminated in a strike in September 1919. Passengers and livestock were stranded, but much was done by volunteers to help, including one chap who wanted to help even though he had no legs; two volunteers had acid thrown in their faces while helping at South Lambeth Goods Depot.

At last the companies were able to order stores and materials for much needed renewals and maintenance of buildings, lines, engines and rolling stock, although it was some time before normality resumed. The work carried out by the GWR for the Government came to a close, and the total cost of these works amounted to approximately £1,031,477. Some of the work was retained by the GWR as it was beneficial to the running of the company, the cost being calculated on a valuation of the completed work (labour and materials having already been paid for by the Government) to a total of £328,902, which included some work in progress that the GWR considered to be of benefit.

With hostilities ended the financial consequences of the war were calculated, but the final statistics were of a greater price: those of the GWR employees who bravely answered their country's call to arms. Up to 30 November 1918 the statistics were as follows:

Joined the forces	25,463
Still with the forces	21,453
Number employed as replacements	11,987
Total employees in 1914	78,084
Total employed in November 1918	69,383
Total number killed in action	1,902
Total number wounded, sick or prisoners of war	2,304

After the Armistice social gatherings were organised throughout the GWR system to welcome home those employees who had been serving in the forces and were lucky enough to have survived. There was music, food, and speeches, after which, at some events, commemoration gifts were presented. Fallen comrades were remembered but it was only in the report of the event at Plymouth that any mention was made of those disabled; of 290 men who had returned, four were seriously and thirty-four slightly disabled.

GWR employees were fortunate to have their jobs guaranteed upon their return, as were others employed in companies with similar arrangements, but one employee found it impossible to return. William Chappell, together with his brothers Albert and George, were GWR men and left to go to war. All three survived, and Albert and George returned to Swindon Works, but William decided to emigrate; he had taken the opportunity to settle an old score with his bully of a foreman prior to leaving for the front line!

Many of the men who had returned from the forces joined comrades associations which enabled some of them to share memories with others who had had similar experiences, something most found hard to do with family and friends who had no idea what had been endured. One association was specific to the Great Western: the GWR Old Contemptibles Association. Presumably the membership was made up of those who had been in the forces since the beginning of the war or the 'out since Mons' men. This association produced an enamel membership badge and for those who like to collect all things Great Western this badge is a rare one that commands a high price – one to look out for when rummaging at a car boot sale!

So ended the Great Western Railway's involvement in the Great War. It was optimistically and naively known as the 'war to end all wars', but without the total defeat of Germany some knew they would rise again, and another war would be inevitable.

Influenza

An influenza epidemic gripped the world in 1918. Men who had survived much in the trenches were struck down by this invisible attacker. With so many travelling to and from various war fronts to their home, the flu rapidly spread. Usually the old and infirm are those at greatest risk, but in 1918 no one was safe. It is difficult to calculate how many GWR employees succumbed to this deadly virus as many were recorded as having died of pneumonia, which was a fairly common consequence of the flu.

Listed are a few employees and the date of their deaths recorded in the *GWR Magazine*:

H.A. Deane, District Superintendents Office, Bristol	December 1918
F.C. Gardiner, Divisional Superintendents Office, Worcester, aged 37	18/11/1918
W.E. Harwood, Chief Booking Clerk, Slough	16/10/1918

Mrs Ellen Louisa Hazell, Telegraph Office, Paddington — 24/10/1918

Alfred Lewis, Foreman Loco Running Shed, Swindon, aged 63 — 19/11/1918

Elsie Annie Lewis, Telegraph Office, Paddington — 4/2/1919

Mr W.E. Marwood, Chief Booking Clerk, Slough, aged 30 — 16/11/1918

Miss Elsie Moody, Telegraph Office, Swindon Works — 23/10/1918

Mrs Nellie Gwendoline Slocombe, Telegraph Office, Paddington — 7/1/1918

Miss Winnie Pascoe, District Goods, Managers Office, Bristol — November 1918

W.E. Wyatt, Road Motor Inspector, Plymouth — December 1918

Frank Potter

It could be said that one of the consequences of the war was the premature demise of GWR General Manager Frank Potter, who died in July 1919.

Born on 30 March 1856, Potter was a Great Western man through and through, having started in the company when he was 13; he had made his way upward from his early beginnings in the Goods Department at Paddington. He was liked by many and his appointment to General Manager in January 1912 was warmly welcomed. Two months later he was gazetted Lieutenant Colonel of the Engineer and Railway Staff Corps.

Frank Potter. (*GWR Magazine*)

Ideally suited to his position as General Manager, he went about his business with confidence, enthusiasm and energy, which he showed in abundance during the war years when he was on numerous committees, including the Railway Executive Committee and the Belgian Trade Committee. Potter was always on the go during the war not only with the routine work, directors' meetings and suchlike, but attending medal ceremonies, welcoming home wounded GWR men – the list was endless, his life being full to the extreme with little time for relaxation. The efficient running of the GWR and its contribution to the country during such trying times was most important to him. He declined a knighthood, not once, but twice!

In February 1919 he was ordered by his medical adviser to take a complete rest, and somewhat reluctantly he journeyed to Cornwall where, it was observed, he appeared to have benefited. Unfortunately his condition, arterial sclerosis, worsened and he died on the morning of Wednesday 23 July 1919, at the Tregenna Castle Hotel, St Ives. His body was taken back to Paddington the following day, and the funeral took place at Harlington on the Saturday.

Frank Potter's successor was Charles Aldington who had held the post of Assistant General Manager.

Remembrance and Memorials

At the end of the war there was a sense of relief in Britain; as there was hardly a single family that had not been affected by it in some way or another, the feelings of the people were mixed: tiredness from years of fighting or hard industrial work at home, pride in what had been achieved, elation at having overcome adversity, resentment by some of those who had been away fighting and wrongly considered that those who remained at home had had a cushy life, plus the anger, brought about by a lack of knowledge and understanding, felt by some who had lost relatives and loved ones, when seeing those returning from the front could not help themselves from thinking 'why didn't my lad survive?' Of course, with so many families touched by tragedy there was an overwhelming sense of grief and sadness in the country which, for some, would never dull with the passing of time.

Unlike today, the war dead were not repatriated. Except for the serving personnel who died at home, the majority of graves were abroad; there was no personal, private place to grieve. There was a need, and a want, to permanently record the names of the fallen and over the next five years or so war memorials appeared like mushrooms in towns, villages and workplaces. The GWR began recording the names of the fallen while the war was in progress (as did many churches etc.) and the first official GWR Roll of Honour appeared on Platform 1, Paddington Station, at the end of 1915, and later copies were placed at main stations. Designed by C.E. Power of the company's Electrical Engineers Department, the roll was housed in a sturdy frame measuring 6ft x 4ft 6in. The roll listed the men by department order, then alphabetical order, together with where on the system they were based. In the centre panel was the following inscription: 'The names shown here are those members of staff of the GWR who have lost their lives in the war. Many of them were called upon to participate in some of the fiercest fighting of the campaign; they upheld the best tradition of their country, and their loss is deplored alike by the Company and their comrades.'

The first Roll of Honour recorded those men who were lost up to 8 November 1915 and, out of necessity, was replaced on a regular basis to ensure that the information was up to date. The roll stated the number of men who had enlisted, together with the percentage of the staff that that number represented, and how many of those enlisted men who had been lost.

The first 'great silence' at Paddington, 1919. (*GWR Magazine*)

Remembrance Day, 1920, platform 1 at Paddington Station. (*GWR Magazine*)

Audit Office memorial.
(*GWR Magazine*)

From October 1917 a feature appeared on the roll which recorded the various honours attained by the employees. A significant change appeared later whereby the phrase 'their loss is deplored alike by the Company and their comrades', was replaced with 'their memory is revered alike by the Company and their comrades'.

In 1918, by request, a copy of the Roll of Honour was sent to France and placed in the war library attached to the Ministry of Education and Fine Arts. Another was said to have been given to the Imperial War Museum, but they have no record of this.

The new millennium saw a restoration project instigated by First Great Western, Network Rail and the Railway Heritage Trust for those few remaining Rolls of Honour housed at stations on the old GWR lines. Originally the rolls at Newton Abbot, Taunton, Exeter (St David) and Bristol Temple Meads were to be conserved, but owing to damp damage and fading an expert conservator decided that they needed replacing. A 10in x 8in colour transparency was taken of the Taunton Roll of Honour and original size digital prints were processed on photographic paper with a plastic backing. The old rolls were taken away and restored by Network Rail's drawing conservation team in Swindon, and mounted on boards.

Unfortunately, some time after the work had finished, a fifth roll was found in the entrance hall of Bristol & Exeter House at Bristol Temple Meads Station in almost perfect condition which, having been indoors for the duration, would have made for a more suitable master for the copies. Although this work is to be applauded, the original Rolls of Honour, a few of which can be found at stations on preserved GWR lines like Didcot, are more appealing to the eye, being of an aged cream colour.

GWR memorial, platform 1 at Paddington Station after the unveiling. (Author's collection)

An impressive service to the memory of all the railwaymen of Great Britain and Ireland who had died during the war was held at 2.30 p.m. on Wednesday 14 May 1919 at St Paul's Cathedral, with King George, Queen Alexandra and Princess Victoria in attendance. Simultaneous services, following the same form of service, were held at other cathedrals and churches with those at Birmingham, Bristol and Cardiff being in the area served by the GWR.

On the first anniversary of the signing of the Armistice a two-minute suspension of all activities was called for by the King, and at 11 a.m. on the eleventh day of the eleventh month a two-minute silence ensued. Trains that were due to depart at 11 a.m. remained in the stations for the two minutes, while those trains already travelling were brought to a stop; such was the strength of feeling at that time. There were then few memorials where people could gather, and at GWR stations staff assembled in front of the Roll of Honour. Some 200 staff assembled at the Roll of Honour on Platform 1 at Paddington Station where, it was reported, 'an impressive silence ruled over the great terminus'.

The following year staff gathered again in front of the Rolls of Honour, and at Newton Abbot wreaths were laid by ex-PO Winsor, who was one of the Arctic expeditionary party of 1875–76, and ex-sergeant C.S. England (RFA). Also in attendance were three of the station's Military Medallists, CSM Winsborrow, CSM Furzeman and Sergeant W. Lethbridge, with the last post being sounded by Bugler Lane.

At Acton Station laurel leaves were picked from the garden to decorate the Roll of Honour.

The GWR produced a number of memorials which varied in size depending on the information inscribed and the department concerned. One of the smaller memorials is the brass Stores

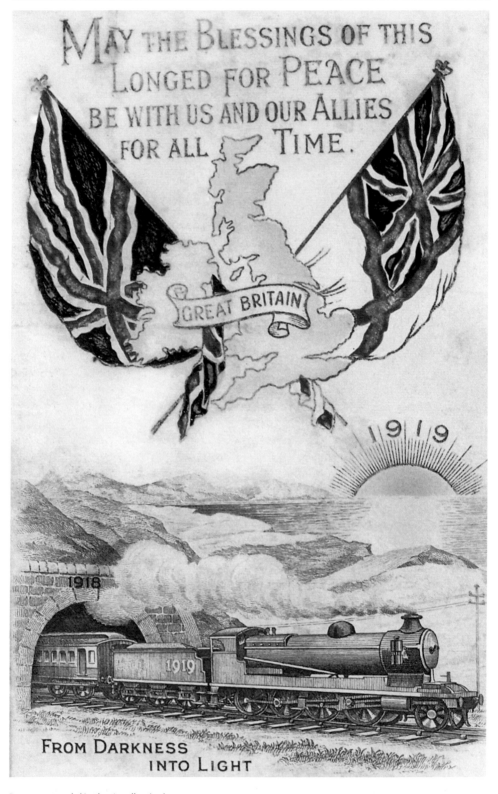

Peace postcard. (Author's collection)

Department Memorial, which records the names of the twenty-four members of this department who lost their lives, and is displayed at the STEAM Museum at Swindon. The elaborate wooden memorial to 'A' Erecting Shop, with the names of all the 217 employees of that shop who answered 'the call to arms', together with the eighteen men who paid the ultimate price, is also displayed here. All the names are recorded for prosperity in gold lettering.

Mr P.E. Lott, a cloakroom attendant at Paddington Station, designed and painted a Roll of Honour for the Paddington Railway Club, which recorded the names of 130 members who had joined the services.

The GWR Audit Office staff at Paddington funded the making of a memorial tablet to the sixteen members of staff who had lost their lives (out of a total of 182) from the office who had enlisted, and was unveiled by the chief accountant, Mr R. Chope, on 23 April 1920.

Many of the memorials were unveiled by local dignitaries, and that of 'A' Erecting Shop was unveiled before several hundred onlookers on 19 February 1921 by the Mayor of Swindon, Alderman E. Jones, accompanied by the Archdeacon of Swindon, Dr Talbot and a number of GWR officials. On 20 October 1923 memorials, in the form of brass tablets, to the fallen of Nos 3, 15, 18 and 19d shops in the Carriage and Wagon Works of Swindon were unveiled in front of some 2,000 of the shops' employees and friends by Mayor A. Harding, with the dedication by the Archdeacon as before. As well as recording the fallen, there was the following inscription: 'A memorial bed was placed in the Victoria Hospital by the men of 3, 15, 18 and 19d shops, September 1923.'

The year 1925 saw the last of the memorials to be unveiled. The 'AM' Shop at Swindon was one of the smallest but it was nonetheless important, with seven names of the fallen inscribed upon it. The 'R' Shop, Swindon Works, was an impressive memorial bearing the names of 166 of the shops' employees who served during the war, and was unveiled on 6 November 1925 by Mr R.G. Hannington, Locomotive Works Manager.

The memorial to all the GWR men who lost their lives during the war can be found on Platform 1, Paddington Station, which was unveiled on 11 November 1922. It was designed and sculptured by Charles Sargeant Jagger (1885–1934), who originally trained as a goldsmith, taking up sculpture in 1906 and winning the Prix de Rome in 1914. He spent the following four years (1914–18) in the army as an infantry officer, during which time he served in Gallipoli and the Western Front, being wounded while in each location, and awarded the Military Cross for heroism during the German spring offensive of 1918. His talent was in great demand after the war and he designed many memorial sculptures such as the large Artillery Memorial (together with architect Lionel Pearson) at Hyde Park Corner, to the smaller, beautifully simplistic Great Western Railway Memorial. The bronze statue depicts a soldier reading a letter he has just received from home, and is set against a background of granite and marble, upon which are engraved the badges of the navy and the RAF.

T.S. Tait, partner in the firm of Sir John Barnet, Tait and Lorne, was responsible for the design of the architectural setting. A student of Paisley Technical College and Glasgow School of Art, where he was a prize winner, he went on to design some notable buildings in London. Wishing to 'do his bit', he enlisted under the Derby Scheme during the war and he was sent to Woolwich where his skills were put to good use as a leading draughtsman.

The unveiling took place in front of some 6,000 assembled persons, who arrived by special and ordinary trains by invitation, primarily made up of grieving relatives. To accommodate this large crowd, and allow them a good view of the proceedings, some temporary alterations had to be made inside Paddington Station, with a stage erected on Platforms 2 and 3, and large type well carriage trucks placed on the lines between Platforms 1 and 2, upon which had been constructed stepped platforms, the total construction forming a continuous stand in front of the War Memorial.

The service itself began just after 10.45 a.m., with a short introduction by the Vicar and Rural Dean of Paddington, followed by the singing of *O God our help in ages past*. Immediately before the two minutes' silence the memorial was unveiled by the Rt Hon. Viscount Churchill, GWR Chairman, accompanied by the Archbishop of Canterbury and officials. Prayers followed with speeches praising the work of the GWR and employees during the war and remembering those who gallantly fought for their country. The ceremony ended with the singing of the National Anthem; then was the time for family and friends to place their own tributes at the memorial: private moments for those who had lost much.

A sealed casket made at Swindon Works was buried beneath the statue, inside which had been placed a vellum roll containing the names of the fallen. Quite why this was considered an appropriate way to record the names is not known, as it would have been more fitting to have had the names inscribed on the wall behind the statue, such as the memorial at Liverpool Street Station.

Officially the war dead had been commemorated but a sad fact often overlooked was that there would be deaths later that could be directly contributed to the trauma of war. Frank Greenaway, who had been mentioned in despatches and awarded the DCM, died on 29 December 1923, his health, it was reported, had been affected by exposure during war service. He and others like him were not classed as casualties of war, and therefore their names are not recorded in any of the databases.

ABBREVIATIONS

2/Cpl	Second Corporal
2/Lt	Second Lieutenant
A/	Acting Rank
A/Mech	Air Mechanic
Acc	Died of accident
Am/Co	Ammunition Column
Apprent	Apprentice
AS	Able Seaman
ASC	Army Service Corps
Ass	Assistant
ATC	Army Troops Company
Att	Attached to
AVC	Army Veterinary Corps
Bde	Brigade
Bn	Battalion
BNS	Burried near this spot
Bom	Bombardier
Br Cem	British Cemetery
Bty	Battery
C&W	Carriage & Wagon Dept
CAO	Chief Accountants Office
Capt	Captain
CDG	Croix de Guerre
Cem	Cemetery
CEO	Chief Engineers Office
CGMO	Chief Goods Manager's Office
CMEO	Chief Mechanical Engineer's Office
Co	Company
Com Cem	Communal Cemetery
CQMS	Company Quarter-master Sergeant
CSM	Company Sergeant Major
CWGC	Commonwealth War Graves Commission
Dac	Died in aerial combat
DCLI	Duke of Cornwalls Light Infantry
Das	Died at sea

DCM	Distinguished Conduct Medal
DDB	Died During Bombing of Chatham
DE	Divisional Engineer
DEO	Divisional Engineer's Office
Dept	Department
Dfa	Died in flying accident
DGMO	District Goods Manager's Office
DLSO	Divisional Loco Superintendent's Office
Dist	District
Div	Divisional
Doi	Died of illness
Dow	Died of wounds
Dr	Drowned
Dsh	Drowned in shell hole
DSO	Divisional Superintendent's Office
D.S.O.	Distinguished Service Order
Dvr	Driver
ERA	Engine Room Artificer
F/Amb	Field Ambulance
Flt/Lt	Flight Lieutenant
Ft/Sub/Lt	Flight Sub-Lieutenant
Fus	Fusiliers
Gdsm	Guardsman
GMO	General Managers Office
Gnr	Gunner
HAC	Honourable Artillery Company
IWT	Inland Water Transport
K	Kings
KIA	Killed in action
KRRC	Kings Royal Rifle Corps
L&C	Loco & Carriage Dept
L/Bomb	Lance Bombardier
L/Cp	Lance Corporal
L/Packer	Leading Packer
L/Sea	Leading Seaman
L/Sgt	Lance Sergeant
L.I.	Light Infantry
Lt	Lieutenant
Lt-Col	Lieutenant Colonel
Maj	Major
MC	Military Cross
Mem	Memorial
MGC	Machine Gun Corps
MID	Mentioned in Despatches
Mil Cem	Military Cemetery
Miss	Missing
MM	Military Medal

MSM	Meritorious Service Medal
NCO	Non Commissioned Officer
NW	New Works Dept
OC	Officer Commanding
Off	Office
OS	Ordinary Seaman
Pnr	Pioneer
POW	Prisoner of War
Pte	Private
QMS	Quarter-master Sergeant
R	Royal
RAF	Royal Air Force
RAMC	Royal Army Medical Corps
R Berks	Royal Berkshire Regiment
R.E.	Royal Engineers
Regt	Regiment
Res	Reserve
RFA	Royal Field Artillery
RFC	Royal Flying Corps
RGA	Royal Garrison Artillery
RHA	Royal Horse Artillery
Rifm	Rifleman
R/Labourer	Relaying Labourer
Rly	Railway
RMA	Royal Marine Artillery
RMLI	Royal Marine Light Infantry
RN	Royal Navy
RNAS	Royal Naval Air Service
RNVR	Royal Naval Volunteer Reserve
ROD	Railway Operating Division
RSM	Regimental Sergeant Major
SDGW	Soldiers Died in the Great War
Sgt	Sergeant
Sgt-Maj	Sergeant Major
S	Ship Lost
S/Lab	Slip Labourer
S/M	Royal Navy Signalman
SOL	Superintendent of the Line
Spr	Sapper
Sqdn	Squadron
Sto	Stoker
Sub-Lt	Sub-Lieutenant
SWB	South Wales Borderers
Temp	Temporary
Tpr	Trooper
UL	Under Locking Lineman
Yeo	Yeomanry

COMMISSIONED OFFICERS

Ablett, David	Paddington Goods St. – Sub-Lt RNVR Att. Trench Mortar Bty
Aldington, Charles	General Managers Assistant – Lt-Col. Engineer & Rly. Staff Corps
Alexander, H.A.	Engineer Dept. Paddington – Capt R.E.
Alford, B.T.	Draughtsman Engineer Dept. Paddington- 2/Lt 4th Somerset L.I.
Anthony, L.	DEO Clerk Neath – 2/Lt Royal Welsh Fus
Apperley, W.H.	Loco Dept. Labourer Swindon – 2/Lt ASC
Aspinall, W.	Packer Engineering Dept. Ponkey – 2/Lt Kings (Liverpool) Regt
Auchterlonie, L.	Veterinary Surgeon Horse Dept Paddington – Lt AVC
Ball, L.P.	SOL Staff Paddington – Maj. RAF
Bassett, R.J.	Clerk Pontypool Road – 2/Lt ROD R.E.
Baugh, J.T.	Traffic Dept. Bedlinog – 2/Lt 6th Manchester Regt
Beckley, H.W.	Surveyor Engineer Dept. Taunton – Capt. 298th Rly. Troops Co. R.E.
Beckley, V.W.	Engineering Dept. Assistant Shrewsbury – Maj. OC 275th (GWR) Rly Co. R.E.
Beesley, R.G.G.	Goods Dept. Clerk Hockley – Lt Norflok Regt
Bennett, W.J.	Tracer DEO. Neath – Capt. RFA
Berry, S.B.	New Works Engineers Off. Paddington – 2/Lt R.E.
Birks, Alfred Owen	L&C Clerk Swindon – 2/Lt 1st Dorset Regt (ex-Sgt-Maj. ASC)
Bishop, B.F.	Estate Dept. Paddington – 2/Lt N. Staffordshire Regt
Blackwell, F.W.K.	GMO Clerk Paddington – Lt Rly. Troops Co. R.E.
Bolter, Charles Albert	Staff of Solicitor – 2/Lt MGC (ex-Sgt Artists Rifles)
Bottomley, J.E.	L&C Swindon – 2/Lt 3/4th Wilts Regt
Bowen, William	DSO Swansea – 2/Lt 3rd Welsh Regt
Bowskill, H.V.	Traffic Dept. Clerk Ammanford – 2/Lt Hussars
Boxall, Alfred	DEO Shrewsbury – 2/Lt 262nd (GWR) Rly Co. R.E.
Boxall, G.F.	Electrical Engineers Off. Paddington – 2/Lt R.E.
Bramham, E.S.	Electrical Engineers Off. – Capt. RAF
Bray, E.W.A.	Drawing Off. Loco Dept. Swindon – Lt 72nd Co. ASC
Bridgen, C.W.	DGMO Clerk London – 2/Lt County of London Regt
Brown, E.T.	Engineers Off. Chipping Sodbury – 2/Lt 11th Gloucestershire Regt
Brown, George	Deeds Off. Paddington – 2/Lt HAC
Brown, R.C.	Estate Dept. Paddington – 2/Lt

Brown, Sidney T.	Deeds Off. Paddington – Capt. HAC (ex-Royal Fus)
Brown, W.H.	Permanent-Way Dept. Reading – 2/Lt 3rd Dorset Regt
Browne, A.G.	Traffic Dept. Clerk Pembroke Docks – 2/Lt Trench Mortar Bty
Brusch, G.	Goods Dept. Hockley – CSM Granted commission in the field 1918
Buchanan, L.G.	CEO Paddington – 2/Lt 1/10th Kings (Liverpool) Regt
Buckingham, W.A.	Audit Off. – 2/Lt 5th Berkshire Regt
Burbidge, S.	GMO Paddington – Lt Rly. Troops Co. R.E.
Cambridge, F.P.G.	DSO Paddington – 2/Lt Berkshire Yeomanry
Cantell, W.J.	Passenger Dept. Clerk Thame Street – 2/Lt 13th W. Yorkshire Regt
Carey, J.S.	Electrical Dept. Paddington – 2/Lt 8th Middlesex Regt
Carter, H.L.	Signal Engineers Off. Reading – Lt RAF
Carus-Wilson, Trevor	New Works Engineers Dept. Paddington – Lt-Col. 5th DCLI
Chaddock, R.S.	GWR Canal Mangers Off. Clerk – 2/Lt E. Lancashire Regt
Challis, H.W.	Goods Dept. Clerk Brentford – 2/Lt Middlesex Regt
Chance, A.H.	DGMO – 2/Lt 7th Warwickshire Regt
Chancellor, J.E.	DGMO Clerk Birmingham – Lt RAMC
Chapman, F.G.	Stores Dept. Clerk Swindon – Lt 3rd Dorset Regt
Chapman, W.G.	GMO – Lt RNVR
Chisholm, K.J.	DSO Paddington – Lt 5th Northamptonshire Regt
Choules, R.B.W.	L&C (Accounts Dept) Swindon – 2/Lt Rly Troops R.E.
Clarke, S.	Signal Dept. Inspector Neath – Capt. & Hon.Major 6th Welsh Regt
Clewett, G.	Stationmasters Off. Clerk Manchester – 2/Lt RFA
Colbourn, H.T.	CGMO Paddington – 2/Lt Shropshire L.I.
Coles, Herbert	Goods Dept. Clerk High Wycombe – 2/Lt 2nd Rifle Brigade
Collcott, E.H.	Parliament Dept. Solicitors Off. – 2/Lt Middlesex Regt
Conway, Harold	Restaurant Car Attendant Paddington – 2/Lt Indian Army (ex-Wilts Regt)
Cooke, George Joshia	Lad Messenger Paddington Goods – 2/Lt RFC (ex-London Regt)
Cookson, Walter J.	Solicitors Off. Clerk Paddington – Lt 31st Signal Co. RE (ex-DCLI)
Cope, Thomas W.O.	Loco Dept. Stafford Road – Lt RN Reserve – Motor Boat Reserve
Court, R.W.S.	Audit Off. Clerk Hereford – 2/Lt 1st Herefordshire Regt
Cousin, D.P.	Stores Dept. Clerk Swindon – 2/Lt Essex Royal Garrison E. Anglia Regt
Cowherd, J.	Parcel Clerk Traffic Dept. Bristol – 2/Lt Worcestershire Regt
Coy, F.C.	DMO Cardiff – 2/Lt Royal Welsh Fus
Crane, H.J.	Goods Dept. Worcester – 2/Lt Loyal N. Lancashire Regt
Crane, Reginald Hooper	DGMO Manchester – 2/Lt 1st E. Yorkshire Regt
Cresswell, F.S.	Surveyor and Draughtsman Engineer Off. Paddington – Major RFC
Cronin, H.W.	Audit Dept. Clerk Paddington – Lt 5th Bedfordshire Regt
Curnow, T.G.	SOL Clerk Paddington – Lt Rly. Transport R.E.
Currivan, E.C.	L&C Clerk Wolverhampton – 2/Lt ASC
Curtis, E.C.	Motor Car Dept. Slough – Lt Seaforth Highlanders
Dalison, Charles Beauvoir	Draughtsman L&C – Maj. RNAS/RAF
Day, Harold	Premium Apprent. L&C Swindon – Ft/Sub/Lt RN Air Service
Dean, George F.	Accounts Dept. Clerk Swindon – 2/Lt 162nd Btty. RFA
Dixon, William H.	Goods Dept. Clerk Hockley – 2/Lt 25 Squadron RAF
Driscoll, R.	Labourer Monmouthshire & Brecon Canal – 2/Lt 3rd SWB
Ducat, G.V.	Audit Off. Paddington – Lt 8th Middlesex Regt
Dulin, W.W. Motta	Loco Works Swindon – Lt RFC

Dunford, B.F.	Traffic Dept. Clerk Radstock – 2/Lt RFC
Dunster, J.E. deM.	GMO Clerk Paddington – 2/Lt 10th Devonshire Regt
Dunton, S.H.	Audit Off. Clerk Paddington – 2/Lt 17th Middlesex Regt
Edwards, C.S.	Parliament Off. Paddington – 2/Lt RFC
Elcombe, S.	SOL Off. – Capt. ASC
Eldred, R.J.	Draughtsman New Works Dept. Paddington – 10th Welsh Regt
Enser, J.W.	SOL Off. – Lt ASC
Evans, Eric H.	Audit Off. Clerk – Lt RAF (ex-RFA)
Evans, P.E.	Traffic Dept. Clerk Worcester – 2/Lt RFC
Faith, C.F.	Stores Dept. Swindon – Lt Army Ordnance Corps
Fardon, T.E.	SOL Off. – 2/Lt RE
Farthing, W.E.	Engineering Dept. Clerk Plymouth – 2/Lt Devon Royal Garrison Artillery
Ferguson, G.W.	Drawing Off. L&C Swindon – 2/Lt RFC (ex-ASC)
Fluck, A.E.S.	L&C Clerk Swindon – Capt. 52nd Warwickshire Regt (father of Diana Dors)
Ford, L.E.	DSO Cardiff – 2/Lt 2nd Monmouthshire Regt
Fortune, H.G.	Traffic Dept. Swindon – 2/Lt 3/6th Welsh Regt
Gallie, A.E.	Goods Dept. Clerk Landore – 2/Lt
Garthwaite, F.	Chief Engineers Off. Paddington – 2/Lt 275th (GWR) Rly Co. R.E.
Gellier, Arthur Berteau	Premium Apprent. Swindon Works – 2/Lt 2/7th Lancashire Fus
Gibb, R.	Divisional Engineers Off. Plymouth – 2/Lt 262nd (GWR) Rly Co. R.E.
Gibson, K.J.	Draughtsman L&C Swindon – Lt 8th Wilts Regt
Gigg, W.G.	Booking Clerk Taunton – 2/Lt Worcestershire Regt
Gilbert, A.J.	Clerk Loco Running Shed Swindon – 2/Lt Berkshire Regt
Gison, A.D.	L&C Newport – 2/Lt 10th SWB
Godfrey, Ernest N.	GMO Paddington – Lt RFA
Godsell, R.F.	District Agents Off. Cork, Ireland – 2/Lt Royal Munster Fus
Good, H.	Traffic Dept. Maidenhead – 2/Lt 15th Middlesex Regt
Grainger, William T.	L&C Clerk Swindon – 2/Lt 3/4th Wilts Regt
Green, H.W.	Goods Dept. Clerk Smithfield – 2/Lt Hampshire Regt
Griddlestone, J.G.L.	Draughtsman Loco Dept. Swindon – Lt 10th Devonshire Regt
Grierson, J.	CGMO – 2/Lt Lonson Scottish
Griffiths, A.	CGMO Clerk Paddington – Lt ASC
Hackman, Clifford	Stores Dept. Clerk Swindon – 2/Lt RAF
Hall, W.H.	Goods Dept. Clerk Hockley – Lt Rly. Troops R.E.
Ham, F.W.	Goods Dept. Clerk Brentford – 2/Lt RFC
Hannington, R.A.G.	Assist. Divisional Superintendent Swindon/Old Oak Common – Capt ROD R.E.
Hards, J.H.	Goods Dept. Clerk Halesowen – Hon. Lt RAMC
Hardy, R.H.W.	DGMO Liverpool – 2/Lt 3rd Welsh Regt
Harper, S.H.V.D.	Goods Dept. Clerk South Lambeth – 2/Lt RFA
Harris, E.J.B.	SOL Off. – 2/Lt 9th Royal W. Surrey Regt
Harris, F.U.J.	Passenger Dept. Clerk Wrexham – 2/Lt Royal Welsh Fus
Harris, Walter Lewis	Traffic Dept. Clerk Newquay – 2/Lt 10th Devonshire Regt
Hart, Frank Squire	DSO Paddington – 2/Lt Somerset L.I. (ex-Public Schools Batt. Middlesex Regt)

Hawker, H.	DGMO Clerk Exeter – Sub-Lt RN Division
Heaton, A.W.	Goods Dept. Victoria & Albert – 2/Lt Northamptonshire Regt
Hicks, Ernest	Chief GMO – 2/Lt London Regt Irish Rifles
Hoates, W.	Fireman Loco Dept. Leamington – Lt Warwickshire Regt
Hodsell, E.J.	Drawing Off. L&C Swindon – Lt RN Flying Corps
Hollinrake, J.C.	Chief Accounts Off. Clerk Paddington – 2/Lt 1st Suffolk Regt
Holttum, W.	Engineering Dept. Chipping Sodbury – Lt 1/1st London Regt Royal Fus
Howarth, A.L.	GWR Wireless Station Weymouth – Flt Lt RN Air Service
Hudson, F.A.	Surveyor CEO Paddington – 2/Lt R.E.
Huggins, E.W.	Hotels Dept. Clerk Paddington – 2/Lt London Regt
Humphrey, B.	Motor Car Dept. Engineering staff Slough – Lt ASC (Mechanical Transport)
Humphrey, W.H.E.	GMO Clerk Paddington – Lt Rly. Transport R.E.
Irwin, Horace C.	Chief Accountants Staff – 2/Lt Argyll & Sutherland Highlanders
Jackson, Edward P.	Chief Accountants Off. Paddington – Capt. Berkshire Regt
Jackson, L.	Signalman Wheatley Oxon – 2/Lt RGA
James, A.H.	Apprent. C&W Swindon – 2/Lt RFA
James, A.S.	DSO Swansea – 2/Lt
James, S.H.	L&C Swindon – 2/Lt RGA
Jarrett, W.G.	Chief Booking Clerk Swansea – 2/Lt ASC
Jobson, W.	Draughtsman L&C Swindon – Lt
Jones, A.J.	Apprent. Loco Works Swindon – 2/Lt Berkshire Regt
Jones, F.H.	L&C Swindon – 2/Lt 4th Wilts Regt
Jones, G.	Assistant Motor Car Dept. Slough – 2/Lt ASC (Motor Transport)
Jones, H.M.	DSO Swansea – 2/Lt Royal Welsh Fus
Jones, H.R.	CGMO – 2/Lt 12th SWB
Jones, John Victor	Labourer L&C Swindon – 2/Lt 3rd Dorset Regt
Jones, M.	Drawing Off. L&C Swindon – 2/Lt 565th (Wilts) Army Troops Co. R.E.
Jones, T.P.	Motor Car Dept. Slough – 2/Lt ASC
Jones, W.H.	Traffic Dept. Cardiff – 2/Lt 3rd Shropshire L.I.
Kelley, G.V.	SOL Clerk Paddington – Lt Rly. Transport R.E.
Kerridge, S.C.	Goods Dept. Weymouth – 2/Lt Northumberland Fus
Kew, D.	Engineering Dept. Reading – 2/Lt 1st Hertfordshire Regt
Keyworth, T.D.	Goods Dept. Wellington (Salop) – 2/Lt 4th Shropshire L.I.
Kindersley, C.H.R.	DSO Bristol – Lt 6th Dorset Regt
King, B.	Stores Dept. Swindon – Lt Warwickshire Regt
Kirkpatrick, R.C.	Chief Assistant to Div. Engineer Wolverhampton – 116th (GWR) Rly Co. R.E.
Knapp, G.E.C.	Loco Dept. Swindon – Capt. 565th (Wilts) Army Troops Co. R.E.
Kneath, David John	Traffic Dept. Aberdare – 2/Lt 5th Cheshire Regt
Lake, E.	DEO Plymouth – Maj. 116th (GWR) Rly Co. R.E.
Lambeth, C.	L&C Swindon – Lt 1st S.W. Brigade RAMC
Lampitt, R.E.	SOL Off. – Lt ASC
Law, E.G.	SOL Off. – 2/Lt Royal Fus
Law, Henry Milner	Goods Dept. Southall – 2/Lt 6th Seaforth Highlanders
Lees, P.B.	Accounts Off. New Works Engineer Dept – 2/Lt 14th Gloucestershire Regt

Lett, John Millard	DSO Pontypool – Lt Worcestershire Regt
Leveson-Gower, R.H.G.	SOL Off. Paddington – 2/Lt 23rd London Regt
Littler, Tom	Apprent. L&C Swindon – 2/Lt 1 Squadron RAF
Lloyd, Alan	DGMO Exeter – Flight Cadet RAF (ex-Devonshire Regt)
Lovelace Waite, W.C.	DSO Paddington – 2/Lt RFA
Lucas, Thomas H.	Draughtsman L&C Swindon – Lt RAF (ex-Wilts Regt)
Ludlow, F.H.	Goods Dept Clerk Smithfield – 2/Lt London Regt
Mackenzie-Brown, W.H.	Engineering Dept. Assistant Reading – Capt. Dorset Regt
Mahony, C.J.	Traffic Dept. Clerk Wadebridge – 2/Lt DCLI
Manley, John	Premium Apprent. Loco Works Swindon – Capt. RFC (4 Sqaudron?)
Maples, Kenneth J.	Solicitors Dept. Paddington – Capt. S. Staffordshire Regt
Martin, C.	Draughtsman Loco Dept. Swindon – Lt Somerset L.I.
Marwood, H.G.	Chief Cashiers Off. Paddington – Assistant Paymaster RN Reserve
Mason, F.B.	CGMO – Capt. 26th Middlesex Regt
Matheson, E.G.	New Works Dept. Birmingham – Maj. (OC) 295th Rly Co. R.E.
Mattock, L.H.	Clerk Trowbridge – 2/Lt Royal W. Surrey Regt
Mauger, E.W.	GWR Continental Agent – Capt. Rly. Transport Division R.E.
May, D.G.	Stores Dept. Swindon – Lt
Mayo, C.D.	Audit Dept. Clerk Paddington – 2/Lt 2nd Royal Scotts Lothian Regt
Mayo, S.H.	CGMO Paddington – 2/Lt Berkshire Regt
Mead, T.T.	DEO Paddington – 2/Lt Rly. Troops R.E.
Meller, S.A.	Engineering Dept. Wolverhampton – 2/Lt 15th Royal Fus
Mildmay, Hon. F.B.	GWR Director – Lt-Col
Miles, Robert William	GMO Paddington – Capt 13th Sherwood Foresters
Millard, E.R.	Drawing Off. L&C Swindon – 2/Lt 3rd Wilts Regt
Mocatta, Frederick C.	Engineering Off. Paddington – Capt. RAF (ex-RFA)
Mockford, Joseph	CGMO – 2/Lt 1st London Regt Royal Fus
Moody, R.G.A.	SOL Off. – 2/Lt 10th S. Lancashire Regt
Morris, G.G.	GWR Receiving Officer King William Street – Capt. RE Rly Traffic Richborough
Morris, H.H.	Drawing Off. Loco Dept. Swindon – Lt 3rd Wilts Regt
Morten, L.J.	Chippenham – 2/Lt Ox & Bucks L.I.
Murray, B.J.	Loco Dept. Newport – Commissioned in Indian Army
Naish, A.H.	New Works Assistant Chief Engineers Off. – Lt Kings Royal Rifles
Nason, Richard Philip	Clerk Cleobury Mortimer Station – 2/Lt Sherwood Foresters
Neville, Reginald	Draughtsman Loco Dept. Swindon – Lt 1st Bedfordshire Regt
Nicholls, E.H.R.	DSO Paddington – 2/Lt Royal Welsh Fus
Norwood, R.H.	CGMO Clerk Paddington – 2/Lt 'C' Co. 9th Batt. Tank Corps
Orpwood, F.R.	CGMO – 2/Lt 4th Royal Inniskilling Fus
Owen, H.S.	Chief Accountants Off. Paddington – 2/Lt Manchester Regt
Parker, A.W.	Hotels Dept. Clerk Paddington – 2/Lt Rly Troops R.E.
Pearman, W.S.	Chief Engineers Off. Paddington – Lt Rly Troops R.E.
Pellow, R.C.	Apprent. Fitter L&C St.Blazey – 2/Lt RAF
Perfect, E.	DEO Newport – 2/Lt 275th (GWR) Rly Co. R.E.
Pester, A.	Goods Dept. Clerk South Lambeth – 2/Lt RFA
Peters, Walter William	L&C Swindon – Engineer Sub-Lt RN Reserve
Phillips, W.J.	Goods Dept. Clerk Newport – 2/Lt 4th Seaforth Highlanders

Piper, H.	DE Dept. Shrewsbury – 2/Lt Royal Fus
Plumb, R.G.	CGMO Paddington – 2/Lt Seaforth Highlanders
Pole, E.R.	Chief Accountants Off. Paddington – Lt R.E.
Pratt, W.G.	Clerk South Lambeth Goods Station – 2/Lt RFA
Price, F.G.	DEO Paddington – 2/Lt 275th (GWR) Rly Co. R.E.
Price, P.A.E.	CGMO Paddington – 2/Lt 'Q' Anti-aircraft Bty RGA
Prowse, J.H.	Traffic Dept. Clerk Paddington – 2/Lt Tank Corps
Quartermaine, Alan S.	Chief Engineers Off. Paddington – Maj. 116th (GWR) Rly Co. R.E.
Randles, W.T.	Goods Dept. Clerk Saltney – 2/Lt RAF (ex-R.E.)
Read, Stanley Charles	Goods Dept. Clerk Reading – 2/Lt 27 Squadron RAF
Rendell, Henry Thomas	Motor Car Dept. Slough – Major ASC (Motor Transport)
Rickard, H.	GMO Paddington – 2/Lt 2/5th DCLI
Roberts, D.C.	Traffic Dept. Clerk Montpelier Station – 2/Lt 10th SWB
Roberts, G.H.	Goods Dept. Cardiff – 2/Lt 14th Worcestershire Regt
Roberts, S.H.	Hotels & Refreshments Dept. Paddington – Lt ASC
Robinson, A.J.	Passenger Dept. Cholsey – Capt. Ox & Bucks L.I. (ex-Middlesex Regt)
Robinson, J.G.	Engineers Off. Paddington – Lt London Rifle Brigade
Robinson, P.G.	Hotels Dept. Assistant Paddington – Lt Rly Troops R.E.
Robinson, S.H.	Chief Engineers Dept. – 2/Lt Labour Unit R.E.
Rodda, H.C.	CMEO Reading – Lt 565th (Wilts) Army Troops Co. R.E.
Rodway, Swinhoe G.	Chief Medical Officer Swindon – Surgeon Major RAMC
Rogers, B.R.C.	Traffic Dept. Clerk Ruabon – 2/Lt 6th Royal Fus Att to 3rd Batt
Rowland(s), F.A.	Booking Clerk Birmingham – 2/Lt York & Lancaster Regt
Rumsey, Vere	Clerk Neyland Station – Lt RGA
Russell, H.A.	Goods Dept. Weymouth – 2/Lt 3rd Dorset Regt
Sainsbury, J.	CEO Paddington – 2/Lt ASC
Sargent, F.	GMO – Lt Railway Troops R.E.
Scarfe, C.G.	Chief Accountants Off. Paddington – 2/Lt 19th Sherwood Foresters
Seaborn, R.H.	Goods Dept. Cardiff – Lt 18th Welsh Regt
Shardlow, C.F.	CGMO (Rates Section) – 2/Lt Royal Welsh Fus
Sharp, Richard	Harbourmaster Fishguard – Capt. (OC) 'A' Co. Pembroke Volunteers
Sharpe, Salisbury	GWR Medical Officer London – Lt-Col. 2nd London Field Ambulance RAMC
Shears, W.H.	Clerk Winchester Station – 2/Lt 3rd Lancashire Regt
Simpkinson, F.V.	Engineering Dept. Wolverhampton – 2/Lt 103rd Field Co. R.E.
Simpson, C.L.	Draughtsman Loco Dept. Swindon – Lt 565th (Wilts) Army Troops Co. R.E.
Simpson, Thomas E.	Apprent. Fitter L&C Newport – 2/Lt 65 Squadron RAF (ex-Monmouthshire Regt & ASC)
Smith, Clark G.T.	Motor Car Dept. Slough – Capt. RAF
Smith, Harold B.	SOL Off. – Lt 3/7th London Regt (Att. to Royal Rifle Corps)
Sorley, G.M.	DSO Paddington – Lt 3rd City of London Regt Royal Fus
Speary, Fred	DGMO Reading – 2/Lt 8th Berkshire Regt
Spittle, George Herbert	Electrical Engineers Dept. Paddington – Maj. 1st Army Signalling School RE (ex-RN Division)
Stanbury, S.J.	Clerk Barnstable – Lt 1/6th Devonshire Regt
Steane, F.	Secretary's Off. – Lt (Acting Capt)

Stephens, Henry Hill	L&C Clerk Newport – 2/Lt 42 Squadron RAF
Stewart, E.W.R.	Goods Dept. Clerk Paddington – Lt 5th E. Surrey Regt
Stocker, F.L.	DEO. Taunton – Lt 28th Royal Fus Att. to 20th Batt
Stuart, Evans J.T.	Goods Dept. Cardiff – 2/Lt 19th Royal Welsh Fus
Tallboys, H.C.	Porter Shunter Ledbury – 2/Lt Worcestershire Regt
Taylor, Joseph H.	Apprent. Loco Works Swindon – Flt Lt RAF
Thomas, H.W.	L&C Swindon – 2/Lt 7th Wilts Regt
Thomas, J.R.	Trffic Dept. Clerk Tirydall – 2/Lt Welsh Regt
Thomas, T.J.	Goods Dept. Swansea – Lt RAMC
Thomson, H.	Engineering Dept. Newport – Lt 12th Scottish Rifles
Tripe, Alfred King	Estate Dept, Clerk Plymouth – Lt RGA Att. to Tank Corps
Turner, G.	Goods Dept. Clerk Hockley – 2/Lt Warwickshire Regt
Turner, T.	Surveyor & Draughtsman Engineer Off. London – 2/Lt Rly Troops R.E.
Turner, T.H.	L&C Superintendents Off. Clerk Swindon – 2/Lt 3/23rd London Regt
Tweedie, M.G.	Signal Engineers Off. Reading – Capt. R.E. (Signals)
Tymms, D.J.	CEO Paddington – 2/Lt Kings Own Scottish Borderers
Tyrwhitt, S.E.	SOL Off. – Lt 565th (Wilts) Army Troops Co. R.E.
Underwood, A.L.	DSO Clerk Worcester – 2/Lt Royal Fus
Veltom, F.S.	GMO Paddington – 2/Lt Rly Transport RE
Vickery, A.	Chief Engineering Dept. Paddington – Lt Rly Troops R.E.
Wadner, Frederick	Porter Goods Dept. Bristol – Capt. Kings Royal Rifle Corps
Warren-King, J.A.	GMO Paddington – Lt Rly. Troops R.E.
Wason, Cyril Ernest	Goods Dept. Clerk Cardiff – 2/Lt 9th Royal Fus
Watkins, H.B.	Clerk Johnstown & Hafod – 2/Lt Shropshire L.I.
Webb, T.H.W.	Ticket Collector Bath Station – 2/Lt E. Surrey Regt
Whitehead, H.M.	DSO Gloucester – 2/Lt Tank Corps
Whitfield, Richard H.	Surveyor & Draughtsman Engineers Off. Neath – Lt 104th Field Co. R.E.
Whitley, H. Stuart	Chief Assistant to Div. Engineer Neath – Maj. (OC) Rly. Survey Section RE (ex-275th GWR Rly Co. R.E.)
Whyte, C.	Rates & Taxes Dept. Clerk Paddington – 2/Lt Leicestershire Regt
Willcock, H.B.	DSO Clerk Paddington – 2/Lt 3rd Essex Regt
Williams, A.V.	Clerk Wrexham – 2/Lt Shropshire L.I.
Williams, David	Drawing Off. L&C Swindon – 353rd Electrical & Mechanical Co. R.E. (ex-565th (Wilts) R.E.)
Williams, F.G.	Porter Herford Goods Station – 2/Lt E. Lancashire Regt
Williams, Kenneth G.	Temp GWR Employee – 2/Lt MGC
Wilson, Cyril Spencer	Assistant Manager C&W Swindon – Maj. No.4 Workshop Co. REOC (ex-565th (Wilts) R.E.)
Wood, J.V.B.	DGMO – Lt 12th SWB
Wood, O.T.	Chief Assist. to Div. Engineer Paddington – Capt. 262nd (GWR) Rly Co. R.E.
Worth, H.A.G.	Chief Engineers Off. Paddington – 2/Lt RFA
Wright, F.G.	Loco Dept Swindon – Maj. & OC 565TH (Wilts) Army Troops Co. R.E.

GALLANTRY MEDALS AND AWARDS

Where there is no indication of the date of the award, dates in brackets refer to when details were published in the *GWR Magazine*.

DISTINGUISHED SERVICE ORDER
Three awarded

Carus-Wilson Trevor   CEO Paddington   Lt-Col 5th Duke of Cornwall's L.I.
     Also MID and Territorial Decoration (2/18)
Rendell Henry Thomas   Motor Car Dept. Slough   Lt (Temp. Major) ASC (Mechanical
     Transport Section). Also MID (2/18)
Spittle George Herbert   Electrical Engineer Dept   Maj. 1st Army Signalling School R.E.
     For distinguished work in connection with the 'recent big push' (7/17)

DISTINGUISHED SERVICE CROSS
One awarded

Day Harold   Premium Apprent/L&C/Swindon   Flt/Sub/Lt RNAS – 10 & 8 Squadrons.
     In recognition of the skills and determination shown by him in aerial combats, in the course
     of which he has done much to stop enemy artillery machines from working. On 6 January
     1918 he observed a new type of enemy aeroplane. He immediately dived to attack, and after
     a short combat the enemy machine went down very steeply, and was seen to crash. On sev-
     eral other occasions he has brought down enemy machines out of control. He had a total of
     eleven victories (some shared)

Telegraphic Address ROBERTS, PADDINGTON STATION

TELEPHONE No 7000 PADDINGTON

Great Western Railway.

Chief Goods Manager's Office.
T.

Paddington Station.

London. W.2.

18th February, 1919.

Dear Sir,

On behalf of the Directors, Chief Officers and Staff of the Great Western Railway I have pleasure in conveying to you a message of congratulation upon the honour conferred upon you by the award of the Military Cross for conspicuous gallantry and devotion to duty.

The distinction must be a source of much gratification to you, as it is to the Company to learn that a member of their staff has merited special recognition in connexion with the operation of the War.

I am,

Yours faithfully,

2nd Lt. F.Spearey,
    8th Battalion Royal Berks Regt,
        B.E.F.
            FRANCE.

Letter of congratulations from the GWR to
Lieutenant Spearey. (Spearey Archives)

Second Lieutenant F. Spearey.
(*GWR Magazine*)

MILITARY CROSS
Thirty-one awarded

Ablett David Clerk Paddington goods Temp Sub-Lt RNVR. Att. Trench Mortar Battery. He assisted in capturing thirty-one prisoners and later put a trench in a state of defence and drove off an enemy attack (5/17)

Beesley R.G.G. Clerk Goods dept. Hockley Lt Norfolk Regt. For gallantry in the capture of Ribecourt 20 Nov. 1917

Bennet W.J. Tracer DEO Neath Lt RFA. For gallantry in action on the Western Front. Also MID - Aged 23 (4/18)

Bishop B.F Estate Off. Paddington 2/Lt N. Staffordshire Regt. Under heavy continuous shell fire he personally led a rescue party to a dug-out that had been blown in by a direct hit. Two of four lives were saved (4/18)

Boxall Alfred Assistant to Div. Engineer Lt 262nd (GWR) Rly Co. R.E. For work on the Ypres Gun Spur under dangerous conditions (4/18)

Browne A.G. Clerk/Traffic/Pembroke Dock 2/Lt Trench Mortar Bty. For exploits on the night of 24 June 1917 when a number of prisoners were taken; also complimented by his General. Although only 20 years of age, he had been wounded several times

Brusch G. Goods Dept Hockley CSM. For distinguished conduct. Also granted a commission (10/18)

Chaddock R.S. Clerk/Canal Manager Bath 2/Lt E. Lancs Regt (ex-Somerset L.I.). For gallantry in the field (11/17)

Cookson Walter J. Solicitors' Office Paddington Lt R.E. Also MID (7/17)

Cowherd J. Parcel Clerk/Traffic/Bristol 2/Lt. For gallantry and distinguished conduct (4/18)

Crane H.J. Goods. Dept Worcester 2/Lt Loyal N. Lancashire Regt. For conspicuous and good service (2/19)

Dawson J. Loco Dept. Swindon Capt. 565th (Wilts) Army Troops Co. R.E.

Ferguson G.W. Drawing Off. L&C Swindon 2/Lt RFC (ex-ASC) – great-nephew of Daniel Gooch (2/18)

Fowles Alfred Carman/Goods/Wolverh'ton CSM Gloucester Regt. when his officers were struck down he took command of the first line, rallying and urging his men forward under heavy fire (11/16)

Gallie A.E. Clerk Goods Dept Landore 2/Lt. For conduct during the Battle of Messines 1917

Green H.W. Clerk Goods Dept Smithfield Lt Hampshire Regt. For work during attack on Kemmel 8-9 August 1918. He led two platoons in the attack and captured a machine gun. When the enemy attempted to return and bring in machine guns he forced them to retire by his initiative

James A.S. Clerk DSO Swansea 2/Lt. For gallantry and services rendered at Mesopotamia (10/17)

Jobson W. Draughtsman L&C Swindon Lt (6/19)

Jobson W. Ass.Analyst/L&C/Swindon (9/19)

Kerridge S.C. Clerk/Goods/Weymouth 2/Lt Northumberland Fus. During an advance in Feb. 1917 his regiment distinguished itself; Kerridge was specially mentioned

Kew D. Engineering Dept Reading 2/Lt Hertfordshire Regt. For gallantry at Achiet-Le-Grand on 23 August in connection with a battery of guns. Also DCM and MID (11/18)

Kirkpatrick R.C.   Chief Ass. to Eng. Dept Wolverh'ton Capt. 116th (GWR) Rly. Co. R.E. (7/17)

Moxham E.T.   Clerk DSO Cardiff   Sgt-Maj. RAMC (7th F/Amb). The
dressing station was in danger and all told to evacuate, but he and colleagues remained to
care for forty serious cases and 400 waiting to be dealt with. Germans took over for a few
hours, but was re-taken by the British. The station was under fire the whole time (3/16)

Rodda Henry C.   CMEO Swindon   Lt 565th (Wilts) ATC R.E. Also Medaille
Militaire (7/19)

Speary Fred   Clerk DGMO Reading   2/Lt 8th R. Berks Regt. For gallantry
and devotion to duty in the attack on Trones Wood 24 (27) Aug. 1918. He manoeuvred his
platoon in a short withdrawal, later successfully attacking through Bernafay Wood

Turner T.H.   Clerk L&C Swindon   Lt 3/23rd London Regt. For bravery in
clearing out forward railhead areas, especially a large supply dump, under heavy fire (9/18)

Wilson Cyril Spencer Ass.Manager/W&C/Swindon   Capt. 565th (Wilts) ATC R.E. For distinguished conduct and gallantry. Twice MID (12/18)

Wood J.V.B.   DGMO Birmingham   2/Lt 12th SWB. On the night of 12-13
Aug. 1916 he was in charge of a party raiding a German Trench, which he did with gallantry
and coolness. When his captain was wounded he took charge of a prisoner, and while under
escort the prisoner was wounded by a shell, but Wood managed to get him to safety. Wood
returned to bring in the wounded under heavy fire, and he was the last man back to the
British Trench

DISTINGUISHED CONDUCT MEDAL
Eighty-three awarded and one bar

Albury A.   Packer/Engineer/Pangbourne   (11/18) POW

Allen W.   Labourer/L&C/Old Oak Common   Acting Sgt 1/3rd London Regt. For
conspicuous gallantry at Neuve Chapelle. On the night of 13 March 1915 he was in charge
of a patrol and discovered a small bridge laid down for an enemy advance. He destroyed the
bridge, holding up the enemy

Arnold F.   Carman/Goods/Lambeth   L/Cpl. For devotion to duty and conspicuous gallantry under fire (4/18)

Askew W.J.   Forage Carman/Horse/Hockley   Cpl 2nd Coldstream Guards. For gallantry (2/15)

Atherton W.J.R.   Rail Motor Conductor/Bristol   (7/19)

Avenell Arthur C.   Carriage Cleaner/L&C/Tondu   Cpl Wiltshire Yeo. For conspicuous
bravery in the field. Aged 25 (7/17)

Balding S.C.   Apprent Fitter/L&C/Stafford Rd   Pte RFA. For brave conduct in the field.
During the battle in June he was serving as a driver and was the only surviving member of his
gun team. He stuck with his gun, and although it was disabled he managed to bring it out of
action (10/17)

Blake A.J.   Labourer/L&C/Swindon   (7/19)

Blythe J.W.   Blacksmith/Wolverhampton   Sgt. (6/19)

Bonner O.C.   Carman/Goods/Hockley   Sgt. For gallantry and bravery on 10
July 1916 during the Battle of the Somme (1/18)

Bowley T.   Carriage Shunter/Old Oak Comm   CSM 6th R. Berks Regt. For rescuing a
wounded soldier after an attempt by two others. Upon leaving the trench he had to lie down

flat for an hour due to heavy fire, but when he got to the wounded man he found he could not move him. Bowley returned to the trench where a group of men dug their way to the wounded man. Also MM and Bar to DCM (3/16)

Bridgwater W. Packer/Engineer/Shrewsbury (9/19)

Brown G. Restaurant Car Attendant/Padd Sgt. 13th Middlesex Regt. For gallant and resourceful work in 1916 (12/18)

Conway Harold Restaurant Car Attendant/Padd 2/Lt Indian Army. Awarded at Messines Ridge June 1917. Also MM

Cripps L.A. Porter/Traffic/Gowerton Cpl. For conspicuous gallantry while in command of two Stokes mortars covering the front line (12/19)

Davies Oswald Locomotive Fitter/Swindon Sgt 565th (Wilts) ATC R.E. Awarded for heroism when repairing a bridge under heavy fire on the Yser Canal, Ypres 1915. This allowed the French to get their wounded to a dressings station.

Dinwiddy L.A. Porter/Exeter St Thomas 3rd Coldstream Guards. For gallantry on the 25/26 April 1915 at Givenchy when he rescued, at great risk, officers and men who were trapped down a mine which was full of gas

Eason A. Fireman/Loco/Wolverhampton Cpl. MGC (5/18)

Eades Henry J. C. Policeman/Plymouth Pte 1st Devonshire Regt – See separate entry

Easty A. Packer/Engineer/Battersea 116th (GWR) Rly Co. R.E. For devotion to duty and services rendered in the field over fifteen months (6/17)

Eddington E. Packer/Engineer/Yarnton Sgt R.E. Awarded on 27 June 1918 for devotion to duty when in charge of men at Ypres. Although subject to heavy fire, and with utter disregard of danger, he set a splendid example to the men ensuring work continued to progress

Edwards A.J. Lampman/Traffic/Chester L/Cpl. 19th Liverpool Regt. (2/17)

Ellias T. Packer/Engineer/Symonds Yat (1/1920)

Ford G.W.R. Piecework Checker/L&C/Swindon Sgt. 5th Wiltshire Regt. Also MID (6/16)

Gage A.E. Telegraph Lineman/Signal/Acton Spr 32nd Motor Air Line R.E. For gallantry on 19 Dec. 1915 at Vlamertinge. During an attack, beginning with gas and shelling most of the day, he spent all day repairing wires, and re-repairing, whilst under constant fire. Also MID

Green W.E.R. Engine Cleaner/Pontypool Road Pte (6/19)

Greenaway F. GMO/Paddington CSM W. Kent Regt (9/17)

Gosling W.J. Apprent Gas Fitter/Swindon (9/19)

Harmer O. Head Shunter/Traffic/Cardif (7/19)

Hart Richard H. Signal Porter/Blaenavon Sgt R. Berks Regt. For gallant work performed at Richebourg where he carried wounded men to safety under fire (11/15)

Hayward J.W. Porter/Traffic/Cropredy Pte. For gallantry at Arleux-en-Gohelle (2/19)

Hughes F.A. Fire Cleaner/Loco/Llanelly L/Cpl 1st Devonshire Regt (4/16)

James George Unknown Cpl. For services at Gaza, March 1917

Jelfs W. Porter/Littleton & Badsey Station Pte Worcestershire Regt (7/17)

Kew D. Engineering Dept/Reading 2/Lt Hertfordshire Regt. Awarded in Oct. 1917 at Arras. Also MC and MID

Kitchen A. Ganger/Engineer/Brill & Lug'shall 116th (GWR) Rly Co. R.E. For devotion to duty and services rendered over fifteen months (7/17)

Law George   Shed Labourer/St Philips Marsh   Pte 1st Gloucester Regt. On 17 Sept. 1914, in front of the trenches, and outpost sentry was wounded and another sentry went to report the casualty. While this was being done the wounded man was seen crawling towards the trench. Law immediately went to the man's aid and, despite heavy fire, carried him to a place of safety

Lehon E.   Parcel Porter/Traffic/Paddington   CSM Middlesex Regt. Although buried by a shell explosion and greatly shaken, he remained on duty throughout an attack, displaying great coolness and courage (4/17)

Lingard S.W.   Staff of DSO Bristol   Cpl. 1st Midland Brigade RFA. (2/16)

Loveday Arthur W.   Fram Builders Ass./Swindon   Sgt 1st Wilts Regt. He volunteered for a raiding party during which time he dispatched two Germans, but others arrived, and although outnumbered he threw two bombs amongst them, giving the party a chance to retreat to safety (3/16). Bar to DCM: For great gallantry and dash in the attack on the Hindenburg Trench on 24 Aug. 1916, which was captured and held after a severe struggle with the Prussian Guard

Meacham A.G.   Clerk S.O.L. Paddington   Sgt. For bringing in a wounded comrade over a quarter of a mile under heavy fire (7/18)

Moore George G.   Shunter/Goods/Wolverhampton   Gnr 3rd N. Midland Bde RFA. For conspicuous bravery in the field (3/16)

Morse A.A.B.   Fireman Loco Dept Truro   (10/19)

Probert   Rd Motor Conductor/Abbergav'y   Sgt-Maj. Awarded for gallant action. His company was overwhelmed by the enemy, and all the officers and men, except two, were killed or wounded. The two men tried to escape but were observed. One man was severely wounded, the other (Probert), although exposed to great danger, stayed with his comrade and eventually carried him to safety (1/19)

Pugh M.M.   Labourer/Sheet/Gloucester   Pte 8th Gloucester Regt. Promoted to Sgt. Also MM and CDG (3/17)

Rabbits F.   Packer/Engineer/Yeovil Pen Mill   Pte Dorset Regt. For maintaining rapid fire on the enemy during an attack, and bringing in a wounded man under fire (9/16)

Randall S.W.S.   Clerk Newport High Street   RSM. Between 27 Oct. & 9 Nov. 1917 he carried out his duties, often under heavy shell fire, with coolness for three days and nights without a break. He performed his duties near Khuweifch Heights cheerfully, although exhausted (9/19)

Sargent S.J.   Instrument Maker/Signal/Reading   (9/19)

Scott A.G.   Machineman/Wagon Shop/Swindon   L/Cpl 5th Wilts Regt. He was one of a party lost outside the British lines at Chunuk Bair for over a fortnight. Although weak, exhausted, and exposed to heavy fire, he returned to base where he volunteered to act as a guide for the rescue party (3/16)

Scott Alfred Keith   CAO/Paddington   RSM 7th Cameron Highlanders. Awarded after the Battle of Loos, where his battalion suffered heavy casualties.

Scott J.W.   Porter Smithfield Goods Station   Gnr 459th Howitzer Bty. At Hooge on 7-8 Aug. 1915 he repaired wires under heavy shelling so that the battery could fire on a redoubt prior to the attack on the 9th. Also, although ordered not to until pause in the fire, he went out to gain valuable information on hostile movements

Sharp Leo M.   Apprent Fitter/Marine/Fishguard   Sgt. R.E. (8/16)

Smith G.C.   Wagon Riveter/L&C/Worcester   Sgt. (6/19)

Smith V.C.   Clerk Gloucester Goods Station   CSM Gloucestershire Regt. (12/17)

Stedman W.B.   Architect's Assistant Paddington   Sgt-Maj. Awarded for his work during the recent German attacks. Also MSM (9/18)

Symes E.   Carriage Cleaner Old Oak Common   Sgt. For bravery during the Battle of the Somme where he served in a machine-gun section (1/18)

Symons Leslie   Clerk GMO Paddington   Sgt KRRC. During an enemy attack on 11 Aug., when slightly wounded and gassed, he encouraged his men and continued to fire his machine gun until the Germans were repulsed (10/18)

Weeks W.   Signalman Kingskerswell   (7/19)

Wells F.   Packer/Engineer/Cardiff   Sgt. For tackling a party of ten of the enemy and, using his rifle as a club, he knocked over seven before being wounded himself (3/19)

Whitehead W.   Permanent Way Foreman Didcot   Sgt 262nd (GWR) Rly Co. R.E. For continued bravery under heavy shell fire in carrying out urgent work on several occasions (12/17)

Williams Henry   Stower/Goods/Paddington   Sgt Grenadier Guards. Also MM (12/16)

DISTINGUISHED SERVICE MEDAL
Three awarded

Harrison C.   Plumber/Engineering/Reading   Engineer HM Airships. For services rendered in connection with submarine sinkings, escorting convoys, and other work in the North Sea & English Channel (1/18)

Huntley John Henry Boilersmith's Helper Swindon Works Gnr 'C' Bty 62nd Bde RFA. Also MID (3/17)

MILITARY MEDAL
278 awarded and 11 bars

Aaron H.   Clerk Goods Dept Hockley   Pte Warwickshire Regt. As a stretcher bearer he attended and retrieved wounded under heavy fire (he later had his leg amputated above the knee) (2/17)

Adams A.E.   Cleaner Loco Dept Ebbw Vale Jct.   Pte. For devotion to duty in the Balkans and rescuing two NCOs (4/19)

Adams W.   Gas Lineman Engineering Worcester (6/19)

Allcott Harold B.   Traffic Dept. Abercarn   Gun. 'D' Bty. 21st Brigade RFA.

Allsworth Frederick J. Mechanics Labourer L&C Oxford   Sgt. 'A' Co. 1st Hampshire Regt.

Ashton J.H.   Clerk Goods Dept Southall   Sgt. Rifle Bde. On 31 July he took charge of a forward command after the officer had been killed, and kept up communications for the following five days, and despite repeated counter-attacks, the battalion did not yield (2/18)

Atlee D.   Clerk Goods Dept Southall   Cpl London Regt. For bravery during a bombing raid on 17 Feb., during which he lost his right arm (7/17)

Ayres E.P.   Parcel Porter Cholsey   L/Cpl. For bravery at Passchendaele in holding a position against the enemy when his party was cut off

Ayres J.H.   Horsekeeper Oxford   Pte. For showing high courage while carrying messages under an intense bombardment, also for astonishing military skill in conducting parties by concealed approaches to previously reconnoitred positions (2/19)

Ayres William Arthur Brass Finisher Signal Dept. Reading   Spr IWT R.E. (ex 8th Berkshire Regt)

Ball E.A.   Parcel Porter Trowbridge   Pte. For devotion during the St
   Quentin attack (10/18)

Beale F.B.   Parcel Porter Kidderminster   (6/19)

Beck V.   Erector Loco Dept Swindon   (6/19)

Beesley V.   Porter Traffic Dept Hockley   L/Cpl. (4/19)

Belsten R.   Clerk L&C Tondu   Cpl. Awarded for conspicuous bravery
   in the last battle of the Somme for sticking to his gun after an order had been given to retreat
   (2/18)

Bettany F.   Clerk Goods Dept Walsall   Pte. For bravery during a bombing raid
   at Maillet (4/19)

Betteridge H.J.   Packer/Engineer/Cheltenham   Cpl. 262nd (GWR) Rly Co. R.E. For
   coolness and perseverance in carrying out duties under heavy fire at Reigersburg Chateau
   Spur and R.E. Park (10 & 11/17)

Betteridge W.   Packer/Engineer/Gloucester   Cpl. 262ND (GWR) Rly. Co. R.E.
   (11/17)

Birch J.   Packer/Engineer/Baschurch   L/Cpl 262nd (GWR) Rly Co. R.E. For
   bravery in carrying out work under heavy shell fire. Awarded Bar to MM in October 1917
   (12/17)

Blake A.C.   Traffic Dept Westbourne Park   Sgt MGC. For remaining in position
   with one machine gun covering the withdrawal of the infantry, and when nearly surrounded,
   successfully extricated his gun (8/18)

Blood B.   Bridgeman Wolverhampton   2/Cpl 262nd (GWR) Rly Co. R.E. For
   displaying great bravery under fire (11/17)

Blythe J.A.   Boilersmith Apprent Wolver'h   (6/19)

Bonehill W.   Traffic Dept Henley   Pte. During a bombing raid on 19 June
   he killed nine of the enemy and captured a machine gun (12/18)

Bowley Tom   Shunter Old Oak Common   CSM R. Berks Regt. Also DCM and Bar
   (3 & 12/16)

Brammer J.   Shunter Shrewsbury   Sgt Shropshire L.I. For conspicuous
   bravery which consisted of bombing a snipers post under heavy fire on 16 Aug. 1917

Brewer Ernest A.   Loco Dept Southall   Pte 7th DCLI. For gallantry and devotion to duty during which time he was wounded (12/16)

Brewer T.V.   Weighbridgeman Lawrence Hill   Battery QMS. For restoring to con-
   sciousness two men who had been gassed, and took them to a field hospital. When he
   returned he was instrumental in saving a gun (9/18)

Brooks R.J.   Porter/Traffic/Southam Road   Pte. (3/18)

Brown G.   Rest'ant Car Attendant Paddington   Sgt 13th Middlesex Regt. For coolness
   and resolve during a gas attack, after which he administered salt and water to his comrades
   who would have otherwise been in a critical condition. He also showed great courage when
   in action for the first time at Loos, assisting two wounded officers to safety, who recommended he be rewarded (7/16)

Brush W.J.D.   Draughtsman Bristol   Cpl 262nd (GWR) Rly Co. R.E. For
   coolness and perseverance while carrying out his duties at Reigersburg Chateau and R.E. Park
   (10 &11/17)

Brust C.A.   Stores Porter/Hotel/Paddington   Pte. Awarded for recent action (9/18)

Bubb E.   Porter Birmingham Snow Hill   Gnr RFA. For bravery under heavy shell
   fire (2/18)

Burford A.   Capstanman/Goods/Hockley   Cpl R.E. For rescuing five trucks of
     ammunition under shell fire. Also Bar to MM (8/18)
Carey A.   Wagon Painter/L&C/Swindon   L/Cpl. (4/19)
Charge Robert R.   Caller-off/Goods/Paddington   Cpl. 5th Bedfordshire Regt
Cheadle F.J.   Carpenter Wolverhampton   Sgt. S. Staffordshire Regt (1/17)
Chester J.H.   Porter Shrewsbury Joint   A/Sgt. (4/17)
Child F.W.   Tinsmith/Signal/Reading   Sgt. For conspicuous good work on
     16-17 Aug. 1917. During an attack on an enemy position north of St Julien a company of
     another battalion was held up, and Child's platoon was ordered to assist. All senior NCO's and
     officers were casualties, and Child took charge of the platoon and led the men on, enabling
     the position to be rushed. Later he moved his platoon to form a defensive flank
Churchman E.G.   Packer/Engineer/W London Jct   L/Cpl R.E. He volunteered to stay
     behind and blow up a bridge to stop the advancing enemy, of which he was successful (7/18)
Clack R.R.P.   Coppersmith/L&C/Swindon   Cpl. For repairing telephone wires
     under heavy fire (4/19)
Clarke A.   Repairer/Sheet/Worcester   Gnr RFA. For bravely preventing the
     explosion of one of the main ammunition dumps (8/18)
Clifford T.E.   Packer/Engineering/Tysley   Pte. For bravery in the fighting on the
     Somme on 15 Sept. 1916.
Cole William   Fireman/Loco/Watlington   L/Cpl W Surrey Regt. For bravery in
     obtaining information on patrol work between 2 & 19 Feb. 1916
Coleman A.E.   Brass Moulder/L&C/Swindon   Gnr. For repairing telephone wires and
     bringing in a wounded man under heavy fire (4/19)
Coleman T.G.   Clerk/Bristol Goods Station   Bom. For meritorious services in
     keeping the lines of communication. Mentioned in the orders for the day after the Battle of
     Messines
Collins T.   Packer/Keinton Mandeville   For gallantry and devotion to duty at
     Ypres April 1918
Collyer B.F.   Telegraph Linesman/Tysley   Awarded for saving guns (3/19)
Conway Harold   Rest'ant Car Attendant Paddington   2/Lt Indian Army. Awarded on the
     Somme 1 Sept. 1916. Also DCM
Cooke E.V.   District Relief Signalman Wellington   Spr R.E. For gallant conduct and excel-
     lent work done in the field (12/17)
Cooksey A.P.   Office Porter Goods Dept S. Lambeth   L/Cpl. For gallantry during a bombing
     raid. When two sergeants were incapacitated he took charge of the platoon, and captured a
     machine gun (4 & 6/19)
Cooper S.A.   Checker Traffic Dept Torre   (7/19)
Cotton W.G.   Carman Goods Dept Leeds   (6/19)
Crouch E.L.   Clerk DGMO Paddington   (7/19)
Culling Ernest Frank 'R' Shop Swindon Works   L/Cpl 565th (Wilts) A.T.C. R.E.
     Awarded in 1918
Darville Tom   Porter Draycott   (8/16)
Davies Hugh   Packer Engineering Dept Crumlin   Gnr RFA. (9/17)
Davis H.J.   Wagon Riveter Worcester   Gnr. For extinguishing fire and saving
     two guns (12/18 & 1/19)
Davis W.C.   Audit Office Paddington   L/Cpl RAMC. For gallant conduct
     during an attack near Ginchy on 19-20 Sept. (11/16)

Day E.J.   Ass. Examiner/Loco/Swindon   (6/19)

Dovaston S.   Gas Fitter/Engineer/Wolverhampton Spr R.E. For duty on 16 April when he
   shot an entire machine-gun crew and silenced it (6/19)

Draper A.E.   Packer Engineering Dept Bewdley   (6/19)

Duke C.H.   R/Laying Ganger/Engineer/St Blazey Sgt 262nd (GWR) Rly Co. R.E. For gallantry under fire (12/17)

Duke E.W.   GWR Concrete Works Taunton   Spr. R.E. (4/18)

Dunn A.   Relaying Labour Engineer Dept Truro Sgt. (6/19)

Dunstone E.J.   Clerk Stationmaster's Off. Paddington Sgt County of London Regt. For gallantry during a night attack at St Julien when seventeen men of his company were disabled by
   heavy shell fire – he was wounded later (12/17)

Dymock George   Packer Engineering W. London Jct. L/Cpl R.E. (12/17)

East S.W.   Porter Traffic Dept Oxford   Pte RAMC. For brining in wounded
   under very heavy shell fire (8/17)

Edwards C.M.   Parcel Porter Moretonhampsted   Sgt. For bravery on the field during the
   Battle of Cambrai on 27 Nov. 1917

Edwards F.J.   Apprentice Loco Dept Stafford Road (6/19)

Edwards H.   Slip Ganger Engineering Reading   Spr R.E. For gallantry and devotion to
   duty at Salonika (11/18)

Eggleton J.   Engine Cleaner Loco Dept Southall Spr R.E. For keeping up communications by signalling with hand lamps to aeroplanes, and repairing lines under heavy fire (4/19)

Elson E.F.   Lad Clerk Goods Dept Bristol   Cpl RFA (1/18)

Enock H.G.H.   Porter Traffic Dept Cardiff

Evans H.   Shunter Traffic Dept Neath   Sgt. For holding a sap against three
   German attacks on the Somme 3 Sept. 1916

Evans H.S.W.   Porter Goods Dept Herford   L/Cpl. For carrying messages under
   heavy fire at Khewilfch (10/18)

Ferris James   Wharfinger Traffic Dept Bullo Pill Pte Gloucester Regt (1/17)

File E.   Clerk Goods Dept Southall   Pte Seaforth Highlanders. For carrying
   despatches under heavy shell fire on 16 Nov. 1916, and for gallantry displayed between then
   and 19 Nov.

Fisher Thomas F.   Apprent. Swindon Works   Dvr RFA. For bringing in a wounded
   man from No Mans Land under fire

Ford A.B.   Platform Attendant Billacombe   L/Cpl. R.E. (3/18)

Ferguson J.   Porter Traffic Dept Kidderminster Cpl. Awarded for good work performed in France during March & April 1918

Gale B.H.   Carman Hockley Goods   Pte. For saving an officer's life and a
   gun team in Belgium April 1917

Gaut H.G.W.   Clerk DSO Bristol   Sgt. (1/19)

Glass R.H.   Apprentice Fitter Loco Dept Swindon Driver. Awarded for rendering assistance to officers and men under great difficulties and danger (4/19)

Goddard Henry C.   Fitter Mate Signal Dept Reading   (12/17)

Godwin H.A.   Gasfitter Engineering Dept Reading Trumpeter Berkshire Yeo. For carrying
   a wounded comrade to safety under heavy fire (6/18)

Gray C.C.   Goods Dept Oxford   L/Cpl. For gallantry in attempting to
   establish telephone communication in the front line at Bapaume-St Quentin while under continuous shell fire in Aug. 1917

Gray W.　　　　　　Porter Traffic Dept Patney & Chirton (7/19)

Greening C.T.　　　Leading Relaying Labourer G'cester　Sgt 262nd (GWR) Rly Co. R.E. For coolness and perseverance while carrying out his duties under heavy shell fire at the Ypres Gun Spur (11/17)

Griffiths H.T.　　　Porter Ashperton Station　　　　　2/Cpl. (8/18)

Gubbins Jessie　　　Grinder L&C Swindon　　　　　　CQMS 7TH Ox 7 Bucks L.I

Hallwell E.　　　　Incandescent Lineman Worcester　　Sgt Artillery. For high qualities displayed in a dangerous situation while in command of a gun on an armoured train (1/19)

Hammacott Wilfred　Labourer Loco Dept Newton Abbot　Pte Wiltshire Regt. For gallantry in 1917; awarded Bar on 15 April 1918 for carrying messages under heavy shell fire, and though wounded and 'blown up' by a shell he was successful in his mission. Taken prisoner Aug. 1918

Hancock J.　　　　Slipper Boy Stourbridge　　　　　L/Cpl. For capturing a German machine gun together with its crew at Messines Ridge

Hanks Joseph L.　　Telegraph Lineman Carmarthen　　Sgt R.E. For bravery when he was in charge of a party laying telephone wires to their new HQ and another place, at great personal risk under heavy barrage fire. Although wounded he worked to the point of exhaustion, returning only when safe communication had been established (3/18)

Harper William T.　Lifters Mate Wormwood Scrubs　　Sgt. 1/3rd London Regiment

Harrison Edward　　Bricklayer/Engineer/Birmingham　　Sgt. S. Staffordshire Regt (1/18)

Harry Howard　　　Plumber's Mate/Old Oak Common　　Pte R. Berks Regt. For meritorious service in action (6/17)

Hayward J.H.A.　　District Relief Porter Birmingham　Sgt R.E. (Att. Guards Div). For bravery at Ypres April 1916 – badly wounded in June

Howard W.B. or W.E.　Dist. Lampman/Traffic/Wrexham　　Pte. For bravery when acting as a despatch runner (1/19)

Head A.J.　　　　　Porter Traffic Dept Southall　　　Pte. For frequently carrying messages under heavy fire, and accompanying his officer into dangerous positions (12/18)

Henken A.W.　　　Timber Inspector/Creostote/Hayes　Awarded for continuous repair of wires under heavy fire (9/18)

Higgs G.　　　　　Deal Porter Wagon & Timber S'don　2/Cpl R.E. For gallant conduct and devotion to duty on 24-25 Sept. 1916 during the Battle of Thiepval

Hill A.A.　　　　　Fireman Loco Dept Southall　　　　Spr R.E. (7/17)

Holdway H.　　　　Packer Engineering Dept Twerton　　Dvr RHA. For an act of conspicuous bravery (4/17)

Holmes Jeremiah　　Vanguard South Lambeth　　　　L/Cpl MGC. On 31 July 1916 he worked his gun after the remainder of his gun team had been placed Hors de Combat, he held the position, and saved the situation when hard-pressed on every side (3/18)

Hubbard C.　　　　R/Labourer/ Engineering/Taunton　　Sgt. For conspicuous bravery on 7 & 8 June (10/17)

Huddison A.E.　　　Engine Cleaner Newton Abbot　　　RFA. (6/16)

Hudson W.　　　　Booking Clerk Abertillery　　　　(6/19)

Hughes E.　　　　Packer Engineering Clee Hill Ludlow　Spr R.E. Awarded for demolition work in recent operations (7/18)

Hughes Edgar Wallace　Packer Engineering Dept Hanwell　Cpl. 4th City of London Regt

Hughes H.　　　　Toolman Engineering Dept Wrexham　Sgt. For saving a mined bridge at Ath Belgium, which the enemy were attempting to blow up (4/19)

Humphrey John C.   Solicitors' Office Paddington   L/Cpl HAC. For gallantry in an attack in which he was cut off and surrounded for four days, without food or water. This award was made immediately (7/17)

Instone F.C.   Porter Traffic Dept Swindon   Pte. For bravery at Messines Ridge March 1918

Irwin Horace C.   Staff of Chief Accountant   2/Lt Argyll & Sutherlands, later with the Seaforths. Awarded for services at Beaumont Hamel Nov. 1916

Joint R.   Packer Engineering Dept Brent   Cpl 262nd (GWR) Rly Co. R.E. For rescuing a wounded man under shell fire (11/17)

Jones F.G.   Clerk Goods Dept Leamington   Pte. For services during a night bombing expedition into enemy trenches (10/17)

Jones J.   Rail Motor Conductor Pontypool Rd   Sgt. For bravery at Beaumont Hamel in taking charge of a platoon after its officer was put out of action, and for making use of a machine gun (12/17)

Jones J.   Porter Goods Dept Hockley   Rifm. For gallantry. Taken prisoner March 1918 (2 & 6/19)

Jones S.H.   Porter Traffic Dept Albrighton   Pte. During an advance under heavy fire an officer was seriously wounded near the German line. Jones fought his way to the spot, captured three Germans, killed a number with grenades, rendered first aid to the officer, and made the prisoners help to take him to a place of safety (11/17)

Johnson B.F.   Lad Porter Goods Halesowen   Cpl DCLI (12/16 & 1/17)

Kettle W.   Lampman Traffic Dept Birmingham   Cpl RAMC. For bravery in Palestine (3/18)

Kew D.   Engineering Dept Reading   2/Lt Hertfordshire Regt. Awarded Aug. 1917. Also MC and DCM

King Albert   Clerk SOL Office   Cpl Div Signal Co. R.E. For conduct and bravery on 20 May when he was wounded in the right shoulder and arm by shrapnel (8/17)

Lang J.F.   Apprentice C&W Dept Swindon   Pte Wiltshire Regt. For carrying messages and doing other useful work during an advance on 29 Sept. (4/18)

Lanham W.   Fitter Electrical Dept Fishguard   Cpl. Awarded Sept. 1918. Also MSM

Lawrence Sydney J.   Packer Engineering Dept Ruislip   Spr. 23rd Div. Signal Co. R.E.

Lee F.   Labourer/Signal (Telegraph)/Newport   Cpl Welsh Regt. For bombing enemy trenches and obtaining valuable information. Also Russian Order (9/19)

Lewis Herbert   Electrical Fitter Swindon   Sgt. 15th Signal Co. R.E.

Leybourne A.S.   Police Detective Paddington   L/Cpl Mobile Police. He successfully negotiated traffic through an exposed post while being bombarded by enemy aircraft and gas shells (2/18)

Lockyear W.G.   Time & Storekeeper Old Oak C'mn   Pte Middlesex Regt. For extraordinary coolness while carrying messages under heavy shell fire (6/18)

Locock A.   Packer Engineer Dept Old Oak C'mn   Sgt R.E. Awarded 9 Sept. for bravery on the Somme when with a party of ten men sent to an advance post 200yds in front of the line to build a road block. The block was shelled three times, and he took charge and completed the work when the officer and seven men were casualties (11/17)

Lomax John   Rest'ant Car Attendant Hotels Dept   Sgt. For bravery at Hessian Wood Sept. 1917

Lyddon A.J.   District Lampman Traffic Llantrisant   (7/19)

Marsh A.G.   Porter Traffic Dept Weymouth   Bom RFA (12/16)

Marsh W.E.   Fitter Loco Dept Swindon   (6/19)

Matthews T.   Chainman Engineer Dept W. Ealing   Cpl. For carrying despatches at Passchendaele Oct. 1917. Five had been killed attempting the same action

McTighe H.G.   Vanguard Paddington Goods   Also awarded Bar to MM (7/19)

Meacham A.G.   SOL Staff   Sgt London Regt. (8/17)

Miller H.T.G.   Clerk DSO Bristol   Cpl Signals R.E. He was in charge of an advanced report centre with no protection against shell fire, and was ordered to remain as long as possible, but leave if shelling became intense, which it did, but he remained for another two hours ensuring continued communications until an alternative line had been laid, when he ordered his men to leave. He remained to disconnect instruments (6/17)

Moody L.W.   Engine Cleaner Old Oak Common   Cpl For gallantry and devotion to duty on 2 April 1917. Also MID

Moore J.   Platelayer Engineering Looe Branch   Cpl R.E. For repairing a railway 'somewhere in France' under heavy shell fire, enabling heavy guns and ammunition to be taken to the firing line (4/18)

Morgan H.L.   Fireman Loco Dept Cardiff   (6/19)

Morgan W.   Clerk Traffic Dept Aberfan   1st Class Air Mechanic. For heroic conduct on 24 Sept. when under heavy shell fire he continued working and intercepting German signals until his instruments were destroyed by a shell (12/17)

Morris Frank E.   Porter Traffic Dept Snow Hill   Pte RAMC. For bravery in carrying a wounded officer from the danger to base under rifle fire (3/18)

Morse Harry Jacob   Clerk Swindon Works   RSM 4th Wiltshire Regt. Served in Egypt and India

Mothersole R.   Packer Engineer Dept Acton   2/Cpl. Also MID (3/19)

Mumford J.J.   Crane Lad Porter G'ds Dept Brentford Pte R.Fusiliers. For gallantry and devotion to duty on 26 Sept. (12/16)

Naish H.T.   Clerk DSO Cardiff   Sgt. For gallantry in assisting in organising men, and placing them in positions to resist a counter-attack under heavy shell fire (11/17)

Neate A.   Gas Fitter Engineer Dept Paddington L/Cpl Also awarded Bar to MM (6/19)

New W.G.   Carriage Cleaner Old Oak Common   Pte (11/17)

Newing A.B.   Clerk Chief GMO Paddington   Rifm. For carrying messages in daylight under heavy machine gun and rifle fire. He was the only means of communication, and never failed to deliver his messages (4/19)

Newman C.S.   Signalman Adderbury   Spr R.E. For special work of great value during which he was wounded (10/17)

Nicholas W.R.   Bricklayer Eng'rs' Dept Shrewsbury   Pte Shropshire L.I. For carrying messages of great importance under heavy shell fire (1 & 2/18)

Nodder H.   Draughtsman/Taunton   Cpl R.E. For carrying out successful operations under heavy fire (10/18)

Normansell W.R.   Under Shunter Traffic Dept Cardiff   Spr R.E. For bravery after being wounded in an air raid on 29 May (1/19)

Norton W.J.   Tinsmith Loco Factory Stafford Road For gallant conduct in the Battle of Arras (12/17)

Ollerinshaw W.E.   Messenger Goods Dept Bristol   Pte (3 & 6/19)

Paddock J.H.   Bricklayer Eng'rs' Dept Shrewsbury   Sgt. For gallantry and devotion to duty on the Somme 1916 and Ypres 5-11 Aug. 1917. Later POW

Palmer W.H.   Engineman Loco Dept Newton Abb't RAMC (1/17)

Paul Frederick George Swindon Works — RAMC. Awarded Dec. 1916

Peats W.F. — Fireman Loco Dept Worcester — Cpl. For saving guns (12/18)

Perham J.K. — Clerk Loco Dept Swindon — Bom. For repairing telephone wires under heavy fire (12/18)

Perks J.H. — Carpenter Engineer Dept Shrewsbury Spr. R.E. (12/16)

Phillips E. — R/Labourer/Engineer/Newton Abbot — L/Cpl R.E. For bravery at the Battle of Loos when he, with two others, was the first to be out of the trench to cut the barbed wire for the bayonet charge. Also MID

Phillips T. — Checker Traffic Dept Milford Haven — Gnr Siege Bty RGA. For laying a cable in an exposed position at night ready for operation in the morning, and repairing it on three occasions under shellfire (8/17)

Pickering L. — Canal Labourer Kings Norton — Pte. Awarded for fine behaviour (8/18)

Piff William Harold — Painter L&C Swindon — Pte. R.E. (12/17)

Pook F. — Passenger Guard Launceston — (9/19)

Powell W.F. — Clerk Goods Dept Bristol — Gnr 48th Midland Div. 1st Gloucester Bty. Also MID (6/19)

Powell W.T. — R'rant Waiter/Birmingham Snow H. — Sgt KRRC. For good work done when a party captured eight German officers and men (7/17)

Price George — Rail Motor Conductor Garnant — Sgt Shropshire L.I. For exceptional bravery when in charge of a bombing party in France (6/17)

Pugh H.M. — Labourer Sheet Dept Gloucester — Pte 8th Gloucester Regt. For successfully going out under fire and securing important despatches. Also DCM and CDG (11/16)

Queeney J. — Carman Goods Dept W'hampton — Pte 2nd Worcestershire Regt. On 13 July, when acting as an officers servant, he volunteered to carry messages from the firing line to the C.O. under heavy rifle and shell fire. Although wounded he got the messages through, and brought in a wounded officer from in front of the German front line (2/17)

Randles W.T. — Clerk Goods Dept Saltney — Sgt R.E. (later Lt, then RFC). For keeping up the lines of communication under heavy bombardment and gas on the Bulgarian Front. He was gassed (4/18)

Reed S.R. — Clerk Traffic Dept Dulverton — Also Bar to MM (6/19)

Reeves F.L. — Packer Engineer Dept Worcester — L/Cpl 262nd (GWR) Rly Co. R.E. For bravery under heavy shellfire (1 & 4/18)

Richards H. — Packer Engineer Dept Reading — (12/19)

Richardson A.W. — Porter Oxford Station — Gnr RGA– brother of W.F. Richardson (1/18)

Richardson E.J. — Clerk L&C Newton Abbot — RAMC. Also Bar to MM (1 & 12/17)

Richardson W. — Packer Engineer Dept Newport — Sgt Monmouthshire Regt (M.G. Section) (8/17)

Richardson William F. Apprentice Loco Works Swindon — Spr R.E. - brother of A.W. Richardson (6/18)

Roberts F. — Packer Engineer Dept Cressage — Pte Gallantry in carrying messages under shell fire (4/19)

Roberts Leonard — Parcel Clerk Leominster — Cpl. Shropshire L.I. Heroism displayed 23 July 1916

Roberts T. — Carman Traffic Oswestry — Sgt Shropshire L.I. While in a support trench the Germans made an overwhelming violent attack. Roberts brought up his platoon to reinforce the line, and succeeded without losing a man (2/18)

Robbins J.T.   Signal Porter Traffic Charlbury   (6/19)

Rogers W.   Ticket Collector Craven Arms   L/Cpl Cheshire Regt. For distinguished
conduct last August, when his officer was wounded he took charge of a number of men and
carried on under a severe bombardment (2/18)

Rogers Walter Ed.   Fireman Loco Dept Shrewsbury   Sgt. 2/1ST Shropshire Brigade RHA

Rotherham W.   Porter Acocks Green   Sgt. During an enemy bombardment
he voluntarily went out to repair telephone wires under heavy fire, and remained on duty in a
house that was struck several times by shells. Also CDG & MID (7/17)

Rouse A.W.   Wagon Builder Worcester   Sgt RFA. On Easter Sunday 1916 his
battery was under fire and a shell entered the gun pit setting it, and the shell dump, on fire. He
was unsuccessful in extinguishing it with sandbags, but obtained some water from a shell hole
and put the fire out. He also helped to dig out six men buried in the next pit, who survived.

Rudd Ernest Henry J. Clerk Goods Dept Southall   L/Sgt. 1/8th Middlesex Regt. Also MID

Russell J.C.   Booking Clerk Brixham   Pte. For repeatedly carrying messages
through an intense barrage at Vaux Vreaucourt, maintaining communications at a critical
period (12/18)

Sargent W.J.   Porter Traffic Dept Grange Court   Pte. Gloucestershire Regt. (2/17)

Sim Vincent D.   Clerk Hotels Dept Paddington   Pte R. Fusiliers. For gallantry and devotion to duty at Houthulst Forest 13 Nov. Also awarded 'A' Parchment

Smart A.   Packer Engineer Dept Cranmore   2/Cpl. For gallantry on the Western
Front (8/18)

Smart G.C.   Sheet Repairer Gloucester Docks   Sgt. For consistent skill in leadership
(2/19)

Smith A.G.   Relaying Labourer Cholsey   QMS. For gallantry and devotion to
duty in France (9/18)

Smith Charles Ed.   Creosoter Engineer Dept Hayes   Sgt RAMC. For gallant conduct and
devotion to duty on 7 June (11/17)

Spurlock E.P.   L&C Swindon   Sgt. Wessex Engineers (9/17)

Staples Jabez Hale   Frame Builder L&C Swindon   Able Seaman Hood Bn RN. For putting
an enemy machine gun out of action (1/19)

Stone J.   Leading Packer Norton Fitzwarren   For work under heavy fire on 6 Oct.
1917

Stott J.A.   Clerk CAO Paddington   L/cpl. For conspicuous gallantry in
hand-to-hand fighting at the Battle of Gazs (2/18)

Stubbs S.   Porter Madeley Station   L/Cpl. For devotion to duty 9-10 April
1918

Sweet R.H.   Signal Dept Newport   Pte. For bravery – promoted to sergeant (12/16)

Symons Leslie   Clerk GMO Paddington   Sgt KRRC. For dash and determination
displayed during a patrol encounter, and assisted in bringing in a wounded man. Also DCM
(10/18 & 2/19)

Tate Basil   Weighbridgeman Cradley Heath   Pte. (9/18)

Taylor C.   Timekeeper Goods Wolverhampton   CSM (9/18)

Taylor W.   Head Shunter Old Oak Common   Spr R.E. For saving an ammunition
train on fire by throwing out lighted charge boxes, and stopping until the last at a depot with
the enemy approaching. Also staying with wounded and helping them to get away for treatment after a shell had fallen amongst a working party killing 11 and wounding 14 (7/18)

Thatcher Alfred   Packer Engineer West London Jtn   Spr R.E. For gallantry and devotion to
    duty in June (9/17)

Thornhill W.   Porter Guard Windsor   L/Cpl. (2/19)

Trew Reginald E.   Wagon Repairer L&C Panteg   Cpl 2nd Monmouthshire Regt. For
    conspicuous bravery in 1917

Tyler G.H.   Loco Fireman Stourbridge   Cpl. For saving several wagons of
    ammunition on a train set on fire by enemy action (12/18)

Vaughan J.   Packer Engineer Dept Berwyn   Cpl R.E. Railway Troops. For rescuing a
    wounded man under heavy shellfire (12/17)

Vickery A.S.   Slip Labourer Engineer Dept Taunton Bom. For saving his gun under heavy
    shellfire (2/19)

Waite Norman G.   Machinist Signal Dept Reading   (12/17)

Walker H.   Gas Engine Driver L&C Swindon   Sgt MGC. Also awarded DCM and Bar
    to MM (1/19)

Wardell L.E.   Goods Clerk Traffic Dept Slough   (7/19)

Warfield J.E.V.   Carman Goods Dept Bristol   Dvr RFA. The Germans had located
    British horse lines and began shelling them. Warfield released as many horses as possible, and
    returned them after shelling had stopped for an hour, but shelling was renewed with fresh vigour,
    and he went back a second time and brought the horses out of the danger zone (2 & 3/17)

Warren J.S.   Road Motor Conductor Penzance   2/Cpl. R.E. (7/18)

Warren J.S.   Porter Traffic Dept Saltash   2/Cpl. (8/18)

Way Walter   Worker GWR Concrete Wks Taunton Spr. R.E. (4/18)

Weaving E.   Leading Packer Engineer Gloucester   Cpl 8th Gloucester Regt. For bravery
    in the field (wounded in action) age 33 (10/16)

Westlake R.E.   Checker Goods Dept Penzance   Battery QMS. For clearing a blocked
    road of various transports under heavy shell fire, and saving many casualties (10/18)

Wheeler W.C.   Packer Engineer Dept. Reading   Spr R.E. For work near Ypres under
    heavy shell fire on 29 Aug. 1917

Whelan J.   Porter Goods Dept Hockley   Cpl. For delivering messages under
    heavy rifle and machine-gun fire. Also 'A' Parchment (2/19)

Williams Henry   Stower Goods Dept Paddington   Sgt Grenadier Guards. Aged 36. Also
    DCM (12/16)

Williams W.R.   Parcel Vanman Traffic Dept Liverpool Motor Driver. At St Julien on 5 Sept.
    1917, with a few others, seeing that stretcher-bearers were overtaxed, drove out with motor
    ambulances and brought in wounded

Williamson A.A.   Labourer Loco Dept. W'hampton   (1/1920)

Winsborrow J.   Carpenter L&C Newton Abbot   Sgt. (4/19)

Wintle F.E.   Clerk Sheet Dept. Worcester   Sgt Worcester Regt. For distinguished
    action at the Battle of St Quentin (6/18)

Wood A.J.   Machinist Loco Dept. Worcester   (6/18)

Woodman Edwin G. Checker Resolven Station   Pte Welsh Regt. During a raid on
    enemy trenches on the night 18-19 May 1917, he displayed cool contempt throughout, and
    did excellent work with bombs killing several of the enemy. He had previously been wounded,
    returning to the front in Jan. 1917

Worrall W.   Gateman Traffic Stratford-u-Avon   (6/19)

Yeo J.W.   Clerk Goods Dept. Hayes   Spr R.E. For meritorious conduct on 25
    Sept. (4/18)

MERITORIOUS SERVICE MEDAL

Fifty-nine awarded

Ault F.H.	Coach-body Maker Swindon	(9/19)
Bell C.F.	Clerk CEO Paddington	(7/19)
Bevan T.G.	T'graph Linesman Signal Dept C'diff	L/Cpl. For keeping communications open between Jan. and June 1916 at Bully
Burrows F.G.	Shunter Traffic Dept Grange Court	Sgt. For organising ability and great gallantry during attacks at Ypres in the autumn of 1917, which contributed to his battalions success
Cliff C.W.	Clerk DEO Wolverhampton	QMS ASC (2/18)
Crutchley H.	Number Taker Goods Dept Bilston	Sgt. For valuable services rendered in France (9/18)
Fletcher N.J.	Clerk Cheltenham (Malvern Road)	(12/19)
Godfrey A.G.	Booking Office Paddington	Also Medaille d'Honneur (10/1920)
Green G.	Carriage Examiner Landore	(9/19)
Greenfield G.H.	Clerk DSO Paddington	For valuable services rendered in France (10/18)
John R.	Div. Loco. Superintendant Off. Neath	(12/19)
Lane A.	Detective Inspector Paddington	(7/19)
Lanham W.	Fitter's Mate Electrical Dept Fishg'd	Cpl. For services in France, awarded 17 June 1918. Also MM
Leighfield W.C.	Machineman L&C Swindon	Also MM (9/19)
Manners R.	Carpenter Engineer Dept Reading	(6/19)
Martin L.P.	Clerk Goods Dept Bikenhead	(6/19)
Owen T.W.	Signalman Wrexham	(7/19)
Peachey H.O.	Clerk Goods Dept Covent Garden	QMS RFA. Awarded by the King for valuable service in the war (12/16)
Perkins J.F.	Clerk Market Drayton	Staff Sgt. Also twice MID (12/19)
Pugh C.T.	Permanent-Way Insp'tor Shrewsbury	Sgt Rly Troops R.E. For work on the Western Front (4/19)
Rodway Herbert J.	Packer Engineering Malvern Link	Sgt. 'B' Company 13th Glos Regt
Savage A.D.	Clerk Goods Dept Taunton	(11/19)
Scott G.G.	Clerk DEO Gloucester	(7/19)
Shorney F.W.	Clerk L&C Bristol	(3/19)
Smith P.A.	Clerk DSO Cardiff	Sgt-Maj. For constant devotion to duty during the German Advance March-May 1918, and for promptitude in saving and removing various supply dumps (3/19)
Squires A.J.	Leading R/Labourer Truro	Sgt 116th (GWR) Rly Co. R.E. (12/180
Stedman W.B.	Architect's Assistant CEO	Sgt-Maj. For work during the recent German attacks (9/18)
Strain C.G.	Stower Goods Dept Hockley	(11/19)
Street F.R.	Messenger Perm-way Dept Reading	(4/1920)
Warner P.W.	Clerk Chief Engineer's Off. Padd'ton	(7/19)
Wigmore F.G.	Rd Motor C'ductor Plym'th Millbay	For valuable services rendered in France & Flanders (4/19)
Williams F.W.	Clerk Goods Dept Hockley	(11/19)
Woolley G.A.	Clerk DGMO Shrewsbury	(3/19)

ALBERT MEDAL 1ST CLASS
One awarded

Broadhurst G. Packer Engineering Portskewett L/Cpl 10th SWB. On 10 Feb. while men were being instructed in bombing, one of them dropped a live bomb, picked it up and in his excitement threw it into the corner of the room where the other men were. Broadhurst immediately placed his foot on the bomb, hoping to minimise the effect of the explosion. He was severely wounded in both feet, but his brave action safeguarded his comrades (8/18)

GINCHY DIAMOND
One awarded

Burge E.E. Painter Swindon Sgt. Royal Dublin Fusiliers. Also MID

'A' PARCHMENT
Three awarded

Lamb H.J. Pte. For conspicuous bravery at Moyenville Aug. 1918

Sim Vincent Clerk Hotels Dept Paddington Pte R. Fusiliers. Awarded in Nov. 1916 for bravery at Beaumont Hamel. Second parchment awarded for gallantry at Houthulst Forest on 13 Nov. 1917. Also awarded MM

Whelan J. Porter Goods Dept Hockley Cpl. Also MM (2/19)

MEDAILLE MILITAIRE
Three awarded

Marshall W.E. Porter Goods Dept Cheltenham Pte. For carrying wounded under heavy fire at High Wood, Somme 9 Sept. 1916

Rodda Henry C. CMEO Swindon 565th (Wilts) ATC R.E. Awarded on 6 Nov. 1915 for valuable work carried out on a survey round Brigade HQ near Verbrandenmolen. Also MC

CROIX DE GUERRE (FRENCH, BELGIAN AND ITALIAN)
Twenty-three awarded

Cotton W.G. Porter Hockley Goods Sgt. For bravery at Albert on 25 Sept. 1915

Dalison Charles B. Draughtsman L&C Dept Maj. RNAS./RAF. Also awarded palms to medal (4/19) Dalison remained in the RAF. (Group Captain in 1939)

Gale B.H. Porter Goods Dept. Hockley (6/19)

Hurford R.F. Booking Clerk Paignton Belgian CDG. For distinguished service in the field (3/19)

Lewis T.A.	Erector Loco Dept Swindon	(6/19)
Mills P.M.	Electrical Engineers Staff	CSM London Regt. Awarded by the

French government for good work in the line (6/18)

Pardoe G.	R/Labourer/Engineering/Ludlow	(6/19)
Pugh H.M.	Labourer Sheet Dept Gloucester	Pte 8th Gloucester Regt. Also MM &

DCM (3/17)

Rambridge C.	Machineman L&C Swindon	(9/19)
Read A.E.	Audit Off. Clerk Paddington	(6/19)
Rotherham W.	Porter Acocks Green Station	Sgt. Also MM and MID (7/17)
Short J.H.	Greaser GWR ship SS *Andrew*	Cpl. (2/19)
Spencer E.	Clerk Ruabon	Flt-Sgt. He rescued two soldiers and

carried them to a dressing station where he himself was overcome by gas (4/19)

Teague Edgar Vivers Lad Clerk Goods Dept Paddington   Sgt. 12th Durham L.I.

Thomas C.F.   Clerk DGMO Shrewsbury   Sgt. For unusual energy and much courage during the severe bombardments during the retreat at the end of March 1918. By his personal work in connection with the French, he assured the working of the Achiet-le-Grand unit until the evacuation of all material.

Thomas Frank G.   Telephone Operator Swansea   Signaller. For bravery and devotion to duty in Palestine. Advancing with the infantry as a signaller, with an observation officer, the detachment captured a hill, but the enemy forced the infantry to retire, but Thomas and observation officer stuck to the hill, from which the could direct a barrage, which enabled the position to be recaptured (9/18)

Tomkiss A.   R/Labourer Engineering Shrewsbury Belgian CDG (10/19)

SERBIAN MEDAL
Three awarded

Evans L.	Fireman Loco Dept Southall	Spr R.E. For devotion to duty (3/17)
Jenks H.G.	Shipper Goods Dept Birkenhead	Sgt. For continuous devotion to duty

(4/18)

RUSSIAN ORDER OF ST GEORGE
One awarded

Lee F.   Telegraph Section Signal Dept Newport   Cpl Welsh Regt. Also MM

(8/17)

RUSSIAN ORDER OF ST ANNE (WITH SWORDS)
One awarded

Knapp G.E.   Locomotive Dept Swindon   Capt. 565th (Wilts) Army Troops Co.

R.E. Also MID

FRENCH MEDAILLE D'HONNEUR
Four awarded

Godfrey A.G.	Booking Office Paddington	Also awarded MSM (10/1920)
Lloyd L.V.	Clerk Goods Dept Shrewsbury	Bom. For bravery (3/19)

GREEK MILITARY CROSS
One awarded

Tomkins A.H.	Engineman Loco Dept Neath	(9/19)

MEDAILLE BARBATIE DI CREDIUTA (RUMANIAN)
One awarded

Trickey J.P.	Passenger Shunter/Newton Abbot	(6/19)

BELGIAN ORDER OF THE CROWN

Rayner-Smith C.   Superintendent of the line office   Awarded Gold order from the King of Belgium for services in connection with transportation of Belgians in England during the war.

Webb E.H.   Chief Booking Clerk Kensington   Awarded Silver Order for his services in connection with the conveyance of Belgians in this country while he was stationmaster at West Brompton (9/1920)

MEDIALLE DU ROI ALBERT

Hearne W.   SOL Office   Awarded by the King of Belgium for services rendered to the Belgian cause (8/1920)

MENTIONED IN DESPATCHES
Ninety-five mentioned in despatches

Bell C.F.   Clerk CEO Paddington   (12/19)

Bennett W.J.   Tracer DEO Neath   Lt R.F.A. Twice mentioned in Sir Douglas Haig's Despatches for distinguished service in June 1917 and Jan. 1918. Also MC

Birch A.G.   L/Packer Engineer. Herford Barton   2/Cpl 116th (GWR) Rly Co. R.E. Mentioned in despatch of 11 June (11/18)

Blick E.E.   Surveyor & D'ghtsman Shrewsbury   Mentioned in Gen. Dir. G.F. Milnes despatches of 1 Jan. 1918 for distinguished service

Bowden H.   L/Packer Engineering Menheniot   Cpl (A/Sgt) 116th (GWR) Rly Co. R.E. Mentioned in despatch of 11 June (11/18)

Bowler Frederick J.   Goods Shunter Reading   Cpl 1st Loyal N. Lancs Regt. On 10

Sept. 1914 at the Battle of Marne, he rescued Lt Knight, and carried him 400yds across open and shell-swept country, and was subjected to heavy rifle fire. For this he was mentioned in one of the first despatches of Sir John French

Brown C.R. — Shunter Brynamman — Mentioned in Haig's despatches Nov. 1917

Burge E.E. — Painter Swindon — Sgt R. Dublin Fus. Mentioned for services at Cambrai. Also Ginchy Diamond

Carus-Wilson Trevor CEO Paddington — Lt-Col. 5th DCLI. Also awarded D.S.O.

Chamberlain G. — Carman Oxford (Goods) — Cpl Ox & Bucks L.I. He rescued a comrade in the field under fire (promoted to Sgt) (6/15)

Cliff Cyril W. — Clerk DEO Wolverhampton — Staff QMS ASC (8/17)

Cookson Walter J. Solicitors Office Paddington — Temp. Lt R.E. Mentioned twice. Also MC (2 & 7/17)

Cox W.S. — Clerk Traffic Dept Avonmouth — L/Cpl. For good work performed while attached to the headquarters staff at Salonika (9/16)

Davey W. — Clerk Goods Bilston — Sgt. For services rendered with the British Forces at Salonika (1/19)

Dawson J. — Loco Swindon — Lt 565th (Wilts) ATC R.E. Mentioned on 31 Dec. 1915. Also MC

Durrant F.W. — Clerk Goods Shrewsbury — (9/19)

Edwards D. — Mason Engineering Clynderwen — (7/19)

Fletcher N.J. — Chief Parcel Clerk Cheltenham S'tion Sgt. Mentioned by Commander-in-Chief in Salonika (3/18)

Forbes P.H. — CAO Paddington — Sgt R.E. Rly Transport Establishment (Military Forwarding Section) at G.H.Q. (2/16)

Ford G.W.R. — Piecework Checker L&C Swindon — Sgt 5th Wiltshire Regt. Also DCM (4/16)

Gage A.E. — Telegraph Linesman Signal Acton — Spr 32nd Motor Airline Section R.E. For conspicuous gallantry at Vlamertinghe. Also DCM (4/16)

Gubbins J. — Grinder No.13 Shop Swindon — Sgt Ox & Bucks L.I. For taking command of a platoon after the officer had been wounded, and although wounded himself, he led the platoon forward to the final assault (5/17)

Greenaway F. — GMO — CSM W. Kent Regt. Also DCM (7/17)

Griffiths P. — Signalman Ketley — (10/19)

Hambley D.S.W. — Clerk Audit Paddington — (7/19)

Huntley John Henry Boilersmiths Helper Swindon Works Gnr 'C' Bty R.F.A. Also DSM (3/17)

Jackson E.W. — Audit Office Paddington — Regt QMS (7/16)

James H.C. — Clerk DEO Gloucester — A/Bty QMS. Mentioned in Haig's despatch 8 Nov. (2/19)

Jarrett W.G. — Chief Booking Clerk Swansea — (6/19)

Jones H.M. — DSO Swansea — 2/Lt. Mentioned in despatch by Sir Douglas Haig (11/17)

Judd C.J. — Coppersmith Motor Dept Slough — Sgt-Maj RAMC. Mentioned in a despatch by Gen. Sir E.H. Allenby (11/18)

Knapp G.E. — Loco Swindon — Lt 565th (Wilts) ATC R.E. Mentioned on 31 Dec. 1915 Also Russian Award

Le Cheminant A.E. CGMO — RSM. Mentioned in despatch by Secretary of State (3/19)

Mattlingly E.J.   GMO   Cpl. Mentioned in Haig's despatch of
    30 April – later promoted to Sgt (9/16)
May D.G.   Clerk Stores Swindon   Lt. Mentioned in Haig's despatch of 8
    Nov. 1918
Mildmay The Hon. F.B. GWR Director   Lt-Col. (7/16)
Moody L.W.   Engine Cleaner Loco Old Oak C'on Cpl. Mentioned on 25 Oct. 1915 for
    services as a stretcher-bearer. Also MM
Morris J.T.   Clerk CEO   (12/19)
Mothersole R.   Packer Engineering Acton   2/Cpl. Twice mentioned and awarded
    MM (3/19)
Perkins J.F.   Clerk Market Drayton   Staff Sgt. Twice mentioned and
    awarded MSM (2/19)
Phillips E.   R/Labourer E'neer Newton Abbot   L/Cpl R.E. Sir John French's despatch
    of 3 Jan. 1916 and Haig's in August. Also awarded MM
Powell W.F.   Invoice Typist Goods Bristol   Gnr 48th S. Midland Div. 1st
    Gloucester Bty. For meritorious conduct while connecting wires in the field under fire. Also
    awarded MM (3/16)
Pritchard G.   Clerk Traffic Ruabon   L/Cpl 53rd Rly Co. R.E. Egyptian
    Expeditionary Force. Specially mentioned by Sir Archibald Murray's despatch 1 June-30 Sept.
    1916
Rendell Henry T.   Motor Car Dept. Slough   Capt. ASC (Mechanical Transport
    Section). Mentioned in June 1916 for gallant and distinguished conduct. Also awarded D.S.O.
Richens W. (aka W. Styles)Shed Man Loco Slough   Pte RAMC. For meritorious conduct
    on 14 Sept. 1914 at Pont Arcy when, under heavy fire, he and L/Cpl Jones brought in Sgt
    Stansfield (49th Bty R.F.A.) who was dangerously wounded
Robinson A.J.   Clerk Cholsey Station   Capt.Ox. & Bucks L.I. – Haig's des-
    patch 7 Nov. 1917
Robinson P.G.   Assistant Hotels Paddington   (10/19)
Roper A.W.   Assist. Examiner L&C Swindon   (9/19)
Rotherham W.   Porter Acocks Green Station   Sgt. Mentioned for bravery during the
    Battle of Neuve Chapelle. Also MM and CDG (7/17)
Roxbee E.C.   Clerk Salisbury Station   (10/19)
Rudd Ernest H.J.   Clerk Goods Southall   Cpl 1/8th Middlesex Regt. He was in
    charge of a wiring party, and knowing the importance of his work, kept his party at it during
    shelling and firing, and once completed his own section he started on another. He carried a
    badly wounded man to the support trench that was being dug, then carried on with his wire
    work in front of the advance trench. His coolness and example had a very good effect on his
    men. Also MM (8/18)
Sargent S.A.   Clerk GMO   (10/19)
Simpkins W.J.   Clerk Goods Gloucester   (10/19)
Staple E.   Carpenter Engineers Taunton   (7/19)
Steane F.   Secretary's Office   Lt. (A/Capt) Sir E.H. Allenby's despatch
    for service with the Egyptian Expeditionary Force (3/19)
Sheppard Ashley F. C. Pilot Guard Traffic Bristol W. Depot CSM 1st Wiltshire Regt.
Tomkins A.H.   Engineman Loco Neath   (9/19)
Whitley Henry S.B.   Chief Assistant Neath   Maj. (Officer Commanding) Rly Survey
    and Reconnaissance R.E. Despatch of Nov. 1917 (7/19)

Wilson Cyril Spencer   Ass. Works Manager C&W S'don   Maj. R.E. Twice mentioned and
    awarded MC
Wye C.W.A.   Draughtsman C.E.O. Paddington   (7/19)

COMMENDATIONS – MILITARY AND CIVILIAN

Cook R.A.   Accountants Off. Clerk L&C SwindonL/Cpl ASC. Highly commended by his
    Major-General for snatching from another man an ignited enemy grenade. He threw it into a
    shell hole some 10yds away, saving the mans life at great risk to his own. He was 16 years old
    when he enlisted (2/18)
Day H.G.   Stationmaster Rodwell   Chairman of the joint war committee
    of the British Red Cross and Order of St John brought the name of Mr Day to the notice of the
    Secretary of State for War for valuable services rendered (12/19)
East F.   Signalman Oxford   Named by Secretary of State for War
    for valuable service. He assisted at Oxford Military Hospital for four hour shifts, twice weekly,
    bandaging and attending to patients
Forbes P.H.   Chief Accountants Office
Granby A.C.   Labour/Electrical/Vic & Albert Docks   Pte RAMC. Highly commended by
    his General for bravery in the field. When acting as a stretcher bearer he went forward into
    a shelled area and remained there dressing and sending down the wounded. The report said
    that he undoubtedly saved the lives of many. (11/18)
Haines (no initial)   Fitter Motor Car Workshops Slough   Sgt. Specially recognised for an act
    of gallantry performed on 12 Dec. 1917 at Bethune. When Bethune station and vicinity was
    being bombed by aeroplanes, he behaved with courage and successfully assisted to rescue a
    wounded comrade
Peck G.F.   Staff GWR. Engineers Off. P'gton   Flt-Sgt (promoted to Sgt-Maj). For
    distinguished services (3/17)
Serjent F.J.   Audit Office Clerk Paddington   Cpl. For gallantry and devotion to
    duty. It was ordered that his name be entered in the record of the Irish Division, to which he
    was attached (12/17)
Sim Vincent D.   Clerk Hotels Dept. Paddington   Pte Royal Fusiliers. For bravery on the
    14-15 Nov. 1916. Also MM and A Parchment
Smith W.H.   District GWR Agent Guernsey   For valuable services rendered on
    Guernsey
Speller W.J.   General Managers Office   (5/15)
Strang A.J.   Parcel Porter Martock Station   Pte. Gilt-edged card presented by his
    Divisional Major-General which stated 'a report has been received of gallant conduct on 16
    Sept. 1916 in carrying messages under shell fire'
Velton F.S.   General Mangers Office

BIBLIOGRAPHY

Bavin, W.D., *Swindon's War Record*, 1922
Carter, E.F., *Railways in Wartime*
Commonwealth War Graves Commission Website (www.cwgc.org)
Earnshaw, Alan, *Britain's Railways at War 1914–18*
Encyclopaedia of the Great Western Railway, Patrick Stephens Ltd
Great Western Railway Magazine, 1914–22
GWR War Reports of the General Manager to the Board of Directors 1914–19
Harris, Michael, *Great Western Coaches 1890–1954*
Henniker, Col. A.M., *Official History of the War – Transportation on the Western Front*, Imperial
    War Museum
History of the Corps of Royal Engineers, Vol. V
Lucking, J.H., *The Great Western at Weymouth*
Naval History Website (www.naval-history.net)
Nock, O.S., *The Great Western Railway in the 20th Century*
Peck, A.S., *The Great Western at Swindon Works*
Plumridge, J.H., *Hospital Ships and Ambulance Trains*
Pratt, Edwin A., *British Railways and the Great War*
Pratt, Edwin A., *War Record of the Great Western Railway*
Railway Correspondence & Travel Society, *Locos of the GWR*, Various Vols
Soldiers Died CD, Naval and Military Press
St Pauls Cathedral Memorial Service Book Railwaymen Roll of Honour, Naval and Military Press
Sutton, Mark, *Tell Them of Us – Remembering Swindon's Sons 1914–18*
The Railway Magazine, Various Issues, 1920–22
Tourret, R., *GWR Goods Wagons*
Trench Map Archive CD, Imperial War Museum/Naval and Military Press

Together with the above references many other sources were used such as war diaries, regimental and battalion histories, general social histories, and battlefield histories and guides.

ROLL OF HONOUR

Where it has not been possible to find a match in official records a note has been made as to where the GWR recorded the name.

NAME	GRADE/DEPT./LOCATION	AGE	MILITARY DETAILS	DEATH DATE	CEM/ MEM/ NOTES
Abbiss Harry	Packer/Engineer/Lostwithiel	18	Pte R Warwick Regt	Died 6/11/18	Lostwithiel Cem
Ackrill William Milburn	Goods Guard/Aberbeeg	37	Pte 2nd Lancashire Fus	Died 7/7/15	Menin Gate Mem
Acland Samuel James	Signalman/Traffic/Truro	24	L/Cpl N. Devon Hussars	KIA 2/11/15	Hill 10 Cem. Gallipoli
Adams Arthur John	Porter/Traffic/Newton Abbot	20	Pte 58th Bn MGC (Infantry)	Died 28/8/18	Vis-en-Artois Mem
Adams G.	Loco Dept./Hereford				GWR Roll of Honour
Adams John Henry	Labourer/Signal/Reading		Pte 3rd R Berks Regt	Died 2/11/18	Reading Cem
Adams William J.	Porter/Traffic/Swindon	24	Cpl 9th R Warwick Regt	Dow 15/11/15	Hill 10 Cem
Adams William Victor	Traffic Dept/Fishguard Harbour		Cpl 'B' Bty. 88th Bde. RFA	KIA 28/7/16	Caterpillar Cem
Adey Cyril Archibald	Engine Cleaner/Loco/Oxley	19	Pte 1/6th S.Staffs Regt	KIA 13/10/15	Loos Mem
Adey Thomas	Porter/Traffic/Wednesbury	19	Pte 17th Sherwood Foresters	Dow 18/9/17	Godewaersvelde Cem
Aggett Henry James	R/Labour/Engineer/Newton Abbot		Pte 8th Devon Regt	Dow 28/7/16	St.Sever Cem. Rouen
Ainge Frank	Locomotive Dept./Evesham		Pte 2/6th Gloucester Regt	Died 2/12/17	Cambrai Mem
Ainger W.	Examiner/L&C/Old Oak Common				GWR Mag. 10/18
Alder Ernest Albert	Labourer/No.23 Shop/Swindon	23	Pte 1st Wilts Regt	KIA 28/6/15	Menin Gate Mem
Alder Walter Gee	Apprent./L&C/Swindon		5th Tank Corps	KIA 23/3/18	Pozieres Mem
Alderson William John	Timber Loader/Goods/Leominster	26	11th Div. Train ASC	Died 25/10/18	Terlincthun Br Cem
Alexander Alfred Moses	R/Labourer/Engineer/Maidenhead	29	116th (GWR) Rly Co R.E.	Died 11/11/18	Cairo War Mem Cem
Alford Adolphe John	Porter/Traffic/Torre	19	Pte 2/8th Worcester Regt	Dow 10/11/18	Torquay Cem
Allaway Albert Ernest	Greaser/L&C/Gloucester	20	Pte 1/5th Gloucester Regt	KIA 23/7/16	Thiepval Mem
Allaway Henry James	Lampman/Traffic/Reading	25	Pte 2/1st Ox & Bucks L.I.	KIA 6/12/17	Fifteen Ravine Cem
Allcott Harold Benjamin	Traffic Dept./Abercarn	25	Gnr D Bty 251st Bde RFA	KIA 18/4/18	Chocques Mil Cem
Allen Alfred John	Messenger/D.S.O./Worcester	23	Cpl 2/8th Worcester Regt	Dow 31/7/16	Merville Com Cem
Allen Arthur	Signalman/Traffic/Dunstall Park	27	Pte 9th Royal Fus	KIA 13/4/16	Loos Mem.
Allen A.V.	Carman/Goods/Plymouth		Gnr 60th Heavy Bty RGA	Died 17/9/19	Delhi Mem-see CWGC
Allen Harry Montague	Fireman/Loco/Llanelly	20	Pte. 15th Welsh Regt	Dow 11/7/16	Heilly Station Cem
Allen James David	Sleep-car Attend/Hotel/Paddington	24	Sgt 25th F/Amb RAMC	Died 15/1/16	Exeter Higher Cem
Allen W.	Locomotive Dept/Southall				GWR Roll of Honour
Allen Y. or V.	Shunter/Traffic/Gowerton				GWR Mag. 7/17
Allin George Francis	Nurseryman/Engineer/Taunton	27	Pte 6th Somerset L.I.	KIA 3/4/18	Pozieres Mem
Allsop/Allsopp F.O./A.O.	Parcel Porter/Traffic/Newport				GWR Mag 3&6/18
Allsworth Fred Joseph	Mechanics Labour/L&C/Oxford	42	Sgt 1st Hampshire Regt	KIA 1/7/16	Redan Ridge Cem No.2
Alner Charlie	Porter Shunter/Traffic/Bruton	29	Pte 1st Somerset L.I.	KIA 1/11/14	Ploegsteert Mem
Alway Frank	R/Labour/Engineer/Wolverhampton	20	L/Cpl. 4th Grenadier Guards	KIA 25/9/16	Thiepval Mem
Amor George	Labourer/L&C/Swindon	33	Pte 7th Wilts Regt	Died 16/9/16	Salonika Military Cem
Anderson William	Carman/Goods/Birmingham				GWR Mag 11/16
Andrews Charles Norman	Labourer/Engineer/Gloucester	20	Pte 1/5th Gloucester Regt	Died 21/7/16	Thiepval Mem
Andrews Edward S.	Packer/Engineer/Fencote	20	Pte 4th Coldstream Guards	KIA 18/10/15	Vermelles Br. Cem
Andrews George William	Porter/Traffic/Danzey	21	Pte 11th R Warwick Regt	KIA 24/4/17	Arras Mem

Name	Occupation/Dept/Location	Age	Regiment/Rank	Death	Memorial/Cemetery
Andrews Herbert	Signalman/West Drayton	29	Sgt 1st Wilts Regt	KIA 24/10/14	Le Touret Mem
Andrews Walter	Labourer/Engineer/Dawlish		Pte 20th Hussars	KIA 23/3/18	Pozieres Mem
Angelinetta Gilbert	Striker/L&C/Danygraig	21	Rifm 7th Rifle Brigade	KIA 30/7/15	Menin Gate Mem
Anstey James	Carman/Traffic/Westbury	33	Gnr 45th Bty RFA	Died 22/10/18	Poznan Old Cem
Anstey Thomas Reginald	Clerk/Goods/Hockley	26	Pte 15th R Warwick Regt	KIA 3/9/16	Thiepval Mem
Anst(e)y Frederick Cecil	Labourer/L&C/Swindon		Pte 2nd Wilts Regt	Dow 15/6/15	Le Touret Mem
Anthony David	Ballast Loader/Eng./Briton Ferry	34	Pte R Berks Regt	KIA 24/4/17	Doiran Mil Cem
Archer Charles Henry	Packer/Engineer/Bampton	36	Pte 2nd Ox & Bucks L.I.	KIA 16/5/15	Le Touret Mem
Arkinstall E. Harry	Engine Cleaner/Stafford Road	18	Pte 1/6th S. Stafford Regt	KIA 13/10/15	Loos Mem
Armfield William Aulty	Carriage Fitter/Old Oak Common	24	Pte 1st DCLI	Dow 7/12/15	Corbie Com Cem
Arrowsmith Henry	Fireman/Loco/Abadare	27	Pte 1st Welsh Guards	KIA 27/9/15	Loos Mem
Arthur William James	Boilermakers Helper/L&C/Swindon	28	Driver 503rd Field Co R.E.	Dow 23/5/17	Mory Abbey Mil Cem
Ash John	Packer/Engineer/Pontardulais		Pte 13th Middlesex Regt	KIA 28/9/15	Loos Mem
Ashbourne John Henry	Packer/Engineer/Warwick	31	2/Cpl 213th ATC R.E.	KIA 30/3/18	Pozieres Mem
Ashby George Edward	Clerk/Goods/Totenham Court Rd.		Rifm 12th London Regt	KIA 7/10/16	Thiepval Mem
Ashford Ernest Harold	Clerk/Goods/Oxford	23	Pte 5th R Berks Regt	KIA 9/4/17	Arras Mem
Ashley Herbert Thomas	Traffic Dept/Bristol	22	Pte 12th Gloucester Regt	KIA 20/9/18	Serre Rd. No.2 Cem
Ashman Henry Douglas	Clerk/Hotels/Paddington	23	Pte 1/1st Berkshire Yeomanry	KIA 21/8/15	Helles Mem
Ashton John Hubert	Clerk/Goods/Southall	35	Sgt 16th Rifle Bde	KIA 21/3/18	Pozieres Mem
Atherton Herbert John	Porter/Traffic/Dorchester	25	L/Cpl MGC (Cavalry)	Dow 11/3/18	Tincourt New Br Cem
Atkins Thomas Henry	Labourer/Signal/Worcester	29	Pte 1st Lincolnshire Regt	KIA 1/11/14	Menin Gate Mem
Attoe Albert Amos	Gang Lad/Signal/Reading		Pte 8th Somerset L.I.	KIA 29/8/18	Vis-en-Artois Mem
Austin Edward	Riveter/Wormwood scrubs		Pte 1/3rd Royal Fus	KIA 10/3/15	Le Touret Mem
Austin William	Packer/Engineer/Bridgend	33	Pte 2nd Welsh Regt	KIA 25/9/15	Loos Mem
Averies Harold	Machineman/L&C/Swindon		Pte 1st Wilts Regt	KIA 23/3/18	Arras Mem
Avery William Henry	Lad Porter/Traffic/Bickleigh	19	L/Cpl 1st Lancaster Regt	Dow 3/10/17	Dozinghem Mil Cem
Axford Frank	Packer/Engineer/Codford		Pte 6th W. Kent Regt	KIA 30/11/17	Cambrai Mem.
Axford William Victor	Machinist/L&C/Swindon		Pte 5th Wilts Regt	KIA 25/1/17	Amara War Cem
Ayling Walter Edward	Porter/Traffic/Menheniot	23	Rifm 21st London Regt	Dow 26/9/16	Etaples Cem
Ayres William Arthur	Brass Finisher/Signal/Reading	19	Spr I.W.T. R.E.	Died 22/7/17	Merville Com Cem
Bache Alfred George	Fitters Apprent/Loco/Tyseley		A/Mech RAF Recruit Depot	Died 21/7/18	Birmingham Cem
Bacon John William	Clerk/Goods/Bristol	23	Pte 2nd Hampshire Regt	KIA 25/5/18	Aval Wood Cem
Baden Frank	Striker/No 14 Shop/Swindon		Pte 5th Wilts Regt	KIA 19/7/15	Pink Farm Cem
Badrick Percy	Porter/Traffic/Paddington	19	Rifm 2nd Rifle Bde	Dow 30/5/18	Mont Huon Mil Cem
Bagg Albert	Traffic Dept/Cardiff	23	Pte 36th Co MGC	KIA 30/11/17	Cambrai Mem
Baggs Arthur	Storekeeper/Loco/Llantrisant		Pte 1st Wilts Regt	Dow 27/10/18	Rocquigny Road Cem
Baggs George Philip	Porter/Goods/Bristol	29	Pte 1st DCLI	KIA 9/9/14	La Ferte-s-Jouarre Mem
Bailey Albert J.	Labourer/Loco/Old Oak Common	30	Pte 2nd Highland L.I.	Dow 23/9/14	Neuilly-s-Seine new Cem
Bailey Claud Thomas	Porter/Goods/Smithfield	31	Rifm 2nd KRRC	Dow 8/7/16	Chocques Mil Cem
Bailey Frank Edward	Driller/Engineer/Shrewsbury	24	Rifm Rifle Bde. Depot	Died 9/1/16	Shrewsbury Gen. Cem
Bailey Frederick	Packer/Engineer/Liskeard	19	Gnr D Bty 296th Bde RFA	Dow 18/3/18	Achiet-le-Grand Cem
Bailey Fred Thomas	Shop Clerk/L&C/Swindon	30	Cpl 10th Tank Corps	KIA 25/8/18	Grevillers Br Cem
Bailey J.F.	Goods Dept/Smithfield				GWR Roll of Honour
Bailey James	Number Taker/Traffic/Rogertone		Pte 1st or 2nd Monmouth Regt	Dow 12/4/18	Aire Com Cem
Bailey Joseph	Labourer/Engineer/Westbury		Pte 1st Wilts Regt	KIA 21/10/16	Regina Trench Cem
Bailey Joseph Henry	Boilersmith/Loco/Stafford Road		Pte RAMC	Died 16/12/18	Wolverhampton Cem
Bailey N.J.	Fitter/Engineer/Taunton	32	ERA HMS Blake RN	Died 23/11/18	Taunton Cem
Bailey Thomas W.	Labourer/L&C/Swindon	42	Spr 565th (Wilts) ATC R.E.	Died 13/3/17	Grovetown Cem Meaulte
Bailey William	Carman/Goods/Handsworth	31	Pte 2nd S. Staffs Regt	KIA 12/11/14	Oosttaverne Wood Cem
Baines G.O.	Shunter/Traffic/Chirk	22	Spr 98th Light Rly Co R.E.	KIA 21/12/17	Alexandria War Cem
Bakehouse William	Packer/Engineer/Tonyrefail	28	Spr 262nd (GWR) Rly Co R.E.	KIA 5/9/17	Ypres Reservoir Cem
Baker Edgar Frank	Loco Dept Off/Swindon		Pte 5th Wilts Regt	KIA 10/8/15	Helles Mem
Baker Ernest George	Packer/Engineer/Leamington	24	Pte 10th R. Warwick Regt	Dow 8/5/17	Lijssenthoek Mil Cem
Baker Henry Clifford	Lad Clerk/Goods/Bristol	19	Pte 249th Co MGC (Infantry)	KIA 22/8/17	Tyne Cot Mem
Baker Hubert Dudley	Clerk/Accounts/Paddington	20	Pte 15th London Regt	KIA 18/1/17	Railway Dugouts Cem
Baker John Ernest	Carriage Cleaner/L&C/Neath	27	Pte 1st W Kent Regt	KIA 24/10/14	Le Touret Mem
Baker R.	Engineer Dept/Nantyderry				GWR Roll of Honour
Baker T.	Wireman/Signal/Newport or Neath				GWR Mag 6/18
Baker W.D.	Signal Dept/Reading				GWR Roll of Honour

Name	Occupation	Age	Unit	Death	Memorial
Baker W.H.	Messenger/Goods/Bristol				GWR Mag 2&6/19
Baldwin E. Charles	Bridge Lab/Engineer/Gloucester	37	Spr 118th Rly Co R.E.	KIA 21/7/16	Calais South Cem
Baldwin Herbert Percy	Invoice Typist/Goods/Cardiff	34	Pnr R.E. att 72nd Bde	Died 16/10/18	Delsaux Farm Cem
Bale Reginald Sydney	Clerk/Goods/Tiverton	19	Pte 6th Wilts Regt	KIA 23/3/18	Arras Mem
Bale William	Labourer/Engineer/Taunton		Pte 2/6th R Warwick Regt	KIA 4/12/17	Cambrai Mem
Ball Arthur	Porter/Traffic/Bridgend	22	Cpl 8th Devon Regt	KIA 25/9/15	Loos Mem
Ball Albert Harold	Packer/Engineer/St Germans	26	Sto HMS Vanguard RN	SL 9/7/17	Plymouth Naval Mem
Ball Frederick	Machineman/L&C/Swindon	23	Gnr D Bty 2nd Bde RFA	KIA 13/10/15	Foss 7 Mil Cem
Ball Harold Sydney	Clerk/Traffic/Clifton Down	21	Gnr G anti-aircraft Bty RFA	KIA 23/10/17	Minty Farm Cem
Ball Isaac	Carman/Goods/Hockley	28	Pte 1st Northumberland Fus	Died 15/11/14	Menin Gate Mem
Ballard John Henry	Hydraulic Press Checker/Swindon	27	Pte Army Cyclist Corps (2nd Div.)	KIA 26/7/15	Beuvry Com Cem
Balmond William Henry	Fireman/Loco/Bristol	31	Spr 2/3rd S Midland Field Co R.E.	Dow 12/12/16	Aveluy Com Cem
Bangs Percival Charles	Finisher/L&C/Swindon	26	Pte 140th F/Amb RAMC	KIA 23/3/18	Achiet-le-Grand C. Cem
Banning William	Packer/Engineer/Cheltenham		Pte 12th Gloucester Regt	KIA 20/8/16	Thiepval Mem
Barker George William	Porter/Traffic/Wednesbury	22	Pte 8th R. Welsh Fus	Dow 26/9/15	Hill 10 Cem Gallipoli
Barlow Thomas	Labourer/Signal/Reading	31	Rifm 33rd London Regt	Died 5/11/18	Terlincthun Br Cem
Barnes A.	Ticket Collector/Traffic/Small Heath				GWR Mag 12/17
Barnes Henry Thomas	Labourer/Engineer/Gloucester	34	Pte 8th Gloucester Regt	Dow 2/11/18	Terlincthun Br Cem
Barnes William H.F.	Machinist/C&W/Swindon	18	Pte 2nd Wilts Regt	Dow 12/4/17	Warlincourt Halte Br Cem
Barnicoat Edwin	Labourer/Engineer/Lostwithiel		Pte 1/4th DCLI	KIA 27/4/18	Ramleh War Cem Israel
Barr Thomas Reginald	Carpenter/Engineer/Gloucester		Pte 1/5th Gloucester Regt	KIA 17/3/17	Asservillers New Cem
Bartlett Walter Frank	Warehouse Clerk/Stores/Reading	26	CQMS 41st Div Train ASC	KIA 29/5/18	Dozinghem Mil Cem
Barson James	Porter/Traffic/Littlemore		Pte 1/4th Ox & Bucks L.I.	KIA 23/7/16	Pozieres Br Cem
Barson William George	Engine Cleaner/L&C/Oxford	17	Pnr 5 Bn Special Bde R.E.	Dow 29/10/16	N. Hinksey Churchyard
Bartholomew D.	Porter/Goods/Paddington				GWR Mag 2/19
Bartlett Alfred	Packer/Engineer/Kingham	40	Gnr 4th Reserve Bde RFA	Died 16/3/18	Oddington Churchyard
Bartlett Oliver Raymond	Fireman/Loco/Danygraig	20	Pte 1/6th Welsh Regt	KIA 2/10/15	Loos Mem
Barton Ernest	Telegraph Lineman/Signal/Swindon	29	Pte 2nd Ox & Bucks L.I.	KIA 16/5/15	Le Touret Mem
Barton Edward C.	Draughtsman/L&C/Swidon		Pte 16th Middlesex Regt	Dow 7/7/16	Abbeville Com Cem
Batchelor E.C. or C.E.	Carman/Goods/S. Lambeth		R.E.		GWR Mag 9/17
Bateman Fred George	Parcel Clerk/Traffic/Birmingham	22	Pte 1st Somerset L.I.	KIA 28/3/18	Roclincourt Valley Cem
Bates Frederick	Packer/Engineer/Honeybourne	26	Pte 1/8th Worcester Regt	KIA 24/4/17	Thiepval Mem
Bathe George	Helper/L&C/Swindon	25	Pte 1st Wilts Regt	KIA 20/2/15	Kemmel Chateau Mil Cem
Bathe William Herbert	Machineman/L&C/Swindon	19	Pte 4th Royal Fus	KIA 9/4/17	Tilloy Br Cem
Batten Albert Leslie	Parcel Porter/Traffic/Newport		Pte 233rd Co MGC	Dow 1/10/17	Brandhoek No 3 Mil Cem
Baugh James Thomas	Platform Attendant/Traffic/Bedlinog	25	2/Lt 6th Manchester Regt	Dow 3/11/18	St Souplet Br Cem
Bayliss Thomas James	Mechanic/L&C/Gloucester	27	L/Cpl 8th Gloucester Regt	KIA 18/11/16	Thiepval Mem
Beale James Sydney	Clerk/Goods/Poplar	19	Pte 1/5th Sherwood Foresters	Dow 4/10/18	Tincourt New Br Cem
Beard Fred	Labourer/R Shop/Swindon	35	AS HMS Good Hope RN	SL 1/11/14	Portsmouth Naval Mem
Beard Henry	Packer/Engineer/Probus	27	Pte 17th Lancashire Fus	Dow 15/4/17	Chapelle Br Cem
Beard Herbert Thomas	Dresser/Sheet/Worcester	42	Pte 1st Worcester Regt	KIA 16/3/15	Le Touret Mem
Beauchamp C.	Under Lineman/Signal/Gloucester				GWR Mag 12/17 & 5/18
Beckett Hubert	Labourer/L&C/Swindon	34	L/Cpl 11th Somerset L.I.	KIA 3/11/18	Obigies Com Cem
Beckett Percy	Storesman/Stores/Didcot	21	L/Cpl 8th Co MGC (Infantry)	Died 14/4/17	Duisans Br Cem
Bedden David Arthur	Porter/Goods/Poplar		Rifm 3rd Rifle Bde	KIA 22/3/18	Pozieres Mem
Beer Alfred John	Porter/Traffic/S. Molton	21	Pte 1/6th Devon Regt	Died 10/8/16	Amara War Cem
Beer David Stanley	Clerk/CGMO/Paddington	21	Rifm 16th London Regt	KIA 1/7/16	Thiepval Mem
Beer J.	Traffic Dept/Alexandra Dock				GWR Roll of Honour
Beer Samuel John	Packer/Engineer/Buckfastleigh	30	Spr I.W.T. R.E.	Died 28/1/19	Terlincthun Br Cem
Belcher Alfred	Porter/Traffic/Gloucester		L/Cpl 2/4th Gloucester Regt	KIA 3/12/17	Cambrai Mem
Belcher Charles	Labourer/L&C/Swindon		Pte 7th Royal Dublin Fus	KIA 17/11/15	Doiran Mem
Belcher Frederick William	Parcel Porter/Traffic/Paddington		Cpl 1st Royal Scots Fus	KIA 19/4/15	Voormezeele 1 & 2
Belcher John	Labourer/Engineer/Didcot	41	Pte 2nd R. Berks Regt	KIA 11/6/18	Soissons Mem
Bellinger Henry Charles	Packer/Engineer/Bassaleg		Pte 2nd Lancashire Fus	KIA 7/7/15	Menin Gate Mem
Bellringer Harold George	Packer/Engineer/Bodmin Road		Pte 1/5th DCLI	KIA 17/4/18	Loos Mem
Benford William	L/Packer/Engineer/Didcot		Pte 1st R. Berks Regt	KIA 31/3/15	Vieille-Chapelle Mil Cem
Benham W.B. or W.H.	Porter/Traffic/Reading				GWR Mag 12/18
Bennett Ernest Harry	R/Labourer/Engineer/Taunton	28	L/Cpl ROD R.E.	Died 1/4/19	Ruishton Church Cem
Bennet H.J.	Clerk/Traffic/Melksham				GWR Mag 3/19

Name	Occupation/Dept/Location	Age	Regiment/Unit	Death	Cemetery/Memorial
Benney James	Packer/Engineer/Drinnick Mill	27	1st Cl. Sto HMS Vivid RN	Doi 13/6/17	St Stephen-in-Brannel
Bent W.	Carman/Goods/Manchester				GWR Mag 9&12/16
Beresford C.	Painter/Engineer/Wolverhampton				GWR Mag 6/19
Berkley Arthur Lucas	Clerk/Goods/Manchester	27	Pte 4th Worcester Regt	KIA 14/4/18	Ploegsteert Mem
Berrett William John	Policeman/Goods/Hockley	22	Pte 6th Wilts Regt	Dow 13/9/16	Etaples Mil Cem
Berry G.H. James	Fireman/Loco/Newport Dock St		Pte 1st Monmouthshire Regt	KIA 8/5/15	Menin Gate Mem
Berry J.E.	Tracer/Signal/Reading				GWR Mag 1/17
Berry Robert	Packer/Engineer/Teignmouth	34	Pte Devonshire Regt	Died 5/4/20	Teignmouth Cem
Berry William Arthur	Packer/Engineer/Alexandra Dock	23	L/Cpl 296th Rly Co R.E.	KIA 7/9/18	Faubourg D'Amiens Cem
Bevan Frederick James	Porter/Goods/Bridgend	20	Pte 4th SWB	Dow 11/8/15	7th F/Amb Cem Gallipoli
Bevan George	Labourer/L&C/Swindon	30	Pte 2nd Wilts Regt	Dow 26/12/16	Birmingham Cem
Bevans Frederick	Engine Cleaner/L&C/Neyland		Dvr 'A' Bty 66th Bde RFA	Died 24/6/16	Amara War Cem
Bezzant Alfred Frederick	Labourer/No 1 Shop/Swindon		Pte 2nd Wilts Regt	Dow 23/6/15	Longuenesse Cem
Bibbings Lewis W.J.	Porter/Goods/Newton Abbot		Dvr 172nd Bde Am/Col RFA	Doi 30/7/17	Pieta Mil Cem Malta
Bickel Claud Trelease	Clerk/Traffic/Highbridge	23	Pte 5th Yorkshire L.I.	KIA 27/7/18	Soissons Mem
Bickerton Walter	Labourer/Engineer/Worcester	38	Pte 3rd Worcester Regt	KIA 7/11/14	Menin Gate Mem
Biffin Albert Samuel	Labourer/Signal/Shrewsbury	21	Pte 1st R. Warwick Regt	KIA 25/4/15	Menin Gate Mem
Bigg Leonard J.	Porter/Goods/Poplar	24	Sgt 'A' Bty 82nd Bde RFA	KIA 28/10/18	Le Cateau Mil Cem
Biggin William Charles	Lad Porter/Goods/Bath		Pte 5th Dorset Regt	Dow 12/10/16	Rocquigny Road Cem
Biggs J.	Signal Porter/Passenger/Coleford				GWR Mag 8/15
Bignall S.	L&C/Swindon				GWR Roll of Honour
Bigwood William Henry	Riveter/L&C/Swindon	24	Pte 1/4th Wilts Regt	Died 6/9/16	Baghdad War Cem
Biles John William	Fireman/Loco/Lydney	22	Pte 2nd Worcester Regt	Dow 8/10/18	Mont Huon Mil Cem
Bill Horace B.	Carman/Goods/Hockley		CSM 9th Devonshire Regt	KIA 1/7/16	Devonshire Cem
Billey William Robert	Clerk/Traffic/Ebbw Vale	19	Pte 2nd Worcester Regt	KIA 21/5/17	Croisilles Br Cem
Billingham William Robert	Goods/Hockley	25	Gnr 'S' Anti-aircraft Bty RFA	KIA 27/9/17	Zuydcoote Mil Cem
Birch James E.	Caller-off/Goods/Birkenhead	20	Pte 1st Cheshire Regt	KIA 19/11/14	Menin Gate Mem
Bircher John	R/Labourer/Engineer/Wolverh'ton	31	7th S Staffordshire Regt	KIA 16/8/17	Tyne Cot Mem
Bird A.	Traffic/Abergavenny				GWR Roll of Honour
Birks Alfred Owen	Clerk/L&C/Swindon	26	2/Lt 1st Dorset Regt	Dow 13/3/18	Haringhe Mil Cem
Birks George Allen	Loco Dept/Swindon	27	Aircraftman 1st Class RAF	Died 14/7/18	Swindon Cem
Bisatt Robert George	Traffic/Cardiff	19	Pte 15th Lancashire Fus	KIA 2/11/18	Ors Br Cem
Bishop Arthur Edward	Labourer/L&C/Swindon	25	Pte 8th Welsh Regt	Died 3/5/17	Basra Mem
Bishop Charles Edward	Secondman/Signal/Newport	25	Spr No.1 Rly Telegraph R.E.	Died 11/12/16	Barlin Com Cem
Bishop Ernest James	Fireman/Loco/Landore	26	Rifm 12th Rifle Bde	KIA 25/9/15	Ploegsteert Mem
Bishop Leonard Edgar C.	Shedman/L&C/Bristol		Gnr B Bty 92nd Bge RFA	KIA 28/7/16	Vlamertinghe Mil Cem
Bishop William Walter	Clerk/Goods/Paddington	17	Pte 1/8th Middlesex Regt	KIA 25/4/15	Menin Gate Mem
Biss Robert George	Goods Clerk/Traffic/Devizes	19	L/Cpl 2nd Wilts Regt	KIA 20/10/18	St Aubert Br Cem
Bizley R.C.	Tinsmith/L&C/Swindon		Pte 125th Army Ordnance Corps	Died 26/11/18	Kirechkoi Cem
Blackmore Reg James	Lad Porter/Goods/Exeter		Pte 9th N Staffordshire Regt	Dow 26/6/18	Bienvillers Mil Cem
Blackmore Russell Henry	Kitchen Porter/Tregenna C. Hotel	22	Pte 5th Connaught Rangers	Died 14/1/16	Sofia War Cem
Blackmore W.	Porter/Traffic/Brislington				GWR Mag 9&10/18
Blackwell Albert Edward	Signalman/Traffic/Garnant	23	Pte RAMC Att. 79th MGC	Died 25/5/17	Salonika Mil Cem
Blake Albert Charles	Traffic/Westbourne Park	22	L/Sgt 20th Batt MGC (Infantry)	KIA 1/4/18	Pozieres Mem
Blake Alfred James	Packer/Engineer/S. Lambeth		Pte 17th Middlesex Regt	KIA 13/11/16	Thiepval Mem
Blake Bernard Norman	Clerk/DGMO/Newgate Street	24	A/Bom 'D' Bty 160th Bde RFA	KIA 7/6/17	La Laiterie Mil Cem
Blake Edward Caleb	Carriage Cleaner/Old Oak Common		Pte 13th Royal Fus	KIA 8/10/18	Vis-en-Artois Mem
Blake Harold George	Clerk/Loco/Gloucester	29	Spr Rly Troops (Longmoor) R.E.	Died 16/3/18	Torquay Cem
Blake James	Parcel Porter/Traffic/Winchester		Pte 15th Hampshire Regt	KIA 8/6/17	Mendingham Mil Cem
Blake J.R.	Porter-Shunter/Winchester				GWR Mag 9/19
Blake Martin James	Carman/Goods/Park Royal	23	Pte 9th Lancers	KIA 22/3/18	Pozieres Mem
Blane Alfred	Clerk/Goods/Paddington	27	Pte 'A' Sqdn Berkshire Yeo	Dow 24/9/15	Alexandria War Cem
Bloxsom Francis H.	Labourer/L&C/Swindon	20	Gnr C Bty 86th Bge RFA	Dow 3/9/18	Ligny-St Flochel Br Cem
Bloxsome W.J.	S/Lab/Engineer/Charlton Kings		Spr 117th Rly Co (Base Depot)	Died 7/8/17	Salonika Mil Cem
Blunsdon Fred Albert	Striker/No 14 Shop/Swindon	36	Pte 1st Wilts Regt	KIA 25/9/15	Menin Gate Mem
Board M. or A.	Signalman/Traffic/Chard		Artillery		GWR Mag 2/20
Boak G.	Loco Dept/Croes Newydd				GWR Roll of Honour
Boden Albert Harry	Shunter/Traffic/Shrewsbury	25	Pte 7th Shropshire L.I.	Dow 2/9/18	Bac-Du-Sud Br Cem
Boden Arthur Charles J.	Lad Porter/Goods/Exeter	21	Pte 24th F/Amb RAMC	KIA 19/11/17	Vlamertinghe Mil Cem

Name	Occupation/Department	Age	Rank/Regiment	Fate	Memorial/Cemetery
Bolas Alfred Birch	Shunt Horse Driver/Hartlebury	28	Pte 2nd Worcester Regt	KIA 7/11/14	Menin Gate Mem
Bolt Frank	Quay Porter/Traffic/Weymouth		Sgt 5th Dorset Regt	KIA 1/10/18	Sucrerie Cem
Bolt J.H.	Blacksmith/Stafford Road				GWR Mag 5/17
Bolter Charles Albert	Solicitor/Paddington	31	2/Lt 29th Bn MGC (Infantry)	KIA 12/4/18	Le Grand Beaumart Cem
Bona Thomas	Striker/Engineer/Carmarthen		Pte 9th Welsh Regt	KIA 25/9/15	Loos Mem
Bond Alfred James	Carriage Cleaner/L&C/Exeter	37	Pte 9th Devonshire Regt	Dow 27/10/17	Lijssenthoek Mil Cem
Boobyer Albert George	Signal Porter/Traffic/Swimbridge	21	S/m HM Trawler Lord Airedale	SL 29/11/16	Plymouth Naval Mem
Bott J.H.	Apprent/Loco/Wolverhampton				GWR Roll of Honour
Bould George	Engine Cleaner/Loco/Shrewsbury	18	Pte 1st Royal Welsh Fus	KIA 3/9/16	Thiepval Mem
Boulton Ernest Rice	Painter/Loco Works/Swindon		Spr 2/2nd S Midland Field Co RE	Dow 28/7/16	Longuenesse Cem
Bounds George Thomas	Packer/Engineer/Dinmore	21	L/Cp 1st Herefordshire Regt	KIA 29/7/18	Raperie Br Cem
Bourn Sidney George	Policeman/Passenger/Paddington	28	Rifm 1st Rifle Bde	Dow 7/7/15	Ferme-Olivier Cem
Bourne Samuel Boulton	Shunter/L&C/Swindon	35	Spr ROD R.E.	Died 17/7/18	Terlincthun Br Cem
Bourton Albert Edward	Parcel Porter/Traffic/Kidderminster	21	Pte 1st Grenadier Guards	Dow 8/12/17	Rocquigny Road Cem
Bovey Walter Percy C.	Shedman/L&C/Kingswear	29	Gdsm 4th Grenadier Guards	Died 16/12/18	Cologne South Cem
Bowen Fred Benjamin	Clerk/Traffic/Ammanford	22	Pte 19th Royal Welsh Fus	KIA 24/11/17	Cambrai Mem
Bowen Gamaliel	Checker/Traffic/Pembrey	23	OS HMS Excellent RNVR	Doi 23/1/18	Haslar RN Cem
Bowen George Allan	Porter/Traffic/Wrexham	22	Pte 16th F/Amb RAMC	KIA 25/10/18	St Souplet Br Cem
Bowen H.	Signal Dept/Gloucester				GWR Roll of Honour
Bowen J.	Packer/Engineer/Port Talbot				GWR Mag 12/18 1/19
Bowen William	Clerk/DSO/Swansea	30	2/Lt 3rd Welsh Regt (att 15th)	Dow 30/8/18	Fienvillers Br Cem
Bowerman Frederick	District lampman/Traffic/Tyseley	28	Gnr 'A' Bty 91st Bde RFA	KIA 9/8/17	Welsh Cem (Ceasars)
Bowles James	Packer/Engineer/Cullompton		Pnr Depot Special Bde R.E.	KIA 27/6/16	Ploegsteert Mem
Bowyer Albert James A.	Clerk/Goods/Hockley	20	Pte 15th Warwick Regt	Died 20/11/17	Penn Fields Churchyard
Boxall Alfred	Engineers Office/Shrewsbury	31	2/Lt 262nd (GWR) Rly Co R.E.	Dow 25/10/17	Bedford House Cem
Boxer Charles	Clerk/Goods/Swansea	30	L/Cpl 3rd Devonshire Regt	Died 31/12/16	Tywardreath Church
Bradford Ernest Walter	Motor Conductor/Falmouth	21	Pte 2nd Warwick Regt	KIA 13/5/17	Arras Mem
Bradley Albert Henry	Shedman/Loco/Stratford-on-Avon	30	Gnr 113th Bty 25th Bde RFA	KIA 11/1/17	Martinpuich Br Cem
Bradley H.	Traffic Dept/Birmingham				GWR Roll of Honour
Bradshaw Albert Edward	Porter/Traffic/Stratford-on-Avon	23	Pte 2nd Coldstream Guards	Dow 30/8/18	St Sever Cem
Braham Victor George	Porter/Goods/S Lambeth	28	Cpl 4th Royal Fus	KIA 16/6/15	Menin Gate Mem
Bramham Ernest Stewart	Tester of electrics of whole GWR	34	Capt Aero Construction RAF	Doi 7/11/18	Brookwood Mil Cem
Branchflower John	Locking Lineman/Signal/Taunton	29	Pte 1st Somerset L.I.	Dow 30/3/15	Cologne South Cem
Branwhite Robert	R/Labour/Engineer/Westbourne Pk		L/Bom D Bty 103rd Bde RFA	Dow 18/6/18	Dueville Com Cem
Brayne John William	Fireman/Loco/Chester	22	Spr 4th Siege Co R.E.	Dow 7/4/16	Lijssenthoek Mil Cem
Brazendale Edwin Oscar	Night Storeman/L&C/Stourbridge	26	Spr Rly Stores R.E.	Died 13/12/18	Mikra Br Cem
Brewer J. Victor	Weighbridgeman/Lawrence Hill		Bty QMS RGA	Died 7/5/18	Bathampton Churchyard
Bridewell Herbert	Packer/Engineer/Patney & Chirton	30	Pte 1st Wilts Regt	KIA 3/5/16	Ecoivres Mil Cem
Bridge Heney George	Passenger Porter/Traff/Patchway	23	Pte 2/5th Gloucester Regt	KIA 30/9/18	Laventie Mil Cem
Bridgeman Arthur John	Wagon Painter/L&C/Swindon		Pte 1st Wilts Regt	Dow 17/6/17	Bailleul Com Cem
Bridgeman Henry	Labourer/Signal/Swindon	28	Pte 1st Wilts Regt	Dow 25/1/15	Loker Churchyard
Bridgwater Thomas H.	Packer/Engineer/Berrington	26	Gnr 20th Bde Am/Col RFA	Dow 19/5/15	Leeds Cem (Lawns)
Bright Alfred John	Porter/Traffic/Slough	21	Pte 1st W. Surrey Regt	KIA 12/4/18	Ploegsteert Mem
Brindley Colin John P.	Clerk/Goods/Cradley		Pte 2/6th R Warwick Regt	Dow 10/4/18	St Sever Cem
Brine G.W.	Porter/Traffic/Marston Magna				GWR Mag 10/19
Brinn Ernest	Fireman/Loco/Goodwick	25	L/Cpl R.E. (Cable Section)	Dow 9/8/16	Vermelles Br Cem
Bristow F.J.	Clerk/Goods/S Lambeth				GWR Mag 5/16
Britt Sydney	Parcel Carman/Traffic/Knowle		Pte 4th SWB	Dow 13/12/17	Amara War Cem
Brittain Harry Varney	Loco Dept/Swindon	24	Dvr ASC XVI Corps Am/Col	Died 3/10/18	Sarigol Mil Cem
Brooker C.A.	Signal Dept/West Ealing				GWR Roll of Honour
Brookman Frank	Loco Dept/Swindon	23	Sgt 12th Gloucester Regt	Died 6/11/17	Tyne Cot Mem
Brookman Sidney George	Telephonist/Passenger/Swansea	15	AS Hood Bn RN Division	KIA 4/6/15	Helles Mem
Brooks/Brookes Charles	Signalman/Traffic/Bedlinog	27	Pte 8th Lincolnshire Regt	Died 19/9/17	Hamburg Cem
Brooks George Fred	Packer/Engineer/Pontypool		Pte 2nd Monmouthshire Regt	KIA 22/7/16	Hamel Mil Cem
Brooks Raymond John	Porter/Traffic/Southam Road	22	Pte 2nd Coldstream Guards	KIA 30/11/17	Gouzeaucourt Br Cem
Brough Thomas T.	Clerk/Goods/Reading	19	Pte 1st Seaforth Highlanders	KIA 22/4/16	Basra Mem
Broughton Albert S./S.A.	Greaser/L&C/Bridgwater	21	Cpl 7th Gloucester Regt	Dow 4/2/17	Amara War Cem
Brown Charles	Bricklayer/Engineer/W Bromwich				GWR Mag 9&10/17
Brown E.S.	Clerk/Goods/Paddington				GWR Mag 2/20

Name	Occupation/Department	Age	Unit	Fate	Memorial/Note
Brown Frank Thomas	Carman/Goods/Hockley	20	Pte 4th (Depot) Worcester Regt	Died 17/7/18	Birmingham Cem
Brown Fred Norman T.	Striker/L&C/Swindon	21	Pte D Co 5th Wilts Regt	Died 29/3/17	Basra Mem
Brown George Easter	Deeds Off./Paddington	25	2/Lt H.A.C.	Dsh 20/4/17	Arras Mem
Brown J.	Carman/Goods/Hockley				GWR Mag 12/18
Brown J.	Packer/Engineer/Ledbury				GWR Mag 3/19
Brown Joseph	Frame Builder/Carriage/Swindon				GWR Mag 3&7/18
Brown Norman Cyril	Office Boy/Signal/Shrewsbury	18	Pte 7th Shropshire L.I.	KIA 13/11/16	Serre Road No 1 Cem
Brown Patrick	Labourer/L&C/Ranelagh Bridge	29	Rifm 1st Royal Irish Rifles	KIA 24/6/15	Aubers Ridge Br Cem
Brown Richard	Bricklayer/Engineer/Shrewsbury				GWR Mag 9&10/17
Brown Thomas	Plumber/Engineer/Wolverhampton				GWR Mag 8&12/17
Browne Alec Trayton S.	Porter/Traffic/Filton		Pte 1st Coldstream Guards	KIA 27/11/17	Cambrai Mem
Browning Walter Henry	Porter/Goods/Gloucester		Pte 1/5th Warwick Regt	KIA 22/8/17	Tyne Cot Mem
Bryan J.	Carman/Goods/Hockley				GWR Mag 2&6/19
Brayant E.F.	Carman/Goods/Bristol				GWR Mag 11/17
Bryant E.G.	Spare Hand/L&C/Swindon				GWR Mag 12/16
Bryant G.F.	Carman/Goods/Bristol				GWR Mag 2/18
Bryant Sidney or Samuel	Packer/Engineer/Burlescombe		Pte 8th Somerset L.I.	KIA 17/7/17	Cabin Hill Cem
Bubb Frank	Labourer/Engineer/Charlton Kings	37	Pte 7th Shropshire L.I.	KIA 28/3/18	Wancourt Br Cem
Buckeldee Frank Lewis	Clerk/Registration Off/Paddington	22	L/Cpl 9th London Regt	Dow 30/11/17	Achiet-le-Grand Cem
Buckingham Albert	Engineering/Ealing Broadway		Pte 1st R. Berks Regt	KIA 3/11/14	Menin Gate Mem
Buckingham William A.	Audit Clerk/Paddington	31	2/Lt 5th R. Berks Regt	Dow 3/10/18	St Sever Cem
Buckle Frank	Porter/Traffic/Gobowen	19	Gdsm 4th Grenadier Guards	KIA 16/9/16	Thiepval Mem
Bufton W.C.	Loco Dept/Hereford				GWR Roll of Honour
Bull Daniel George	L&C/Swindon	27	L/Cpl 5th Wilts Regt	Died 31/8/16	Basra War Cem
Bunce Arthur Robert	Machinist/L&C/Swindon	21	Pte 5th Wilts Regt	KIA 10/8/15	Helles Mem
Bunney Mark	Carpenter/Engineer/Camborne	32	Cpl 2/4th DCLI Att. Signals	Died 20/11/18	Baghdad War Cem
Bunstone Richard	Yard Foreman/Traffic/Bridgend		Staff Sgt RAMC	Died 14/10/17	Bridgend Cem
Burchell John Yockney	Telephone Attendant/L&C/Swindon	20	Pte 2/8th Worcester Regt	KIA 27/8/17	Tyne Cot Mem
Burchell William Eli	Labourer/L&C/Swindon	35	Pte 2nd Wilts Regt	KIA 15/6/16	Thiepval Mem
Burden Edward Harley	Bricklayer/Engineer/Leamington		Pte 1/7th R Warwick Regt	Dow 8/11/16	Bezentin-le-Petit Cem
Burls Ernest	L&C/Old Oak Common	31	Pte 2nd Essex Regt	KIA 26/8/14	La Ferte-s-Jouarre Mem
Burlton Leslie Victor	Chairer/Engineer/Hayes	28	Pte 1st R Scots Fus	Died 23/8/18	La Ferte-s-Jouarre Mem
Burnett George Fred A.	Porter/Traffic/Bristol Joint		Pte 2nd Ox & Bucks L.I.	Dow 9/7/18	Bellacourt Mil Cem
Burrason David	Engine Cleaner/Loco/Oxley		Pte 7th S Staffordshire Regt	Das 23/8/15	E Mudros Mil Cem
Burridge E.J.	Parcel Porter/Traffic/Paddington				GWR Mag 9/17
Burrows Samuel	Labourer/Engineer/Stroud	21	Pte 1st Goucester Regt	KIA 23/12/14	Brown Road Mil Cem
Burrup Alfred	Temp Excavator/Newport	24	Pte 1st SWB	KIA 21/10/14	Bedford House Cem
Burt Ernest George	Porter/Traffic/Bath	20	Pte 24th Bn MGC (Infantry)	Dow 17/10/18	Delsaux Farm Cem
Burton John	Bricklayer/Engineer/Newnham	40	Gnr 119th Siege Bty RGA	KIA 10/12/17	Ypres Reservoir Cem
Busby Maurice Fred	Engine Cleaner/Loco/Banbury	21	Pte 1st Coldstream Guards	KIA 28/9/15	Loos Mem
Bush Ernest Frederick	Signalman/Traffic/Llangennech	23	Pte 15th Welsh Regt	KIA 25/1/16	St Vaast Post Mil Cem
Bush Harry E. or F.	Shunter/Traffic/Acton	28	Pte 1st Royal Fus	Died 18/11/15	Reninghelst N Mil Cem
Bush W.	Horsekeeper/Goods/Bristol				GWR Mag 1/19
Bush W.S.U.	Fireman/Loco/Tondu	24	A/Bom B Bty 87th Bde RFA	Died 21/11/18	Solesmes Br Cem
Bushnell Benjamin	Labourer/Engineer/Port Talbot	28	Pte 1st R. Berks Regt	KIA 26/6/16	Cabaret-Rouge Br Cem
Butcher Albert Edward	Machinist/L&C/Swindon	18	Pte 6th Wilts Regt	KIA 2/7/16	Thiepval Mem
Butcher Albert Stewart	Apprentice/L&C/Swindon	21	Pte 2nd Wilts Regt	Dow 29/10/17	Bailleul Com Cem
Butcher George Edward	Moulder/L&C/Swindon	28	Pte 2nd Wilts Regt	KIA 26/4/18	Tyne Cot Mem
Butcher William George	Porter/Traffic/Wilton	25	L/Cpl 1st Wilts Regt	Dow 15/10/14	Le Touret Mem
Butler Alfred George	Brakesman/Traffic/Bullo Pill		L/Cpl 1/5th Gloucester Regt	KIA 21/7/16	Thiepval Mem
Butler C.A.	Accounts Clerk/Paddington				GWR Mag 2/19
Butler John	Carpenter/L&C/Swindon	21	Spr 1/1st Wilts Fortress R.E.	Dow 23/3/15	Swindon Cem
Butler T.E.	Traffic Dept/Old Oak Common				GWR Roll of Honour
Butler Victor	Packer/Engineer/Tintern	22	L/Cpl 2nd Monmouth Regt	KIA 2/12/17	Cambrai Mem
Buxton James F.	Porter/Traffic/Bristol	29	AS H.M.T.B. 18 RN	Died 31/12/18	Bari War Cem Italy
Cain H.W.	Restaurant Car Atten/Paddington				GWR Mag 3/18
Cale Frederick Harold	Engine Cleaner/Loco/Cardiff		Pt 7th (Cyclist) Bn Welsh Regt	Died 5/5/15	Cardiff Cathays Cem
Campbell T.C.	Fireman/Loco/Cardiff				GWR Mag 4&7/19
Candler Francis John	Porter/Traffic/Lustleigh		L/Cpl 14th R Warwick Regt	KIA 27/9/18	Vis-en-Artois Cem

Name	Occupation	Age	Rank/Regiment	Death	Memorial
Cann Richard George F.	Apprentice/L&C/Swindon	19	Pte 1st Wilts Regt	Dow 30/6/15	Boulogne E. Cem
Cannon William	Ticket Collector/Paddington	29			GWR Mag 1/16
Cannons Sidney	Labourer/L&C/Swindon		Sgt 1st Wilts Regt	Dow 8/8/17	Mendinghem Mil Cem
Canter Tom	Boilersmith Helper/L&C/Swindon	30	Pte 8th R Berks Regt	KIA 25/9/15	Loos Mem
Card James	Packer Engineer/Lawrence Hill	29	Rifm 1st Rifle Bde	KIA 13/9/14	Vauxbuin Fr Cem
Carey John	Frame Bulder/21A Shop/Swindon		Pte 1st Wilts Regt	Dow 27/6/15	Harlebeke New Br Cem
Carpenter Richard J.V.	Porter/Traffic/Whitchurch (Hants)	20	Pte 9th Lancers	KIA 11/3/18	Jeancourt Com Cem
Carr Edward	Striker/Engineer/Port Talbot	24	Spr 136th ATC R.E.	Died 18/6/18	Longuenesse Cem
Carroll Richard	Packer/Engineer/Saltney	31	Pte 10th Cheshire Regt	KIA 26/4/16	Ecoivres Mil Cem
Carter Charles Alfred	Restaurant Car Atten/Paddington		L/Cpl 36th Bn MGC (Infantry)	Dow 24/4/18	Ham Br Cem
Carter John Gilbert	Engine Cleaner/Loco/Bristol	19	Pte 1st Dorset Regt	KIA 11/4/18	Ayette Br Cem
Carter Philip	Labourer/L&C/Swindon	31	Pte 1st Wilts Regt	Dow 8/7/16	Puchevillers Br Cem
Carter R.G. or G.R.	Signalman/Traffic/Abercanaid				GWR Mag 7&8/18
Carter Reginald James W.	Sheet Repairer/Goods/Worcester	22	Pte 3rd Worcester Regt	KIA 7/6/17	Wulverghem-L Rd Cem
Carter Simeon John	Shunter/Traffic/Llantrisant	28	Pte 1st Somerset L.I.	KIA 26/8/14	La Ferte-s-Jouarre Mem
Carter William Charles	Boilersmiths Mate/L&C/Llanelly	36	L/Cpl 1st R. Berks Regt	Dow 6/2/16	Chocques Mil Cem
Cartwright Arthur	Porter/Traffic/Churchill & B'down	20	Pte 14th Worcester Regt	Dow 23/3/18	Dernancourt Com Cem
Cartwright C.	Porter/Traffic/Gowerton				GWR Mag 3/19
Cartwright F.	Shunter/Traffic/Shrewsbury				GWR Mag 11/18 & 3/19
Carus-Wilson Trevor	Assistant/New Works/Swindon	48	Lt-Col 1/5th DCLI	Dow 27/3/18	St Sever Cem
Caseley Henry Francis	Fireman/Loco/Swansea	19	L/Cpl 2nd Devonshire Regt	KIA 10/5/15	Ploegsteert Mem
Casey Dennis H.	Sheet Labourer/Goods/Swansea	19	Pte 6th Welsh Regt	KIA 5/9/15	Lindenhoek Chalet Cem
Castle A.	Carriage Cleaner/Loco/Cardiff	27			GWR Mag 2/15
Castle Ernest George	Wagon Examiner/L&C/Landore	32	Pte 1st Wilts Regt	Dow 29/10/14	Le Touret Mem
Caswell Charles Harry J.	Oil-pad Examiner/L&C/Bordesley	22	Pte 6th Yorkshire L.I.	Died 20/9/15	Poperinghe New Mil Cem
Caswell Ernest Edward	Porter/Traffic/Swindon	19	Pte 5th Wilts Regt	Died 4/12/15	Hill 10 Cem Gallipoli
Caswell John Edward	Call-Boy/Traffic/Shrewsbury		Cpl 2/1st Shropshire Bty RHA	KIA 29/11/17	Tyne Cot Cem
Catherall Edward	Carriage Cleaner/L&C/Chester	20	Pte 19th Liverpool Regt	KIA 1/7/16	Thiepval Mem
Cattle Frederick T.J.	Slipper-Boy/Goods/Bridgwater		Rifm 17th KRRC	KIA 18/11/17	Tyne Cot Mem
Chalkley Reginald George	Restaurant Car Attend/Plymouth	20	Pte 2nd Bn RMLI	Dow 20/2/17	Etaples Mil Cem
Chamberlain A.	Porter/Traffic/Round Oak				GWR Mag 10/15
Chamberlain A.	L&C/Stourbridge				GWR Roll of Honour
Chamberlain Ernest C.	Clerk/C.A.O./Paddington	23	Sgt 13th London Regt	KIA 9/5/15	Ploegsteert Mem
Chamberlain George	Carman/Goods/Oxford	34	Sgt 7th Ox & Bucks L.I.	KIA 17/3/17	Karasouli Mil Cem
Champion George William	Restaurant Car Attend/Paddington	25	Pte 2nd Wilts Regt	Dow 28/8/15	Lillers Com Cem
Chance Albert Henry	Clerk/Goods/Birmingham	26	2/Lt 2/7th R Warwick Regt	KIA 22/3/18	Pozieres Mem
Chandler Charles E.	Machineman/L&C/Swindon	22	Pte 1st R. Berks Regt	Dow 5/4/18	Le Quesnoy Com Cem
Chandler Fred James	Apprent Coppersmith/L&C/Swind'n	22	Spr 565th (Wilts) ATC R.E.	Died 30/10/16	Grove Town Cem
Chandler Samuel Thomas	Fireman/Loco/Plymouth	21	Pte 2nd Wilts Regt	KIA 24/10/14	Menin Gate Mem
Chanter Sydney Harold	Machineman/L&C/Swindon	25	L/Cpl 2nd Wilts Regt	KIA 11/3/15	Le Touret Mem
Chaplin Cyril L.	Apprent/L&C/Swindon	20	Spr 142nd ATC R.E.	KIA 2/12/17	Hermies Br Cem
Chapman Frank	Fireman/Loco/Abingdon		Gnr 31st Siege Bty RGA	KIA 10/3/18	Ypres Reservoir Cem
Chapman James George	Axlebox Pad Maker/L&C/Swindon	26	Sgt 8th Royal Fus	Dow 3/9/16	Etaples Mil Cem
Chapman W.	Porter/Goods/Birkenhead				GWR Mag 12/14 & 9/16
Chapman William James	L&C/Swindon	23	Gnr D Bty 147th Bde RFA	Dow 24/6/16	Doullens Com Cem
Chappell Alfred	Engine Cleaner/Loco/Cardiff		Pte 6th R. Irish Fus	Dow 15/8/15	Helles Mem
Chappell Arthur Stanley	Erector/Engineer/Newport	32	Pte 7th SWB	Dow 24/9/15	St Perre Cem Amiens
Charge Robert Richard	Caller-off/Goods/Paddington		Cpl 5th Brdfordshire Regt	Dow 17/11/17	Cairo War Mem Cem
Charles Raynor H.L.	Fireman/Loco/Lydney	20	A.S. HMS Vala RN	SL 21/8/17	Plymouth Naval Mem
Charlwood Harry	Packer/Engineer/Droitwich		Spr 275th Rly Co R.E.	Died 23/10/18	Pershore Cem
Cheesley Percy Joseph	Motor Attendant/L&C/Swindon	23	Bom 45th Bty RFA	Dow 23/8/16	S. Marston Churchyard
Chenoweth Sidney	Clerk/Goods/Oxford Street London	24	Rifm 1/5th London Regt	KIA 15/8/17	Buttes New Br Cem
Chequer Herbert Jeffrey	Wagon Painter/L&C/Swindon	28	Gnr RGA	Died 31/12/17	Alexandria War Cem
Cheshir(e) W.R.	Porter Guard/Traffic/Paddington				GWR Mag 2/19
Chesterman John	Carpenter/Engineer/Westbury		Pte 2/4th Ox & Bucks L.I.	KIA 20/4/18	St Venant-Robecq Cem
Chesterman Percy T.	L&C/Swindon	24	Dvr 28th Div (HQ) ASC	Died 6/6/18	Lahana Mil Cem
Child Frank W.	Tinsmiths Mate/Signal/Reading		Sgt 1/4th R. Berks Regt	KIA 4/10/17	Tyne Cot Mem
Chillingworth Fred W.	Lamp Fitter/Electrical/Paddington	24	Cpl 7th Essex Regt	Dr 17/8/15	Alexandria Mil War Cem
Chinn Samuel Arthur	Porter/Traffic/Newquay	31	Pte 1st DCLI	KIA 21/11/14	Menin Gate Mem

Name	Role/Department/Location	Age	Regiment	Death	Memorial/Cemetery
Chipp Edward John	Lad Clerk/L&C/Old Oak Common	17	L/Cpl 2/10th Middlesex Regt	Dow 23/9/15	Helles Mem
Chisholm Ken James	Clerk/Traffic/Paddington		Lt 5th Northampton Regt	Dow 18/8/16	Puchevillers Br Cem
Chiswell Stanley J.	Engine Cleaner/Loco/Weston-S M		Pte 1st Coldstream Guards	KIA 27/11/17	Cambrai Mem
Christian Arthur Lewis	Porter/Traffic/Trowbridge	19	Pte 1st Wilts Regt	Died 14/10/18	Cologne South Cem
Chubb Harold	Motor Driver/Traffic/Plymouth	26	Pte 18th Co MGC (Infantry)	Died 31/5/19	Baghdad War Cem
Church Charles F.G.	Ticket Collector/Traffic/Paddington	28	Pte 20th Royal Fus.	KIA 20/7/16	Thiepval Mem
Claridge Hubert Cecil	Packer/Engineer/Fairford	19	Sto HMS Indefatigable RN	SL 31/5/16	Plymouth Naval Mem
Clark A.A.	L&C/Swindon				GWR Roll of Honour
Clark F.W.	Fireman/Loco/Llantrisant				GWR Mag 8/16
Clark(e) Henry	Packer/Engineer/Pangbourne				GWR Mag 3/15
Clark William Arthur	Clerk/Rates Off/Paddington	23	Rifm 6th London Regt	KIA 20/4/15	Guards Cem Windy C.
Clarke Alfred	Boiler Washer/L&C/Newton Abbot	30	Pte 1st R. Berks Regt	Dow 11/12/17	Grevillers Br Cem
Clarke A.H.	Boilersmith Ass/L&C/Worcster				GWR Mag 10/16&2/17
Clarke Ernest Frank	Sand Loader/L&C/Littlemore	32	Pte 2/4th R. Berks Regt	Dow 17/8/16	Littlemore Churchyard
Clarke F.	Parcel Poter/Traffic/Cardiff				GWR Mag 2&3/18
Clarke N.A.	Wagon Repairer/L&C/Port Talbot				GWR Mag 10/19
Clarke Sydney Edgar	Carriage Cleaner/Newton Abbot	28	Pte 5th Dorset Regt	KIA 1/10/18	Sucrerie Cem
Clarke W.	Porter/Goods/Exeter				GWR Mag 4/18
Clarke W.	Porter/Traffic/Stratton				GWR Mag 4&7/19
Clasper J.	Traffic Dept/Round Oak				GWR Roll of Honour
Cleave Fred Thomas	Carpenter/Engineer/Pontardulais		Pte 10th Devonshire Regt	KIA 4/9/16	Thiepval Mem
Cleaver Edward	Horsekeeper/Goods/Hockley	27	Pte 1st Gloucester Regt	KIA 29/10/14	Menin Gate Mem
Cleaver George	Labourer/Engineer/Reading		Pte 5th Ox & Bucks L.I.	KIA 9/4/17	Tilloy Br Cem
Clements A.J.	Labourer/L&C/Swindon				GWR Mag 5/16
Clements G.H.	Porter/Traffic/Halesowen				GWR Mag 4&6/19
Clements Joseph Henry	Porter/Goods/Smithfield	21	L/Cpl 5th R. Inniskilling Fus	KIA 15/8/15	Helles Mem
Cleverly W.G.	Clerk/Traffic/Wells				GWR Mag 7/19
Clifford Thomas Edwin	Packer/Engineer/Tyseley		L/Cpl 2nd Coldstream Guards	KIA 27/8/18	Mory Street Mil Cem
Clifford William	Brakesman/Traffic/Tondu				GWR Mag 12/14
Clinkard Kenneth Cyril	Clerk/Traffic/Witney	21	L/Cpl 1/4th Ox & Bucks L.I.	KIA 15/6/18	Boscon Br Cem
Cloke James Thomas	Packer/Engineer/Porthcawl	22	AS HMS Bittern RN	SL 4/4/18	Plymouth Naval Mem
Coe Thomas	Carriage Cleaner/Old Oak Common	24	Pte 7th Bedford Regt	Dow 19/1/16	Corbie Com Cem
Coe Walter Henry	Policeman/Traffic/Paddington	35	Cpl RFA	Died 5/11/18	Upton-cum-Chalvey
Cogan Frank Albert	Porter/Traffic/Kingswear	22	Pte 9th Devonshire Regt	Dow 15/6/17	Vraucourt Copse Cem
Coker George David	R/Labourer/Engineer/W Ealing	28	Pte 20th Royal Fus.	Dow 12/7/17	Kensal Green Cem
Coldrick Wyndham James	Parcel Porter/Traffic/Newport		L/Cpl 2nd S Lancashire Regt	KIA 20/9/17	Potijze Chateau Cem
Cole A.B.	Lad Clerk/Goods/Brentford				GWR Mag 10/17 & 2/18
Cole Charles	Packer/Engineer/Evesham	33	Pte 1/8th Worcester Regt	KIA 5/4/17	Templeaux-le-Grand Cem
Cole James	Forgeman Ass/18 Shop/Swindon		Pte 1st Wilts Regt	KIA 16/6/15	Menin Gate Mem
Cole R.A.	Parcel Porter/Traffic/Bristol				GWR Mag 10/19
Cole Robert George	Wagon Repairer/L&C/Bristol	24	Spr ROD R.E.	Died 26/4/17	Calais South Cem
Cole W.J.	L&C/Swindon				GWR Roll of Honour
Cole William Thomas	Traffic/Dudley	26	Pte 1st Grenadier Guards	Dow 20/11/16	Grove Town Cem
Coleman Ernest	Frame-Builder/21A Shop/Swindon		Pte 2/1st Ox & Bucks L.I.	KIA 19/7/16	Loos Mem
Coleman E.J.B.	Clerk/Goods/Frome	22	Spr 51st Broad Gauge Rly Co RE	Died 16/11/18	St Pol Br Cem
Coles Charlie	Labourer/L&C/Swindon	24	Cpl B Bty 161st Bde RFA	Dow 14/7/18	Bagneux Br Cem
Coles Ernest T.	Labourer/Engineer/Twyford	27	Pte 137th Co MGC (Infantry)	KIA 14/6/17	Maroc Br Cem
Coles Frank	Checker/Goods/Weymouth		Sgt A Bty 84th Bde RFA	KIA 25/4/17	Arras Mem
Coles G.	Engineer/Bristol				GWR Roll of Honour
Coles George Walter	Halt Attendant/Traffic/Lambourn	23	Pte Queens Oxford Hussars	KIA 21/3/18	Pozieres Mem
Coles Harry Henry	Signal Dept/West Ealing	33	Pte 17th Middlesex Regt	KIA 13/11/16	Serre Road No.1 Cem
Coles Herbert	Clerk/Goods/High Wycombe	19	2/Lt 2nd Rifle Brigade	KIA 18/11/17	Tyne Cot Mem
Collcott Ernest Harry	Solicitors Clerk/Paddington	34	2/Lt 1/8th Middlesex Regt	KIA 11/6/16	Bray Mil Cem
Collett Ernest George	Machinist/21A Shop/Swindon		Pte 1st Wilts Regt	KIA 12/3/15	Menin Gate Mem
Colley Edward	Porter/Traffic/Ironbridge	24	Pte 8th Shropshire L.I.	KIA 18/9/18	Doiran Mem
Colley Ernest	Carman/Goods/Hockley	24	Sgt 1/8th Worcester Regt	KIA 24/4/17	Thiepval Mem
Collins Albert Henry	Porter/Traffic/Grange Court		Pte 1st Gloucester Regt	KIA 9/9/16	Thiepval Mem
Collins F.J.	Porter/Traffic/Washford				GWR Mag 5/18
Collins W.	Packer/Engineer/Marlborough				GWR Mag 6/18

Name	Occupation	Age	Regiment/Unit	Death	Memorial/Cemetery
Collis Leonard Alfred	Clerk/Registration Off/Paddington	26	Rifm 9th London Regt	KIA 1/7/16	Gommecourt No.2 Cem
Colwill Francis	Porter/Passenger/Exeter				GWR Mag 8/15
Comer Lewis George	Fireman/Loco/Pontypool Road	22	Spr 123rd Field Co R.E.	Dow 14/7/16	Abbeville Com Cem
Comley Fred Harold	Vanguard/Goods/Bristol	18	Sto HMS Indefatigable RN	SL 31/5/16	Plymouth Naval Mem
Comley John F.	L&C/Swindon	37	Pte 5th Wilts Regt	KIA 10/8/15	Helles Mem
Comley Jessie Gueseppe	L&C/Swindon	24	Pte 7th Wilts Regt	KIA 24/4/17	Doiran Mem
Comley Percy Harold	Staff Clerk/L&C/Swindon	28	Spr 2nd Light Rly Co R.E.	Dow 1/10/17	Lijssenthoek Mil Cem
Condren (Condon) L.	Carriage Cleaner/L&c/Cardiff	38	Pte 6th R. Munster Fus	KIA 15/8/15	Helles Mem
Congdon Joseph Percy	Pacler/Engineer/Doublebois	24	Sgt 1/5th DCLI	KIA 27/10/17	Sunken Road Cem
Conibear Bruce	Hydraulic Engineman/L&C/Bath		Spr 204th Field Co R.E.	KIA 16/5/17	Bellicourt Br Cem
Connett Richard Victor	Engine Cleaner/Loco/Exeter		Pte 8th Devonshire Regt	KIA 1/7/16	Devonshire Cem
Conway William John	Packer/Engineer/Skewen	22	Pte 13th Middlesex Regt	KIA 28/9/15	Loos Mem
Cook Albert Edward	Gaugeman/L&C/Swindon	27	Pte 6th Wilts Regt	KIA 24/7/16	London Cem Longueval
Cook Edward Harry	Traffic Dept/Albrighton	22	Pte 2/6th Gloucester Regt	Died 2/12/17	Fifteen Ravine Cem
Cook George	Labourer/No.14 Shop/Swindon	20			GWR Mag 6/16
Cook H.	L&C/Swindon				GWR Roll of Honour
Cook Herbert J.	Horsekeeper/Goods/Paddington	24			GWR Mag 2/16
Cook Hubert James	U.L.L./Signal/Newport	25	Cpl 88th Bty 14th Bde RFA	KIA 3/12/17	The Huts Cem
Cook J.	R/Labourer/Engineer/Wolverh'ton	31			GWR Mag 7&9/16
Cook J.	Carman/Goods/Minories London				GWR Mag 1&7/18
Cook John Robert	Clerk/Goods/Hereford	23	Pte 1/8th Worcester Regt	KIA 4/11/16	A.I.F. Burial G. Flers
Cook Reginald William	Chief Clerk/Engineer/Paddington	26	Bom 7th London Bde RFA	KIA 2/3/16	Vermelles Com Cem
Cook S.J.	Packer/Engineer/Barnstaple		Spr 10th Rly Co R.E.	Died 28/2/19	Theux Com Cem
Cook T.W.	Labourer/L&C/Wormwood Scrubs				GWR Mag 11/16 & 1/17
Cook William Charles	Clerk/L&C/Swindon	34	Pte 7th Bn Tank Corps	Dow 8/10/18	Terlincthun Br Cem
Cooke Frank Guest	R/Labourer/Engineer/Wolverh'ton	34	Bom 55th Bty 33rd Bde RFA	KIA 12/11/17	White House Cem
Cooke George Josiah	Lad Messenger/Goods/Paddington	20	2/Lt R.F.C.	KIA 23/11/17	Zuydcoote Mil Cem
Cooke James Henry	Packer/Engineer/Kingsland	24	Pte 7th Shropshire L.I.	KIA 26/9/17	White House Cem
Coole Lionel Walter	Apprent Fitter/15 Shop/Swindon	18	Pte 1st Wilts Regt	KIA 11/12/14	Menin Gate Mem
Coombes J.F.	Goods/Bristol				GWR Roll of Honour
Coombs/Coombes E.J.	Porter/Traffic/Bodmin Road	22	Pte 7th DCLI	KIA 14/10/17	Fins New Br Cem
Coombs George Henry	Carman/Traffic/Ilminster		Gnr 132nd Heavy Bty RGA	KIA 30/8/18	Hem Farm Cem
Cooper Arthur	Angle-iron Apprent/L&C/Swindon	22	Pte 5th Wilts Regt	Dow 31/1/17	Amara War Cem
Cooper Arthur Llewellyn	Clerk/Traffic/Solihul	20	Pte 6th F/Amb RAMC	Dow 19/3/18	Mont Huon Mil Cem
Cooper Fred Charles	Traffic Dept/Cardiff		Pte 1st E Lancashire Regt	Died 23/5/18	Anzac Cem
Cooper H.	Stable Lad/Traffic/Walsal				GWR Mag 3/17
Cooper Robert Cecil	Clerk/Goods/Bristol	19	Cpl 1/6th Gloucester Regt	KIA 21/7/16	Pozieres Br Cem
Cooper R.J.	Traffic Dept/Paddington				GWR Roll of Honour
Cooper T.C.	Van Boy/Traffic/Cardiff				GWR Mag 8/19
Corbett Arthur	Fireman/Loco/Llanelly		Pte 2nd Wilts Regt	KIA 23/2/15	Rue-David Mil Cem
Corbett Edward	Riveter/No 13 Shop/Swindon		Cpl 6th R. Munster Fus	Dow 16/8/15	Alexandria Mil War Cem
Corbin James	Porter/Traffic/Portland	18	Pte 16th Devonshire Regt	KIA 2/9/18	Vis-en-Artois Mem
Corfield William Fred	Apprent Painter/L&C/Wolverh'ton		CSM 2/6th S. Staffordshire Regt	Died 16/7/18	Niederzwehren Cem
Corner Stephen T.	Apprent Boilersmith/L&C/Swindon		ERA HMS Sandhurst RN	Acc 27/2/17	Kensington Cem
Cornock Hubert William	Clerk/Goods/Bristol	26	Cpl 6th Gloucester Regt	Dow 26/6/15	Bailleul Com Cem
Corser Horace	Finisher/L&C/Swindon	25	Spr 79th Field Co R.E.	Dow 11/1/18	Bleuet Farm Cem
Corser Reginald	Fitter/L&C/Swindon	25	ERA HMS Defence RN	SL 31/5/16	Plymouth Naval Mem
Cosnett John	Carman/Goods/Newport	33	Pte 1st Welsh Regt	Dow 27/5/15	Bailleul Com Cem
Couldrey Horace Arthur	Erector/L&C/Swindon	22	Pte 6th Wilts Regt	KIA 7/4/17	Elzenwalle B Cem
Court Reginald Walter S.	Clerk/Audit Off/Hereford		2/Lt 1st Hereford Regt	KIA 26/3/17	Jerusalem Mem
Court Stanley	Checker/Traffic/Newbridge	20	Pte 11th SWB	KIA 11/4/18	Vieille-Chapelle Mil Cem
Court Stan William Claude	Clerk/Accounts/Paddington	19	Cpl 2/16th London Regt	Dow 30/7/16	Ecoivres Mil Cem
Cowherd John	Parcel Clerk/Traffic/Bristol	22	2/Lt 5th (4th) Worcester Regt	KIA 29/9/18	Hooge Crater Cem
Cowley Charles	Warehouse Lad/Stores/Swindon		Pte 5th R Berks Regt	Dow 18/10/16	Longueval Road Cem
Cowley James Fred	Boilermaker/L&C/Swindon		Sgt 1/4th Wilts Regt	Dow 13/11/17	Gaza War Cem
Cox Albert Harry	L&C/Swindon	25	Pte 5th Wilts Regt	Died 8/3/17	Baghdad War Cem
Cox Arthur James	Machineman/L&C/Swindon	22	Gnr 35th Bty RFA	Dow 16/9/16	Dartmoor Cem
Cox Charles Ben Joseph	Timekeeper/L&C/Bristol	21	Pte 8th R. Berks Regt	KIA 24/7/16	Thiepval Mem
Cox Edmund	Porter/Traffic/Oxford	31	Gnr 128th Heavy Bty RGA	KIA 6/6/16	Brandhoek Mil Cem

Name	Occupation/Location	Age	Regiment	Death	Memorial/Cemetery
Cox Francis G.	Porter/Traffic/Cranmore	22	Pte 5th Irish Regt	Dow 22/9/15	Alexandria Mil War Cem
Cox Isaac	Helper/L&C/Swindon	31	Pte 1st Wilts Regt	KIA 11/8/17	Menin Gate Mem
Cox John	Fitter Assist/L&C/Severn Tunnel J	32	Pte 6th SWB	KIA 15/5/16	Arras Mem
Cox Joseph H.	Shunter/Traffic/Abertillery	31	Pte 1st SWB	KIA 25/1/15	Le Touret Mem
Cox Leonard Arthur	Fireman/Loco/Trowbridge	22	Cpl 5th Wilts Regt	Dow 10/8/15	Helles Mem
Cox Thomas	Machinist/No.13 Shop/Swindon		L/Cpl 1st Coldstream Guards	Dow 29/12/14	Wimereux Com Cem
Cox William Percival	Turner/L&C/Swindon	19	Cpl 106th Field Co R.E.	KIA 18/11/15	London Rifle Bde Cem
Coxhead William Arthur	Fireman/Loc/Southall		Gdsm 3rd Grenadier Guards	KIA 14/9/16	Thiepval Mem
Crago Richard	R/Labourer/Engineer/Truro	33	Pte 22nd Northumberland Fus	KIA 19/10/17	Tyne Cot Mem
Crane Reginald Hooper	DGMO/Manchester	28	2/Lt 1st E Yorkshire Regt	KIA 4/10/17	Tyne Cot Mem
Crathern T.W.B.	Audit Off/Paddington	32	Cpl R.E.	Died 1/12/19	Hanwell Cem
Creber Stafford W.V.	Erector/L&C/Swindon	21	Airman 1st Class R.F.C.	Died 7/10/17	Mikra Br Cem
Cresswell H.	Stower/Goods/Hockley				GWR Mag 6/17
Crew Alfred Rowland	Under Shunter/Traffic/Bewdley		Pte Qeens Worcester Hussars	KIA 23/4/16	Jerusalem Mem
Crews Hector	Clerk/Goods/Cardiff	19	Pte 20th Royal Fus.	KIA 20/7/16	Thiepval Mem
Cridge Henry William G.	Packer/Engineer/W London Jct		Spr 130th Field Co R.E.	KIA 21/5/16	Ecoivres Mil Cem
Cridge Walter Percy	Fireman/Loco/Bristol		Cpl 3rd Worcester Regt	Dow 19/4/18	Cologne South Cem
Cripps Albert Burr	Packer/Engineer/Pontllanfraith	22	AS Hawke Bn RN Div	Dow 7/2/17	Varennes Mil Cem
Crocker A.C.	Riveter Assist/L&C/Wormwood S				GWR Mag 12/16
Crocker Cyril	Porter/Traffic/Hele & Bradninch	23	Gnr 126th Siege Bty RGA	Dow 24/8/18	Beacon Cem
Crocker George A.	Clerk/L&C/Swindon	29	Pte 100th F/Amb RAMC	Dow 15/3/18	St Sever Cem
Crocker Herbert	Packer/Engineer/W London Jct	25	Pte 2nd Wilts Regt	KIA 12/3/15	Le Touret Mem
Crocker Henry Robert	Porter/Traffic/Wellington	35	Pte 12th Somerset L.I.	Died 9/7/17	Kantara War Mem Cem
Crockett Ralph Henry	Machinist/L&C/Swindon	21	Pte 5th Wilts Regt	Died 29/6/16	Basra Mem
Crockett S.	Labourer/Engineer/Cradley				GWR Mag 3&4/16
Crockett Sam Thomas	Vanguard/Goods/Paddington	21	Dvr B Bty 108th Bde RFA	Died 27/11/18	Terlincthun Br Cem
Cronin Harold William	Travelling Auditor/S Wales Dist	37	Lt 5th Bedford Regt	Dow 2/12/17	Gaza War Cem
Crook A.	Machineman/L&C/Swindon	30			GWR Mag 3&4/16
Crook A.G.	L&C/Swindon				GWR Roll of Honour
Crook William	Packer/Engineer/W London Jct		L/Cpl 128th Field Co R.E.	KIA 2/7/17	Menin Gate Mem
Cross T.	Engineer/Nantyglo				GWR Roll of Honour
Cross Thomas V.	Porter/Traffic/Bristol Joint Station	27	Gnr Howitzer Bde RMA	Dow 20/6/15	Bully-Grenay Com Cem
Crossman Frank	Labourer/Signal/Taunton		L/Cpl 1st DCLI	KIA 8/5/17	Arras Mem
Crouch Norman C.E.	Clerk/Traffic/W Drayton	21	Pte 8th R Berks Regt	KIA 27/5/16	Loos Mem
Cruise Charles Thomas	Porter/Traffic/Birmingham		Pte 45th Royal Fus.	KIA 10/8/19	Archangel Mem Russia
Crump Fred George	Packer/Engineer/Exminster	32	L/Bom Howitzer Bde RMA	KIA 10/7/18	Esquelbecq Mil Cem
Cude Arthur Frederick	Porter/Traffic/Tilehurst	19	Pte 1/4th R Berks Regt	KIA 16/5/16	Hebuterne Mil Cem
Cull Cyril C.	Engine Cleaner/Loco/Danygraig	18	Pte 1/6th Welsh Regt	KIA 21/2/16	St Patricks Cem Loos
Cummings J.W.	Porter/Traffic/Acton				GWR Mag 11/18
Cumner Victor George	Apprent Boilermaker/L&C/Swindon	22	Spr 478th Field Co R.E.	KIA 4/6/17	Tilloy Br Cem
Cunningham John J.	Porter/Traffic/Paddington		Gnr C Bty 317th Bde RFA	Dow 23/9/18	Etaples Mil Cem
Curtis Alfred	Refresh Room Waiter/Bristol T.M.	22	Pte 12th Gloucester Regt	KIA 6/5/17	Arras Mem
Curtis Eric Calvin	Motor Car Dept/Slough	26	2/Lt 5th Seaforth Highlanders	KIA 28/7/18	Buzancy Mil Cem
Curtis G.	Steward/Marine/Weymouth				GWR Mag 6/19
Curtis G.	Packer/Engineer/Tyseley				GWR Mag 11/16 & 2/17
Curtis Sydney Herbert	Labourer/L&C/Swindon	23	Pte 1/4th Wilts Regt	Died 11/12/18	Ramleh War Cem Israel
Curtis W.T.	Wagon Painter/L&C/Swindon				GWR Mag 5/16
Cuss Charles Henry	Labourer/L&C/Swindon	37	Sgt 5th Wilts Regt	Died 31/1/19	Mikra Br Cem
Dadge Gilbert George	Smiths Apprent/14 Shop/Swindon	21	Pte 2nd Wilts Regt	Dow 15/6/15	Le Touret Mem
Dance Walter W.S.	Machinist/Signal/Reading	19	Pte 1/4th R Berks Regt	KIA 16/5/16	Hebuterne Mil Cem
Daniel Fred	Clerk/Goods/Paddington				GWR Mag 11/17 & 2/18
Daniels E.I.	Clerk/Accounts/Paddington		Spr 98th Light Rly Crew R.E.	Das 31/12/17	Chatby Mem
Darke Leonard Thomas	Machinist/L&C/Swindon	23	L/Sgt 1/8th Worcester Regt	KIA 5/10/18	Beaurevoir Com Cem
Darling Arthur Lancelot	Machineman/L&C/Swindon	22	Pte 7th Wilts Regt	KIA 24/4/17	Dorian Mem
Darville Thomas Newman	Porter/Traffic/Draycott	20	Gnr D Bty 93rd Bde RFA	KIA 20/5/16	Ypres Reservoir Cem
Darville William Ewart	Porter/Traffic/Bristol	20	Pte 7th Somerset L.I.	Died 28/8/18	Niederzwehren Cem
Davenport Horace	Clerk/L&C/Swindon				GWR Mag 6/18
Davey Wilfred Thomas	Clerk/Goods/Hockley	18	Pte 2/6th R Warwick Regt	KIA 12/4/18	Ploegsteert Mem
David Henry James	Labourer/Engineer/Taunton	33	Pte 6th Somerset L.I.	KIA 3/9/16	Thiepval Mem

Davidge Alfred Ernest	Labourer/Engineer/Taunton	32	L/Sea HMS Columbella RN	Doi 17/3/17	Taunton Cem
Davie William Edward	Wagon Repairers Assist/Bristol		L/Cpl 6th Somerset L.I.	KIA 22/10/17	Tyne Cot Mem
Davies (Davis) A.G.	Packer/Engineer/Bransford Road		Sgt 162nd Depot Worcester Regt	Died 12/8/18	Leigh Cem Bransford
Davies Bertie Edward	Storesman/Stores/Wolverhampton		Pte 12th Durham L.I.	Dow 20/9/17	Lijssenthoek Mil Cem
Davies Francis Victor	Engine Cleaner/Loco/Goodwick	17	Pte 3rd R. Welsh Fus	Died 19/9/16	Narberth Cem
Davies G.D.	Traffic/Haverfordwest				GWR Roll of Honour
Davies George R.	Carriage Cleaner/Loco/Chester				GWR Mag 6&8/18
Davies J.	Porter/Traffic/Wrexham				GWR Mag 3&4/19
Davies J.	Traffic Dept/Swansea				GWR Roll of Honour
Davies J.H.	Brick Archman/L&C/Oxley				GWR Mag 12/16 & 4/17
Davies J.H.	Fireman/Loco/Landore				GWR Mag 11/17
Davies J.J.	Porter/Goods/Ludlow				GWR Mag 11/16
Davies M.C.	Goods/Langley Green				GWR Roll of Honour
Davies Oscar Harold	L&C/Shrewsbury		Pte 14th Worcester Regt	Died 31/10/18	St Pol Br Cem
Davies P.	Clerk/Traffic/Newport				GWR Mag 11/18&3/19
Davies R.	Traffic/Fishguard				GWR Roll of Honour
Davies R.	L&C/Swindon				GWR Roll of Honour
Davies R.	Traffic/Llanelly				GWR Roll of Honour
Davies R.E.	Signal Lineman/Wrexham				GWR Mag 6&7/15
Davies Rowland	Engine Cleaner/Loco/Newport		1st Monmouthshire Regt	KIA 8/5/15	Menin Gate Mem
Davies Thomas Philip	R/Labourer/Engineer/Wrexham	19	Pte 3/4th R. Welsh Fus	Died 8/7/15	Wrexham Cem
Davies W.	L&C/Wolverhampton				GWR Roll of Honour
Davies William	Iron Frame Repairer/L&C/Coleham				GWR Mag 12/17 & 6/18
Davies William George	Brakesman/Lydney Severn & Wye		Pte 7th Gloucester Regt	KIA 8/8/15	Helles Mem
Davies W.H.	Wagon Repairer/L&C/Panteg	17			GWR Mag 2&4/15
Davis A.	Parcel Porter/Traffic/Paddington				GWR Mag 11/16 & 2/17
Davis A.E.	Labourer/L&C/Swindon				GWR Mag 9/16
Davis Albert E.	Carriage Cleaner/L&C/Paddington				GWR Mag 7/18
Davis C.C.	Porter/Goods/Langley Green				GWR Mag 1/18
Davis(es) Henry T.	Policeman/Goods/Hockley	35	Pte 1st R. Warwick Regt	KIA 9/12/14	Prowse Point Mil Cem
Davis J.	Porter/Kington Station				GWR Mag 10/15
Davis Sidney	Packer/Engineer/Cheltenham	22			GWR Mag 8/16
Davis S.J.	Labourer/W&C/Swindon	30		Doi	GWR Mag 9/16
Davis W.	Shunter/Traffic/Old Oak Common				GWR Mag 7&10/17
Davis W.J.	Gasfitter/L&C/Swindon				GWR Mag 2/19
Daw William Gilbert	Goods/Swindon	27	Pte 2nd H.A.C.	Dow 13/7/18	Magnaboschi Br Cem
Dawes Reginald	Labourer/L&C/Swindon	21	Pte 6th Shropshire L.I.	Dow 1/12/17	Tincourt New Cem
Dawson William C.	Clerk/Audit/Paddington	39	Spr ROD R.E.	Died 13/10/18	Upton-cum-Chalvey
Day Albert William G.	Clerk/Traffic/Abingdon	19	Pte 2nd R. Berks Regt	KIA 26/10/16	Thiepval Mem
Day George Moore	Packer/Engineer/Aynho	36	Sto HMS Laforey RN	SL 23/3/17	Chatham Naval Mem
Day Harold	Apprent/L&C/Swindon	20	Ft/Sub/Lt 8 Squadron RNAS	Dac 5/2/18	St Marys Cem Haisnes
Day Mark	L&C/Swindon		Pte 2nd Grenadier Guards	KIA 31/7/17	Menin Gate Mem
Day R.	Rail Motor Conductor/Southall				GWR Mag 9/19
De La Mothe Percy J.	Goods/Guernsey	29	Pte 1st R. Guernsey L.I.	KIA 13/4/18	Ploegsteert Mem
Deacon William James	Shedman/L&C/Swindon	35	AS HMS Good Hope RN	SL 1/11/14	Portsmouth Naval Mem
Deakin Albert Ernest	Porter/Goods/Hockley	27	L/Cpl 1st Worcester Regt	KIA 26/10/16	Thiepval Mem
Deal(e)y William Alfred	Porter/Goods/Hockley	22	Gnr 160th Siege Bty RGA	Died 19/10/18	Abbeville Com Cem
Dean Charles Conrad	Clerk/Goods/Brettell Lane	20	Pte 16th R. Warwick Regt	Dow 15/9/16	La Neuville Br Cem
Dean George Frederick	Clerk/Accounts/Swindon	28	2/Lt 162nd Bde RFA	KIA 16/10/17	Tyne Cot Mem
Dean William James	Porter/Traffic/Birmingham		Pte 14th R. Warwick Regt	KIA 3/9/16	Thiepval Mem
Dearle Horace	Signal Porter/Traffic/Dousland	19	Pte 20th Northumberland Fus	Died 17/10/17	Tyne Cot Mem
Dearlove Ernest W.	Porter/Traffic/Cholsey	19	Pte 2/4th R Berks Regt	Dow 30/10/18	St Aubert Br Cem
Denham H.	Labourer/Signal/Taunton				GWR Mag 2/19
Dennis Ernest	Coal Trimmer/Electric/Park Royal	27			GWR Mag 9/15
Denton Walter William	Machinist/L&C/Swindon	23	Pte 1/4th Wilts Regt	KIA 10/5/18	Ramleh War Cem
Dermott Alfred William	Clerk/DGMO/London	18	Pte 1/13th London Regt	KIA 9/5/15	Ploegsteert Mem
Derrick Albert James	Restaurant Car Conductor/Padd	26	L/Cpl 8th E. Surrey Regt	Died 18/5/17	Mons (Bergen) Cem
Dew Herbert	Packer/Engineer/Salisbury	35	Spr No.4 Tramway Co R.E.	KIA 29/4/18	Nine Elms Br Cem
Dewland George	Packer/Engineer/Dunkerton	30	Pte 1st Dorset Regt	KIA 22/10/14	Le Touret Mem

Name	Role/Location	Age	Rank/Regiment	Death	Memorial
Dicken/Dickin W.	Fireman/Loco/Wolverhampton				GWR Mag 6/16
Didcock George	Engineer/Cholsey		Pte 5th R. Berks Regt	KIA 28/4/17	Arras Mem
Didcock Mark	R/Labourer/Engineer/Cholsey		Pte 1st R. Berks Regt	KIA 16/5/15	Le Touret Mem
Diggory Edwin Thomas	Clerk/Goods/Cardiff	25	QMS 1/2nd Welsh F/Amb RAMC	KIA 20/8/15	Hill 10 Cem
Dimond Albert Victor	Labourer/Engineer/Wiveliscombe	28	Pte 1/4th Devonshire Regt	Died 4/1/16	Kirkee Mem India
Dinwiddy Leonard Arthur	Porter/Traffic/Exeter St Thomas	20	L/Cpl 3rd Coldstream Guards	KIA 8/10/15	Loos Mem
Diver Albert Edward	R/Labourer/Engineer/Plymouth NR	33	Pte 8th Devonshire Regt	KIA 25/9/15	Loos Mem
Dixon Arthur Edward	Lampman/Traffic/Shrewsbury	20	Pte 55th Co MGC (Infantry)	Dow 12/10/17	Dozingham Mil Cem
Dixon Edmund	Packer/Engineer/Tyseley				GWR Mag 12/16&1/17
Dixon Edgar Arnold	Clerk/L&C/Swindon	19	Pte 2/4th Ox & Bucks L.I.	KIA 12/9/18	Ploegsteert Mem
Dixon Norman Reg W.	Apprent/L&C/Swindon	22	Spr 565th (Wilts) ATC R.E.	Dow 19/9/18	Beaumetz C Road Cem
Dixon W.	Clerk/Goods/Hockley				GWR Mag 8/18
Dobson Arthur	Machinist/L&C/Swindon	18	Pte 93rd Training Reserve	Died 22/3/17	Froxfield Cem
Dobson Arthur Alan	L&C/Didcot	21	Pte 1st R. Berks Regt	KIA 28/9/15	Loos Mem
Dobson Arthur James	Wagon Painter/W&C/Swindon		Pte 1st Wilts Regt	KIA 6/7/16	Thiepval Mem
Dodd F.	Shedman/L&C/Chester				GWR Mag 12/16
Dodson George Cecil	Traffic/Wellington (Salop)	25	Sgt 234th MGC (Infantry)	KIA 9/10/17	Tyne Cot Mem
Dodson Joseph	Shipper/Goods/Manchester	34	Pte 17th Manchester Regt	Dow 26/4/17	Mont Huon Mil Cem
Doran Edward Hammett	Clerk/Traffic/Swansea	37	Cpl 10th Rifle Bde	Dow 10/3/17	Grove Town Cem
Dorchester Edward J.	Clerk/Engineer/Chipping Sodbury		Rifm 1st KRRC	Dow 23/8/18	Vis-en-Artois Mem
Dore Frederick W.H.	Engine Cleaner/Loco/Newton Ab't	18	Pte Plymouth Bn RMLI	Dow 28/5/15	Lancashire Landing Cem
Dormer George	Traffic/Princess Risborough	33	Gnr D Bty 78th Bde RFA	Dow 6/9/18	Lebucquiere Com Cem
Dorrell R.	Engine Cleaner/Loco/Tyseley				GWR Mag 10/20
Doughty F.	Clerk/Goods/Bilston				GWR Mag 7/18
Doughty Joseph	Painter/Engineer/Wolverhampton		Cpl 9th R. Scots	KIA 1/8/18	Raperie Br Cem
Dowell Frederick James	L/Packer/Engineer/Evershot	33	Cpl 5th Dorset Regt	KIA 21/8/15	Helles Mem
Dowers Francis John	Wheelwright/L&C/Swindon	26	Spr 565th (Wilts) ATC R.E.	Died 18/11/18	Douai Br Cem
Dowley Richard George	Labourer/Signal/Shrewsbury	26	Pte 7th Shropshire L.I.	Dow 19/7/16	Boulogne East Cem
Dowman Henry	Bricklayer/Engineer/Banbury		Pte 2nd Ox & Bucks L.I.	KIA 16/5/15	Le Touret Mem
Downes Charles Fred	Labourer/Engineer/Shrewsbury	30	Pte 2nd S Lancashire Regt	KIA 27/5/18	Soissons Mem
Downing Francis	Fireman/Loco/Southall	21	Spr 126th Field Co R.E.	KIA 14/7/16	Thiepval Mem
Drake E.B.	Fitters Apprent/Marine/Fishguard				GWR Mag 2/19
Drew H.	Packer/Engineer/Salisbury				GWR Mag 8/18
Drew William Fred	Clerk/Accounts/Paddington	30	2/Cpl ROD R.E.	Dow 4/9/18	Aubigny Com Cem
Drewett Stan George	Machinist/L&C/Swindon	20	Pte 1/2nd London Regt	KIA 27/8/18	Summit Trench Cem
Drinkwater Harry	Packer/Engineer/Warwick		Pte 1/5th R. Warwick Regt	KIA 17/11/16	Thiepval Mem
Driver W.	Packer/Engineer/Weston-s-Edge				GWR Mag 10/19
Drury Philip C.	Labourer/L&C/Swindon		Gnr 86th Bde Am/Col RFA	KIA 30/9/17	The Huts Cem
Drury Robert	Shed Porter/Goods/Cardiff		Pte 1st Lincolnshire Regt	KIA 4/6/15	Menin Gate Mem
Duck Fred Ernest	Apprent Boilermaker/L&C/Swindon	23	Pte 2/4th R Berks Regt	KIA 22/8/17	Tyne Cot Mem
Dudman Albert Victor	Letterpress Printer/Paddington	24	Rifm 12th London Regt	KIA 7/10/16	Thiepval Mem
Duffus John Victor	Clerk/Traffic/Llandilo		Pte 1st SWB	KIA 23/9/16	Thiepval Mem
Duke Frederick	R/Labourer/Engineer/Taunton	25	Pte 6th Somerset L.I.	KIA 16/9/16	Thiepval Mem
Dulin William Walter M.	Apprent/L&C/Swindon		Lt Central Despatch Pool RAF	Died 29/7/18	Terlincthun Br Cem
Dunbar Walter E.	Porter/Traffic/Taunton		L/Cpl 8th Somerset L.I.	KIA 10/4/17	Arras Mem
Dunford Ernest Frank	Traffic/Radstock	22	Pte 8th Gloucester Regt	KIA 13/1/16	St Vaast Post Mil Cem
Dunn Horace	Wagon Painter/L&C/Swindon				GWR Mag 6/19
Dunstan Paschal Palmer	Messenger/D.S.O./Plymouth	19	Pte 15th Hampshire Regt	KIA 9/8/18	Tyne Cot Mem
Durant Robert Henry W.	Vanguard/Goods/Poplar		Pte 8th W. Kent Regt	Dow 4/10/15	Valenciennes Com Cem
Dyde John Henry	Dist Lampman/Traffic/Handsworth	26	Pte 2nd Coldstream Guards	KIA 27/8/18	Croisilles Br Cem
Dyment William Clifford	Carpenter/Signal/Newport	29	Pte 17th Lanashire Fus	KIA 22/5/18	Varennes Mil Cem
Eade Frederick C.	Packer/Engineer/R. Albert Dock	29			GWR Mag 2&3/15
Eades Henry James C.	Policeman/Traffic/Plymouth Millbay	25	Pte 1st Devonshire Regt	Dow 1/9/18	Varennes Mil Cem
Eagle Arthur Walter F.	Carriage Cleaner/L&C/Paddington	27	L/Cpl 227th Co MGC (Infantry)	KIA 30/11/17	Cambrai Mem
Eames W.A.	Traffic/Windsor & Eaton				GWR Roll of Honour
Eason A.G.	L&C/Wolverhampton				GWR Roll of Honour
East W.	Packer/Engineer/Notgrove				GWR Mag 9/20
Eastlick W.H.	Porter/Goods/Devonport				GWR Mag 6/20
Eaton George Harry	Wheelwright/L&C/Westbourne Pk		Sgt 4th Army Workshops R.E.	KIA 30/3/18	Pozieres Mem

Name	Occupation	Age	Regiment	Death	Memorial
Eaton Walter F.	Shunter/L&C/Neath				GWR Mag 6/17
Eddy William James	R/Labourer/Engineer/W Ealing	26	Pte 1st Cameronians	KIA 20/1/15	Ploegsteert Mem
Edge Charles	Boilermaker/L&C/Swindon		Pte 7th Wilts Regt	K 16-18/10/18	Highland Cem
Edmonds A.T.	Fireman/Loco/Newport Dock St.				GWR Mag 6/15
Edwards Alfred Ernest	Porter/Goods/Bristol	32	L/Cpl 1st SWB	Dow 2/4/15	Bethune Town Cem
Edwards Alfred Thomas	Mason/Engineer/Cinderford		Rifm 23rd Entrench Bn Irish Rifles	KIA 24/3/18	Pozieres Mem
Edwards Arthur William	Porter/Goods/Hockley		Pte 9th R. Warwick Regt	KIA 9/4/16	Basra Mem
Edwards Ellis	Porter/Traffic/Blaenau Festiniog	19	Pte 13th R. Welsh Fus	KIA 22/4/18	Bouzincourt Com Cem
Edwards Ernest William	Horse Loader/Traffic/Oxford	29	Pte 5th Ox & Bucks L.I.	Dow 21/9/15	Etaples Mil Cem
Edwards F.G.	Porter/Traffic/Pill				GWR Mag 3/19
Edwards G.F.	Carman/Goods/Handsworth				GWR Mag 9/17
Edwards Herbert H.W.	Porter/Traffic/Praze	22	Pte 7th DCLI	KIA 11/4/16	Menin Gate Mem
Edwards Henry James	Fireman/Loco/Trowbridge	23	Sgt 5th Wilts Regt	Died 1/10/18	Kirkee Mem India
Edwards John Henry	Boilermaker/L&C/Swindon		Spr 565th (Wilts) ATC R.E.	KIA 18/9/18	Ruyaulcourt Mil Cem
Edwards L.	Traffic/Oxford				GWR Roll of Honour
Edwards Percival S.A.	Porter/Traffic/Devizes		Pte 13th R. Welsh Fus	KIA 31/7/17	Dragoon Camp Cem
Edwards Robert Lloyd	Porter/Traffic/Maentwrog Road	20	Pte 17th R. Welsh Fus	KIA 13/5/16	Loos Mem
Edwards W.	L/Packer/Engineer/Wood End				GWR Mag 9&12/19
Edwards William Ernest	Audit Clerk/Paddington	39	Spr 19th Light Rly Co R.E.	Dow 29/3/18	Aubigny Com Cem
Eggleton H.	Engineer/Bristol				GWR Roll of Honour
Elderfield H. E.	Storesman/Stores/Swindon	24			GWR Mag 4/15 & 5/16
Eldridge T.H.	Locomotive/Oxford	33	Cpl 135th Heavy Bty RGA	Died 25/2/19	Oxford Cem
Ellis Arthur Cecil	Fitters Apprent/L&C/Swindon	19	Spr 6th Reserve Bn R.E.	Died 24/9/18	Swindon Cem
Ellis C.	Traffic/Bristol				GWR Roll of Honour
Ellis Harold John Henry	Porter/Traffic/Loddiswell	22	Pte 17th Manchester Regt	KIA 22/3/18	Pozieres Mem
Ellis Walter John	Porter/Traffic/Newton Abbot	26	Pte 19th Welsh Regt	Died 6/11/18	Rocquigny Road Cem
Ellison Walter J.	Assist Wheelwright/L&C/Swindon	25	Spr 133rd ATC R.E.	Dow 1/10/17	Godewaersvelde Cem
Elston John Crouch	Porter/Goods/Poplar	31	Pte 4th Royal Fus	KIA 26/10/14	Le Touret Mem
Eltham Ernest L.	Traffic/Oxford		L/Sgt 2nd R. Berks Regt	KIA 25/9/15	Ploegsteert Mem
Emanuel Victor	Clerk/L&C/Neath	20	Pte 2nd SWB	KIA 16/8/17	Tyne Cot Mem
Emson Arthur Charles	Rail Motor Conduct/Kidderminster	27	Spr 19th Rly Operating Co R.E.	Died 15/9/18	Mikra Br Cem
Escott Frederick	Labourer/Signal/Chippenham	21	Pte 2nd Wilts Regt	KIA 12/3/15	Le Touret Mem
Escott Frederick Arthur	Porter/Goods/Lawrence Hill	28	Pte RMLI HMS Goliath	SL 13/5/15	Plymouth Naval Mem
Esmond Stephen	Motorman/Goods/Paddington	33	Pte 14th Anti-aircraft ASC	KIA 26/1/15	Houplines Com Cem
Essex V.	Storesman/Stores/Didcot	40	Dvr 75th Bty 46th Bde RFA	Died 14/3/19	Cairo War Mem Cem
Etheridge Charles	Packer/Engineer/Rowley Regis		Sgt 1/6th R Warwick Regt	KIA 4/2/17	Asservillers New Cem
Evans Arthur Alexandra	Dist Lampman/Traffic/Newport DS	19	Rifm 1st Monmouthshire Regt	KIA 24/4/15	Menin Gate Mem
Evans A.H.	Boiler Washer/L&C/Danygraig				GWR Mag 1&6/18
Evans Arthur Sydney	Porter/traffic/New Radnor	19	Pte 63rd Bn MGC (Infantry)	KIA 5/4/18	Englebelmer Com Cem
Evans David	Packer/Engineer/W London Jct	23	Pte 2nd Grenadier Guards	Dow 23/11/14	Cambridge City Cem
Evans E.D.	Traffic/Hodnet				GWR Roll of Honour
Evans Eric Henry	Clerk/Accounts/Paddington	23	Ft/Cadet 53rd Training RAF	DFA 13/9/18	N. Sheen Cem
Evans Fred William	Porter/Goods/Reading	24	Pte 1st RMLI	KIA 2/9/18	Vis-en-Artois Mem
Evans G.B.	Traffic/Cardiff				GWR Roll of Honour
Evans George Loveridge	Signal Porter/Traffic/Blaenavon	23	Tpr Household Bn H. Guards	Died 13/12/17	Happy Valley Br Cem
Evans Herbert Charles	Fireman/Loco/Cardiff	23	Gnr 112th Bty 24th Bde RFA	Died 20/9/16	Bronfay Farm Mil Cem
Evans Henry W.A.	Lad Porter/Goods/Poplar				GWR Mag 2&4/17
Evans J.	Striker/Engineer/Aberavon				GWR Mag 12/16 & 3/17
Evans J.	Wireman/Signal/Worcester				GWR Mag 12/19
Evans John	L/Packer/Engineer/Craven Arms				GWR Mag 5&7/17
Evans John Trevor S.	Clerk/Goods/Carfiff	26	Temp Capt 19th/R Welsh Fus	Dow 7/5/18	Serre Road No.1 Cem
Evans N.	Locomotive/Swindon				GWR Roll of Honour
Evans P.E.	Clerk/Traffic/Hartlebury				GWR Mag 3/17
Evans Robert H.	Labourer/Sheet/Bridgwater	30	Pte 2nd Highland L.I.	KIA 6/12/17	Hermies Hill Br Cem
Evans Rowland W.	Fireman/Loco/Chester		Sgt 9th Cheshire Regt	KIA 4/7/16	Thiepval Mem
Evans Thomas David	Apprent/L&C/Swindon	19	Pte 2nd Wilts Regt	KIA 5/11/18	Cross Roads Cem
Evans Thomas Henry	Foreman Parcel Porter/Shrew'bury	35	Pte 2nd Shropshire L.I.	KIA 10/3/15	Menin Gate Mem
Evans W.	Packer/Engineer/Shrewsbury				GWR Mag 10/19
Evans William Edward	Booking Clerk/Traffic/Llandilo	36	Pte 26th Royal Fus	KIA 10/10/16	Thiepval Mem

Name	Role/Location	Age	Regiment	Death	Cemetery/Memorial
Evans W.E.	Loco/Worcester				GWR Roll of Honour
Evans W.L.	Clerk/Traffic/Pontardulais				GWR Mag 6/20
Everest E.	Porter/Traffic/Acton				GWR Mag 11&12/18
Ewell Edward	Packer/Engineer/Shrewsbury		Pte 5th Shropshire L.I.	KIA 24/8/16	Delville Wood Cem
Faithorn Samuel Thomas	Porter/Traffic/Plymouth		L/Cpl 1st Middlesex Regt	KIA 25/9/15	Loos Mem
Fantham Edward	Parcel Porter/Traffic/Birmingham	21	L/Cpl 2nd Coldstream Guards	Dow 20/9/16	Ste Marie Cem
Faraday James	Helper/L&C/Swindon	34	Pte RMLI	Doi/w14/10/14	Gillingham Cem
Farlow James Edward	Packer/Engineer/Buildwas		Pte 1st Shropshire L.I.	Dow 10/7/18	Niederzwehren Cem
Farmer George Enos	Bridge Labourer/Shrewsbury		Spr 275th (GWR) Rly Co R.E.	Dow 28/9/18	Varennes Mil Cem
Farmer H.	Traffic/Handborough				GWR Roll of Honour
Farmer Thomas	Fitters Helper/B Shop/Swindon		Pte 5th Wilts Regt	KIA 10/8/15	Helles Mem
Farndell Charles	Labourer/No 6 Shop/Swindon		L/Cpl 12th Gloucester Regt	KIA 30/7/16	Thiepval Mem
Farr James	Clerk/Traffic/Bromborough				GWR Mag 12/18
Farr James Alfred	Clerk/DGMO/Cardiff	18	Pte 6th K Scottish Borderers	KIA 9/7/16	Peronne Road Cem
Farrington Charles Henry	Packer/Engineer/Ealing	27	Pte 1st Royal Fus	KIA 27/9/14	La Ferte-s-Jouarre Mem
Farthing Henry James	Riveter/L&C/Bridgwater	20	Pte 15th Durham L.I.	KIA 9/9/18	Vis-en-Artois Mem
Farthing William Edgar	Clerk/Engineer/Plymouth	24	2/Lt 159th Heavy Bty RGA	Died 8/2/17	Ford Pk Cem Plymouth
Fell Christopher William	Fireman/Loco/Slough	27	Bugler 1/1st Ox & Bucks L.I.	KIA 10/3/17	Eclusier Com Cem
Fell Thomas Curtis	Horse Box Builder/L&C/Swindon	20	Pte 17th Lancashire Fus	KIA 28/9/18	Hooge Crater Cem
Fellenden Thomas	Porter/Traffic/Wolverhampton		Gdsm 2nd Grenadier Guards	KIA 9/10/17	Tyne Cot Mem
Felton C.E.	Porter/Traffic/Paddington				GWR Mag 1/19
Fennell Frank	Clerk/Signal/Reading	24	Pte 1/4th R. Berks Regt	KIA 5/4/17	Lempire Com Cem
Ferreday/Ferriday W.	Labourer/L&C/Wolverhampton				GWR Mag 9/17
Fewings Herbert Reg	Porter/Traffic/Churston	19	Pte 10th Cheshire Regt	Dow 27/5/18	Soissons Mem
Fidoe Arthur Oliver	Carriage Cleaner/L&C/Leamington		Pte 2/7th R Warwick Regt	Dow 4/12/17	Fins New Br Cem
Field F.H.	Shunter/Traffic/Cwmbran				GWR Mag 12/17 & 2/18
Finch J.	Vanguard/Goods/Paddington				GWR Mag 11/19
Fincken William Henry	Porter/Goods/Paddington		Pte 3rd London Regt	KIA 2/7/16	Hebuterne Mil Cem
Finley William Reginald	Clerk/Traffic/Stourbridge Jct	25	Cpl 1st Life Guards	Dow 20/5/18	Etaples Mil Cem
Finn John Joseph	Shunter/Traffic/Southall	33	L/Cpl 1st Devonshire Regt	KIA 24/7/16	Thiepval Mem
Fisher Harold Ernest	Apprent/L&C/Swindon	18	Pte 7th Wilts Regt	K 16-18/10/18	Highland Cem
Fisher James Charles H.	Coach Painter Apprent/Swindon		Pte 6th R. Dublin Fus	KIA 17/10/18	Forest Com Cem
Fisher R.T.	Chief Accountants Dept				GWR Roll of Honour
Fitzpatrick Thomas	Fixer/Signal/Newport	37	Pte 1st SWB	Dow 2/12/15	St Sever Cem
Fleet William	Parcel Carman/Traffic/Chester	21	L/Cpl 9th Cheshire Regt	Dow 3/7/16	Heilly Station Cem
Fletcher C.G.	Bricklayer/Engineer/Wolverh'ton				GWR Mag 6&12/18
Florey Henry	Hydraulic Forgeman/L&C/Swindon		Pte 5th Wilts Regt	KIA 17/1/17	Amara War Cem
Flower Edwin Brian	Wheelwright/C&W/Swindon		Spr 9th Light Rly Co R.E.	Dow 4/10/17	Rocquigny Road Cem
Ford Albert Thomas	Labourer/Engineer//Reading		L/Cpl 6th R. Berks Regt	KIA 17/2/17	Thiepval Mem
Ford Edward	Carriage Cleaner/Old Oak Common	42			GWR Mag 10/16
Ford E.B.	Locomotive/Trowbridge				GWR Roll of Honour
Ford George James	R/Labourer/Engineer/Brent	31	Pte 1/7th Devonshire Regt	Died 19/2/15	Exeter Higher Cem
Ford George William R.	Piece-work Checker/L&C/Swindon	37	Sgt 5th Wilts Regt	Dow 10/8/15	Helles Mem
Ford William Frank	Locomotive/Swindon	26	Pte 9th Devonshire Regt	KIA 26/10/17	Tyne Cot Mem
Fortune Henry George	Clerk/Traffic/Morrison	21	2/Lt Att 132nd MGC	KIA 17/1/17	Amara War Cem
Forskett Edward George	Finance Clerk/Paddington	20	Pte 2/22nd London Regt	Dow 4/11/17	Kantara War Mem Cem
Foster Frank	Porter/Traffic/Evesham	24	Pte 5th Ox & Bucks L.I.	KIA 25/9/15	Menin Gate Mem
Foster Mathew	Porter/Goods/Poplar		Gnr 88th Bty 14th Bde RFA	Died 8/5/17	Bethune Town Cem
Fowler Herbert James	Coach Finisher/L&C/Swindon	24	Pte 2nd Wilts Regt	Dow 8/7/16	Thiepval Mem
Fowles Albert Victor	Signal Porter/Traffic/Aberdylais	20	Pte 2nd Coldstream Guards	Died 16/4/18	Bac-du-Sud Br Cem
Fox A.	Porter/Traffic/Shrewsbury				GWR Mag 6/16
Fox H.J.	Porter/Traffic/Lawrence Hill				GWR Mag 6/19
Foxhall Reg Stanley	Porter/Goods/Cardiff	24	Pte 12th Gloucester Regt	KIA 28/6/18	Ploegsteert Mem
Foynes E.F.	Clerk/Goods/Smithfield				GWR Mag 10/17
Francis George Henry	Vanguard/Goods/Poplar	18	Pte 9th Essex Regt	Dow 12/8/18	Mont Huon Mil Cem
Francis Herbert William	Painter/L&C/Coton Hill		Pte 15th Sherwood Foresters	KIA 20/10/18	Harlebeke New Br Cem
Frankum Charles W.M.	Under-Lineman/Signal/Wrexham	28	Shoeing Smith K Bty R.H.A.	Dow 2/4/18	St Sever Cem
Frankum Jessie	Machinist/Signal/Reading	33	L/Sgt 1st Seaforth Highlanders	KIA 22/4/16	Basra Mem
Freeman Henry Frank	Labourer/L&C/St Blazey		Pte 8th Gloucester Regt	KIA 30/5/18	Soissons Mem

Name	Occupation	Age	Regiment	Death	Memorial
French A.W.	Telegraph Relief Staff/Paddington		Despatch Rider R.E.	Doi 31/1/19	Unknown
Friday Thomas Charles	Ticket Collector/Traffic/Paddington	27	Dvr 20th Bty 7th Lond'n Bde RFA	Died 19/6/16	Paddington Cem
Frost A.W.	Porter/Traffic/Cardiff		Pte 3rd Hampshire Regt	Das 4/5/17	Hyeres New Com Cem
Frowen Ernest Harry	Packer/Engineer/Lydney	24	L/Cpl 10th Gloucester Regt	KIA 25/9/15	Loos Mem
Fry William Herbert	Helper/L&C/Swindon	20	Dvr 84th Bde Am/Col RFA	Dow 4/11/17	Wimereux Com Cem
Fudge Andrew Hector	Traffic/Acton	29	Pte 4th Royal Fus	KIA 14/9/14	La Ferte-s-Jouarre Mem
Fuller John	Frame-Builder/21A Shop/Swindon		Pte 1st R. Berks Regt	KIA 25/10/14	Menin Gate Mem
Fuller W.	Labourer/Engineer/Didcot				GWR Mag 5&7/17
Gale Alfred John	Porter/Traffic/Highworth		Pte 1st RMLI	KIA 25/8/18	Vis-en-Artois Mem
Gale Bruce Arthur	Porter/Traffic/Salisbury	20	Gdsm 4th Grenadier Guards	Dow 13/4/18	Longuenesse Cem
Gale Walter	Canalman/Engineer/Burlescombe	22	Pte 8th Devonshire Regt	KIA 4/9/16	Thiepval Mem
Gale W.W.	Labourer/L&C/Swindon				GWR Mag 11/16 & 1/17
Galloway F.	Shunter/Traffic/Port Talbot				GWR Mag 8/15
Gamlen Arthur William	Fireman/Loco/Bristol	22	Spr 3/1st S Midland Field Co R.E.	KIA 9/6/16	Rue-des-Berceaux Cem
Gardiner Charles William	Locomotive/Swindon		Gnr D Bty 62nd Bde RFA	KIA 3/5/17	Bunyans Cem
Gardiner F.	Boiler Cleaner/L&C/Sudbrook				GWR Mag 9/16
Gardiner F.F.	Locomotive/Cardiff				GWR Roll of Honour
Gardiner Herbert	Shunter/Traffic/Swansea Docks	32			GWR Mag 12/14
Gardner Edwin Charles	Signal Porter/Traffic/Washford	26	Pte 1/5th Somerset L.I.	KIA 10/4/18	Ramleh War Cem
Gaul James	Trimmer/Marine/Fishguard	32	L/Sea SS Emlyndene RN	Das 12/12/17	Plymouth Naval Mem
Gee George Wilfred	Warehouse Clerk/Stores/Swindon	20	L/Cpl 2nd Wilts Regt	KIA 15/6/15	Le Touret Mem
Gee William Henry	Wagon Painter/L&C/Swindon	32	Pte 1st Wilts Regt	KIA 26/10/14	Le Touret Mem
Geen William Henry	Wharf Labourer/Engineer/Dunball		Pte 10th Devonshire Regt	KIA 10/2/17	Doiran Mem
Gentle Alfred H.	Clerk/Goods/Avonmouth Docks		Pte 1st Gloucester Regt	KIA 27/8/16	Thiepval Mem
George E.	Porter/Goods/Hockley				GWR Mag 12/17 & 2/18
George Llewellyn	Gasman/L&C/Danygraig	45	Sto HM Trawler Thuringia RN	SL 11/11/17	Plymouth Naval Mem
Gerrard Walter P.	Porter/Goods/Bristol	28	Pte 1st SWB	KIA 26/9/14	Le Ferte-s-Jouarre Mem
Gibbons David Thomas	Porter/Traffic/Cardigan	23	L/Cpl 1/4th Welsh Regt	KIA 11/8/15	Helles Mem
Gibbons/Gibbens Walter	Packer/Engineer/Reading	30	Pte 13th F/Amb RAMC	Doi 21/11/16	St Sever Cem
Gibbs Harry	Locomotive/Swindon		Pte 15th Welsh Regt	KIA 4/8/17	Menin Gate Mem
Gibbs Joseph	Labourer/L&C/Swindon		Pte 7th Wilts Regt	KIA 7/10/18	Vis-en-Artois Mem
Gibbs John Charles B.	Clerk/L&C/Swindon	19	Pte 1st Wilts Regt	Died 10/2/17	Bailleul Com Cem
Gibbs Oliver Stephen	Packer/Engineer/Cheltenham		Pte 9th Cheshire Regt	KIA 24/3/18	Delsaux Farm Cem BNS
Gibbs Vincent Frederick	Porter/Traffic/Evesham		Pte 20th London Regt	KIA 30/8/18	H.A.C. Cem Ecoust
Gibson Frederick James	Porter/Goods/Frome	20	Dvr 3rd Air Line Section R.E.	Died 23/10/18	Doiran Mem
Giddings Stanley N.G.	Ticket Collector/Newbury	23	Sgt 8th R. Berks Regt	Dow 7/4/18	Picquigny Br Cem
Gilbert R.W.	Locomotive/Wormwood Scrubs				GWR Roll of Honour
Giles Arthur Edward	Engine Cleaner/L&C/Swindon	19	Pte Motor Transport ASC	Died 8/11/17	Dae es Salaam Cem
Giles H.	Goods/Wolverhampton				GWR Roll of Honour
Giles Herbert	Labourer/Engineer/Stratton		Rifm 21st London Regt	KIA 4/9/18	Voormezeele No 3
Giles Howard Russell	Clerk/Goods/Worcester	20	Pte Worcester Yeomanry	KIA 23/4/16	Jerusalem Mem
Giles John Samuel	Sheet Repairer/Goods/Worcester	26	Gnr 3rd Bty 45th Bde RFA	KIA 2/8/17	Belgian Bty Corner Cem
Giles William Ewart	Time & Storekeeper/L&C/Oxford		Pte 19th Middlesex Regt	KIA 1/9/18	Sailly-Saillisel Br Cem
Gilkes Charles Thomas	Messenger/Engineer/Paddington	19	Pte 1st London Regt	KIA 10/5/15	Ploegsteert Mem
Gilks William Henry	Packer/Engineer/Warwick	35	Pte 7th R Warwick Regt	Doi 11/4/16	Warwick Cem
Gill Giles	Apprent Boilermaker/L&C/Swindon	20	Pte 1st Wilts Regt	KIA 23/1/15	Wytschaete Mil Cem
Gillam Ernest Arthur	Engine Cleaner/L&C/Yeovil	19	Pte 1st Somerset L.I.	Dow 26/4/16	Humbercamps Com Cem
Gillard Samuel Tyler	Brass Finisher/L&C/Swindon		Pte 8th Somerset L.I.	Dow 31/7/17	Menin Gate Mem
Gillett A.H.	Labourer/L&C/Swindon				GWR Mag 12/18
Gillett Thomas Charles W	Labourer/L&C/Swindon	34	Cpl 1/5th Gordon Highlanders	KIA 1/8/18	Raperie Br Cem
Gillett William Francis	Labourer/L&C/Swindon		Pte 1st Garrison Warwick Regt	Died 5/7/16	Khartoum War Cem
Gillingham M.W.	Clerk D.S.O./Traffic/Bristol		Cpl 3rd Gloucester Regt	Died 25/10/17	Bristol Canford Cem
Gingell George	Slip Labourer/Engineer/Dauntsey				GWR Mag 10/16 & 1/17
Given Sydney James	Clerk/Goods/Birmingham		Sgt 14th R Warwick Regt	KIA 11/9/16	Serre Road No.2 Cem
Glass A.E.	Spare Hand/L&C/Swindon				GWR Mag 10/17
Glass Philip	Porter/Goods/Paddington	27	Pte 9th Queens R. Lancers	KIA 13/5/15	Div Collecting Post Cem
Glover G.	Porter/Goods/Hockley				GWR Mag 11&12/17
Godbeer Percival John	Porter /Goods/Plymouth	29	Pte 1st Devonshire Regt	KIA 24/12/14	Menin Gate Mem
Goddard Bertram	L&C/Swindon		Pte 3rd Wilts Regt	Died 17/10/15	Swindon Cem

Name	Occupation/Dept	Age	Regiment/Rank	Date	Memorial/Cemetery
Goddard E.E.	Trimmer/Marine/Fishguard				GWR Mag 1/16
Godwin Harold John	Driller/L&C/Swindon		Sgt 6th Wilts Regt	Doi 10/8/18	Hamburg Cem (POW)
Godwin Joseph William	Labourer/Hydraulic/Hockley	37	Cpl 10th W. Yorkshire Regt	KIA 1/7/16	Thiepval Mem
Golby Horace Lett	Carpenter/L&C/Swindon		Airman 2nd Class R.F.C.	Died 30/3/18	Swindon Cem
Golder Albert	Shunter/Traffic/Old Oak Common	25	Pte 2nd Ox & Bucks L.I.	KIA 16/9/14	Vailly Br Cem
Golding W.	Packer/Engineer/Hirwain	35			GWR Mag 1/15
Goldsborough Ernest G.	Fireman/Loco/Bristol	25	L/Cpl 2nd Wilts Regt	KIA 10/3/15	Le Touret Mem
Gomm Edwin Hubert	Locomotive/Southall	35	Pte 4th Royal Fus	KIA 23/8/14	Le Ferte-s-Jouarre Mem
Gooding Thomas W.	Goods Clerk/Traffic/Cambourne	20	Spr ROD R.E.	Died 10/6/18	Blargies Com Cem
Goodman A.F.	Locomotive/Swindon				GWR Roll of Honour
Goodman Harold W.H.	L2 Shop/Swindon		Pte 1st Wilts Regt	Dow 28/6/15	Boulogne East Cem
Goodman J.	Under-Lineman/Signal/Portobello				GWR Mag 8&9/18
Goodwin Thomas Harold	Clerk/Goods/Worcester	20	Pte Queens Worcester Hussars	KIA 23/4/16	Jerusalem Mem
Gore James Bonsey	Signalman/Severn & Wye Joint	23	Sgt 10th Gloucester Regt	KIA 25/9/15	Loos Mem
Gosling William Henry	Trimmers Apprent/L&C/Swindon	19	Pte 1st Hampshire Regt	KIA 22/4/18	St Venant-R Road Cem
Gough Daniel	R/Labourer/Engineer/Ludlow		L/Cpl 58th Bn MGC (Infantry)	Dow 24/4/18	Hangard Com Cem
Gough Frank	Labourer/L&C/Swindon	19	Pte 5th Wilts Regt	KIA 19/7/15	Pink Farm Cem
Gould Bert	Labourer/Engineer/Taunton		L/Cpl 12th Somerset L.I.	Dow 8/11/17	Kantara War Mem Cem
Goulding James Henry	Carman/Goods/Newport	28	Pte G Training Co MGC	Died 21/11/18	St Woolos Cem Newport
Gover Fred Charles	Packer/Engineer/Reading	28	Pte 2nd Ox & Bucks L.I.	KIA 21/10/14	Menin Gate Mem
Granger William Thomas	Clerk/L&C/Swindon	24	Lt 4th Wilts Regt	Dow 21//9/17	Bus House Cem
Grant Edmund James	Engine Cleaner/Loco/Trowbridge		Pte 5th Wilts Regt	KIA 23/11/15	Green Hill Cem
Grant Herbert Edwin	Invoice Clerk/Goods/Bristol		Pte 7th Somerset L.I.	KIA 7/8/17	Menin Gate Mem
Grant John	Engine Cleaner/L&C/Old Oak Com				GWR Mag 11/16
Gray Charles Casswell	Clerk/Goods/Oxford	24	L/Cpl 1/4th Ox & Bucks L.I.	Dow 24/6/18	Montecchio Com Cem
Gray Thomas Charles	Frame-Builder/13 Shop/Swindon		L/Cpl 2nd Wilts Regt	KIA 13/3/15	Le Touret Mem
Greedy William John	Packer/Engineer/Dulverton	26	Cpl 1/5th Somerset L.I.	KIA 10/4/18	Ramleh War Cem
Green Arthur	Porter/Goods/Hockley	30			GWR Mag 11/15 & 4/16
Green Benjamin Joseph	Packer/Engineer/Cradley	32	Sgt 18th Lancashire Fus	KIA 31/10/18	Harlebeke New Br Cem
Green C.R.B.	Locomotive/Swindon				GWR Roll of Honour
Green Charles William	Porter/Goods/South Lambeth	24	Rifm 18th London Regt	Dow 11/6/15	Noeux-L-Mines Cem
Green Hubert	Fireman/Loco/Stourbridge	20	Pte 9th Worcester Regt	KIA 10/8/15	Helles Mem
Green J.H.	Traffic/Ludlow				GWR Roll of Honour
Green Nelson Tom	Viceman/Signal/Reading		Pte 8th R Berks Regt	KIA 13/10/15	Loos Mem
Greenaway Alfred	Bolt Maker/Signal/Reading	35	Spr 86th Field Co R.E.	Dow 14/10/17	Solferino Farm Cem
Greenway William	Packer/Engineer/Worcester	33	Sgt 4th Worcester Regt	Died 28/4/18	Ebblinghem Mil Cem
Greenway William G.	Number Taker/Traffic/Banbury	21	Pte 6th Ox & Bucks L.I.	KIA 20/2/17	Thiepval Mem
Greer Henry Arthur	Apprent Coach Bodymaker/Swind	23	Pte 22nd (Depot) Middlesex Regt	Died 5/11/18	Swindon Cem
Gregory Frederick John	Shop Clerk/L&C/Swindon	32	Sgt C Bty 227th Bde RFA	Died 18/8/16	Bangalore Cem
Gregory Thomas	Porter/Goods/South Lambeth	24			GWR Mag 3/16
Grellier Arthur Berteau	Premium Apprentice/Swindon	19	2/Lt 2/7th Lancashire Fus	KIA 26/3/18	Pozieres Mem
Grieve Frank	Warehouse Clerk/Westbourne Pk	22	Pte 1st DCLI	KIA 17/12/16	St Vaast Post Mil Cem
Griffiths A.	Traffic/Shrewsbury				GWR Roll of Honour
Griffiths Alfred Edward	Striker/Signal/Reading	23	Pte 1/5th Essex Regt	Died 14/11/18	Beirut War Cem
Griffiths Herbert Stanley	Traffic/Dorrington	18	Pte 6th K Liverpool Regt	Dow 22/6/18	Etaples Mil Cem
Griffiths Ivor Monroe	Fireman/Loco/Llanelly	19	Pte 1/4th Welsh Regt	Doi 28/10/15	Alexandria War Cem
Griffiths John	Blacksmith/Signal/Newport	34	Spr 262nd (GWR) Rly Co R.E.	Died 12/5/17	St Woolos Cem Newport
Griffiths John Howell	Traffic/Birkenhead	20	Pte 11th Cheshire Regt	KIA 10/4/18	Ploegsteert Mem
Griffiths John Thomas	Signalman/Traffic/Oakengates		L/Cpl 14th Div Signal Co R.E.	Died 4/4/18	Cambrai E. Mil Cem
Grimes James Thomas	Labourer/Engineer/Westbourne Pk	32	Pte 8th Royal Fus	KIA 7/7/16	Thiepval Mem
Grimmer George Victor	Porter/Traffic/Henwick	23	Pte 1/8th Worcester Regt	KIA 24/10/18	Pommereuil Br Cem
Grindley Frederick	Painter/Engineer/Birmingham		Pte 7th Shropshire L.I.	KIA 13/11/16	Serre Road Cem No.1
Grist Albert Edward	Porter/Goods/Paddington	21	Pte 13th Royal Fus	KIA 14/11/16	Thiepval Mem
Gristock John	Timekeeper/L&C/Bristol	24	Pte 2nd R. Berks Regt	KIA 28/5/18	Soissons Mem
Gristock Robert William	Timekeeper/L&C/Bristol		Pte 1st R. Berks Regt	KIA 29/11/17	Cambrai Mem
Gritt A. James P.	Carriage Cleaner/W. London	20	Pte 13th Royal Fus	KIA 8/7/16	Thiepval Mem
Grove Ernest W.L.	Wagon Builder/L&C/Neath	32	Pte 19th (Depot) Welsh Regt	Died 21/5/18	Cardiff West Cem
Groves Edgar W.	Lampman/Traffic/Swansea				GWR Mag 12/19
Gubbins Jesse	Grinder/L&C/Swindon	40	CQMS 7th Ox & Bucks L.I.	Died 20/10/18	Mikra Br Cem

Name	Occupation	Age	Military	Death	Memorial
Guest H.	Labourer/Engineer/Taunton				GWR Mag 5/17
Guley Edward George	Carriage Fitter/L&C/Swindon		Pte 5th Wilts Regt	KIA 29/3/17	Basra Mem
Gulley James	Striker/L&C/Newton Abbot	30	Pte RMLI HMS Goliath	SL 13/5/15	Plymouth Naval Mem
Gulliver E.W.	Clerk/Goods/Smithfield				GWR Mag 3&7/18
Gully Thomas	Labourer/Engineer/Swansea	26	Pte 1st E. Lancashire Regt	Dow 14/5/15	Bailleul Com Cem
Gundry Alfred J.	Shunt Horse Driver/Goods/Yeovil	33	L/Cpl 1st Somerset L.I.	KIA 26/4/15	Menin Gate Mem
Gunning J.	Carman/Goods/Smithfield				GWR Mag 3&6/18
Gunter Charles Edward	Porter Shunter/Traffic/Witney		L/Cpl 2nd Ox & Bucks L.I.	Dow 3/5/17	Aubigny Com Cem
Gurney Reginald George	Fireman/Loco/Gloucester	30	Sgt 10th Worcester Regt	Dow 8/1/16	Merville Com Cem
Guthrie Richard C.	Apprent/L&C/Swindon		Airman 2nd Class 30 Sqdn R.F.C.	Died 5/12/17	Baghdad N War Cem
Gwilliam George	L/Packer/Engineer/Shrewsbury	41	Cpl 264th Rly Co R.E.	Died 26/12/17	Longuenesse Cem
Gwilt R.T.	Traffic/Easton Court				GWR Roll of Honour
Gye Albert	Porter/Traffic/Brentford		Cpl 13th London Regt	KIA 14/12/16	Laventie Mil Cem
Hacker George Thomas	Apprent/L&C/Swindon		Spr 565th (Wilts) ATC R.E.	Died 29/4/15	Swindon Cem
Hacker Ladas Tom	Coach-Finisher/L&C/Swindon		Dvr 3/3rd Wessex A/Col RFA	Died 24/12/15	Swindon Cem
Hackman Clifford	Clerk/Stores/Swindon	20	2/Lt 92 Squadron RAF	Dfa 7/4/18	Winchcombe Cem
Haines Albert Percy	Porter/Traffic/Hanwell	25	Pte 8th Royal Fus	KIA 7/7/16	Thiepval Mem
Haines James	Locomotive/Swindon	28	Pte 1st Wilts Regt	KIA 24/10/14	Le Touret Mem
Haines Reginald Alfred	Parcel Porter/Traffic/Bristol	26	Gnr 199th Siege Bty RGA	Dow 20/9/18	Thilloy Road Cem
Hale Alfred	Machineman/L&C/Swindon				GWR Mag 6/19
Hale Charles	Labourer/Engineer/Taunton		Pte 1/5th Somerset L.I.	KIA 23/11/17	Jerusalem War Cem
Hall A.C.	Messenger/Electrical/Paddington				GWR Mag 12/17 & 2/18
Hall H. Harold	Clerk/Traffic/Glyn Neath	31	Pte 12th Middlesex Regt	KIA 26/9/16	Thiepval Mem
Hall J.	Storeman/L&C/Llanelly Docks				GWR Mag 10/16
Hall Percy Victor	Engine Cleaner/Loco/Tyseley		L/Cpl 1/6th R Warwick Regt	KIA 27/8/17	Tyne Cot Mem
Hall Samuel Stanley	Porter/Traffic/Littleton & Badsey	19	Pte 19th Bn MGC (Infantry)	KIA 31/5/18	Chambrecy Br Cem
Ham Frederick William	Clerk/Goods/Brentford	30	2/Lt 158th Reserve Sqdn RFC	Dac 6/5/17	Suez War Mem Cem
Hambridge George	Fireman/Loco/Lydney		L/Sgt 10th Worcester Regt	KIA 3/7/16	Thiepval Mem
Hamman/Hammon F.W.	Boiler Washer/L&C/Oxley				GWR Mag 2/16
Hammacott Alfred G.	Porter/Traffic/Swansea High St	28	L/Cpl 8th Devons Att 95th R.E.	KIA 2/10/15	Vermelles Br Cem
Hammett George Henry	Labourer/Engineer/Dawlish	25	Gnr 14th Siege Bty RGA	KIA 23/5/17	La Targette Br Cem
Hammond Arthur John	Mileage Porter/Goods/Avonmouth	24	Pte 1/4th Gloucester Regt	KIA 19/10/15	Hebuterne Mil Cem
Hammond Frederick	Telegraph Labour/Signal/Newport	27	L/Cpl 1st Monmouthshire Regt	KIA 24/4/15	Menin Gate Mem
Hancock Arthur Percy	Porter/Traffic/Slough	29	L/Cpl 1st R Berks Regt	KIA 25/10/14	Menin Gate Mem
Hancock Fred Mead	Clerk/Traffic/Pershore	29	L/Cpl Worecstershire Yeo	Died 25/6/15	Broughton Churchyard
Hancock Horatio G.	Gateman/Traffic/Ely	28	Pte 1st Lancashire Fus	KIA 9/10/17	Tyne Cot Mem
Hancock John William	Rail Motor Conductor/Stourbridge	28	Spr 9th Light Rly Co R.E.	KIA 5/5/18	Houchin Br Cem
Hancock/Handcock Wm	Engine Cleaner/L&C/Old Oak Com	22			GWR Mag 10/16
Hancocks William John	Packer/Engineer/Hall Green	33	Pte 2nd Worcester Regt	KIA 16/5/15	Le Touret Mem
Hann Francis Arthur	Signalman/Traffic/Gilfach		Pte 1st Grenadier Guards	KIA 10/9/16	Thiepval Mem
Hannaford William Henry	Rail Motor Conductor/Plymouth MB	25	Sgt 10th R Warwick Regt	KIA 10/4/18	Tyne Cot Mem
Harding C.P.	Brakesman/Pontypool Crane St				GWR Mag 9/19
Harding Ernest Arthur	Limewasher/Engineer/Reading		Pte 5th R Berks Regt	KIA 19/9/18	Epehy Wood Farm Cem
Harding Frederick Percy	Traffic/Cardiff	21	Pte 1st Lancashire Fus	KIA 12/4/18	Ploegsteert Mem
Harding Joseph Frederick	Packer/Engineer/Hall Green		Pte 10th Gloucester Regt	KIA 13/10/15	Loos Mem
Harding Thomas Neate	Signal/Swindon	32	L/Cpl I.W.T. R.E.	Died 12/2/20	Swindon Cem
Hardman A.	District Lampman/traffic/Gloucester				GWR Mag 3/17
Hardy Reg Herbert W.	Clerk/DGMO/Liverpool	29	Lt 3rd Welsh Regt	Died 4/11/18	Caldicot Churchyard
Harford Edward Henry	Porter/Traffic/Norton Fitzwarren	19	Pte 10th or 16th Essex Regt	Dow 16/7/18	Picquigny Br Cem
Harley James Henry	Office Porter/Paddington Goods	20	Pte 3rd London Regt	KIA 13/10/15	Gorre Br & Indian Cem
Harman Charles	Helper/V Shop/Swindon Works	28	Pte 1st R Berks Regt	KIA 11/11/14	Menin Gate Mem
Harper John Francis	Dist Lampman/Traffic/Shifnal	25	L/Bom 56th Bde RFA	KIA 21/10/18	Harlebeke New Br Cem
Harper William Arthur	Porter/Traffic/Swan Village		Gdsm 1st Scots Guards	KIA 23/8/18	Bucquoy Road Cem
Harper William T.	Lifters Mate/L&C/Wormwood Sc		Sgt 1/3rd London Regt	KIA 11/4/17	London Cem N-Vitasse
Harpin John	Porter/Goods/Bilston		CQMS 1/6TH S Stafford Regt	Dow 7/5/18	Etaples Mil Cem
Harries T.	Engineer/Pembrey				GWR Roll of Honour
Harris A.	Gas Linesman/Engineer/Tysley				GWR Mag 6/15
Harris B.A.	Porter/Traffic/Handsworth				GWR Mag 1&6/18
Harris D.	Locomotive/Carmarthen				GWR Roll of Honour

Name	Occupation/Location	Age	Regiment	Death	Memorial
Harris Ernest Herbert	Labourer/Signal/Reading		Pte 8th R Berks Regt	Dow 19/8/16	Thiepval Mem
Harris George	R/Labourer/Eng/Stourbridge Jct	34	AS HMS Good Hope RN	SL 1/11/14	Portsmouth Naval Mem
Harris George Alwyn	Porter/Traffic/Bearley	19	Pte 1st Hampshire Regt	Dow 2/11/18	Villers-en-Cauchies Cem
Harris Melville George	Shedman/L&C/Moorswater	26	Rifm 1/21st London Regt	KIA 15/9/16	Thiepval Mem
Harris William Duncan	DGMO/Manchester	23	Pte 8th Loyal N Lancashire	Dow 30/11/15	Bailleul Com Cem
Harris William H.	Fitters Labour/L&C/Llanelly Dock				GWR Mag 11&12/17
Harris Walter Lewis	Clerk/Traffic/Newquay	26	2/Lt 10th Devonshire Regt	KIA 10/2/17	Doiran Mem
Harrison Charles Robert	Fireman/Loco/Chester	23	Sgt 1/5th Cheshire Regt	KIA 23/10/15	Suzanne Com Cem
Harrison Edward	Bricklayer/Engineer/Birmingham	36	Sgt 9th S Stafford Regt	KIA 27/8/17	Tyne Cot Mem
Harrison S.	Capstanman/Goods/Hockley				GWR Mag 12/17
Harrop T.W. or G.	Traffic/Penygraig				GWR Roll of Honour
Hart Frank Arthur S.	Clerk/DSO/Paddington	22	2/Lt 9th Somerset L.I.	KIA 16/9/16	Thiepval Mem
Hart George Fred	Traffic/Ogmore Vale		Pte 8th SWB	KIA 9/11/17	Karasouli Mil Cem
Hart H.	Porter/Traffic/Acton				GWR Mag 11/18
Hart Richard Humphrey	Signal Porter/Traffic/Blaenavon	29	Sgt 1st R Berks Regt	KIA 23/6/15	Vieille-Chapelle Mil Cem
Hart Stanley Philip	Goods/Brompton Road	27	Cpl 19th Light Rly Co R.E.	Died 13/2/19	Cambrai E. Mil Cem
Hartall Reginald Charles	Porter/Traffic/Pershore	25	Pte 9th Worcester Regt	KIA 21/4/16	Basra Mem
Hartwell Frederick Ryan	Clerk/Traffic/Trowbridge	19	Pte 905th Motor Transport ASC	Das 4/5/17	Savona Town Cem
Hartwell William Walter	Machinist/L&C/Swindon	20	Pte 5th Wilts Regt	Died 24/8/16	Basra Mem
Hathrill William James	Traffic/Talywain	21	Pte 1st Wilts Regt	KIA 10/3/15	Le Touret Mem
Harvey A.T.	Brakesman/Traffic/Aberbeeg				GWR Roll of Honour
Harvey Frank	Office Porter/Victoria & Albert				GWR Mag 3&8/17
Harvey Nicholas	Porter/Traffic/St Erth	25	L/Cpl 1st DCLI	Died 24/8/18	Bagneux Br Cem
Hatcher Fraser	Clerk/Accounts/Paddington		Rifm 1/12th London Regt	KIA 4/5/15	Menin Gate Mem
Hatcher George Leonard	Premium Apprentice/Swindon	22	Spr 565th (Wilts) ATC R.E.	KIA 18/9/18	Ruyaulcourt Mil Cem
Hatherall A.P.	Locomotive/Swindon				GWR Roll of Honour
Hatton Frederick Henry	Engine Cleaner/Old Oak Common	23	Rifm 16th London Regt	Dow 20/10/18	Longuenesse Cem
Hatton Thomas Alfred	Labourer/Signal/Reading	30	Pte 1st R Berks Regt	KIA 26/8/14	Maroilles Com Cem
Havell H.E.	Mileage Porter/Traffic/Withington				GWR Mag 2&4/19
Hawcutt E.	Porter/Engineer/Purton	27	Gnr Clearing Office RGA	Died 4/2/19	Milton-U-Wychwood
Hawker F.	Porter/Traffic/Cardiff Riverside				GWR Mag 4/17
Hawkes George James	Yard Labourer/Signal/Reading	26	Pte 1st R Berks Regt	KIA 15/5/15	Guards Cem Windy C.
Hawkins C.	Locomotive/Swindon				GWR Roll of Honour
Hawkins Charles John	Porter/Traffic/Reading	19	Pte 6th Wilts Regt	Died 3/12/18	Tournai Com Cem
Hawkins Horace James	Signal/Wolverhampton	33	Pte 5th Lincolnshire Regt	KIA 21/3/18	Arras Mem
Hawkins Tom	Boilersmith Helper/L&C/Swindon		Sgt 5th Wilts Regt	Dow 19/1/17	Amara War Cem
Hayes John Reginald	Lad Clerk/Goods/Chippenham		Pte 15th R Warwick Regt	KIA 24/8/18	Adanac Mil Cem
Haylock Fred Charles	Boilersmiths Apprent/Swindon		L/Cpl 5th Wilts	Dow 1/2/17	Amara War Cem
Haynes A.T.	Porter/Traffic/Birmingham				GWR Mag 4/18
Haynes Henry W.C.	Clerk/Goods/South Lambeth		Pte 13th Middlesex Regt	KIA 21/6/17	Menin Gate Mem
Hayter William Augustus	Carriage Cleaner/Old Oak Common	24	Pte 3rd Royal Fus	KIA 24/5/15	Menin Gate Mem
Hayward Fred	Bridge Labour/Engineer/Newport				GWR Mag 3&6/18
Hayward William Alfred	Apprent Boilermaker/L&C/Swindon	19	Pte 2nd Wilts Regt	KIA 4/11/18	Cross Roads Cem
Hazell Edward James	Wagon Painter/19E Shop/Swindon	27	Pte 1st R Berks Regt	KIA 15/11/14	Menin Gate Mem
Hazell Frederick Peter P.	Dist Lampman/Traffic/Oxford	22	Pte 9th R Inniskilling Fus	Dow 17/9/18	La Kreule Mil Cem
Head A.E.	Passenger Shunter/Bristol Joint				GWR Mag 8&9/18
Headington Albert	Packer/Engineer/Keynsham	38	Spr 116th (GWR) Rly Co R.E.	Doi 4/9/15	Keynsham Cem
Heal Norman H.	Porter/Traffic/Cardiff	23	Pte 9th Devonshire Regt	KIA 22/10/15	Guards Cem Windy C.
Heap Richard William	Apprent Fitter/L&C/Swindon		2/Cpl 154th Field Co R.E.	KIA 16/11/16	Thiepval Mem
Heard H.	Porter/Redcap Receiving Office				GWR Mag 11/17
Heath George	Wagon Builder/L&C/Swindon	25	Pte 2nd Welsh Fus	KIA 5/11/16	Thiepval Mem
Heath Harry Thomas	Engine Cleaner/L&C/Swindon	20	Cpl 5th Wilts Regt	Died 29/12/16	Amara War Cem
Heath Jeffrey	Labourer/Signal/Shrewsbury	23	Sgt 10th Cheshire Regt	KIA 21/7/17	Vlamertinghe N Mil Cem
Heath John Alfred	Clerk/Goods/Paddington	20	Sgt 1st London Regt	Dow 23/5/17	St Sever Cem
Heath Thomas	Packer/Engineer/Market Drayton		Pte 6th Shropshire L.I.	KIA 10/8/16	Sucrerie Mil Cem
Heather Albert Philip	Stower/Goods/Paddington	36	Pte 6th Bedfordshire Regt	Dow 12/7/16	Becourt Mil Cem
Heavens Sidney H.	Labourer/L&C/Swindon		AS HMS Pegasus RN	Dr 1/10/18	Dunfermline Cem
Heaver Fred Charles	Locomotive/Swindon	26	Pte 2nd Wilts Regt	KIA 21/3/18	Savy Br Cem
Hedge Norton F.C.	Apprent/L&C/Danygraig	19	Pte 1st Devonshire Regt	KIA 3/9/16	Guillemont Rd Cem

Hedges William Edward	Locomotive/Swindon	21	Pte 2nd Wilts Regt	KIA 9/4/17	Bucquoy Road Cem
Hemming A.	Signal/West Ealing				GWR Roll of Honour
Hemmings Royston A.	Telegraphist/Traffic/Bristol	19	Cpl 2/6th Gloucester Regt	KIA 28/9/16	Pont-du-Hem Mil Cem
Hemmins Roy Allnutt	Machinist/L&C/Swindon	21	Pte 2nd Wilts Regt	KIA 8/7/16	Thiepval Mem
Henken Albert William	Timber Inspector/Engineer/Hayes	36	L/Bom 13th Siege Bty RGA	Died 19/10/19	Cologne Mem
Herbert F.	Sawyer Labour/Engineer/Newport				GWR Mag 4/19
Herbert George H.	Brakesman/Tarffic/Aberbeeg	30			GWR Mag 6&7/15
Herman Jesse	Machinist/L&C/Swindon		Pte 1st Coldstream Guards	KIA 15/9/16	Thiepval Mem
Hibbard Ernest J.	Frame-Builders Assist/Swindon				GWR Mag 3/15
Hibberd Fred Francis A.	Porter/Goods/Frome	19	Pte 1st Somerset L.I.	KIA 24/10/18	Vis-en-Artois Mem
Hickey Daniel Francis	Yard Porter/Paddington Goods	21	Pte 9th Div Army Cyclist Corps	Dow 17/4/16	Etaples Mil Cem
Hickman Harry	Labourer/Stafford Road Factory		Gnr 17th Trench Mortar Bty RGA	KIA 22/6/16	Thiepval Mem
Hicks Ernest	Clerk/Goods/Paddington	33	2/Lt 2/8th London Regt	KIA 9/10/16	Ecoivres Mil Cem
Hicks George	R/Labourer/Engineer/Hereford	42	Pte 1st Hereford Regt	KIA 23/7/18	Raperie Br Cem
Higby C.M.	Clerk/Goods/Bristol	22	L/Cpl 8th Gloucester Regt	Dow 21/9/17	Locre Hospice Cem
Hignett George	Coalman/L&C/Chester	32	Pte 1/4th Cheshire Regt	KIA 26/3/17	Jerusalem Mem
Hill Albert James	Riveter/L&C/Bridgwater	20	Pte 18th Lancashire Fus	KIA 29/3/18	Pozieres Mem
Hill Francis	Bridge Labourer/Engineer/Neath	20	L/Cpl 1st Devonshire Regt	KIA 23/4/17	Arras Mem
Hill Frank	R/Labourer/Engineer/Ledbury	28	Pte 7th Shropshire L.I.	KIA 28/3/18	Arras Mem
Hill Frederick Walter	Striker/Engineer/Camborne	20	Gnr 16th Heavy Bty RGA	KIA 11/9/17	Bard Cottage Cem
Hill G.	Clerk/Goods/Withymoor(Netherton)				GWR Mag 11/18
Hill G.	L&C/Hockley				GWR Roll of Honour
Hill G.S.	Porter/Paddington Goods Station				GWR Mag 6/17
Hill J.H.	Fixer/Signal/Wolverhampton				GWR Mag 5/17
Hill Percy Ronald	Clerk/Goods/Bristol		Gnr 129th Bristol Heavy Bty RGA	Died 29/1/17	Morogoro Cem Africa
Hill R.N.	L&C/Bristol				GWR Roll of Honour
Hill Reg Victor Witheridge	Smoke Box Cleaner/St Philips M.	20	Pte 2/5th Gloucester Rgt	KIA 17/4/18	Loos Mem
Hill Roland Voden	Warehouse Lad/Westbourne Park	16	Pte 9th DCLI	Doi 31/1/16	Kensal Green Cem
Hill William	Firman/Loco/Stourbridge				GWR Mag 4/17
Hillard Herbert Charles	Frame-Builders Assist/Swindon		Dvr B Bty 52nd Bde RFA	KIA 19/7/16	Peronne Road Cem
Hillier Bertie	Labourer/Engineer/W. Ealing	29	Pte 2nd R. Berks Regt	KIA 9/5/15	Ploegsteert Mem
Hillier Christopher Thorpe	Hydraulic Forgeman/L&C/Swindon	21	Pte 1st Wilts Regt	KIA 31/12/14	Ploegsteert Mem
Hillier R.R.	Apprent/L&C/Swindon	21	L/Cpl 19th Bn MGC	Died 6/1/19	Etaples Mil Cem
Hillier W.	Engineer/Bristol				GWR Roll of Honour
Hind Frederick William	Locomotive/Swindon	22	Pte 14th Gloucester Regt	Died 25/7/18	Valenciennes Com Cem
Hinder Percy	Pad Maker/L&C/Swindon	32	Pte 12th Gloucester Regt	Died 7/8/17	St Sever Cem
Hine Albert William T.	Porter/Goods/Port Talbot	23	Pte 13th Cheshire Regt	KIA 10/8/17	Menin Gate Mem
Hing Harry E.	Fitter/L&C/Slough		Tpr Household Bn Cavalry	Dow 11/4/17	Arras Mem
Hinton Fred Thomas	Vanguard/Goods/Hockley	21	Pte 1/7th Worcester Regt	KIA 16/8/17	New Irish Farm Cem
Hinton Sidney	Porter/Traffic/Cradley Heath		Gnr 118th Siege Bty RGA	Dow 29/10/17	Bedford House Cem
Hiram Albert Edward	Signal/Reading	21	Pte 3rd Dorset Regt	Died 13/8/18	Weymouth Cem
Hitchcock W.	Stower/Goods/Smithfield				GWR Mag 12/16
Hitchings Albert M.	Fireman/Loco/Hereford		Pte 10th Worcester Regt	KIA 3/7/16	Thiepval Mem
Hoar Frank	Packer/Engineer/Menheniot		Pte 1/5th DCLI	KIA 31/3/18	Pozieres Mem
Hobbs Albert Edward	Carriage Cleaner/Old Oak Common	27	Pte 3rd London Regt	Dow 24/7/16	Mont Huon Mil Cem
Hobbs H.T.	Packer/Engineer/W London Jct				GWR Mag 6/19
Hockins F.J.	Traffic/Resolven				GWR Roll of Honour
Hodge John Walter	Porter/Goods/Bristol	19	Pte 2/7th R. Warwicks Regt	KIA 8/8/18	Merville Com Cem
Hodges Arthur	R/Labourer/Engineer/Ledbury	25	L/Cpl 1st Hereford Regt	KIA 2/9/15	Helles Mem
Hodges D.A.	Clerk/Goods/Llanelly				GWR Mag 9/19
Hodson George Fred	Ticket Collector/Traffic/Reading		Rifm 9th London Regt	Dow 2/7/16	Couin Br Cem
Hogg Harry William	Clerk/Engineer/Paddington	20	Pte 2/13th London Regt	KIA 21/8/16	Maroeuil Br Cem
Hoggins Percy Herbert	Fitters Labour/L&C/Stafford Road	35	Pte 2nd S. Stafford Regt	Dow 30/7/16	Corbie Com Cem
Holbrook William T.H.	Painter/Signal/Neath		Pte 24th Welsh Regt	KIA 7/9/18	Tincourt New Br Cem
Holland Harry	Carriage Cleaner/L&C/Oxford		Pte 1st R Berks Regt	Dow 1/11/14	Boulogne East Cem
Holley Albert George	Striker/Engineer/W. Ealing	30	Cpl 11th Royal Fus	Died 14/8/15	Chipilly Com Cem
Holley Francis T.J.	Fitter Turner/L&C/Swindon	22	Spr 1st S Midland Field Co R.E.	Died 23/5/15	Trois Arbres Cem
Holley Gilbert	Porter/Traffic/Exeter	23	Pte 274th Co MGC (Infantry)	Died 13/5/18	Basra Mem
Hollick Benjamin C.J.	Machineman/L&C/Swindon	20	Spr 96th Light Rly Co R.E.	Died 20/1/19	Les Baraques Mil Cem

Name	Occupation/Location	Age	Unit	Death	Memorial
Hollick Percy William	Helper/V Shop/Swindon Works	21	Gnr 14th Siege Bty RGA	KIA 20/6/15	Pink Farm Cem
Holliday Frank	Engine Cleaner/L&C/Didcot	20	Pte 110th Co MGC (Infantry)	KIA 23/1/17	Guards Cem
Holliday William Joseph	Police Constable/Paddington	27	Rifm 1st KRRC	Dow 14/1/15	Bethune Town Cem
Hollow William Edward	Masons Labour/Engineer/Plymouth	24	Pte 1st Devonshire Regt	Dow 15/4/15	Bedford House Cem
Holloway Herbert John	Porter/Traffic/Cardiff	27	Cpl 1st Dorset Regt	KIA 2/9/17	Coxyde Mil Cem
Holly Sidney Harry	Clerk/Goods/South Lambeth	20	Pte 23rd Middlesex Regt	KIA 24/3/18	Arras Mem
Holman Dennis James	Oil Gas Fitter/L&C/Bristol	21	Pte 1/6th Gloucester Regt	Dow 18/7/16	Gezaincourt Com Cem
Holmes Frederick William	Fireman/Loco/Chester	32	Pte 13th Cheshire Regt	Dow 8/8/17	The Huts Cem
Holton Frank	Gas Fitter/L&C/Swindon	36	Spr 105th Field Co R.E.	Dow 20/5/18	Paris City Cem Pantin
Homeyard Reginald	Packer/Engineer/Exminster	22	Spr No 1 Reserve Bn R.E.	Died 12/4/16	Starcross Churchyard
Honeywill Walter Reg	Labour/Engineer/Newton Abbot		Cpl 15th R.Warwick Regt	Dow 3/11/17	Boulogne East Cem
Honeywill William Charles	Engine Cleaner/Loco/Bristol		Pte 1st Dorset Regt	KIA 25/5/18	Bucquoy Road Cem
Hook William	Carman/Traffic/Abingdon	34	Pte 2nd R Berks Regt	Dow 28/5/17	La Chapelette Cem
Hookins Charles	Fireman/Loco/Tondu	23	A/Bom RFA	Died 9/1/19	Pawlett Churchyard
Hope Charles Henry	Shoeing Smith/Goods/Hockley	44	Pte 65th Remount Sqdn ASC	Died 13/11/18	Birmingham Cem
Hope Henry James	Carriage Washer/L&C/Worcester		Rifm 1/5th London Regt	KIA 13/4/17	Arras Mem
Hopes Luther William	Carriage Cleaner/L&C/Bristol		Pte 9th Devonshire Regt	KIA 2/4/17	Arras Mem
Hopkins George	Rail Motor Conductor/Cheltenham	25	L/Cpl 9th Worcester Regt	KIA 10/8/15	Helles Mem
Hopwood Albert Edwin	Packer/Engineer/Market Drayton	36	Spr I.W.T. R.E.	Died 19/11/18	Ramleh War Cem
Horn(e) Bertie	Parcel Porter/Traffic/Paddington	35	Pte 2nd Coldstream Guards	KIA 16/9/16	Thiepval Mem
Hornblow Edward A.F.	Shunter/Traffic/Didcot	28	Sgt B Bty 84th Bde RFA	KIA 17/8/17	Artillery Wood Cem
House Harold James	Fitters Mate/Signal/Reading	20	L/Cpl 1/4th R Berks Regt	KIA 16/5/16	Hebuterne Mil Cem
House Oswald Leopald	Machinist/Signal/Reading	19	Pte 1/4 R Berks Regt	KIA 14/8/16	Thiepval Mem
How George William	Clerk/Traffic/Paddington	22	Pte 1/1st Berkshire Yeomanry	KIA 21/8/15	Helles Mem
Howard Frank Henry	Engine Cleaner/Loco/Exeter		Pte 1/4th Devonshire Regt	Died 4/2/17	Basra Mem
Howe F.J.	Fireman/Loco/Tondu				GWR Mag 10/16
Howell Charles	Packer/Engineer/Stourbridge	34	Pte 4th Worcester Regt	Dow 30/11/15	Hill 10 Cem
Howell Edward Colston	Engine Cleaner/Loco/Bristol	20	Pte 2/6th Gloucester Regt	KIA 19/7/16	Rue-du-Bois Mil Cem
Howell George	Apprent/L&C/Swindon	20	Pte 2nd Wilts Regt	KIA 5/11/18	Cross Roads Cem
Howell G.F.	Springsmith/L&C/Worcester				GWR Mag 11/16 & 1/17
Howells Charles	Fireman/Loco/Newport Dock St.	23	Pte 1st Monmouth Regt	KIA 1/7/16	Thiepval Mem
Howells Trevor L.R.	Clerk/Goods/Newport Dock St.		L/Cpl 1st Monmouth Regt	KIA 8/5/15	Menin Gate Mem
Howes Walter Sidney	Slip Labour/Engineer/Cheltenham	28	Pte 9th Gloucester Regt	Died 25/4/17	Doiran Mem
Howland Alfred Robert	Porter/Goods/Hockley	34	Sgt 1st Royal Fus	Dow 4/8/17	Brandhoek No 3 Cem
Howse George	Packer/Engineer/Hook Norton		Rifm 14th R Irish Rifles	Dow 6/12/17	Rocquigny Road Cem
Howse Walter George	Apprent Boilersmith/L&C/Swindon	19	Pte 116th Co MGC	Dow 4/11/16	Contay Br Cem
Hubbard Clifford	Sheet Repairer/Goods/Bridgwater		AS S.S. Lynburn RNVR	SL 29/8/17	Plymouth Naval Mem
Hudson Harold	Shunter/Traffic/Oxley Sidings	29	Pte 3rd Worcester Regt	KIA 12/3/15	Menin Gate Mem
Hughes Arthur Stanley	Shop Clerk/L&C/Swindon	19	Pte 10th East Kent Regt	KIA 21/9/18	Vis-en-Artois Mem
Hughes Bertram Francis	Platform Porter/Worcester Shrub H	27	L/Cpl 4th Worcester Regt	Dow 22/4/17	Duisans Br Cem
Hughes D.	Packer/Engineer/Bryndu				GWR Mag 5/17
Hughes Edgar Wallace	Packer/Engineer/Hanwell	28	Cpl 4th Royal Fus	KIA 20/11/17	Favreuil Br Cem
Hughes Sidney Gordon	Packer/Engineer/Acrefair		Pte IX Corps Army Cylclist Corps	KIA 5/10/18	Busigny Com Cem
Hughes T.L.	Traffic/Abertillery				GWR Roll of Honour
Hughes W.	Porter/Goods/Shrewsbury				GWR Mag 10/17
Hughes Walter G.D.	Labourer/L&C/Swindon	23	Spr 97th Field Co R.E.	KIA 26/6/16	Ville-sur-Ancre Cem
Hughes William John	Signalman/Traffic/Newport Dock S	21	Pte 14th R Welsh Fus	KIA 10/12/16	Essex Farm Cem
Huish William	Boilersmith s Mate/L&C/Exeter		Pte 2nd Bn RMLI	KIA 26/10/17	Tyne Cot Mem
Hullin John	Shunter/Traffic/Swansea High St.	23	L/Sgt 10th Welsh Regt	KIA 2/8/17	New Irish Farm Cem
Humphreys J.	Porter/Traffic/Princess Risborough				GWR Mag 6&10/19
Humphreys J.C.	Traffic/Hereford				GWR Roll of Honour
Humphreys(ies) H.	Carriage Cleaner/L&c/Cardiff				GWR Mag 9&12/18
Humphries H.J.	Fixer/Signal/Reading				GWR Mag 4&6/19
Hunt A.E.	Traffic/Swansea				GWR Roll of Honour
Hunt Alfred John	Shunter/Traffic/Westbury	27	Cpl 4th Middlesex Regt	Died 21/10/14	Bethune Town Cem
Hunt Alfred W.	Carman/Goods/Bristol	27	Pte 2nd R Welsh Fus	Died 26/5/15	Reading Cem
Hunt Arthur Frederick	Clerk/Traffic/Tondu	19	Pnr 56th Div Signal Co R.E.	Dow 20/9/16	Corbie Com Cem
Hunt C.S.	Craneman/L&C/Plymouth				GWR Mag 11/18
Hunt Edgar	Lampman/Traffic/Mountain Ash	20	Pte 10th Reserve Cavalry Regt	Died 1/2/15	Curragh Mil Cem

Name	Occupation/Department/Location	Age	Rank/Regiment	Death	Memorial/Cemetery
Hunt Frank	Goods Porter/Traffic/Abertillery		Pte Tank Corps att 242nd RFA	KIA 9/10/17	La Clytte Mil Cem
Hunt George	Porter/Goods/Oxford	22	Sgt 5th Ox & Bucks L.I.	KIA 15/10/15	Menin Gate Mem
Hunt W.	Porter/Traffic/Purton				GWR Mag 6&10/18
Huntingdon Maurice J.	Carriage Oiler/Old Oak Common	23	Pte 1st R West Kent Regt	KIA 22/2/15	Poelcapelle Br Cem
Huntley John Henry	Boilersmith Helper/L&C/Swindon	26	Gnr C Bty 62nd Bde RFA	KIA 25/10/16	Guards Cem
Hurford A.J.	R/Labourer/Engineer/Taunton				GWR Mag 3&4/19
Hurley Harold	Labourer/Engineer/Wiveliscombe		Pte 1/4th Devon Regt	KIA 24/5/17	Basra Mem
Hursey Thomas H.	Carriage Cleaner/Old Oak Common		Pte 1st Wilts Regt	KIA 4/5/16	Ecoivres Mil Cem
Hussey P.A.	Locomotive/Trowbridge				GWR Roll of Honour
Hurst William James	Labourer/L&C/Swindon		Cpl 2nd East Kent Regt	KIA 11/5/15	Menin Gate Mem
Hutchings Frank Ernest	Labourer/Signal/West Ealing	23	Sto Submarine L10 RN	SL 4/10/18	Chatham Naval Mem
Hutchin(e)s William	Canal Labour/Engineer/Devizes		Pte 165th Labour Corps	KIA 10/7/17	Coxyde Mil Cem
Hutchinson Harry	Fireman/Loco/Tondu	21	Pte 6th Somerset L.I.	Dow 26/9/15	Menin Gate Mem
Hutson J.	Masons Labour/Engineer/Newport				GWR Mag 2&4/19
Hutt Thomas Stroud	Craneman/L&C/Plymouth Docks	40	L/Sgt 1st Somerset L.I.	KIA 30/8/18	Eterpigny Br Cem
Hyde Leonard Lever	Clerk/CGMO/Paddington	18	Pte 15th London Regt	Das 30/12/17	Chatby Mem
Hyett Herbert James J.	Engine Cleaner/Loco/Gloucester	19	Pte 2/4th Dorset Regt	KIA 9/4/18	Jerusalem Mem
I'anson William Barker	Checker/Traffic/Ammanford		Cpl 9th Royal Fus	KIA 7/10/16	Thiepval Mem
Ilsley John George	Riveter/Signal/Reading	29	Pte 1st R Scots Fus	Dow 19/11/14	Boulogne East Cem
Ingram Francis Edwin	Parcel Porter/Traffic/Birmingham	27	OS S.S. Baku Standard RNVR	SL 11/2/18	Plymouth Naval Mem
Ireland Alfred	Carriage Cleaner/Old Oak Common		Pte 7th Gloucester Regt	KIA 12/1/17	Amara War Cem
Ireland Clifford Robert	Porter/Traffic/Gloucester	28	Pte 1st Gloucester Regt	Dow 29/1/15	Beuvry Com Cem
Ireland Thomas William	Engine Cleaner/Loco/Gloucester		Pte 8th Gloucester Regt	KIA 29/12/17	Ribecourt Br Cem
Ireland William Henry	Packer/Engineer/Speech House	29	Pte 1st Gloucester Regt	Dow 25/12/14	Lillers Com Cem
Irwin Horace Charles	Accounts Clerk/Paddington	27	2/Lt 10th Argyl att 1/4th Sea'f	KIA 20/7/18	Marfaux Br Cem
Isaacs Fred Bartholomew	Carman/Goods/Paddington	24	Pte 1/6th W Riding Regt	KIA 1/11/18	Preseau Com Cem
Isaacs Fred Holloway	Labourer/L&C/Swindon		Pte 2nd Wilts Regt	Dow 3/8/17	Mendinghem Mil Cem
Ivatts George	Guard/Passenger/Port Talbot		L/Cpl 9th Worcester Regt	KIA 10/8/15	Helles Mem
Iverson John Henry	Labourer/Signal/Newport		Gnr 120th Bty RFA	KIA 22/8/18	Vis-en-Artois Mem
Ivins William	Machinist/Signal/Reading		Pte 8th R Berks Regt	KIA 8/4/17	Thiepval Mem
Jackson Edward Philip	Chief Accountants Off/Paddington	27	Capt 1st R Berks Regt	KIA 30/11/17	Cabaret-Rouge Br Cem
Jackson Harold Walter	Fitters Apprent/L&C/Gloucester	20	Dvr C Bty 240th Bde RFA	Dow 17/8/17	Brandhoek No 3 Cem
Jackson James Fred	Carriage Cleaner/Old Oak Common	17	Pte 3rd London Regt	Died 28/11/15	Helles Mem
Jackson Sy(i)dney John	Bricklayer/Engineer/West Ealing	39	Gnr D Bty 59th Bde RFA	KIA 12/3/18	Philosophe Br Cem
Jacobs D.	Clerk/Traffic/Crumlin		CQMS R Welsh Fus	Died 5/12/18	Pontypool (Panteg) Cem
Jago Reginald	Warehouseman/Stores/Swindon	45	Bty QMS 218th Bde RFA	Died 16/5/18	Delhi War Mem
James Albert Hazelwood	Fitter/L&C/Swindon	24	2/Lt RFA	Died 20/12/18	Swindon Cem
James A.W.	R/Labourer/Engineer/Hereford				GWR Mag 9/20
James David M.	Engine Cleaner/Loco/Bristol				GWR Mag 6/19
James Edgar Lewis	Signalman/Traffic/Ammanford	22	Dvr B Bty 119th Bde RFA	KIA 28/5/17	Dickebusch Mil Cem
James G.T.	Packer/Engineer/Titley				GWR Mag 11/18 & 3/19
James H.	Labourer/Engineer/Bath				GWR Mag 3&4/17
James James	Lad Porter/Goods/Llanelly	20			GWR Mag 3&10/16
James Joseph Dennis	Clerk/Traffic/Thatcham	25	Cpl 8th Middlesex Regt	KIA 28/10/16	Rue-du-Bacquerot No1
James T.	Engineer/Lapworth				GWR Roll of Honour
James Thomas Henry	Engine Cleaner/Loco/Llanelly	20	Rifm 8th KRRC	Dow 5/8/15	Menin Gate Mem
James W.A.	Porter/Goods/Windsor				GWR Mag 9/19
James William C.W.	Booking Clerk/Traffic/Maesteg	27	Pte 16th Welsh Regt	KIA 27/8/17	Tyne Cot Mem
James W.F.	Canal Labour/Engineer/Bearley				GWR Mag 1&7/18
Jancey Reginald	Traffic/Hereford	20	L/Cpl 2nd Leinster Regt	Dow 13/5/18	Hereford Cem
Jarvis George Henry	Carman/Goods/Handsworth	19	Gnr 173rd Siege Bty RGA	Died 16/4/18	Etaples Mil Cem
Jayne Alexander	Engineer/Newport		L/Cpl 1st SWB	KIA 25/10/14	Menin Gate Mem
Jefferies A.A.	Packer/Engineer/Cardiff				GWR Mag 12/18 & 1/19
Jefferies Henry Reginald	Labourer/L&C/Swindon	22	Pte 1st Wilts Regt	KIA 24/10/14	Le Touret Mem
Jefferies William J.B.	Labourer/L&C/Swindon	23	Pte 5th Wilts Regt	Dow 29/11/15	Green Hill Cem
Jefferies William Tom	Shedman/L&C/Trowbridge	26	Pte 5th Wilts Regt	KIA 25/9/15	Loos Mem
Jefferson Frank	Carman/Goods/Hockley	31			GWR Mag 12/15 & 1/16
Jefferson James	Chief Claims Clerk/Goods/Birkenh'd	36	CSM 1/7th Liverpool Regt	KIA 16/5/15	Le Touret Mem
Jeffery Robert H.	Refresh Room Page/Leamington	21	Pte 65th F/Amb RAMC	Dow 8/4/18	Etaples Mil Cem

Name	Occupation	Age	Regiment	Death	Cemetery/Memorial
Jeffries A.A.	Engineer/Cardiff				GWR Roll of Honour
Jeffryes Fred Joseph	Lad Clerk/Goods/Paddington	19	Gnr B Bty 190th Bde RFA	Dow 19/9/17	The Huts Cem
Jeffs E.	Hotels/Paddington				GWR Roll of Honour
Jeffs Percy William	Carriage Cleaner/Old Oak Common	38	Pte 1st London Regt	KIA 17/6/18	Wanquetin Com Cem
Jenkins A.E.	Platform Porter/Traffic/Risca				GWR Mag 7&9/17
Jenkins J.	Carriage Cleaner/Loco/Penzance				GWR Mag 11/15
Jenkins W.S.	Porter/Traffic/Theale				GWR Mag 12/18
Jenner Arthur John	Storesman/Stores/Swindon		Pnr 5th Army H.Q. Signals R.E.	KIA 27/10/17	Bard Cottage Cem
Jenner Luther	Labourer/L&C/Old Oak Common				GWR Mag 12/19
Jenner William John	Shunter/Traffic/Severn Tun. Jct	22	Pte 6th SWB	KIA 10/10/16	Thiepval Mem
Jennings Charles J.	Examiner/L&C/Princess Risbo'gh	32	Pte 4th Royal Fus	KIA 6/6/16	Dickebusch Mil Cem
Jennings Fred	Signal Porter/Henly-in-Arden	23	OS HMS Montagua RNVR	Das 19/3/18	Plymouth Naval Mem
Jennings George	Cleaner/L&C/Cardiff		Pte 2nd S Lancashire Regt	KIA 15/4/18	Trois Arbres Cem
Jennings John Reginald	Porter/Traffic/Raglan	18	Pte 4th S Lancashire Regt	Died 6/10/18	Ewyas Harold Church
Jerome Alfred	Bricklayer/Engineer/Reading		Pte 2nd Ox & Bucks L.I.	Dow 27/7/16	Dernancourt Com Cem
Jerram William Charles	Boilersmiths Mate/L&C/Landore		Pte 14th Welsh Regt	KIA 10/7/16	Flatiron Copse Cem
Jerrett George Edward	Time-Keeper/L&C/Cardiff	21	Pte 12th Yorkshire L.I.	KIA 15/5/17	Bailleul Road E. Cem
Jerrett William	Porter/Goods/Cardiff	23	Pte 255th MGC (Infantry)	Dow 29/11/17	Grevillers Br Cem
Jinks Ernest Frederick	Parcel Porter/Traffic/Hereford	36	Pte 4th Worcester Regt	Died 5/2/17	Baghdad N War Cem
John Chris Clifford	Clerk/Traffic/Swansea	20	Pte 14th Welsh Regt	Dow 15/9/16	Lijssenthoek Mil Cem
John F.W.	Porter/Traffic/Johnston				GWR Mag 7/19
John J.	Depot Labourer/Engineer/Neath				GWR Mag 12/19
Johnson Albert	Apprent Boilermaker/L&C/Swindon		Spr 565th (Wilts) ATC R.E.	KIA 18/9/18	Ruyaulcourt Mil Cem
Johnson Henery Edward	Machinist/C&W/Swindon		Dvr A Bty 104th Bde RFA	KIA 25/11/17	The Huts Cem
Johnson J.	Incandescent Lineman/Wrexham				GWR Mag 2&4/17
Johnson Lawrence Sam	Packer/Engineer/Ruislip	21	Dvr Labour Co ASC	Died 21/10/14	Nantes Cem
Johnston Cecil W.T.	Apprent/L&C/Swindon	21	Spr 565th (Wilts) ATC R.E.	Died 17/4/17	Varennes Mil Cem
Jones A.	3rd Group Fireman/Loco/Tondu				GWR Mag 4/19
Jones A.B.	Locomotive/Swindon				GWR Roll of Honour
Jones Arthur	Carriage Cleaner/L&C/Shrewsb'y		Pte 1/4th Shropshire L.I.	KIA 31/10/17	Tyne Cot Mem
Jones C.B.	Parcel Porter/Traffic/Kidderminster				GWR Mag 1/19
Jones C.F.	Porter/Goods/Charing Cross				GWR Mag 10/16
Jones C.J.	Packer/Engineer/Kemble				GWR Mag 10/19
Jones D.	Number Taker/Goods/Port Talbot				GWR Mag 7&12/18
Jones D.	Checker/Traffic/Brynamman				GWR Mag 1&2/19
Jones David Charles	Fireman/Loco/Landore	27	Rifm 12th Rifle Bde	KIA 12/2/16	Menin Gate Mem
Jones David Nathaniel	Fitters Labourer/L&C/Neath	24	Pte 7th R Berks Regt	Died 17/10/17	Karasouli Mil Cem
Jones D.R.	Fitters Apprent/Marine/Fishguard				GWR Mag 11/18
Jones Edward	Packer/Engineer/Ruabon	32	Spr 278th Rly Co R.E.	Died 13/7/18	Les Baraques Mil Cem
Jones E.	Goods Checker/Traffic/Blaengarw				GWR Mag 4&7/19
Jones E.	Helper/L&C/Swindon				GWR Mag 6/19
Jones E.G.	Booking Clerk/Traffic/Glyn Neath				GWR Mag 10/17
Jones Fred	Clerk/L&C/Swindon	19	L/Cpl 2nd Wilts Regt	KIA 30/5/18	Soissons Mem
Jones F.G.	Lad Clerk/Goods/Leamington				GWR Mag 3/18
Jones G.	Packer/Engineer/Kings Sutton				GWR Mag 10&12/17
Jones George Frederick	R/Labour/Engineer/Haverfordwest	23	Pte 1st Welsh Guards	KIA 28/4/16	Potijze Burial Ground
Jones G.H.	Engine Cleaner/Loco/Lydney				GWR Mag 3/19
Jones G.W.	Lad Clerk/Goods/Paddington				GWR Mag 2&3/19
Jones Harold Burcher	Shunter/Traffic/Crumlin	21	L/Cpl 2nd Monmouthshire Regt	KIA 28/1/17	A.I.F. Burial Flers
Jones Henry M. (brother 1)	Clerk/Traffic/Swansea	25	2/Lt 10th R Welsh Fus	KIA 13/11/16	Euston Road Cem
Jones Henry McPherson	Porter/Traffic/Neath	20	Pte 2nd Bn RMLI	KIA 28/4/17	Arras Mem
Jones Hugh M.	Fitters Labour/L&C/Weymouth				GWR Mag 8&9/18
Jones Humphrey	Shunter/Traffic/Brymbo	33	Pte 8th R Welsh Fus	Dow 17/8/15	Alexandria War Cem
Jones H.R.	Traffic/Neath				GWR Roll of Honour
Jones Isaac	Lad Porter/Traffic/Bala	19	L/Cpl 1/7th R Welsh Fus	Died 3/1/16	Pieta Mil Cem
Jones J.	Carman/Goods/Smithfield				GWR Mag 1&4/17
Jones John	Engine Cleaner/Loco/Corwen				GWR Mag 6/20
Jones John	Porter/Goods/Birkenhead				GWR Mag 10&12/16
Jones J.M.	Traffic/Hereford				GWR Roll of Honour

Name	Role/Location	Age	Regiment	Death	Cemetery/Memorial
Jones J.M.	Traffic/Shrewsbury				GWR Roll of Honour
Jones John Victor	Labourer/L&C/Swindon		2/Lt 3rd Dorset Regt	KIA 14/7/16	Thiepval Mem
Jones Joseph	Porter/Traffic/Tipton		Pte 1st S Stafford Regt	KIA 14/7/16	Thiepval Mem
Jones J.W. or J.N.	Clerk/Goods/Moss				GWR Mag 10/18
Jones P.	Fireman/Loco/Swindon				GWR Mag 9/17
Jones Philip	Fireman/Loco/Croes Newydd	23	AS Drake Bn R.N.D.	KIA 20/10/16	Thiepval Mem
Jones R.	Locomotive/Croes Newydd				GWR Roll of Honour
Jones Reg Herbert G.	Porter/Traffic/Upwey	23	Gdsm 2nd Grenadier Guards	Dow 1/3/18	Etretat Churchyard
Jones R.E.	Invoice Typist/Goods/Swansea				GWR Mag 1&6/18
Jones S.G.	Locomotive/Bristol				GWR Roll of Honour
Jones S.J.	Greaser/L&C/Swindon				GWR Mag 6/20
Jones Samuel W.J.	Crane Driver/L&C/Swindon	27	Dvr 3rd Wessex Bde Am/Col	Acc 24/1/15	Swindon Cem
Jones Thomas Henry	Packer/Engineer/Peplow	26	Pte 46th Bn MGC (Infantry)	KIA 22/3/18	Sailly-Labourse Cem
Jones W.	Carriage Cleaner/L&C/Coton Hill				GWR Mag 3&12/18
Jones W.	Signal Porter/Traffic/Monmouth T				GWR Mag 8&9/18
Jones Wilfred Arthur	Machineman/No 3 Shop/Swindon	25	Pte 3rd Wilts Regt	Died 11/3/16	Portland RN Cem
Jones W.David (brother 2)	Clerk/Traffic/Briton Ferry	28	Pte 13th R Welsh Fus	KIA 31/7/17	Artillery Wood Cem
Jones W.H.	Greaser/L&C/Pontypool Road				GWR Mag 4/16
Jordan Albert Victor	Labourer/L&C/Swindon	22	Dvr C Bty 69th Bde RFA	Died 15/8/16	Alexandria War Cem
Jordan Frank Ernest	Porter/Traffic/Oswestry	23	Pte 1st Shropshire L.I.	KIA 24/9/18	Chapelle Br Cem
Jordan John	Porter/Traffic/Liskerd	21	Rifm 21st London Regt	KIA 15/9/16	Thiepval Mem
Joseph(e)s Bertie	Porter/Traffic/Codsall	21	Pte 23rd Royal Fus	KIA 27/7/16	Thiepval Mem
Joslin Robert Luke	Caller-off/Goods/Exeter		Pte 2nd Devonshire Regt	Dow 30/10/16	Grove Town Cem
Joy W.	Engineer/Handsworth				GWR Roll of Honour
Joyce William Henry	Labourer/L&C/Swindon	21	L/Cpl 2nd Wilts Regt	KIA 2/9/15	Loos Mem
Joyner Percy James	Shunt Horse Dvr/Traffic/Bristol	26	Pte 25th Co MGC (Infantry)	KIA 21/3/18	Arras Mem
Joynes James	Packer/Engineer/Cheltenham	42	Spr 262nd (GWR) Rly Co R.E.	Dow 14/11/17	Brandhoek No.3 Cem
Justice Charles Joseph	Painter/Engineer/Wolverhampton	30	L/Cpl 14th Highland L.I.	KIA 26/4/17	Bray Mil Cem
Kean/m Frank	Porter/Traffic/South Brent	21	Pte 9th Devonshire Regt	KIA 26/10/17	Hooge Crater Cem
Keats Albert	Storesman/Stores/Didcot		Cpl 1st Royal Fus	Dow 16/4/17	Bully-Grenay Com Cem
Keegan T.H.	Helper/L&C/Swindon	29			GWR Mag 4/15
Keel Harold Arthur	Erector/L&C/Swindon	21	Pte 1st Wilts Regt	KIA 12/3/15	La Laiterie Mil Cem
Keeling Samuel James	Clerk/Goods/Great Bridge	25	Pte 3rd Worcester Regt	KIA 16/6/17	St Quentin Mil Cem
Keen F.	Bricklayer/Engineer/Princess Ris'b				GWR Mag 12/16 & 3/17
Keen Thomas	Packer/Engineer/Witney	29	Pte 2nd Ox & Bucks L.I.	Dow 30/11/14	Ypres Town Cem
Keenan Owen D.L.	Examiner/L&C/Swansea		Pte 8th R Berks Regt	KIA 18/8/16	Thiepval Mem
Keetch Edward James	Clerk/Goods/Bristol		Pte 16th Gloucester Regt	Died 3/3/16	Bristol Greenbank Cem
Kelland Arthur Fitzwalter	Porter/Goods/Plymouth		Sto HMS Vivid RN	Doi 20/4/17	Galmpton Churchyard
Kelloway Archibald	Porter/Traffic/Nancegollan	20	Cpl 4th DCLI	Died 20/1/15	Karachi Cem/Delhi Mem
Kemp Frederick	Packer/Engineer/Scorrier	25	Pte 15th Hampshire Regt	KIA 7/6/17	Bedford House Cem
Kempster Herbert	Clerk/Accounts/Paddington	18	Pte 2/10th Middlesex Regt	KIA 10/8/15	Helles Mem
Kempster John	Porter/Traffic/Ruabon		Rifm 2nd KRRC	Dow 23/7/16	Thiepval Mem
Kench Alfred Arthur	Ticket Collector/Traffic/Paddington	25	Pte 13th Middlesex Regt	KIA 8/6/17	Voormezeele No.3
Kendall Bertram Henry	Clerk/Goods/Paddington	31	Pte 2nd Scots Guards	Dow 19/5/18	Doullens Com Cem 2
Kennedy E.C.	Clerk/Traffic/Banbury				GWR Mag 6/18
Kent C.	L&C/Swindon	36	Fitter 31st Bde HQ RFA	Died 27/11/18	Kirechkoi-H Mil Cem
Kent E.	Engineer/Didcot				GWR Roll of Honour
Kent Robert	Carriage Cleaner/L&C/Truro	37	Spr 4th Light Rly Co R.E.	Died 4/2/18	Kenwyn Churchyard
Kenworthy George T.	R/Labour/Engineer/Shrewsbury		Pte 8th S Lancashire Regt	KIA 7/6/17	Menin Gate Mem
Kerkhoff John D.	Stower/Goods/Birmingham	32	Sto 1st Class HMS Majestic	SL 27/5/15	No Record of Kirkhoff
Kibblewhite Charles J.	Labourer/L&C/Swindon	30	Pte 1st Wilts Regt	KIA 24/8/14	La Ferte-s-Jouarre Mem
Killingback Henry	Mileage Porter/Goods/Pontypool	20	Pte 11th SWB	KIA 10/7/17	Flatiron Copse Cem
Kimber George William	Packer/Engineer/Pontardulais		Spr 264th Rly Co R.E.	Dow 23/7/16	Lijssenthoek Mil Cem
Kimmiens William R.	Packer/Engineer/Yatton	28	Pte 6th Somerset L.I.	Dow 13/9/15	Le Treport Mil Cem
Kinder P.	Pad Maker/L&C/Swindon				GWR Mag 11/17
King Arthur Thomas R.	Carriage Cleaner/Newton Abbot	22	Pte 5th Devonshire Regt	Died 31/1/18	Highweek Churchyard
King Frank	Packer/Engineer/Reading	39	Sgt 5th Dorset Regt	KIA 11/1/17	Thiepval Mem
King Fred	Frame-Builders Assist/Swindon				GWR Mag 1&3/17
King H.	Under Lineman/Signal/Lawrence H				GWR Mag 2&4/19

Name	Occupation	Age	Regiment	Death	Memorial/Cemetery
King Sydney Alfred	Parcel Porter/Traffic/Paddington	28	Gnr 144th Siege Bty RGA	KIA 28/11/17	Bard Cottage Cem
King S.H.	L&C/Swindon				GWR Roll of Honour
King William Henry	Messenger/Goods/Bristol	18	L/Cpl 8th Somerset L.I.	KIA 29/6/16	Norfolk Cem
King William John	Porter/Goods/Bristol		Pte 2/6th R Warwick Regt	KIA 19/8/18	Tannay Br Cem
Kingdom J.H.	Caller-off/Goods/Cardiff				GWR Mag 4&10/19
Kinnerley Arthur Charles	Incandescent Lineman/Banbury	17	Pte 6th Ox & Bucks L.I.	KIA 3/9/16	Thiepval Mem
Kirk J.	Striker/Signal/Wolverhampton				GWR Mag 7&10/17
Kirk Ralph Henry	Train Porter/Hotel/Paddington	32	Gnr 153rd Siege Bty RGA	Dow 2/8/18	Vignacourt Br Cem
Knapp Charles Edward	Clerk/L&C/Swindon	39	2/Cpl 20th Broad Gauge Rly RE	KIA 16/4/18	Lijssenthoek Mil Cem
Kneath David John	Traffic/Aberdare	22	2/Lt 5th Cheshire Regt	Dow 3/8/18	St Sever Cem
Knee Archibald Edward	Wagon Painter/W&C/Swindon	25	L/Cpl 1st Wilts Regt	Dow 29/5/16	Etaples Mil Cem
Knight Charles E.V.	Porter/Traffic/Natyderry	19	Pte 2nd SWB	KIA 10/3/18	Poelcapelle Br Cem
Knight Ernest Henry	Packer/Engineer/Cheltenham	40	CSM 4th Worcester Regt	KIA 12/4/18	Le Grand Beaumart Cem
Knight Frank	Coremaker/L&C/Swindon	35	Pte 7th Wilts Regt	KIA 24/4/17	Doiran Mem
Knight George Edward	Striker/L&C/Swindon	24	Pte 7th Wilts Regt	KIA 24/4/17	Doiran Mem
Knight H.	R/Labourer/Engineer/Reading				GWR Mag 11&12/16
Knight John Lionel	Dist Relief Porter/Traffic/Westbury		Pte 7th Somerset L.I.	KIA 16/8/17	Tyne Cot Mem
Knight W.	Bridge Painter/Engineer/Chepstow				GWR Mag 9/20
Knight William George	Off Porter/Goods/Plymouth	18	Pte 14th R Warwick Regt	KIA 8/7/18	Tannay Br Cem
Knowles Alfred J.T.	Porter/Traffic/Coalpit Heath	18	Pte 2/6th R Warwick Regt	KIA 12/4/18	Ploegsteert Mem
Knowles G.	Engineer/Plymouth				GWR Roll of Honour
Lamacroft(craft) Walter	R/Labourer/Engineer/S. Brent	33	1ST Class Sto HMS Goliath RN	SL 13/5/15	Plymouth Naval Mem
Lamb Harold William	Call-boy/Traffic/Gloucester	20	Pte 1/4th Gloucester Regt	KIA 24/4/17	Ste Emilie Valley Cem
Lambdin Reginald George	Machinist/L&C/Swindon	19	Pte 2nd Wilts Regt	KIA 4/11/18	Eth Com Cem
Lambert C.A.	Traffic/Abersychan				GWR Roll of Honour
Lambert Henry James	Shedman/L&C/Hereford	48	Cpl Welsh Regt Depot	Doi 15/9/15	Hereford Cem
Lambert William George	Fireman/Loco/Slough	22	Rifm 8th KRRC	KIA 4/8/15	Menin Gate Mem
Lambourne Alfred Henry	Apprent Boilermaker/L&C/Swindon	17	Pte 5th Wilts Regt	Dow 8/8/15	Helles Mem
Lambourne Ernest	Storekeeper/Stores/Swindon	23	Dvr 1st S W Mounted Bde F/Amb	Acc 3/6/15	Swindon Cem
Lambourne Walter F.	Striker/Signal/Reading		Pte 1/4th R. Berks Regt	Dow 27/8/16	Thiepval Mem
Lam(b)son William	Carriage Cleaner/L&C/Bristol	38	Pte 2nd R Scots Fus	Died 16/6/15	Le Touret Mem
Lamerton William Evelyn	Porter/Traffic/St Germans	19	Spr 2nd Light Rly Co R.E.	Dow 8/9/17	Bard Cottage Cem
Lancaster Albert Edward	Labourer/Engineer/Weston-s-Mare		Pte 7th Somerset L.I.	Dow 1/4/17	London Cem Longueval
Lancett E.	Engineer/Ledbury				GWR Roll of Honour
Lane H.W.	Traffic/Gloucester				GWR Roll of Honour
Lane P.F.	Signalman/Traffic/Campden				GWR Mag 1&2/19
Lane Sidney Ernest	Packer/Engineer/Uxbridge	32	L/Cpl 2nd Royal Fus	KIA 20/4/17	Arras Mem
Lane William Eaton	Clerk/Traffic/Ebbw Vale		Sgt 11th SWB	KIA 23/8/16	Essex Farm Cem
Lang Alfred Charles	Lampman/Traffic/Newport High St		Pte 10th SWB	Dow 14/11/17	Cite Bonjean Mil Cem
Lang Cecil	Coach-Builder/L&C/Swindon	26	Pte 1st Wilts Regt	KIA 16/6/15	Menin Gate Mem
Langford Edgar	Clerk/Traffic/Much Wenlock	21	L/Cpl 2nd Worcester Regt	KIA 29/9/18	Pigeon Ravine Cem
Langford Frederick	R/Labourer/Engineer/Small Heath	27	L/Cpl 4th Grenadier Guards	KIA 27/9/15	Loos Mem
Larcombe Donald C.	Poter/Traffic/Exeter		Pte 2nd Devonshire Regt	KIA 14/4/17	Villers Hill Br Cem
Lavis Charles W.	Porter/Goods/Bristol	31	Sgt B Bty 87th Bde RFA	Dow 23/9/17	Outtersteene Com Cem
Lavis Frederick W.	Policeman/Traffic/Plymouth Millbay	21	Cpl 8th Devonshire Regt	KIA 7/5/16	Citadel New Mil Cem
Lavis John M.	Carriage Cleaner/L&C/Newport	21	L/Cpl 1st Monmouthshire Regt	KIA 25/3/15	Wulverghem-L Rd Cem
Law Harold George	Gang Labourer/Signal/Swindon		Pte 5th Wilts Regt	KIA 25/1/17	Amara War Cem
Law Henry Milner	Clerk/Goods/Southall	25	2/Lt 6th Seaforth Highlanders	KIA 9/4/17	Maroeuil Br Cem
Law Thomas	Packer/Engineer/Birkenhead		Pte 1st Shropshire L.I.	KIA 21/3/18	Queant Road Cem
Lawless Jack	Clerk/Traffic/Newport High St.		Rifm 18th KRRC	KIA 26/10/18	Heestert Mil Cem
Lawrence Charles	Parcel Porter/Traffic/Birmingham	23	Pte 1st Coldstream Guards	KIA 28/9/15	Loos Mem
Lawrence Fred Charles	Porter/Goods/Bristol	23	Dvr 474th Field Co R.E.	KIA 10/8/17	Menin Gate Mem
Lawrence Henry Charles	Porter/Goods/Swindon	25	Pte 1st Wilts Regt	Dow 20/10/14	Le Touret Mem
Lawrence John	Gas Stoker/L&C/Swindon				GWR Mag 12/17
Lawrence Sidney Jones	Packer/Engineer/Ruislip	21	Spr 23rd Div Signal Co R.E.	KIA 15/6/18	Granezza Br Cem
Lay F.	Carriage Cleaner/Old Oak Common				GWR Mag 4/19
Le Vasseur Reg Clifford	Casual Docker/Goods/Guernsey	32	Pte 1st Leicester Regt	Dow 15/12/14	Ration Farm Mil Cem
Lea Arthur Henry Ormond	Clerk/Traffic/Kensington	31	L/Cpl 2nd H.A.C.	KIA 26/10/18	Tezze Br Cem
Lea Thomas	Labourer/L&C/Swindon	26	Pte 6th Leinster Regt	KIA 11/8/15	Helles Mem

Name	Role/Location	Age	Service	Death	Memorial/Cemetery
Leach Thomas Henry	Porter/Traffic/Corsham	20	Pte 2nd Wilts Regt	Dow 26/9/15	Loos Mem
Leaman Henry	Fireman/Loco/Bristol		Spr 1/3rd or 2/1st Field Co R.E.	Dow 21/12/16	Aveluy Com Cem
Leavens Charles Fred	Clerk/Goods/Paddington	18	Pte 10th London/Post Off Rifles	KIA 25/7/18	Pozieres Mem
Leddo(e)n Joseph	Carman/Goods/Dublin	26	Gnr 21st Bty 2nd Bde RFA	KIA 12/2/16	Ypres Reservoir Cem
Lee Alfred Henry	Carman/Goods/South Lambeth		Rifm 8th KRRC	Dow 24/8/17	Tyne Cot Mem
Lee Edmund Osborne	Carman/Goods/Acton	29	Sgt 30th Bn MGC (Infantry)	Dow 25/8/18	Arneke Br Cem
Lee Frederick	Labourer/Signal/Newport		L/Sgt 2nd Welsh Regt	Died 12/3/18	Minty Farm Cem
Lee George Francis	Carriage Cleaner/Old Oak Common	33	1st Class Sto HMS Aboukir RN	SL 22/9/14	Chatham Naval Mem
Lee Sidney George	Porter/Traffic/Bristol Joint	20	Bom B Bty 58th Bde RFA	KIA 1/12/15	Helles Mem
Lee Sidney George	Apprent Painter/L&C/Swindon	19	Spr 205th Field Co R.E.	KIA 20/10/18	Harlebeke New Br Cem
Lees Percival Booth	Account Off/New Works Engineer	28	2/Lt 16th Hamps/14th Glos	KIA 19/7/16	Thiepval Mem
Legg Gilbert John Ephram	Attendant/Electrical/Park Royal		Spr 11th Field Co R.E.	Dow 21/8/16	Dantzig Alley Br Cem
Leggett Ernest George	Fitter/No 3 Shop/Swindon	21	L/Cpl 1st Wilts Regt	KIA 3/9/15	Menin Gate Mem
Leggett William Stephen	Coach Body Maker/No 19 Shop	22	L/Cpl 1st Wilts Regt	KIA 16/6/15	Menin Gate Mem
Lehon/Leharne Edward	Parcel Porter/Traffic/Paddington		CSM 1st Middlesex Regt	Dow 11/11/16	St Sever Cem
Leighfield Sydney Francis	Wagon Painter/L&C/Swindon	22	Dvr 31st Bde Am/Col RFA	Died 19/9/18	Mikra Br Cem
Leonard Fred Charles	Frame-Builders Assist/Swindon		Dvr 3rd Wessex Bde RFA	Died 6/10/18	Kirkee Mem India
Leonard Percy Harold	Helper/L&C/Swindon	19	Gnr A Bty 173rd Bde RFA	KIA 18/7/17	Vlamertinghe N Mil Cem
Lett John Millard	Clerk/DSO/Pontypool Road	26	Temp Capt 3rd Worcester Regt	KIA 23/3/18	Arras Mem
Lewis A.	Engineer/Purton				GWR Roll of Honour
Lewis Arthur William	Fireman/Loco/Landore	22	Sgt B Bty 91st Bde RFA	KIA 12/8/17	Dragoon Camp Cem
Lewis Charles Gorvin	Police Constable/Plymouth Docks		Pte Plymouth Div RMLI	Died 8/11/14	Gillingham Cem
Lewis David	Seaman/Marine/Fishguard	31	Gnr 114th Siege Bty RGA	KIA 5/8/16	Peronne Road Cem
Lewis David James	Signalman/Traffic/Henllan	22	Pte 1/4th Welsh Regt	KIA 23/8/15	Hill 10 Cem
Lewis E.	Signalman/Traffic/Llandilo				GWR Mag 3/19
Lewis Frederick James	Electrical Fitter/L&C/Swindon	30	Sgt 15th Signal Co R.E.	KIA 1/7/18	Anzin-St Aubin Br Cem
Lewis H.	Porter/Goods/Wellington				GWR Mag 1/19
Lewis Herbert	Clerk/Goods/Gloucester	18	Pte 1/5th DCLI	KIA 14/4/18	Ploegsteert Mem
Lewis Henry Stephen	Machineman/L&C/Swindon	20	Pte 1st Wilts Regt	KIA 12/4/18	Strand Mil Cem
Lewis John	Labourer/L&C/Coleham				GWR Mag 6&12/19
Lewis Llewellyn John	Engineman/L&C/Old Oak Common	35	Spr 117th Rly Operating Co R.E.	Died 21/7/16	Salonika Mil Cem
Lewis T.	Incandescent Lineman/Banbury				GWR Mag 2&4/19
Lewis T.A.	Clerk/Goods/Cardiff				GWR Mag 12/18 & 1/19
Lewis Thomas Arthur	Apprent Fitter/L&C/Swindon	24	Cpl 6th Siege Co R.E.	Died 2/11/18	Terlincthun Br Cem
Lewthwaite Stan Basil	Clerk/Goods/Poplar	24	Rifm 9th London Regt	Dow 22/7/17	Metz-en-Couture Cem
Liddy William H.	Parcel Vanman/Traffic/Manchester		Pte 14th Welsh Regt	Dow 12/4/18	Gezaincourt Com Cem
Lihou Thomas Elisha	Docker/Goods/Guernsey		AS HMS Good Hope RN	SL 1/11/14	Portsmouth Naval Mem
Lillington Claude Clement	Porter/Traffic/Oxford		Pte 2nd R Berks Regt	KIA 31/7/17	Menin Gate Mem
Lindsey Ernest Albert	L2 Shop/Swindon	19	Pte 6th Wilts Regt	KIA 2/7/16	Thiepval Mem
Lin(g)field William James	Porter/Traffic/Paddington	30	Pte 16th Bn MGC	KIA 4/4/18	Pozieres Mem
Ling James Henry	Messroom Attendant/Stafford Rd	36	Pte 8th S Staffordshire Regt	KIA 25/8/15	Voormezeele No 3
Linton Albert Edward	Chairer/Creosoting Works/Hayes	27	Pte 4th Middlesex Regt	KIA 24/2/15	Godezonne Farm Cem
Lissiman William Henry	Packer/Engineer/Ledbury	34	Pte 1/5th Gloucester Regt	Died 11/10/17	St Sever Cem
Little Henery George	Labourer/L&C/Swindon		Pte 9th K Own Yorkshire L.I.	KIA 25/4/17	Cojeul Br Cem
Little W.R.A. (A.W.R.)	Patcher/L&C/Swindon	25	Sgt Royal Engineers	Died 7/2/18	Rodbourne Churchyard
Littler Tom	Apprent/L&C/Swindon	19	2/Lt 1 Sqdn R.F.C.	KIA 3/7/17	Bailleul Com Cem
Lloyd Alan E.	Clerk/Goods/Exeter	20	Lt RAF	Dfa 1412/18	Highweek Churchyard
Lloyd Henry	Packer/Engineer/Newnham Bridge				GWR Mag 8&9/18
Lloyd Richard	Bricklayer/Engineer/Shrewsbury				GWR Mag 2&3/18
Lloyd S.	Traffic/Crumlin				GWR Roll of Honour
Lloyd S.	Packer/Engineer/Saltney				GWR Mag 6/19
Lloyd Thomas Mansell	Clerk/Goods/Wellington	21	Pte 1/4th Shropshire L.I.	KIA 30/12/17	Thiepval Mem
Lobb Arthur John	Packer/Engineer/St Agnes	27	Pte Devon/168th Labour Corps	Died 17/11/18	St Sever Cem
Lock Henry Davidson	Porter/Goods/Smithfield	30	L/Cpl 1st E Lancashire Regt	KIA 26/8/14	La Ferte-s-Jouarre Mem
Lock Sydney Victor	Traffic/Maidenhead	24	Pte 14th R Warwick Regt	KIA 26/10/17	Hooge Crater Cem
Lock W.	L&C/Bristol				GWR Roll of Honour
Lockey Thomas	Furnaceman/L&C/Swindon	34	Pte 5th Wilts Regt	KIA 10/8/15	Helles Mem
Lockley Ernest	Shunter/Traffic/Merthyr	29	Pte 3rd Worcester Regt	KIA 21/9/14	La Ferte-s-Jouarre Mem
Lockley Walter	Porter/Traffic/Ruabon	25	Rifm 2nd KRRC	KIA 25/9/15	Loos Mem

Lockley William	Porter/Goods/Chester	27	Spr 134th ATC R.E.	KIA 26/10/17	Tyne Cot Mem
Loder G.	Engineer/Uffington	37	Cpl 4th R Berks Regt	Died 16/1/16	Baulking Churchyard
Loder Reginald Arthur	Dresser/L&C/Swindon		Pte 5th Wilts Regt	Dow 28/1/17	Amara War Cem
Long Thomas	Labourer/L&C/Swindon	29	Pte 1st Wilts Regt	KIA 16/6/15	Menin Gate Mem
Looker Samuel G.G.	Machinist/L&C/Swindon		Gnr D Bty 107th Bde RFA	Died 4/4/18	Moreuil Com Cem
Lord Robert Charles	Apprent Fitter/L&C/Swindon	19	Pte 1st Somerset L.I.	KIA 21/10/18	Vis-en-Artois Mem
Lott Arthur Herbert	Foreman/Loco/Neath		Pte 3rd R Berks Regt	Died 10/10/18	Kirk Patrick Churchyard
Lough Harold G.	Draughtsman/Signal/Reading	26	Pte 4th Seaforth Highlanders	KIA 9/5/15	Le Touret Mem
Loveday Arthur William	Frame-Builders Assist/Swindon	31	CSM 1st Wilts Regt	KIA 18/9/18	Gouzeaucourt N Br Cem
Loveday Frederick	Carpenter/L&C/Swindon	29	A/Mech 1 Motor Transport RAF	Doi 6/11/18	Swindon Cem
Loveday Hedley Uriah	L&C/Swindon	20	Pte DCLI Infantry Depot	Died 6/10/19	Swindon Cem
Loveday Ray Charles	Fitter/L&C/Swindon	28	Staff Sgt C Bty 3rd Wessex RFA	Died 20/10/18	Delhi War Mem
Lovelock E.C.	Passenger Porter/Traffic/Pilning	21	Cpl 57 Sqdn RAF	Died 1/4/18	St Pol Br Cem
Lovelock Ernest John	Clerk/Goods/Paddington	19	Rifm 12th KRRC	Dow 16/5/18	Sucrerie Cem
Lovelock George Henry	L&C/Swindon		Pte 1st Wilts Regt	Died 1/6/16	Etaples Mil Cem
Loveridge Edward	Steam Hammerman/L&C/Swindon	24	L/Cpl 5th Wilts	KIA 18/4/16	Basra Mem
Lowe Reginald John	Clerk/Goods/Cardiff	21	Gnr H.Q. 78th Bde RFA	Died 10/9/18	Varennes Mil Cem
Loynes Edward F.	Clerk/Goods/Smithfield	26	Rifm 16th London Regt	KIA 1/7/16	Thiepval Mem
Lucas Charles John	Porter/Traffic/Evershot	18	L/Cpl 14th R Warwick Regt	Dow 27/8/18	Bagneux Br Cem
Lucas Thomas Henry	Daughtsman/L&C/Swindon	27	Lt RAF	Dfa 15/5/18	Cairo War Mem Cem
Lucock John Joseph	Seaman/Marine/Plymouth	35	L/Sea HM Trawler 'Sapper' RN	SL 29/12/17	Plymouth Naval Mem
Ludlow Frank Hubert C.	Clerk/Goods/Smithfield		2/Lt 20th London Regt	KIA 23/11/17	Cambrai Mem
Lugg Richard George	Porter/Traffic/Ashton	18	Pte 2/4th R Berks Regt	KIA 7/6/18	St Venant-R Road Cem
Lugg William John	Machineman/L&C/Swindon	24	Pte 1st E Surrey Regt	KIA 6/11/17	Hooge Crater Cem
Lukins John	Porter/Bristol Goods	19	Pte 1st Somerset L.I.	Dow 18/5/15	Wimereux Com Cem
Lunn Harold Clifford	Clerk/Traffic/Hirwain	19	Pte 2/8th Lancashire Fus	KIA 9/10/17	Tyne Cot Mem
Lynch Adolphus	Porter/Traffic/Martock Station	30			GWR Mag 3/15
Lynn Henry Thomas	Labourer/No 23 Shop/Swindon	23	Pte 2nd Wilts Regt	KIA 17/5/15	Le Touret Mem
Mace William	Incandescent Lineman/Oxford				GWR Mag 6&8/18
Maddocks Joseph	Packer/Engineer/Llandenny	28	Pte 4th SWB	KIA 30/4/17	Basra Mem
Major George Cecil	Porter/Traffic/Oxford	19	Cpl 1st Hampshire Regt	Dow 4/9/18	Ligny-St Flochel Br Cem
Malin W.	Porter/Traffic/Birmingham				GWR Mag 12/16 & 3/17
Manley John	Premium Apprent/L&C/Swindon	20	Capt 19 Sqdn R.F.C.	KIA 18/9/17	Bailleul Com Cem
Mann Edwin Richard	Checker/Traffic/Tavistock	28	Cpl 23rd Northumberland Fus	KIA 18/10/17	Cement House Cem
Manners Bertrand	Frame-Builders Assist/Swindon	36	Pte 2nd Wilts Regt	KIA 17/5/15	Le Touret Mem
Manners William Fred G.	Helper/V Shop/Swindon Works	28	Sgt 1st Wilts Regt	KIA 18/10/14	Le Touret Mem
Manning John Thomas	Clerk/L&C/Swindon	31	Pte 10th F/Amb RAMC	KIA 13/4/17	Athies Com Cem
Mansell W.	Traffic/Hanwood				GWR Roll of Honour
Mant Frank	L&C/Swindon		L/Cpl 5th Wilts Regt	Dow 8/4/16	Basra Mem
Maples Kenneth James	Solicitors Office/Paddington	37	Capt 3rd S Stafford Regt (att 2nd)	KIA 16/5/15	Le Touret Mem
March E.J.	Porter/Goods/Badminton				GWR Mag 4&12/18
Marchant Alfred	Boilersmiths Helper/L&C/Swindon	34	Pte 2nd Wilts Regt	KIA 22/10/14	Perth Cem (China Wall)
Marchant Eiddon Thomas	Bricklayer/Engineer/Bontnewydd	21	L/Cpl 233rd Co MGC (Infantry)	KIA 4/10/17	Tyne Cot Mem
Marga(e)ry Sydney G.	Mileage Porter/Goods/Radstock		Pte 1st Somerset L.I.	KIA 1/9/14	Verberie French Cem
Marks Robert Edward	Engine Cleaner/Loco/Bristol		Pte 2nd R Irish Regt	KIA 31/8/16	Thiepval Mem
Marienberg Abraham G.	Clerk/Goods/Port Talbot	19	Pte 13th Liverpool Regt	KIA 12/12/17	Favreuil Br Cem
Marlow Albert Edward	Packer/Engineer/Southam Road	20	Spr 110th Rly Co R.E.	Died 31/7/16	Dernancourt Com Cem
Marsh Albert George	Porter/Traffic/Weymouth	30	Cpl D Bty 83rd Bde RFA	Dow 23/8/18	Noyon New Br Cem
Marsh Herbert John	Packer/Engineer/Toller	38	Spr I.W.T. R.E.	Died 7/7/18	Toller Churchyard
Marsh Jesse Llewellyn	Stampers Assist/L&C/Swindon	20	L/Cpl 2nd Bedford Regt	KIA 23/10/18	Highland Cem
Marsh Lemuel Enos	Boilersmiths Apprent/Swindon		Pte 5th Wilts Regt	KIA 17/1/17	Amara War Cem
Marshall John	Porter/Goods/Tiverton	21	Pte 1st Coldstream Guards	KIA 22/12/14	Le Touret Mem
Marshman William George	Porter/Goods/Frome	21	AS Hawke Bn RNVR	KIA 3/9/18	Vis-en-Artois Mem
Martin A.C.	Packer/Engineer/Ashley Hill				GWR Mag 7/19
Martin Bertie Edward	Porter/Traffic/Reading		L/Cpl 1st Bn RMLI	KIA 25/8/18	Vis-en-Artois Mem
Martin Harold	Porter/Traffic/Plymouth N. Road	25	Gnr 32nd Bty 33rd Bde RFA	KIA 28/5/18	Soissons Mem
Martin Walter Sidney S.	Messenger/Goods/Shrewsbury	18	Pte 2nd York & Lancs Regt	Dow 24/9/18	Trefcon Br Cem
Maslen Fred George	Frame-Builders Assist/Swindon		Pte 1st Wilts Regt	KIA 11/2/15	Rue-du-Bois Mil Cem
Mason George Henry	Packer/Engineer/Bordesley		Pte 1/7th Worcester Regt	KIA 16/8/17	Tyne Cot Mem

Name	Occupation	Age	Regiment	Death	Cemetery/Memorial
Mason William James	Passenger Porter/Traffic/Saltford	24	Gnr D Bty 232nd Bde RFA	Died 9/2/18	Bradenstoke Churchyard
Massey Allen	Checker/Goods/Birkenhead	32	Pte 1st Wilts Regt	KIA 21/10/14	Le Touret Mem
Masson Joseph	Assist Foreman/L&C/Old Oak Com	37	Sgt 11th Middlesex Regt	KIA 7/7/16	Thiepval Mem
Matthews F.	Lifter/L&C/Swindon				GWR Mag 5&7/16
Matthews H.	Porter/Traffic/Knightwick				GWR Mag 2/19
Matthews Percy Charles	Boilersmith/V Shop/Swindon	18	Pte 2nd Wilts Regt	KIA 15/6/15	Le Touret Mem
Matthews Stan Welcome	Forgemans Assist/Swindon		Pte 1st Wilts Regt	KIA 16/6/15	Menin Gate Mem
Matthews Sydney Philip	Clerk/C.A.O./Paddington		Pte 12th R Sussex Regt	Dow 17/10/17	Voormezeele No 1 & 2
Matthews W.	Patcher/L&C/Swindon				GWR Mag 3/18
Matthews Walter	Boilermaker/L&C/Swindon	22	Pte 2nd Wilts Regt	Dow 21/9/15	Chocques Mil Cem
Mattock Frederick Ernest	L&C/Swindon	24	Pte 2nd Wilts Regt	KIA 21/3/18	Pozieres Mem
Maunder William Henry	Chief Accountants Office		Sgt-Maj RAMC	Died 10/12/16	Highgate Cem London
Maunder William John	Clerk/Solicitors Off/Paddington	34	Rifm 1/9th London Regt	KIA 9/9/16	Thiepval Mem
Max Thomas Ewart	Carpenter/Engineer/Newport Mill St	24	Pte 87th F/Amb RAMC	KIA 14/10/18	Ypres Reservoir Cem
May Ernest Alfred	Packer/Engineer/Ide	32	Spr 119th Rly Co R.E.	Died 23/8/16	Acheux Br Cem
May W.J.	Goods/Paddington				GWR Roll of Honour
Mayhew George W.	Messenger/Goods/Paddington				GWR Mag 8&10/16
Mayo Ernest W.(brother)	Clerk/Traffic/Basingstoke	27	Pte 4th Grenadier Guards	KIA 25/9/16	Delville Wood Cem
Mayo Reginald F(brother)	Clerk/Goods/Paddington	21	Pte 4th Grenadier Guards	Doi 7/12/16	Allonville Com Cem
McCabe J.	Capstanman/Goods/Smithfield				GWR Mag 12/18
McCarthy John Patrick	Fitters Labourer/L&C/Ebbw Jct	29	Pte 3rd Worcester Regt	KIA 28/4/16	Arras Mem
McDonald W.	Goods/Smithfield				GWR Roll of Honour
McIlvride George	Greasemaker/C&W/Swindon		Cpl 10th Hussars	Dow 17/12/17	Tincourt New Br Cem
McMeeken Arthur F.	Clerk/Hotels/Paddington		Pte 9th Royal Fus	KIA 7/10/16	Beaulencourt Br Cem
McNally George	Machinist/L&C/Swindon		Pte R Wiltshire Yeo	KIA 23/3/17	Thiepval Mem
McNish John	Off Porter/Engineer/Wolverh'ton	20	OS HMS Pembroke RNVR	DDB 3/9/17	Gillingham Cem
Mead William Charles	Parcel Porter/Traffic/Stoke Canon	24	Gnr 3A Res Bde RFA	Died 12/10/18	Stoke Canon Churchyard
Megraw William James	Packer/Engineer/Mortimer	21	Pte 1st R Berks Regt	KIA 15/5/15	Le Touret Mem
Melhuish Edward Charles	Porter/Traffic/Paddington	31	Rifm 15th R Irish Rifles	KIA 22/11/17	Thiepval Mem
Meredith Ernest Mitchell	Clerk/Rates & Taxes/Paddington		Pte R Buckingham Hussars	KIA 21/8/15	Helles Mem
Meredith John Lionel	Clerk/Traffic/Mountain Ash	19	Pte 3rd Coldstream Guards	Dow 11/10/17	Dozinghem Mil Cem
Meredith William	Packer/Engineer/Codsall	25	Spr 116th (GWR) Rly Co R.E.	Doi 26/8/15	Codsall Churchyard
Merrifield Alec T.	Packer/Engineer/Glyn Neath		Pte 7th Gloucester Regt	Dow 30/3/17	Basra Mem
Merry Ernest	Spring Maker/L&C/Worcester	23	Cpl 1/8th Worcester Regt	KIA 9/10/18	Busigny Com Cem
Merritt Henry	Issuer/Stores/Swindon		L/Cpl 5th Wilts Regt	Died 15/4/17	Chatby Mem
Metcalf George Norman	Carriage Cleaner/Old Oak Common	26	Cpl 3rd London Regt	Dow 15/8/17	Lijssenthoek Mil Cem
Michael 'Jack' Samuel J.	Chainman/Engineer/Neath	34	Pte 8th S Lancashire Regt	Dow 17/10/16	Puchevillers Br Cem
Middle Richard Henry	Engine Cleaner/L&C/Bristol	18	Pte 12th Gloucester Regt	Dow 8/9/16	Abbeville Com Cem
Middleton James Charles	Carman/Traffic/Basingstoke	27	L/Cpl 1st R Berks Regt	KIA 16/5/15	Le Touret Mem
Middleton William	Packer/Engineer/Skewen		Pte 2nd R Welsh Fus	KIA 13/10/17	Messines Ridge Br Cem
Miles Albert George	Porter/Traffic/Paddington	27	L/Cpl 7th Rifle Brigade	KIA 2/7/15	Bedford House Cem
Miles Francis George	Engine Cleaner/L&C/Banbury	20	Pte 7th Ox & Bucks L.I.	Died 28/12/15	Salonika Mil Cem
Miles Frederick Henry	Packer/Engineer/Pangbourne	29	Pte 1st R Berks Regt	KIA 23/5/16	Zouave Valley Cem
Miles Rupert E.H.	Fitter/No 15 Shop/Swindon	22	Spr 77th Field Co R.E.	Dow 14/2/16	Bedford House Cem
Miles Robert William	GMO/Paddington	21	Cpt 13th (11th) Sherwood F	KIA 1/6/17	Railway Dugouts Burial
Miller Henry Albert	S/Lab/Engineer/Weymouth		Pte 1st DCLI	KIA 17/4/17	Arras Mem
Miller Herbert Ed Bowen	Police Detective/Paddington	24	Gdsm 1st Grenadier Guards	Dow 28/9/17	St Sever Cem
Miller John Benjamin	Traffic/Shrewsbury	31	Spr ROD R.E.	KIA 15/2/17	Poperinghe New Mil Cem
Millin Herbert George	Porter/Traffic/Llwydcoed		Pte 12/13th Northumberland Fus	KIA 25/8/18	Vis-en-Artois Mem
Millman Frederick Charles	Labourer/Engineer/Westbourne Pk		Pte 7th R Dublin Fus	KIA 23/9/16	Struma Mil Cem
Mills A.	Labourer/Engineer/Gloucester				GWR Mag 6&11/18
Mills Alfred George	Cleaner/Traffic/Slough	23	L/Cpl 1st E Surrey Regt	KIA 22/8/18	Queens Cem Bucquoy
Mills E.	Engineer/Cwm				GWR Roll of Honour
Mills Harry George	Porter/Traffic/Highworth	22	Pte 1st Wilts Regt	Died 15/7/18	Braine-le-Comte Cem
Milton Charles	Labourer/Engineer/Watchet		Pte 1/5th Somerset L.I.	KIA 23/11/17	Jerusalem War Cem
Milton Clifford	Labourer/Engineer/Watchet		Pte 1/5th Somerset L.I.	Died 1/11/15	Kirkee Mem India
Milton Henry Frank	Signal Porter/Traffic/Pyle	26	Pte 1st Gloucester Regt	KIA 21/10/14	Menin Gate Mem
Minett John	Wagon Builder/L&C/Swindon	27	A/Mech No10 Acceptance Pk RAF	Doi 1/11/18	Swindon Cem
Minnett John C. Septimus	Loader/Goods/Kidderminster		Pte 5th R Berks Regt	KIA 20/11/17	Cambrai Mem

Name	Role/Location	Age	Rank/Unit	Fate	Cemetery/Memorial
Minton Thomas	Traffic/Market Drayton		Pte 161st Supply Depot ASC	Died 15/6/16	Cairo War Mem Cem
Mitcham William Charles T	Machinist/Signal/Reading	20	Pte 1/4th R. Berks Regt	KIA 23/7/16	Pozieres Br Cem
Mitchell Charles	Porter/Traffic/Paddington				GWR Mag 10/19
Mitchell F.	Traffic/Abertillery				GWR Roll of Honour
Mitchell William A.	Road Motor Conductor/St Austell	19			GWR Mag 3/16
Mizon Samuel	Vanguard/Goods/Paddington		Dvr B Bty 122nd Bde RFA	Dow 17/11/18	Caudry Br Cem
Mobey Francis Richard	Stores/Swindon	32	Pte 25th Bn MGC (Infantry)	KIA 10/4/18	Ploegsteert Mem
Mocatta Frederick Elias	Engineer/Paddington	29	Capt RAF	Doi 26/8/19	Golders Green Cem
Mockford Joseph	Clerk/Goods/Paddington		2/Lt 1st London Regt	Dow 8/4/17	Warlincourt Halte Br Cem
Moger Albert Charles	S/Lab/Engineer/Pensford	23	L/Cpl 8th Somerset L.I.	KIA 1/7/16	Thiepval Mem
Molloy John Edward	Clerk/Engineer/Wolverhampton		L/Bom 131st Heavy Bty RGA	KIA 21/3/18	Arras Mem
Monk John	Packer/Engineer/Stroud	23	Pte 1st Gloucester Regt	KIA 21/10/14	Oosttaverne Wood Cem
Montague Percy Robert	Lad Clerk/Goods/Paddington	19	Rifm 2/9th London Regt	KIA 1/9/18	Vis-en-Artois Mem
Moody William Joseph	Storesman/Stores/Swindon	31	Pte 5th Wilts Regt	KIA 5/4/16	Basra Mem
Moon Alfred Edward	Off Porter/Goods/Birkenhead		L/Sgt 12th Liverpool Regt	Dow 10/9/16	Corbie Com Cem
Moon A.G.	Examiner/L&C/Savernake				GWR Mag 1/15
Moore F.W.	Signal/Reading				GWR Roll of Honour
Moore George Grange	Shunter/Goods/Wolverhampton	22	Sgt 4th Bty 1/3rd Bde RFA	Dow 24/4/16	Aubigny Com Cem
Moore H.J.	Goods/Hockley				GWR Roll of Honour
Moore Sydney James	Staff Clerk/L&C/Newton Abbot	31	Pte 140th F/Amb RAMC	Dow 2/8/16	Wolborough Churchyard
Moore William Arthur C.	Carpenter/Engineer/Neath		Sgt 12th Rifle Brigade	KIA 23/3/18	Pozieres Mem
Moran Thomas	Fireman/Loc/Didcot		Sgt 1st Co MGC (Infantry)	KIA 14/7/16	Thiepval Mem
Moreton Arthur Charles	Booking Clerk/Traffic/Old Hill		Pte 1st Wilts Regt	KIA 27/5/18	Soissons Mem
Morgan Alfred Charles	Issuer/Stores/Swindon		Pte 1st Wilts Regt	KIA 21/10/16	Regina Trench Cem
Morgan D.	Packer/Engineer/Port Talbot				GWR Mag 9/20
Morgan E.	Ticket Collector/Traffic/Caerleon				GWR Mag 11/18
Morgan Edward James	Striker/Signal/Newport	24	Rifm 1st Monmouthshire Regt	KIA 8/5/15	Menin Gate Mem
Morgan F.	Fitter/L&C/Swindon				GWR Mag 8/15
Morgan Frederick John	Apprent Fitter/L&C/Swindon	20	2/Cpl 571st or 1st Field Co R.E.	Dow 15/2/15	Dickebusch Mil Cem
Morgan H.A.	Traffic/Newport				GWR Roll of Honour
Morgan James	Packer/Engineer/Woodstock		Pte 40th F/Amb RAMC	Died 31/7/17	Baghdad N War Cem
Morgan Richard Stanley	Clerk/Traffic/Bristol	26	CSM 2nd Light Rly Co R.E.	Died 18/3/18	Roye New Br Cem
Morgan William J.	Packer/Engineer/Aberavon	33	Pte 1st Welsh Regt	KIA 5/5/15	New Irish Farm Cem
Morris F.C.	Carman/Goods/Slough				GWR Mag 8&9/18
Morris Richard	Labourer/L&C/Swindon		Spr 117th Rly Co R.E.	Died 9/9/15	Aldershot Mil Cem
Morris W.T.	L&C/Swindon				GWR Roll of Honour
Morris William	Ganger/Engineer/Ponkey	40	Pte 1st Welsh Guards	Died 15/5/16	Poperinghe New Mil Cem
Morris William Frank	Lad Porter/Traffic/Resolven	19	Gnr A Bty 122nd Bde RFA	Died 27/7/17	Mendinghem Mil Cem
Morse Frederick William	Porter/Traffic/Yetminster	24	Pte 1/4th Gloucester Regt	Died 15/8/16	Cayeux Mil Cem
Morse Henry	Wagon Painter/L&C/Swindon		Pte 6th Wilts Regt	Dow 15/4/18	Tyne Cot Mem
Morse John	Fire Cleaner/L&C/Swansea	32	Pte 2nd Welsh Regt	KIA 25/9/14	La Ferte-s-Jouarre Mem
Morse Richard Hunt D.	Angle-Iron Smith/L&C/Swindon	24	L/Cpl 6th Wilts Regt	Dow 13/11/16	Pozieres Br Cem
Morshead Leonard	Plumber/Engineer/St Blazey		Spr 101st Field Co R.E.	Died 23/8/18	Montecchio Com Cem
Morten Lewis James	Clerk/Goods/Chippenham	27	2/Lt Bucks Bn Ox & Bucks LI	KIA 4/11/18	Le Rejet-de-Beaulieu
Mosby/Morby Ernest	Packer/Engineer/Adderbury				GWR Mag 8/15
Moss Sydney Christopher	Fireman/Loco/Swindon	20	Gnr 166th Seige Bty RGA	Died 6/1/17	Varennes Mil Cem
Mott S.	Clerk/Traffic/Hayes				GWR Mag 6/19
Moulden Ernest George	Labourer/Stores/Swindon	40	Sgt 1st Wilts Regt	KIA 12/3/15	Menin Gate Mem
Mound John Thomas	Signal Lineman/Stratford-on-Avon	37	L/Cpl 15th Signal Co R.E.	Dow 4/10/15	Lillers Com Cem
Moyses Archibald Winter	Packer/Engineer/Roche	23	Spr Railways R.E.	Died 9/11/18	Roche Cem
Mugford H.N.	L&C/Swindon	23	Spr 565th (Wilts) ATC R.E.	Dow 19/9/18	Sunken Road Cem
Mulcahy Daniel Patrick	Parcel Porter/Traffic/Bristol	20	Pte 2nd Devonshire Regt	KIA 27/7/17	Menin Gate Mem
Mullings Wilfred Henry	Clerk/Goods/Bristol		Pte 25th Co MGC (Infantry)	KIA 18/4/18	Tyne Cot Mem
Mullis George Thomas	Porter/Goods/Hockley		Sgt 2nd W Yorkshire Regt	KIA 25/3/18	Brie Br Cem
Mulloy James Patrick	Stores Lad/Engineer/Wolverhampt		Pte 13th Yorkshire Regt	KIA 1/3/17	Thiepval Mem
Mund(a)y Francis Harold	Labourer/Engineer/Taunton	29	A/Bom 267th Siege Bty RGA	Dow 27/8/18	Fienvillers Br Cem
Murley Charles	L&C/Cardiff	27	Pte 17th Lancers	Died 3/10/18	Bac-du-Sud Br Cem
Muton Charles Henry J.	Packer/Engineer/Weston-s-Mare	29	Pte 1st Somerset L.I.	KIA 9/11/14	Ploegsteert Mem
Naish Alfred Herbert	Assist/New Works/Paddington	39	Lt 20th KRRC	KIA 13/7/16	Carnoy Mil Cem

Nall Thomas	Invoice Typist/Goods/Birkenhead	24	Sgt 19th Liverpool Regt	KIA 22/3/18	Pozieres Mem
Nash Charles	Moulder/L&C/Swindon	33	Spr 63rd Field Co R.E.	Dow 19/10/18	Kortrijk Com Cem
Nash G.	Traffic/Malvern Link				GWR Roll of Honour
Nason Richard Philip	Clerk/Traffic/Cleobury Mortimer	20	2/Lt Nottinghamshire Yeo	KIA 16/4/18	Ploegsteert Mem
Naylor Arthur P.	Clerk/Goods/West Bromwich		Pte 7th Bedfordshire Regt	KIA 10/8/17	Menin Gate Mem
Neale Charles John	Signalman/Traffic/Henley-in-Arden	27	Pte 4th Coldstream Guards	KIA 19/6/17	Artillery Wood Cem
Neale George	Bridge Labour/Engineer/Wolver'h	28	Pte 2nd S Staffordshire Regt	KIA 27/10/14	Menin Gate Mem
Neil G.	Labourer/Engineer/Westbourne Pk				GWR Mag 10&11/17
Nelson A.V.	Secretary's/Paddington				GWR Roll of Honour
Nethercleft Hugh Kirk	Clerk/Marine/Fishguard		2/Lt 2nd SWB	Dow 25/12/17	St Sever Cem
New Percy Victor	Porter/Traffic/Pyle	26	Pte 12th Lancers	KIA 18/5/15	Menin Gate Mem
Newbury Edward M.	Platform Porter/Traffic/Newport	22	Pte 2nd Dragoon att Westminster	KIA 31/10/17	Beersheba War Cem
Newell George Albert	Sheet Repairer/Goods/Worcester	24	L/Cpl 10th Worcester Regt	Dow 28/10/15	St Sever Cem
Newman Bennett	Warehouseman/Stores/Swindon		Pte 4th Bn Tank Corps	KIA 10/8/18	Vis-en-Artois Mem
Newman Frank	Carriage Cleaner/L&c/Cardiff	33	Pte 1st Wilts Regt	KIA 22/6/15	Menin Gate Mem
Newman Fred James	Cellarman/Hotels/Paddington	30	Pte 13th Middlesex Regt	Dow 15/3/16	Brandhoek Mil Cem
Newman F.W.	Machinist/L&C/Swindon	20	Pte 6th Bn MGC	Died 5/4/19	Swindon Cem
Newman John	L&C/Swindon	24	Pte 2nd Wilts Regt	Dow 7/12/14	Merville Com Cem
Newman Reginald Gerald	Porter/Traffic/Henwick	21	L/Cpl 23rd Royal Fus	KIA 27/5/17	Orchard Dump Cem
Newman Wilfred Thomas	Passenger Porter/Traff/Badminton	18	Pte 1st Hampshire Regt	KIA 22/4/18	Loos Mem
Newport William Stephen	Linesman Lad/Signal/W. Drayton	18	Pte 1/5th Devonshire Regt	Dow 21/10/18	Grevillers Br Cem
Newton Albert Edward	Labourer/L&C/Swindon	40	Cpl 2nd Wilts Regt	KIA 31/7/17	Menin Gate Mem
Newton Sidney Lazarus	Shunter/Traffic/Westbury	33	Pte 2nd Wilts Regt	KIA 24/10/14	Menin Gate Mem
Newton William George	Carriage Cleaner/L&C/W. London		Pte 7th London Regt	KIA 8/8/18	Heath Cem Harbonniers
Nicholas Edgar John	Frame-Builders Assist/Swindon	20	Dvr D Bty 79th Bde RFA	KIA 1/4/17	Maroeuil Br Cem
Nicholls A.	Labourer/L&C/Stafford Road	25			GWR Mag 7&10/16
Nicholls Frederick	Fireman/Loco/Southall				GWR Mag 8/18
Nicholls Henry Arthur	Carman/Goods/Hockley		Pte 2nd Coldstreams att RGA	Dow 31/10/15	Bethune Town Cem
Noble Edwin George	Relief Clerk/Traffic/Pontypool Road	27	L/Cpl 1/1st Hereford Regt	KIA 6/11/17	Beersheba War Cem
Noble Thomas	Horsekeeper/Goods/W Ealing	31	Pte 8th Royal Fus	Dow 16/5/17	Etaples Mil Cem
Norman James Charles	Carriage Cleaner/L&C/Weymouth	28	Pte 9th Devonshire Regt	KIA 10/10/17	Tyne Cot Mem
Norris Henry	Packer/Engineer/Pantyffynon	31			GWR Mag 2/15
Norris John Herbert	Packer/Engineer/Caerleon		Rifm 1st Monmouthshire Regt	KIA 27/12/16	Foncquevillers Mil Cem
Norris Percy	Packer/Engineer/Andoversford	26	Pte 12th or 14th Worcester Regt	KIA 30/10/17	Tyne Cot Mem
North F.J. or R.J.	Number Taker/Traffic/Banbury				GWR Mag 3&4/19
Northcote Ernest Percy	Fireman/Loco/Landore	20	Pte 1/6th Welsh Regt	KIA 20/7/16	Flatiron Copse Cem
Northcott Frank Leonard	Porter/Traffic/Devonport		Pte 2nd Devonshire Regt	KIA 1/7/16	Thiepval Mem
Norton Edgar George	Wagon Painter/L&C/Swindon	31	Pte 2nd Coldstream Guards	KIA 16/9/16	Delville Wood Cem
Norton Stanley Gorge	Clerk/Traffic/Aylesbury		Pte 2/1st Ox & Bucks L.I.	KIA 21/3/18	Pozieres Mem
Norwood Reg Harold	Clerk/Goods/Paddington	24	2/Lt C Co 9th Bn Tank Corps	KIA 29/9/18	Bellicourt Br Cem
Nurden W.J.	Striker/L&C/Swindon	51	L/Cpl 1st Wilts National Reserve	Acc 11/12/14	Swindon Cem
Nye Percival	Brakesman/Traffic/Aberbeeg	29	Pte 1st R Berks Regt	KIA 3/11/14	Menin Gate Mem
Oakley Hubert Charles	Engine Cleaner/L&C/Hereford	19	L/Cpl 55th Co MGC (Infantry)	Dow 1/3/17	Pozieres Br Cem
O'Brien Harold Frederick	Apprent Brassfitter/L&C/Swindon	19	Gnr D Bty 82nd Bde RFA	KIA 21/10/17	Minty Farm Cem
O'Callaghan Michael J.	Fireman/Loco/Newport Dock St.	21	Pte 1st SWB	Dow 25/7/16	Puchevillers Br Cem
O'Callaghan W.	Porter/Goods/Hockley				GWR Mag 3/18
Ockwell Edward William	L&C/Hereford	20	Rifm Rifle Bde/2/10th London Reg	KIA 31/3/18	Pozieres Mem
O'Hagan Richard J.	Packer/Engineer/Camborne		Pte 25th F/Amb RAMC	Died 14/1/18	Nine Elms Br Cem
O'Keeffe Timothy	Boilermaker/L&C/Swindon	22	L/Cpl 1st Wilts Regt	Dow 24/9/15	Brandhoek Mil Cem
Old Felis Henry	Porter/Goods/Poplar		Pte 2/4th London Regt	Dow 27/9/17	Dozinghem Mil Cem
Oldham Arthur	Porter/Paddington Goods Station	35	Sgt 2nd Grenadier Guards	KIA 27/8/18	Mory Abbey Mil Cem
Oliver W.	Porter/Traffic/Filton				GWR Mag 3&6/19
Ollis James Albert William	Fireman/Loco/Bristol		L/Cpl 1/4th Somerset L.I.	Died 28/7/16	Basra War Cem
Onions Charles Frederick	Porter/Traffic/Whittington		Pte 18th Welsh Regt	KIA 11/4/18	Ploegsteert Mem
Opie John S.	Porter/Traffic/Plymouth Mill Bay		Pte 9th Devonshire Regt	KIA 1/7/16	Thiepval Mem
Oram Frank	Labourer/C&W/Swindon		Gnr C Bty 186th Bde RFA	KIA 16/8/17	Vlamertinghe N Mil Cem
Oram Percival Lorenzo	Clerk/Traffic/Trowbridge	20	Pte 166th Co MGC (Infantry)	KIA 31/7/17	Menin Gate Mem
Orders Horace Melville	Gasfitter/Engineer/Newport		Pte 19th Lancashire Fus	KIA 1/11/18	Vis-en-Artois Mem
Osborn(e) Ernest William	Engine Cleaner/L&C/Southall	19	Pte 11th W Yorkshire Regt	KIA 9/1/16	Ration Farm Mil Cem

Osborn George Henry	Gasfitter Apprent/L&C/Swindon	22	Pte 11th Liverpool Regt	KIA 21/3/18	Pozieres Mem
Osborn George William	L&C/Neath	40	Pte 6th Northampton Regt	KIA 22/1/17	Tyne Cot Mem
Osborne Frank	Ash-loader/L&C/Westbury		Pte 2nd Leinster Regt	KIA 6/6/17	Irish House Cem
O'Shea T.	Carriage Cleaner/Old Oak Common				GWR Mag 11/16
Outrimm W.G.	Labourer/Engineer/Hayes				GWR Mag 3/19
Overton Frederick John	S/Labourer/Engineer/Trowbridge		Pte 8th E. Yorkshire Regt	KIA 26/12/17	Mory Abbey Mil Cem
Overton William Harold	Clerk/Goods/Wolverhampton	22	Pte 10th Lincolnshire Regt	KIA 28/4/17	Roeux Br Cem
Overy William Henry	Porter/Goods/Smithfield	29	Pte 4th Royal Fus	Dow 24/11/14	Bailleul Com Cem
Owen Clarke	Lamp Trimmer/Electrical/Swansea	25	Pte 1st W. Surrey Regt	Dow 10/5/18	Esquelbecq Mil Cem
Owen F.W.	Engineer/Caerau				GWR Roll of Honour
Owen Horre Solle	Clerk/Accounts/Paddington	31	2/Lt 3rd Manchester Regt	KIA 23/11/16	Hamel Mil Cem
Owen T.R.	Clerk/Goods/Swansea Valley Jct				GWR Mag 10/19
Packer Edward George	Wagon Writer/C&W/Swindon		L/Cpl 14th R Warwick Regt	KIA 26/9/18	Neuville-Bourjonval Cem
Packer L.H.	Examiner/L&C/Port Talbot				GWR Mag 9&12/18
Packer W.M.	Labourer/L&C/Swindon				GWR Mag 9&12/19
Padbury Ernest	Restaurant Car Conductor/Padd	30	Pte 6th Ox & Bucks L.I.	KIA 9/10/16	Thiepval Mem
Padbury Henry	Packer/Engineer/Honeybourne		Cpl 13th Gloucester Regt	Dow 5/8/17	Dozingham Mil Cem
Paget George	Painter/Signal/Newport	26	Pte 8th SWB	KIA 2/8/17	Doiran Mil Cem
Pagett Leonard George	Shunter/Traffic/Oxley Sidings	21	Pte 12th Gloucester Regt	KIA 3/9/16	Thiepval Mem
Paginton George Arthur	Labourer/No 1 Shop/Swindon	28	Pte 7th R Dublin Fus	KIA 16/8/15	Helles Mem
Paine Frank Vincent	Lad Porter/Traffic/Staines	16	Pte 8th Royal Fus	KIA 7/7/16	Thiepval Mem
Painter William Edward	Shop Clerk/L&C/Swindon	22	L/Cpl 1st London Regt att 4th Bn	KIA 18/9/18	Flesquieres Hill Br Cem
Palmer Ralph Henry	Signalman/Traffic/Briton Ferry	35	Spr ROD R.E.	Died 24/8/18	Bagneux Br Cem
Palmer Richard Thomas	Labourer/L&C/Swindon	20	L/Cpl 1st Wilts Regt	KIA 12/3/15	La Laiterie Mil Cem
Pardell John	R/Lab/Engineer/Shrewsbury		Sgt 17th R Welsh Fus	Dow 2/11/18	St Sever Cem
Pardington Fred	Platform Porter/Traffic/Cardiff	30	Pte 2/6th Gloucester Regt	Dow 29/1/18	Ham Br Cem
Pardon Leonard	Carpenter/L&C/Newton Abbot	23	Spr 27th Div Signal Co R.E.	KIA 5/5/15	Menin Gate Mem
Parish Arthur John	Porter/Traffic/Kingswear	20	Pte 10th Devonshire Regt	KIA 24/4/17	Doiran Mem
Park Frederick Joseph	Clerk/Traffic/Devizes	19	Pte 6th Somerset L.I.	KIA 21/3/18	Pozieres Mem
Parker Cecil Francis	Clerk/Traffic/Hengoed	21	Pte 33rd Bn MGC (Infantry)	Dow 21/9/18	Villers Hill Br Cem
Parker Ernest Albert	Carriage Cleaner/Old Oak Common		AS HMS Cressy RN	SL 22/9/14	Chatham Naval Mem
Parker Henry J.	Messenger/S.O.L./Paddington				GWR Mag 9&11/16
Parker J.	Porter/Goods/Hockley				GWR Mag 12/17 & 6/18
Parker J.G.	L&C/Swindon				GWR Roll of Honour
Parmenter Ernest	Porter/Traffic/Oxford	21	Pte 5th Ox & Bucks L.I.	KIA 3/5/17	Arras Mem
Parr John W.	Clerk/Goods/South Lambeth	22			GWR Mag 6&9/16
Parry Percy Samuel	Engine Cleaner/Loco/Sudbrook	20	Rifm 1st Monmouthshire Regt	KIA 8/5/15	Menin Gate Mem
Parsonage Edward	Fireman/Loco/Slough	25	Sto 1st Class HMS 'Recruit' RN	SL 9/8/17	Chatham Naval Mem
Parsons Arthur Collins	Lampman/Traffic/Birkenhead	18	Pte 15th Lancashire Fus	Dow 21/6/18	Gezaincourt Com Cem
Parsons A.J.	Fireman/Loco/Chester				GWR Mag 10/16
Parsons Frank	L&C/Swindon		Pte 1st Wilts Regt	KIA 31/10/14	Le Touret Mem
Parsons George	L/Packer/Engineer/Brislington		L/Cpl SS Sicilly RMLI	Doi 14/10/16	Edinburgh Seafield Cem
Parsons Thomas Arthur	Clerk/Goods/Cardiff	19	Pte 2nd SWB	KIA 27/8/18	Borre Br Cem
Parsons William	Porter/Traffic/Bristol				GWR Mag 12/17 & 6/18
Parsons W.S.	Traffic/Weston-super-Mare				GWR Roll of Honour
Partridge Percy John	Porter/Traffic/Totnes		Pte 12th Gloucester Regt	Died 25/8/18	Adanac Mil Cem
Partridge W.G.	Timekeeper/Goods/Hockley				GWR Mag 7&10/18
Pascoe Herbert	Road Motor Conductor/Maidenhead	19	L/Cpl 1st R Berks Regt	Dow 25/3/15	Bethune Town Cem
Pate William Charles	Boilersmiths Mate/L&C/Chester	24	Pte 1/5th Cheshire Regt	KIA 21/9/16	Delville Wood Cem
Pattemore Fred William	Packer/Engineer/Caerleon	41	Pte 1st Dorset Regt	KIA 2/5/15	Bailleul Com Cem
Patten Joseph	Signal Porter/Traffic/Cardiff	20	Dvr 85th small arms A/Col RFA	Died 23/10/16	Lahana Mil Cem
Paul Alfred William	Porter/Goods/Weymouth	19	Pte 107th Co MGC (Infantry)	KIA 16/8/17	Tyne Cot Mem
Payne Albert	Shunter/Goods/Wolverhampton	29	2/Cpl 14th Light Rly Co R.E.	KIA 21/3/18	Reninghelst N Mil Cem
Payne Bertram	Packer/Engineer/Hele & Bradninch	22	Pte 1st Coldstream Guards	Died 27/11/17	Cambrai Mem
Payne C.H.	Fireman/Loco/Trowbridge				GWR Mag 10/16 & 5/17
Payne Henry William	Porter/Traffic/Stourbridge				GWR Mag 6/20
Payne R.A.	Clerk/Traffic/Reading				GWR Mag 1/19
Paynter Albert Edward	Frame-Builders Assist/Swindon		Gnr 'Y' 9th Trench Motar Bty RFA	KIA 9/5/17	Point-du-Jour Mil Cem
Payton William John	Fireman/Loco/Worcester	25	Pte 2nd Worcester Regt	KIA 24/10/14	Perth Cem (China Wall)

Name	Occupation/Depot	Age	Regiment	Death	Memorial
Pearce A.J.	Engine Cleaner/L&C/Cardiff				GWR Mag 9&12/19
Pearce Ernest George	Porter/Bristol Goods Station	27	Pte 1st Somerset L.I.	KIA 17/5/15	Menin Gate Mem
Pearce F.W.	Road Motor Car Cleaner/Slough				GWR Mag 1/19
Pearce George	Packer/Engineer/West Drayton	33	Pte 1st Middlesex Regt	KIA 8/11/14	Rue David Mil Cem
Pearce W.	R/Labourer/Engineer/Newport				GWR Mag 9/20
Pearce Walter John	Machineman/L&C/Swindon		Pte 5th Wilts Regt	KIA 5/4/16	Basra Mem
Pearce William Henry	Painter/L&C/Swindon	24	Spr 503rd Field Co R.E.	Dow 5/3/17	Warlincourt Halte Br Cem
Pearman D.	Painter/L&C/Wormwood Scrubs				GWR Mag 11/16
Pelling(s) Arthur George J	Bufferman/L&C/Swindon	27	L/Sgt 2nd Wilts Regt	KIA 9/4/17	Bucquoy Road Cem
Pellow Richard Carter	Apprent Fitter/L&C/St Blazey	21	2/Lt RAF	Dfa 9/7/18	Biscovey Churchyard
Pepperell Fred John G.	Clerk/Goods/Oxford	20	Pte 1st Seaforth Highlanders	Dow 24/4/16	Amara War Cem
Perrett Francis Sidney	Clerk/Traffic/Cwmbran	20	Spr 29th Div Signal Co R.E.	KIA 14/10/18	Dadizeele New Br Cem
Perrett Henry/Harry L.H.	Canal Labour/Engineer/Ystalfera	35	Sgt 3rd Coldstream Guards	KIA 9/10/17	Artillery Wood Cem
Perry Charles	Bricklayer/Engineer/Craven Arms				GWR Mag 6&8/18
Perry George	Depot Labourer/Engineer/Neath	21	AS Drake Bn R.N.D.	Died 13/11/16	Ancre Br Cem
Perry H.	Striker/L&C/Worcester				GWR Mag 1&6/19
Perry J.R.	Caller-off/Goods/Smithfield				GWR Mag 9&12/18
Perry Thomas Henry	L&C/Swindon	34	Pte 2nd Wilts Regt	KIA 21/3/18	Savy Br Cem
Perry T.J.	Carriage Cleaner/Old Oak Common				GWR Mag 3&7/18
Pettifer E.A.	Goods/Hockley				GWR Roll of Honour
Phillips Arthur Bertram	Clerk/Goods/Swansea	20	Rifm 1st Monmouthshire Regt	KIA 28/8/17	Loos Mem
Phillips B.	Engineer/Dinmore				GWR Roll of Honour
Phillips Frank Gordon	Clerk/DEO/Paddington	28	Bom C Bty 82nd Bde RFA	KIA 18/9/18	Peronne Com Cem
Phillips Ivor Christmas	Chief Accountants Office	20	Pte 13th London Regt	KIA 9/5/15	Ploegsteert Mem
Phillips W.	Packer/Engineer/Malvern Link				GWR Mag 11/19
Phillips William Henry	Stower/Goods/Hereford		Pte 11th Border Regt	KIA 18/11/16	Waggon Road Cem
Phillips William James	Clerk/Goods/Newport		2/Lt 4th Seaforth Highlanders	KIA 25/7/16	Thiepval Mem
Phipps Albert Frederick	Wagon Repairers Assist/Oxford	18	Pte 1/4th Ox & Bucks L.I.	Dow 25/11/16	St Sever Cem
Pickering Victor G.A.	Telegraphist/Traffic/Swindon	19	Sgt 1st Wilts Regt	KIA 31/5/17	St Quentin Cabaret Cem
Pickett Samuel George	L&C/Swindon	21	Pte 7th Wilts Regt	KIA 24/4/17	Doiran Mem
Pickford Ernest Charles W	Porter/Traffic/Cornwood	21	Pte 8th Devonshire Regt	Dow 10/11/15	Boulogne East Cem
Picton W.	Toolboy/Engineer/Haverfordwest				GWR Mag 11/19
Pidden Frederick	Parcel Carman/Traffic/Dorchester	30	Rifm 8th R Irish Rifles	Dow 2/10/16	Bailleul Com Cem
Pidgeon Arthur	R/Labourer/Engineer/Aberavon	35	Cpl 15th Welsh Regt	KIA 18/9/18	Vis-en-Artois Mem
Pierce Arthur George	Booking Clerk/Traffic/Torre	26	Cpl 2/4th Devonshire Regt	KIA 29/3/16	Kut War Cem
Pile James	L&C/Swindon	37	Pte 1st Wilts Regt	KIA 20/10/18	Terlincthun Br Cem
Pill Percy Herbert	Boilersmiths Helper/L&C/Swindon		Sgt 7th Wilts Regt	KIA 24/4/17	Doiran Mem
Piper Reginald	L&C/Trowbridge	20	Pte 1/4th Wilts Regt	Died 31/12/16	Basra Mem
Pitman Ernest Henry	Brassfitter Apprent/L&C/Swindon	20	Sgt 1st DCLI	Dow 20/4/18	Etaples Mil Cem
Pitt Frederick Guy	Porter/Traffic/Patchway	21	Gnr 25th Bty 35th Bde RFA	Dow 2/11/17	Etaples Mil Cem
Pitt W.	Packer/Engineer/Ashperton				GWR Mag 6&10/19
Pitt W.	Helper/L&C/Swindon				GWR Mag 10/17
Pitts Edgar Carew	L/Packer/Engineer/Ashburton	28	Pte 1st Devonshire Regt	KIA 20/10/14	Arras Road Cem
Pitts George Henry	Porter/Traffic/Pyle	27	Dvr 65th Div A/Col RFA	Died 1/6/18	Torquay Cem
Plane Ernest Clifford	Machinist/L&C/Neath	16	Pte 6th Welsh Regt	KIA 30/11/15	Dud Corner Cem Loos
Pocock Edwin M.	Porter/Traffic/High Wycombe	22	Sgt 2/4th Ox & Bucks L.I.	KIA 21/3/18	Chappelle Br Cem
Pollard W.S.	Porter/Goods/Lawrence Hill				GWR Mag 12/18 & 1/19
Pomeroy Stephen	Porter/Goods/Newport High St	23	Rifm 1st Monmouthshire Regt	KIA 4/10/17	Philosophe Br Cem
Pond Montague Percy	Clerk/Audit Off/Paddington	28	2/Cpl Rly Transport Section R.E.	KIA 6/5/17	Faubourg D'Amiens Cem
Ponting Arthur Francis	Labourer/L&C/Swindon	22	Pte 14th Bn MGC	Dow 28/3/18	Doullens Com Cem 1
Ponting Albert James	Plumber/L&C/Swindon	26	L/Sgt 1st Wilts Regt	Dow 20/5/16	Aubigny Com Cem
Poole Alfred James	Creosoter/Engineer/Hayes	27	Pte 1st Loyal N Lancs Regt	KIA 21/7/16	Thiepval Mem
Poole William Ernest	Wagon Painter/19E Shop/Swindon		Pte 2nd Ox & Bucks L.I.	KIA 25/9/15	Loos Mem
Pope William Ernest	L/Packer/Engineer/Thatcham	40	L/Cpl 5th R Berks Regt	KIA 13/10/15	Loos Mem
Porter Thomas Edgar	Labourer/No12 Shop/Swindon		Pte 1st Wilts Regt	KIA 27/10/14	Le Touret Mem
Porter F.G.	Goods/Bristol				GWR Roll of Honour
Postings J.E.	Parcel Porter/Traffic/Birmingham				GWR Mag 8/19
Potter Reginald	Packer/Engineer/Totnes	24	Spr 81st Field Co R.E.	KIA 6/6/18	Marfaux Br Cem
Poulter Arthur William	Parcel Porter/Traffic/Paddington	19	Rifm 3rd Rifle Brigade	Dow 25/3/18	Rosieres Br Cem

Name	Occupation/Dept/Location	Age	Rank/Regiment	Death	Cemetery/Memorial
Pouncett Arthur	Packer/Engineer/Hartlebury	28	Gdsm 3rd Grenadier Guards	KIA 27/9/15	Loos Mem
Pounds Arthur	Chairer/Engineer/Hayes	24	L/Cpl 9th Royal Fus	Dow 14/7/16	Boulogne East Cem
Povey Albert G. (son)	Machinist/Signal/Reading	17	Pte 6th R Berks Regt	KIA 23/9/15	Becourt Mil Cem
Povey Charles J. (father)	Blacksmith/Signal/Reading	47	Cpl 2/1st Berks Bty R.H.A.	Doi 16/4/15	Buxton Churchyard
Powditch Thomas Herbert	Restaurant Car Conductor/Padd		Pte 13th Middlesex Regt	KIA 18/8/16	Thiepval Mem
Powell Edwin	Road Motor Cond'tor/Abergavenny		L/Cpl 9th R Welsh Fus	KIA 31/7/17	Menin Gate Mem
Powell Frederick James	Packer/Engineer/Bicester	33	Pte 2nd Ox & Bucks L.I.	Died 19/6/15	Bucknell Churchyard
Powell George Winton	Clerk/Surveyors/Paddington	19	Pte 8th Somerset L.I.	KIA 28/4/17	Arras Mem
Powell Joseph H.	Packer/Engineer/Risca		Pte 1st SWB	KIA 22/12/16	A.I.F. Burial Flers
Powell Thomas	Packer/Engineer/Reading	30	Pte 2nd Manchester Regt	Dow 23/10/14	Gorre Br & Indian Cem
Powers James	Porter/Traffic/Shirley	19	Pte 2/7th R Warwick Regt	KIA 24/10/18	Canonne Farm Br Cem
Pratley Frederick Walter	Carman/Goods/Hockley	22	Pte 2nd Hampshire Regt	Das 13/8/15	Helles Mem
Pratt Edgar Charles	R/Labourer/Engineer/Taunton	27	Pte 1st DCLI	KIA 12/5/15	Menin Gate Mem
Pratt Reginald Edward V.	Machinist/Signal/Reading		Pte 1/4th R. Berks Regt	KIA 23/7/16	Thiepval Mem
Prattley Reginald	Clerk/Goods/Handsworth	18	Pte 8th R Berks Regt	Dow 5/9/18	Heilly Station Cem
Preece Bernard Arthur	Clerk/Goods/Oldbury	19	OS RN Depot Crystal Palace	Died 10/12/18	Beckenham Cem
Preece Walter	Traffic/Hallatrow	29	Pte 1st Wilts Regt	KIA 6/7/16	Thiepval Mem
Prescott Harold	Porter/Goods/Banbury	28	Sgt 5th Ox & Bucks L.I.	KIA 25/9/15	Menin Gate Mem
Press William Henry	L&C/Swindon		Spr 565th (Wilts) ATC R.E.	Died 7/10/17	Malo-les-Bains Com Cem
Price Charles Francis	Fireman/L&C/Merthyr or Aberdare	26	Sgt 9th Welsh Regt	KIA 15/1/16	Le Touret Mem
Price Edwin	Packer/Engineer/Hockley	39	Pte 1/6th N Staffordshire Regt	KIA 1/7/16	Gommecourt Wood Cem
Price F.	Goods/Hockley				GWR Roll of Honour
Price Harold P.	Booking Clerk/Traffic/Worcester		Pte 6th Somerset L.I.	Died 25/5/28	Annois Com Cem
Price James George	R/Labourer/Engineer/Bristol	27	Pte 1st Gloucester Regt	KIA 21/1/15	Guards Cem Windy C.
Price James William	Painter/L&C/Swindon		Gnr 2nd Wessex Bde RFA	Died 8/2/15	Swindon Cem
Price John	Ganger/Engineer/Llanvihangel		Sgt 116th (GWR) Rly Co R.E.	Died 3/11/18	Gaza War Cem
Price John Henry	Painters Labourer/Signal/Newport	25	Rifm 1st Monmouthshire Regt	KIA 4/10/17	Philosophe Br Cem
Price John P.	Boilersmiths Apprent/Swindon		Gnr 134th Bty 32 Bde RFA	KIA 1/11/16	Thiepval Mem
Price Paul Adrian Edward	GMO/Paddington	21	2/Lt Q Anti-aircraft Bty RGA	KIA 23/4/17	Beaumetz Cross Rd Cem
Price T.R.	Issuer/Stores/Wolverhampton				GWR Mag 2/19
Price William A. or H.	Fireman/Loco/Bristol		Gloucester Regt		GWR Mag 3/17
Priest Cyril William	Porter/Traffic/Stourbridge Jct	20	Gnr 155th Army Bde RFA	Dow 4/11/18	Caudry Br Cem
Pringle William Henry	Shunter/Traffic/Old Oak Common	24	Cpl 70th F/Amb RAMC	KIA 7/6/17	Railway Dugouts Burial
Prior James	Labourer/Signal/Reading		Spr ROD R.E.	Died 9/10/18	Cairo War Mem Cem
Pritchard George E.	Porter/Goods/Halesowen	34	L/Cpl 2nd S Staffordshire Regt	KIA 16/5/15	Le Touret Mem
Probert F.	Labourer/Signal/Newport				GWR Mag 4/19
Proctor F.	Labourer/Engineer/Maidenhead				GWR Mag 6/19
Prosser Wilfred James A.	Traffic/Risca		Pte 1st R Lancaster Regt	KIA 12/10/17	Tyne Cot Mem
Protheroe Arthur John	Apprent/L&C/Newton Abbot	21	L/Cpl 1/5th Devonshire Regt	Dow 20/11/17	Ramleh War Cem
Provis Nelson H.G.	Labourer/L&C/Swindon	34	Pte 1st Wilts Regt	KIA 20/11/14	Menin Gate Mem
Prow(u)le Arthur T.J.	Porter/Traffic/Bristol	26	Pte 1st Devonshire Regt	Died 22/9/14	La Ferte-s-Jouarre Mem
Prowse George Henry	Porter/Goods/Oxford	30	Pte 2nd Ox & Bucks L.I.	KIA 23/10/14	Ypres Town Cem
Pryor Herbert	Packer/Engineer/Scorrier	31	Pte 1st DCLI	KIA 30/10/17	Tyne Cot Mem
Pudner William Basil Lynn	Striker/L&C/Neath		Pte 6th SWB	KIA 19/7/17	Dickebusch Mil Cem
Pugh Josiah Charles	Incandescent Lineman/Worcester	33	Pte 5th Essex Regt	Died 31/3/17	Worcester (Astwood)
Pugh R.	Incandescent Lineman/Worcester				GWR Mag 8&12/18
Pullen Percy William	Porter/Goods/Swindon		A/Bom 3rd Echelon HQ RFA	Died 15/7/17	Basra War Cem
Pulman Edgar Tom	Clerk/Goods/Oxford	26	Pte 1st Middlesex Regt	Dow 17/4/17	Bucquoy Road Cem
Pumphrey Oswald John	Clerk/Traffic/Newport		Pnr Base Signal Depot R.E.	Das 31/12/17	Chatby Mem
Purdy Richard	Porter/Traffic/Reading	19	Pte 1st Devonshire Regt	KIA 22/8/18	Vis-en-Artois Mem
Purvey George Edwin	Goods Clerk/Traffic/Tyseley		Pte 10th R Warwick Regt	KIA 1/1/18	Thiepval Mem
Pusey Harry	Labourer/Signal/Reading	30	L/Cpl 2nd R Berks Regt	KIA 25/9/15	Ploegsteert Mem
Putman George	Capenter/Engineer/Westbourne Pk	20	Rifm 1st R Irish Rifles	KIA 29/4/18	Tyne Cot Mem
Pycock Herbert Edwin	Clerk/Goods/Paddington		Cpl 2/10th Middlesex Regt	Dow 23/9/15	East Mudros Mil Cem
Pymble Francis James	Labourer/L&C/Hereford	21	L/Cpl 1st Shropshire L.I.	KIA 15/9/16	Essex Farm Cem
Quance Clifford Thomas	Engine Cleaner/L&C/Cardiff	19	Sgt 6th R Irish Fus	Dow 15/9/15	Pieta Mil Cem
Quelch William Henry	Labourer/Signal/Reading	27	L/Cpl 5th R Berks Regt	KIA 21/7/17	Monchy Br Cem
Raftery Albert Luke	Porter/Traffic/Paddington	28	Pte 2nd Suffolk Regt	Dow 27/3/18	St Hilaire Cem
Ralphs Arthur	Number Taker/Traf/Market Drayton	24	Cpl 2/10th R Scots Regt	KIA 11/11/18	Archangel Mem Russia

Name	Occupation/Dept/Depot	Age	Unit	Fate	Cemetery/Memorial
Rampton James	Labourer/L&C/Wormwood Scrubs		Rifm 16th Rifle Brigade	KIA 3/9/16	Hamel Mil Cem
Rand A.J.H.	Labourer/L&C/Swindon				GWR Mag 2/20
Randall Ernest Thomas	Under Lineman/Signal/Aberavon	25	L/Cpl 8th Somerset L.I.	KIA 25/9/15	Loos Mem
Randall George	Canal Labour/Engineer/Trowbridge	42	L/Cpl 5th Wilts Regt	KIA 10/8/15	Helles Mem
Randall George E.	Shunter/Traffic/Bristol				GWR Mag 9/16
Rankin William Wyley	Horsekeeper/Goods/Hockley	27	Dvr 3rd Bde R.H.A.	KIA 27/9/14	Vendresse Br Cem
Ratcliffe Ernest Albert	Goods/Wolverhampton	23	Cpl 1st Field Survey Co R.E.	Died 15/2/19	Etaples Mil Cem
Ravenhill Edward John	Parcel Porter/Traffic/Maesteg	23	Pte 24th Welsh Regt	Died 6/10/18	Lapugnoy Mil Cem
Rawle Alfred William	Labourer/Engineer/Bristol	20	Pte 1st Bedfordshire Regt	KIA 13/6/15	Larch Wood (Rly Cutting)
Rawlings Francis Henry	Labourer/L&C/Swindon		Pte 5th Wilts Regt	KIA 31/1/17	Amara War Cem
Rawlingson Frank	Porter/Goods/South Lambeth	26	Pte 1st SWB	Died 13/11/14	Bimingham Cem
Ray William Frederick	Signalman/Traffic/Swan Village		L/Cpl 19th R Warwick Regt	Dow 29/9/18	Grevillers Br Cem
Read A.E.	Porter/Traffic/Codford				GWR Mag 7/17
Read Arthur Edward	Apprent/L&C/Swindon	22	Pte 1st Wilts Regt	KIA 5/7/16	Thiepval Mem
Read John Archibald	Restaurant Car Attend't/Paddington	26	Pte 1st R West Surrey Regt	KIA 23/4/17	Arras Mem
Read Stanley Charles	Clerk/Goods/Reading	19	2/Lt 27 Sqdn RAF	Died 25/9/18	Grand-Seraucourt Cem
Read Walter Henry	Clerk/Goods/Reading	20	Berkshire Yeomanry	KIA 21/8/15	Green Hill Cem
Reader C.	Carman/Goods/Smithfield				GWR Mag 5/18
Reeks Frederick Herbert	Vanguard/Goods/Paddington	18	Pte 1/3rd London Regt	KIA 10/3/18	Le Touret Mem
Rees William N.	Engine Cleaner/L&C/Pontypool Rd				GWR Mag 4/17
Reeves Frederick John	Timber Yard Labourer/Swindon	26	Pte 1st Wilts Regt	KIA 31/10/14	Le Touret Mem
Reeves H.J.	L&C/Swindon				GWR Roll of Honour
Remphry Joseph Charles	Carriage Cleaner/L&C/Penzance	37	Trimmer HM Star of Freedom RN	SL 19/4/17	Plymouth Naval Mem
Renison Edgar Harold	Clerk/Goods/Birkenhead	21	Pte 10th Loyal N Lancashire Regt	KIA 11/4/17	Windmill Br Cem
Renowden Charles Caine	Carriage Cleaner/L&C/Penzance	32	Pte 1st R Warwick Regt	KIA 15/4/18	Ploegsteert Mem
Revell George (twin	Fireman/Loco/Newton Abbot	23	Pte 1/6th Devonshire Regt	Doi 1/7/17	Basra War Cem
Revell Harry brothers)	Fireman/Loco/Llanelly	23	Pte 9th Devonshire Regt	KIA 30/9/15	Loos Mem
Reynolds A.	Carman/Goods/Hockley				GWR Mag 11/18 & 3/19
Reynolds Frederick	Porter/Traffic/Redruth	23	Spr 27th Broad Gauge Rly Co RE	Died 17/1/19	Abbeville Com Cem
Reynolds Herbert	Fireman/Loco/Worcester	21	Spr ROD Longmoor R.E.	Died 23/1/17	Kidderminster Cem
Reynolds Hubert Harry	Labourer/L&C/Swindon	19	Rifm 1/8th Rifle Bde/Post Off Rifle	KIA 9/9/18	Epehy Wood Farm Cem
Reynolds Sam Sturgess	Telegraph Clerk/Traffic/Reading	25	Spr 17th Div Signal Co R.E.	Died 29/12/17	Baghdad N War Cem
Reynolds Wilfred	Porter/Traffic/Tintern	19	Pte 52nd Bn MGC (Infantry)	KIA 16/7/18	La Targette Br Cem
Reynolds William John	Cart Lad/Traffic/Birmingham	20	Pte 12th Hampshire Regt	KIA 18/9/18	Doiran Mem
Rich Douglas Tom	Call Boy/Traffic/Cardiff		Pte 9th Yorkshire L.I.	Dow 28/4/18	Esquelbecq Mil Cem
Richards E.	Shunter/Traffic/Swansea				GWR Mag 3&4/17
Richards Edwin	R/Labourer/Engineer/Newport				GWR Mag 6&10/18
Richards Frederick W.	Engine Cleaner/Old Oak Common				GWR Mag 2&3/17
Richards George	Labourer/Engineer/Wolverhampton	22	Pte 3rd N Midland F/Amb R.A.M.C	Doi 8/9/14	Wolve. Cem
Richards J.	Carriage Cleaner/Old Oak Common				GWR Mag 10/16 & 2/17
Richards J.	Messenger/D.S.O./Paddington				GWR Mag 10&12/17
Richardson F.	Porter/Goods/Paddington				GWR Mag 2/18
Richardson F.A.	Traffic/Gerrards Cross				GWR Roll of Honour
Richardson John William	Carman/Goods/Paddington	23	OS HMS Pembroke RN	Doi 7/3/18	Paddington Cem
Richings Frederick A.	Signal Porter/Brynmenyn	20	Pte 7th Gloucester Regt	Died 12/2/15	Brookwood 14-18 Mem
Rickets Percy Thomas	Labourer/L&C/Swindon	30	Pte 1st Wilts Regt	KIA 19/10/14	Le Touret Mem
Ridgway George Edwin	Packer/Engineer/Exeter		Pte 8th Devonshire Regt	KIA 25/9/15	Loos Mem
Ridgway James	Porter/Traffic/Lustleigh	19	Pte 51st Hampshire Regt	Died 3/4/19	Exeter St Thomas Cem
Ridley F.W.	Clerk/Goods/Paddington				GWR Mag 2/20
Rigby Norman	Policeman/Traffic/Paddington	31	Pte 1st Scots Guards	KIA 11/11/14	Menin Gate Mem
Riley Arthur James	Carman/Goods/Walsall	31	Pte 9th S Staffordshire Regt	Died 5/11/18	Staglieno Cem Italy
Rixon Walter John	Riveter/L&C/Swindon		Pte 23rd F/Amb RAMC	Dow 25/10/17	Lijssenthoek Mil Cem
Roaf Arthur Box	R/Labour/Engineer/Westbourne Pk	23	Pte 2nd Hampshire Regt	Dow 7/12/17	Mont Huon Mil Cem
Robbins David	Frame-Builders Assist/Swindon	35	Sgt 1st Wilts Regt	KIA 29/7/16	Thiepval Mem
Robbins Jesse Roland	Clerk/Traffic/Abertillery	22	L/Cpl 6th Siege Co (Monmouth)RE	Dow 1/10/17	Lijssenthoek Mil Cem
Robbins Oliver Augustus	Turner/Signal/Reading	24	L/Cpl MGC (Infantry)	Died 19/9/17	Mapledurham Churchy'd
Roberts Albert	Restaurant Car Porter/Paddington				GWR Mag 5/17
Roberts Charles W. Henry	Clerk/L&C/Swindon	26	Sgt 34 Sqdn R.F.C.	Died 26/12/17	Giavera Br Cem Italy
Roberts David Charles	Clerk/Traffic/Montpelier	20	2/Lt 10th SWB	KIA 19/7/16	Sucrerie Mil Cem

Name	Occupation	Age	Military	Death	Memorial
Roberts George	Ticket Collector/Traffic/Ruabon	25	Cpl 1st Welsh Mounted F/Amb	Died 14/2/18	Ramleh War Cem
Roberts John	L/Packer/Engineer/Birkenhead	33			GWR Mag 4/15
Roberts J.A.	Traffic/Tysley				GWR Roll of Honour
Roberts Leonard	Parcel Clerk/Traffic/Leominster	21	L/Cpl 7th Shropshire L.I.	Dow 3/9/16	Bruay Com Cem
Roberts Victor James	Engine Cleaner/Loco/Gloucester		Pte 8th Gloucester Regt	KIA 2/3/16	Rue-du-Bacquerot No1
Roberts W.J.	Carman/Goods/Smithfield				GWR Mag 5/18
Robins Harold Richard	Apprent Wheelwright/Swindon	20	Aircraftman RNAS Dunkerque	Died 19/10/17	Dunkirk Town Cem
Robinson Arthur John H.	R/Labourer/Engineer/Taunton	24	2/Cpl 54th Light Rly Co R.E.	Died 12/6/18	Bac-du-Sud Br Cem
Robinson Frederick Isaac	Coach Trimmer/L&C/Swindon		Dvr A Bty 55th Bde RFA	Dow 7/4/17	Basra Mem
Robinson Fred Stephen	L&C/Swindon	19	Pte 1/4th Wilts Regt	Dow 19/11/17	Deir El Belah War Cem
Robinson James	Porter/Goods/Rowley Regis	29	Pte 3rd Worcester Regt	KIA 7/11/14	Menin Gate Mem
Robinson T.	Bridge Labour/Engineer/Wolver'h				GWR Mag 7/17
Robinson William James	Coach Trimmer/L&C/Swindon		A/Mech 45 Sqdn RAF	Died 8/10/18	Charmes Mil Cem
Rochell George	Boilersmith Assist/L&C/Wolver'h	39	Pte 2nd S Staffordshire Regt	KIA 18/5/15	Le Touret Mem
Rodbourne William Henry	Warehouse Lad/Stores/Swindon		Pte 13th R Welsh Fus	KIA 2/9/17	Poelcapelle Br Cem
Rodham Cuthbert Alfred	Clerk/S.O.L. Office/Paddington	20	Pte 2/3rd London Regt	Doi 8/12/15	Portianos Mil Cem
Rod(e)rick James E.	Fireman/Loco/Hereford		Pte 13th Gloucester Regt	KIA 18/10/16	A.I.F. Burial Flers
Rodway Herbert James	Packer/Engineer/Malvern Link	36	Sgt 13th Gloucester Regt	Died 2/5/18	Dendermonde Com Cem
Rogers Andrew	Labourer/Engineer/Plymouth Docks	39	Pte 1st Gloucester Regt	Dow 22/10/14	Cement House Cem
Rogers Benjamin R.C.	Clerk/Traffic/Ruabon	28	2/Lt 6th att 3rd Royal Fus	KIA 17/10/18	Highland Cem
Rogers Christopher John	Porter Shunter/Traffic/Kingham		Pte 1st Welsh Guards	Dow 12/9/18?	Bac-du-Sud Br Cem
Rogers E.	Engineer/Melksham				GWR Roll of Honour
Rogers Frank	Packer/Engineer/W London Jct				GWR Mag 10/16 & 2/17
Rogers George	Off Porter/C.GMO./Paddington	23			GWR Mag 8&10/16
Rogers George	Messenger/Accounts/Paddington				GWR Mag 6&7/18
Rogers Walter Edward	Fireman/Loco/Shrewsbury	24	Sgt 2/1st (Shropshire) R.H.A.	Dow 23/8/17	Coxyde Mil Cem
Rogers William	Porter/Goods/Smithfield	28			GWR Mag 12/14 & 4/16
Rolfe Francis William	Traffic/Landore		L/Cpl 7th Norfolk Regt	KIA 12/10/16	Thiepval Mem
Rooke J.	Restaurant Car Attend't/Paddington				GWR Mag 12/19
Roper Alfred Marshall	Clerk/Goods/Hockley	29	Cpl 15th R Warwick Regt	KIA 30/7/16	Thiepval Mem
Roper Walter	Porter/Traffic/Wednesbury		L/Cpl 6th Bn MGC (Infantry)	KIA 2/5/18	Tyne Cot Mem
Rose Edward Victor	Engine Cleaner/L&C/Bristol	19	Pte 12th Gloucester Regt	KIA 3/9/16	Thiepval Mem
Rose J. T. or V.	Clerk/Traffic/Torre				GWR Mag 6/19
Rouse Arthur John	Labourer/Signal/Newport		Rifm 1st Monmouthshire Regt	KIA 8/10/18	Sequehart Br Cem 1
Rowe Rupert Charles	Parcel Porter/Traffic/Wotton B'sett	32	CSM 5th Wilts Regt	KIA 21/1/17	Amara War Cem
Rowland Emmanuel	Porter/Traffic/Exeter	28	Bom No 3 Depot RGA	Died 23/4/15	Plymouth Efford Cem
Rowland E.F.	L&C/Swindon				GWR Roll of Honour
Rowland Eli Thomas	Hydraulic Forgeman/L&C/Swindon	37	L/Sgt 7th Wilts Regt	KIA 24/4/17	Doiran Mem
Rowswell C.	Docker/Goods/Guernsey				GWR Mag 6/20
Rudd Ernest Henry John	Clerk/Goods/Southall	24	L/Sgt 1/8th Middlesex Regt	KIA 1/7/16	Thiepval Mem
Ruddle Herbert George	L&C/Swindon		Cpl 5th Wilts Regt	KIA 25/1/17	Amara War Cem
Ruse Thomas William	Docker/Goods/Guernsey	24	Pte 1st R Guernsey L.I.	Dow 1/12/17	Ribecourt Br Cem
Russell A.	Fixer/Signal/Reading	34			GWR Mag 6&7/15
Russell Edward	Clerk/Goods/Manchester	20	Pte 21st Manchester Regt	KIA 1/7/16	Thiepval Mem
Russell Frederick George	Carman/Goods/Leamington		Pte 1st R Warwick Regt	KIA 10/5/17	Level Crossing Cem
Russell Frederick John	L&C/Weymouth		Pte 5th Dorset Regt	KIA 21/8/15	Helles Mem
Russell R.W.	Labourer/L&C/Swindon				GWR Mag 10/17
Rustell George Bramwell	Stores Labourer/L&C/Llantrisant	22	Pte 2nd R Sussex Regt	KIA 4/10/18	Berthaucourt Com Cem
Rutley Harold James	Engine Cleaner/Loco/Bristol	19	Gnr 1st Bty 45th Bde RFA	KIA 30/11/17	Tyne Cot Mem
Ryder Bertram Thomas	Booking Clerk/Traffic/Torquay	28	L/Cpl 9th Devonshire Regt	Dow 11/5/17	Boulogne East Cem
Rymell Francis William	Porter/Goods/Paddington	27	Pte 2nd S Lancashire Regt	KIA 20/9/14	Vailly Br Cem
Sadler Alexander Ernest	Porter/Goods/South Lambeth	28	Pte 3rd Coldstream Guards	KIA 24/3/16	White House Cem
Sadlier G.H.	Carriage Cleaner/L&C/Shrewsb'y				GWR Mag 2/17
Salisbury Albert Edward	Signalman/Traffic/Highley	25	L/Cpl 11th Signal Co R.E.	Died 27/3/19	Shipton-on-Stour Cem
Saloway William Luke	L&C/Swindon	17	Signal Boy HMS Hampshire RN	SL 5/6/16	Portsmouth Naval Mem
Salter Frederick Henry	Signal Porter/Traffic/Washford	21	Pte 1/5th Somerset L.I.	KIA 28/9/15	Basra Mem
Samuel E.	Clerk/Paddington Goods Station				GWR Mag 12/19
Samuels R.F.	L&C/Swindon				GWR Roll of Honour
Samways Fred William	Carriage Cleaner/L&C/Weymouth	36	Sto 1st Class HMS Rocket RN	Doi 12/10/18	Melcombe Regis Church

Samworth John Alfred	Clerk/Cashiers/Paddington	21	Pte 1st H.A.C.	KIA 13/11/16	Thiepval Mem
Sanders David	Wagon Builder/L&C/Swindon	34	L/Cpl 34th Bn MGC (Infantry)	KIA 11/4/18	Ploegsteert Mem
Sanders H.	Goods/Hockley				GWR Roll of Honour
Sandford Walter Edgar	Packer/Engineer/Woodborough	30	Gnr 14th Siege Bty RGA	Dow 4/10/17	Bruay Com Cem
Sanger John	Packer/Engineer/Bishops Nympton	29	Spr 275th (GWR) Rly Co R.E.	Died 31/7/19	Le Quesnoy Com Cem
Sansom Albert John	Wagon Painter/L&C/Swindon	38	Pte 1/6th R Warwick Regt	KIA 18/8/17	Tyne Cot Mem
Sansom C.R.	Traffic/Henley-on-Thames				GWR Roll of Honour
Sargood William George	Carman/Goods/Hayes	26	Pte 1st Royal Fus	KIA 17/1/16	Menin Road S Mil Cem
Saunders Charles Henry	Labourer/Engineer/Bilston		Pte 4th Worcester Regt	KIA 6/8/15	Helles Mem
Saunders Ernest Jesse	Tracer/Signal/Reading	20	L/Cpl 1/4th R Berks Regt	KIA 23/7/16	Thiepval Mem
Sawyer George Francis	Stationary Engine Driver/Swindon		Pte 1st Wilts Regt	KIA 13/10/14	Le Touret Mem
Scammell Sidney Harry	L&C/Swindon	41	Pte 1st Wilts Regt	KIA 21/3/18	Arras Mem
Scarborough Ray Joseph	Clerk/Goods/Wednesbury		Pte 14th R Warwick Regt	KIA 24/9/16	Flatiron Copse Cem
Schofield Stanley William	Coach-body Maker/L&C/Swindon	24	Pte RAMC	Died 23/12/18	Swindon Cem
Scoble Lewis Samuel	Mason/Engineer/Totnes	33	Pte 1/5th Devonshire Regt	KIA 7/11/17	Gaza War Cem
Scott Alexander	Carman/Goods/Cardiff				GWR Mag 3&7/18
Scott Alfred Keith	Clerk/Accounts/Paddington	25	RSM 7th Cameron Highlanders	KIA 13/10/16	Adanac Mil Cem
Scott Douglas John	Clerk/CGMO/Paddington	32	Sgt 2/14th London (Scottish) Reg	KIA 30/4/18	Jerusalem War Cem
Scott Frederick William	Lampman/Traffic/Swindon	30	Gnr 228th Siege Bty RGA	Dow 24/10/17	Menin Road S Mil Cem
Scott Harold James	Porter/Traffic/Kidderminster	19	Pte 6th Wilts Regt	KIA 10/4/18	Tyne Cot Mem
Scott S.	CGMO/Paddington				GWR Mag 3/17
Scott Thomas Henry	Dist Lampman/Traff/Bransford Rd	23	Pte 1/7th R Warwick Regt	KIA 8/10/17	Cement House Cem
Scragg J.H.	L&C/Llanelly				GWR Roll of Honour
Scrivens Frank Edward	Restaurant Car Attend't/Birmingham		Gnr 234th Heavy Bty RGA	Dow 19/7/17	Dozinghem Mil Cem
Scull James T. (brother)	Hammer Driver/L&C/Swindon	21	Pte 2/1st Ox & Bucks L.I.	KIA 19/7/16	Loos Mem
Scull Reginald W.(brother)	Engine Cleaner/L&C/Swindon	18	Pte 2/4th R Berks Regt	KIA 16/4/18	St Venant-R Road Cem
Seager John	Striker/No 14 Shop/Swindon		Sgt 5th Wilts Regt	Dow 12/8/15	Helles Mem
Sealey Frank	Packer/Engineer/Newport	30	Pte 1st SWB	Dow 8/11/14	Netley Hospital Mil Cem
Searle Albert G.	Packer/Engineer/Worle	40	Pte 2nd Gloucester Regt	KIA 19/3/15	Menin Gate Mem
Sedgbeer Ernest John	Labourer/Signal/Reading	24	Pte 1st Dorset Regt	Dow 7/7/16	Taunton Cem
Sedgwick Oliver	Reataurant Car Attend't/Paddington	27	L/Cpl 1st Wilts Regt	Dow 12/3/15	Menin Gate Mem
Selby Arthur Henry	Fitters Labourer/L&C/Swindon	36	Pte 2nd Wilts Regt	KIA 26/9/15	Loos Mem
Sellars Ashley William	Apprent Boilersmith/L&C/Swindon		Pte 1/4th Hampshire Regt	KIA 24/2/17	Basra Mem
Serls George Ernest	Fitters Labour/L&C/St Blazey	21	Pte 7th DCLI	KIA 16/9/16	Thiepval Mem
Seymour Fred William	Packer/Enginer/Pangbourne		Pte 17th Manchester Regt	KIA 12/10/16	Thiepval Mem
Seymour John Henry	Packer/Engineer/Reading	27	Pte 1st Cameronians	KIA 9/2/15	Bois-Grenier Com Cem
Shadwell Mark Brown	Creosoter/Engineer/Hayes	32	Pte 1st Middlesex Regt	KIA 12/11/14	Rue-David Mil Cem
Shakespeare Walter F.	Apprent Boilermaker/L&C/Swindon	20	A/Cpl 1st Wilts Regt	KIA 12/3/15	Menin Gate Mem
Shambrook Felix Thomas	Porter/Traffic/Birmingham	21	Gnr 28th Siege Bty RGA	KIA 27/5/17	Bailleul Road E. Cem
Sharland Charles	Carriage Cleaner/Old Oak Common	28	Pte 1/3rd London Regt	Died 29/9/16	Ste Marie Cem
Sharland Joseph Henry	Wagon Painter/L&C/Swindon	26	Pte 5th Wilts Regt	KIA 5/4/16	Helles Mem
Sharp Vivian King	Clerk/GMO/Paddington	24	Spr Postal Section France R.E.	Doi 20/6/15	South Ealing Cem
Sharpe F.	Shunter/Traffic/Portishead				GWR Mag 9&12/16
Shaw Benjamin	Porter/Goods/Bristol	27	Pte 1st Somerset L.I.	KIA 9/11/14	Ploegsteert Mem
Shaw W.	Loader/67 Gresham Street Office				GWR Mag 1/16
Sheather Frederick Arthur	Restaurant Car Page/Paddington		Pte 1/4th London Regt	KIA 12/5/17	Arras Mem
Shelton Gilbert Henry	Apprent/L&C/Wolverhampton	20	L/Sea Hawke Bn RN Div	KIA 13/11/16	Thiepval Mem
Shelvey Edward James	Parcel Porter/Goods/Paddington	28	Gnr 383rd RGA att Signal R.E.	Died 8/12/19	Beirut War Cem
Shepherd G.	Traffic/Brynmenyn				GWR Roll of Honour
Shepherd John George	R/Labourer/Engineer/Reading		Pte 5th R Berks Regt	KIA 3/7/16	Aveluy Com Cem
Sheppard Archibald W.	Coach Finisher/L&C/Swindon	28	Spr 455th Field Co R.E.	Dow 18/4/17	Duisans Br Cem
Sheppard Ashley F.C.	Pilot Guard/Traffic/Bristol W Depot	35	CSM 1st Wilts Regt	KIA 10/4/18	Ploegsteert Mem
Sheppard W.J.	Traffic/Brynmenyn				GWR Roll of Honour
Shergold Reginald Donald	Electrical Fitter/L&C/Swindon	21	Pnr 81st Field Co R.E.	KIA 26/7/16	Dantzig Alley Br Cem
Sherlock Leopald William	Clerk/CGMO/Paddington	24	L/Cpl 1/9th London Regt	KIA 8/6/18	Dainville Br Cem
Sherston(e) Albert James	Packer/Engineer/Frome	23	Rifm 20th KRRC	KIA 17/6/17	Arras Mem
Shields Edward	Packer/Engineer/Port Talbot	29	Pte 23rd Welsh Regt	Dow 2/10/16	Struma Mil Cem
Shipley George W.	Audit Off/Paddington	37	CSM 2/10th Middlesex Regt	Doi 2/12/15	Alexandria War Cem
Shipley Samuel Bernard	Clerk/Estate/Paddington	23	Rifm 1/8th London Regt	KIA 29/5/15	Le Touret Mem

Name	Role/Department	Age	Rank/Regiment	Fate	Memorial/Cemetery
Shuker Alexander George	L&C/West London		Pte 2nd Border Regt	KIA 26/10/14	Menin Gate Mem
Shuker H.	L&C/Wormwood Scrubs				GWR Roll of Honour
Sidnell William	Time & Storekeeper/Westbury	29	L/Cpl 155th Field Co R.E.	Dow 28/6/16	Bethune Town Cem
Simmonds Albert Henry	Shunter/Traffic/Skewen	28	Pte 1st Liverpool Regt	KIA 28/10/14	Menin Gate Mem
Simmonds J.	Signal/Reading				GWR Roll of Honour
Simmonds T.W.	Porter/Traffic/Hartlebury				GWR Mag 5&12/18
Simmonds William Thomas	Engine Cleaner/L&C/Oxford	21	Pte 1/1st Middlesex Hussars	Died 23/10/18	Damascus War Cem
Simpkins Frederick Albert	Horse-box Builder/L&C/Swindon	20	Dvr 303rd Bde RFA	KIA 7/11/17	Gaza War Cem
Simpson A.	Traffic/Shrewsbury				GWR Roll of Honour
Simpson C.E.	Packer/Engineer/Winchcombe				GWR Mag 2&4/19
Simpson John Ernest	Packer/Engineer/Toddington		Pte 7th Gloucester Regt	KIA 10/2/17	Amara War Cem
Simpson Thomas Edmund	Fitters Apprent/L&C/Newport	23	2/Lt 65 Sqdn RAF	Dfa 1/6/18	Vignacourt Br Cem
Sims Daniel William	Labourer/L&C/Swindon	23	Dvr C Bty 69th Bde RFA	KIA 4/10/18	Tehran War Cem
Sims James William	Striker/No 14 Shop/Swindon	40	Pte 2nd Wilts Regt	KIA 15/6/15	Le Touret Mem
Singer William Harold	Apprent Fitter/R Shop/Swindon	21	Sgt 2/4th Wilts Regt	Died 5/3/17	Kirkee Mem India
Sinnett S.A.	Apprent Fitter/L&C/Swindon		Spr 565th (Wilts) ATC R.E.	KIA 18/9/18	Ruyaulcourt Mil Cem
Skarratt J.	Labourer/Signal/West Ealing				GWR Mag 2&10/19
Skelly William Harold	Shed Porter/Goods/Cardiff	22	Pte 11th Lancashire Fus	KIA 16/5/16	Arras Mem
Skinner William Robert	Porter/Traffic/Brimscombe	23	Sgt 2nd Lancashire Fus	Dow 4/5/18	Lapugnoy Mil Cem
Skipper James	Office Porter/Paddington Goods	36	L/Cpl 2nd R Sussex Regt	KIA 9/5/15	Guards Cem Windy C.
Skipper Percy Ernest A.	Fireman/Loco/Old Oak Common	22	Pte 8th R Berks Regt	KIA 13/10/15	Mazingarbe Com Cem
Slade Joseph John	Connector/Traffic/Old O. Common	28	Pte 1/3rd London Regt	KIA 10/3/15	Le Touret Mem
Slade Lewis Henry	L&C/Swindon		Pte 1st R Warwick Regt	KIA 15/4/18	Ploegsteert Mem
Slade M.J.	Stores/Swindon				GWR Roll of Honour
Slade Walter	Machineman/L&C/Swindon	21	Pte 5th Wilts Regt	Died 19/9/18	Baghdad N War Cem
Slater Henry Ernest	Pantry Boy Fishguard Restau't Car	19	Pte 1st Wilts Regt	KIA 25/12/14	La Laiterie Mil Cem
Slocombe Ralph	Lad Clerk/Goods/Bristol	19	Pte 2nd Hampshire Regt	Dow 3/9/18	Longuenesse Cem
Sloman Frank	Signal Porter/Traffic/S. Molton				GWR Mag 8/18
Slucutt William Albert	Engine Cleaner/Loco Depot/Bristol		Spr 475th S Midland Field Co R.E.	Dow 19/8/17	Duhallow A.D.S. Cem
Small William Henry	Packer/Engineer/Bassaleg	27	Rifm 1st Monmouthshire Regt	Dow 1/7/16	Foncquevillers Mil Cem
Smerdon George	Porter/Goods/Taunton		L/Cpl 1/6th Devonshire Regt	Died 10/6/16	Kirkee Mem India
Smith A.	Labourer/Signal/Reading				GWR Mag 10&11/17
Smith Archibald	Machineman/L&C/Swindon	26	Pte 2nd Wilts Regt	KIA 8/7/16	Thiepval Mem
Smith Albert E.	Shunter/Traffic/Alexandra Dock	20	Gnr 232nd Bty 74th Bde RFA	Died 11/1/15	Cahir Mil Plot R of Ireland
Smith Charles Edward	Creosoter/Engineer/Hayes		Sgt 76th F/Amb RAMC	KIA 17/4/18	Mont Noir Mil Cem
Smith Cyril Charles B.	Clerk/S.O.L. Office/Paddington	25	Rifm 9th London Regt	Dow 29/4/18	Crouy Br Cem
Smith Edward	Lifters Mate/L&C/Wormwood Sc	28	Sgt 10th Border Regt	Doi 6/10/15	Lewisham Cem
Smith Ernest James	R/Labourer/Engineer/Maidenhead	36	Sgt 116th (GWR) Rly Co R.E.	Died 25/9/18	Ramleh War Cem
Smith Frederick	Machineman/L&C/Swindon				GWR Mag 8&10/17
Smith Frederick	Porter/Traffic/Witney	22	Pte 1st R Irish Fus	KIA 11/4/18	Tyne Cot Mem
Smith Frederick Leonard	Machinist/L&C/Wolverhampton		Sgt 2/6th S Staffordshire Regt	KIA 21/3/18	Arras Mem
Smith G.J.	Timekeeper/L&C/Banbury				GWR Mag 12/18
Smith Harold Benjamin	S.O.L. Off/Paddington	22	2/Lt 7th London Regt	Dow 20/5/17	H.A.C. Cem
Smith J.	Carman/Goods/Smithfield				GWR Mag 5/18
Smith John	Timber Porter/C&W/Swindon	34	Pte 7th Wilts Regt	KIA 24/4/17	Doiran Mem
Smith Sidney Rowland	Bolt Maker/L&C/Swindon	18	Pte 5th Wilts Regt	KIA 10/8/15	Helles Mem
Smith Sydney Albert	Parcel Porter/Traffic/Swansea	19	Pte 11th SWB	Dow 1/5/18	Swansea Cem
Smith Sydney Austin G.	Clerk/Goods/Bridgwater	19	A/Mech 2nd class 34 Sqdn RAF	Died 24/7/18	Tezze Br Cem
Smith W.	Traffic/Reading				GWR Roll of Honour
Smith William H.	Brakesman/Traffic/Rogerstone	30			GWR Mag 12/14 & 4/16
Smith W.J.	L&C/Swindon				GWR Roll of Honour
Smith Walter Joseph	Packer/Engineer/Hall Green	25	Pte 10th Gloucester Regt	KIA 25/9/15	Loos Mem
Smithers Henry	Packer/Engineer/Bassaleg	32	Pte 4th SWB	KIA 9/8/15	Basra Mem
Soane John	Machinist/Signal/Reading		Pte 1/1st Hereford Regt	KIA 23/7/18	Raperie Br Cem
Solman George A.	Messenger/Goods/Cardiff		Pte 1st Welsh Guards	KIA 27/9/15	Loos Mem
Souch John Henry	Halt Attendant/Traff/Sarsden Halt	25	Pte 6th Ox & Bucks L.I.	KIA 16/8/17	Tyne Cot Mem
Soundy John Edward	Packer/Engineer/Oxford	33	Spr 273rd Rly Co R.E.	Died 5/10/18	Bralo Br Cem Greece
Southan Tom	Porter/Traffic/Stroud	20	Pte 1st Worcester Regt	KIA 6/6/18	Soissons Mem
Southwell Harry Asher	Fitter &Turner/L&C/Swindon	21	Spr 89th Field Co R.E.	Dow 13/7/15	Lijssenthoek Mil Cem

Name	Occupation/Dept	Age	Regiment	Death	Memorial
Spackman Edwin C.	Fitters Labour/L&/Newton Abbot		Pte 6th R Berks Regt	Acc 17/2/17	Thiepval Mem
Spackman Harold	Porter/Traffic/Charlton Mackrell	17	Pte 10th Gloucester Regt	Died 12/3/15	Bath (Locksbrook) Cem
Spackman William Edward	L&C/Swindon		Pte 2nd Wilts Regt	KIA 18/10/16	Thiepval Mem
Spalding E.J.	L&C/Worcester	41	Gnr 2nd S Midland Bde RFA	Died 24/7/19	Worcester (Astwood)
Sparkes Richard	Porter/Traffic/Bristol	22	Gnr 6th Siege Bty RGA	KIA 24/9/17	Trois Arbres Cem
Sparks Harry	Packer/Engineer/Ledbury		Pte 2nd E Yorkshire Regt	KIA 16/4/15	Menin Gate Mem
Speck George Frederick	Wagon Smith/L&C/Swindon		Cpl 4th Anti-airc'ft Workshop ASC	KIA 30/5/18	Longuenesse Cem
Spicer Arthur	Slipman/Engineer/Port Talbot	30	Pte 19th Welsh Regt	Died 22/12/15	Aire Com Cem
Spiller William Henry	Carman/Goods/Yeovil	26	L/Cpl 1st Somerset L.I.	KIA 1/7/16	Thiepval Mem
Spreadborough Arthur G.	Packer/Engineer/Abbeydore		Pte 7th Shropshire L.I.	KIA 26/3/18	Arras Mem
Spreadbury Bertram B.	Coach Painter/L&C/Swindon	25	Spr 565th (Wilts) ATC R.E.	KIA 18/9/18	Ruyaulcourt Mil Cem
Sprules Nelson George	L&C/Swindon	26	Pte 1st Wilts Regt	KIA 28/3/15	Voormezeele No 3
Spurdens Frederick W.	Off Porter/Goods/Victoria & Albert		Pte 1/13th London Regt	Dow 27/9/16	Grove Town Cem
Spurway Arthur George	Cartage Loader/Goods/Cardiff	26	Sgt D Bty 149th Bde RFA	KIA 5/5/18	Brandhoek Mil Cem 3
Squibb George	Mason/Engineer/Weymouth		Pte 1st Dorset Regt	Dow 16/4/17	Foreste Com Cem
St.Cyre Herbert Alphonse	Clerk/Engineer/Paddington	19	Pte 1/14th London Regt	KIA 7/10/16	Thiepval Anglo-Fr Cem
Stack T.	Carman/Goods/Paddington				GWR Mag 11/17
Stacey Edward Ernest	Labourer/Engineer/Bristol		Pte 1/6th Gloucester Regt	KIA 21/7/16	Thiepval Mem
Stacey Edward Tom	Apprent Blacksmith/L&C/Swindon	22	Pte 1/4th Wilts Regt	Died 31/7/16	Baghdad N War Cem
Stacey Gabriel W.	Goods Porter/Traffic/Bridgend	21			GWR Mag 5&9/16
Stacey George Herbert	Boilersmiths Mate/Newton Abbot		Pte 5th Devonshire Regt	KIA 28/7/18	Chambrecy Br Cem
Staddon A.	Traffic/Exeter				GWR Roll of Honour
Stallwood Albert	Carman/Traffic/Windsor & Eton		Tpr Guards Machine Gun Regt	Dow 24/10/18	Premont Br Cem
Stanbury William James A.	Clerk/Goods/Plymouth	21	Pte 8th Devonshire Regt	KIA 25/9/15	Loos Mem
Stanley William Thomas	Mileage Porter/Goods/Oxford	33	Pte R Army Ordnance Corps	Died 14/1/18	Wolvercote Churchyard
Stanton Thomas	Engine Cleaner/L&C/Newport	18	Pte 1st SWB	KIA 25/1/15	Le Touret Mem
Staples Herbert	Frame-Builders Assist/Swindon		CSM 7th Wilts Regt	KIA 13/10/18	Maurois Com Cem
Staple(s) James	R/Labourer/Engineer/Taunton		Pte 6th Somerset L.I.	KIA 18/8/16	Delville Wood Cem
Staples Jabez Hale	Frame-Builders Assist/Swindon	20	AS Hood Bn RN Division	KIA 29/9/18	Anneux Br Cem
Steel John	Fireman/Loco/Fishguard		Sto 1st Class HMS Goliath RN	SL 13/5/15	Plymouth Naval Mem
Steer Frederick	Carriage Cleaner/L&C/Plymouth	31	Pte 5th Devonshire Regt	KIA 21/12/17	Jerusalem Mem
Stephens Edgar William	Signal Porter/Traffic/Coleford	24	Sgt 10th Gloucester Regt	KIA 20/4/16	St Patricks Cem Loos
Stephens Henry Hill	Clerk/L&C/Newport	19	2/Lt 42 Sqdn RAF	Dow 28/6/18	Aire Com Cem
Stephens R.	GMO/Paddington				GWR Roll of Honour
Steptoe G.	Packer/Engineer/Soho		Spr Signal Co R.E.	Died 24/2/19	Defford Churchyard
Stevens Alfred	Painter/L&C/Swindon		Pte 1st Wilts Regt	Dow 10/7/16	Puchevillers Br Cem
Stevens F.R.	Sleeper Chairer/Engineer/Hayes				GWR Mag 10&12/16
Stevens George	Poter/Traffic/Landore	22			GWR Mag 12/14 &1/15
Stevens J.E.	Apprent Boilermaker/L&C/Swindon				GWR Mag 1/18
Stevens R.	Wages Clerk/L&C/Swindon				GWR Mag 11/18 & 3/19
Stevens R.	Messenger/GMO/Paddington				GWR Mag 12/18
Stevens W.H.	Porter/Traffic/Yeovil				GWR Mag 10/19
Stevenson Fred Arthur	Clerk/Paddington Goods Station	20	Pte 1/14th London Regt	Dow 8/10/17	St Sever Cem
Stevenson Harold Leslie	Porter/Goods/Hockley		Pte 3rd Worcester Regt	KIA 24/8/14	La Ferte-s-Jouarre Mem
Steventon Alfred	Porter/Goods/Wednesbury	22	Pte 2/6th S Staffordshire Regt	Dow 5/12/17	Etaples Mil Cem
Stewart Edward Henry C.	Clerk/Audit Off/Paddington		Rifm 1/5th London Regt	KIA 1/7/16	Thiepval Mem
Stewart Thomas	Lifters Mate/L&C/Danygraig	25	Pte 10th R Welsh Fus	KIA 17/2/16	Menin Gate Mem
Stieber Frederick Richard	Policeman/Goods/Paddington	24	Sgt 6th R Berks Regt	Dow 23/7/16	Abbeville Com Cem
Stile George James	Fitter/L&C/Newton Abbot		Pte 5th Devonshire Regt	KIA 31/12/16	Basra Mem
Stinchcombe E.	Clerk/Goods/Paddington				GWR Mag 3&4/19
Stinton John Ashley	Labourer/L&C/Worcester	30	Bom A Bty 165th Bde RFA	Dow 9/8/18	Terlincthun Br Cem
Stocker Frederick Luff	Clerk/DEO/Taunton		Lt 28th att 20th Royal Fus	KIA 23/8/18	Douchy-les-Ayette Cem
Stokes Frank William	Carman/Goods/Paddington		Bom 213th Siege Bty RGA	KIA 23/10/17	Birr Cross Roads Cem
Stokes William Laurence	Engine Cleaner/Loco/Bristol	20	Spr 1st S Midland Field Co R.E.	Died 23/5/15	Trois Arbres Cem
Stone H.	Parcel Porter/Traffic/Cardiff				GWR Mag 10/20
Stone Joseph	Labourer/L&C/Swindon	43	Sgt 3rd Wilts Regt	Died 23/7/18	Swindon Cem
Stone J.E.	Hotels/Paddington				GWR Roll of Honour
Stone J.F.	Carman/Goods/Bristol				GWR Mag 3/17
Stoneman Charles Henry	Packer/Engineer/Exeter		L/Cpl 16th Devonshire Regt	Dow 6/10/18	Grevillers Br Cem

Name	Occupation	Age	Regiment	Death	Memorial/Cemetery
Stoneman F.	Carman/Goods/Park Royal				GWR Mag 2/18
Stote Charles James H.	Messenger/Traffic/Paddington	18	Pte 1/13th London Regt	KIA 7/9/16	Thiepval Mem
Stoten Arthur	Carriage Cleaner/Old Oak Common	28	Pte 13th Royal Fus	KIA 9/7/16	Thiepval Mem
Strange Augustus J.	Apprent/L&C/Swindon	21	Spr 211th Field Co R.E.	Died 29/10/18	Pont-de-Nieppe Com Cem
Strange Clem J. (brother 1)	Helper/L&C/Swindon	22	Pte 2nd Wilts Regt	KIA 3/9/17	Torreken Farm Cem 1
Strange Leonard George	R/Labourer/Engineer/Narberth	29	Pte 2nd Grenadier Guards	KIA 1/12/17	Cambrai Mem
Strange T.	Stores/Swindon				GWR Roll of Honour
Strange Zenas (brother 2)	Helper/L&C/Swindon	18	Pte 5th Wilts Regt	KIA 10/8/15	Helles Mem
Strangward Harold John	Clerk/Solicitors Off/Paddington	32	Cpl 9th London Regt	KIA 30/5/16	Hebuterne Mil Cem
Strat(f)ford William Fred	L&C/Swindon		Cpl 8th Somerset L.I.	KIA 5/4/18	Gommecourt Br Cem 2
Street F.	L&C/Swindon				GWR Roll of Honour
Strickland W.	Ticket Collector/Traffic/Exeter				GWR Mag 12/17 & 6/18
Stringer A.	Shunt Horse Driver/Withymoor				GWR Mag 3/19
Stringer Alfred James	Porter/Traffic/West Bromwich	19	Pte 1/5th R Warwick Regt	KIA 10/8/17	Menin Gate Mem
Stringer Charles Henry	Shed Sweeper/Severn Tunnel Jct	34	L/Cpl 5th SWB	KIA 23/9/17	Spoilbank Cem
Stroud A.J.	L&C/Swindon				GWR Roll of Honour
Stroud Charles Edward	Fitter &Turner/L&C/Swindon	21	Cpl 2nd Wilts Regt	Dow 6/3/16	Swindon Cem
Stroud Walter Thomas	Porter/Traff/Grimstone & Frampton		Pte 1/5th Lancashire Fus	Died 26/2/19	Charleroi Com Cem
Stroud Walter Timothy	Fireman/Loco/Didcot	23	Pte 1st Wilts Regt	Dow 11/1/17	Hazebrouck Com Cem
Stuckey Fred	R/Labourer/Engineer/Taunton		Pte 1/5th Somerset L.I.	KIA 31/12/16	Basra Mem
Styles Frederick George	Porter/Goods/South Lambeth	32	Pte 1st R Berks Regt	Dow 10/9/14	Bois Guillaume Com Cem
Sullivan Joseph	Labourer/L&C/Swindon		Pte 5th Wilts Regt	KIA 25/1/17	Amara War Cem
Summerfield James Henry	Goods/Wolverhampton		Pte 2/5th Lincolnshire Regt	Died 2/8/18	Le Quesnoy Com Cem
Summers Maynard	Labourer/L&C/Swindon	27	L/Cpl 1st Wilts Regt	KIA 12/3/15	Menin Gate Mem
Sumner Frank	Porter/Traffic/Leamington	18	Signalman SS Daybreak RN	SL 24/12/17	Plymouth Naval Mem
Sutton Henry	Parcel Vanman/Traffic/Manchester	21	Pte 1/7th Lancashire Fus	KIA 6/6/15	Helles Mem
Sutton William Edward G.	Electrical Fitter/L&C/Swindon	19	Pte 6th Shropshire L.I.	KIA 10/6/18	Sucrerie Cem
Sutton W.G.	L&C/Severn Tunnel Junction				GWR Roll of Honour
Swain Alfred J.	Carman/Goods/Paddington	25			GWR Mag 7&9/16
Swain G.	Packer/Engineer/Dunstall Park				GWR Mag 8/19
Swanborough Francis E.	L&C/Swindon	25	Pte 1st Wilts Regt	KIA 15/6/15	Menin Gate Mem
Sweetland Kiwen Barnes	Clerk/Traffic/Weston-super-Mare	22	Cpl 1st Somerset L.I.	KIA 2/11/18	Preseau Com Cem
Sweetzer H.D. (brother)	Fireman/Loco/Reading	24	Sto 1st Class HMS Hampshire RN	SL 5/6/16	Portsmouth Naval Mem
Sweetzer Louis (brother)	Call Boy/L&C/Reading	20	Pte 7th R Berks Regt	KIA 25/9/18	Doiran Mem
Swift Horace Arthur	Clerk/CGMO/Paddington	19	Pte 9th Norfolk Regt	KIA 29/4/18	Tyne Cot Mem
Symons A.	Watering-up man/Elect/Old Oak C				GWR Mag 12/18 & 1/19
Talbot P.	Goods/Leamington				GWR Roll of Honour
Tame Charles Gilbert	Machinist/Signal/Reading		Pte 3rd Worcester Regt	Dow 24/6/17	Bailleul Com Cem
Tamplin J.	Striker/L&C/Neath	20	Spr 124th Field Co R.E.	KIA 11/7/16	Flatiron Copse Cem
Tandy Wilfred	Packer/Engineer/Broadway	30	Pte 9th R Warwick Regt	KIA 7/8/15	Helles Mem
Tansill Fred G. (brother)	Signal/Carmarthen	19	Pte 4th E Yorkshire Regt	KIA 8/9/18	St Erme Com Cem
Tansill William J. (brother)	Engine Cleaner/L&C/Carmarthen	22	Spr 437th (Welch) Field Co R.E.	Died 29/7/17	Alexandria War Cem
Tarr William Jesse	Wagon Repairers Assist/Taunton	19	Pte 6th Somerset L.I.	KIA 21/3/18	Pozieres Mem
Tasker Frederick	Carman/Traffic/Southam Road	25	Pte 10th R West Surrey Regt	KIA 14/6/17	Menin Gate Mem
Taverner Percy	Machineman/L&C/Swindon	24	Pte 2/6th Devonshire Regt	Died 20/10/18	Kirkee Mem India
Taylor Edward	Carriage Cleaner/L&C/Wolverh'ton				GWR Mag 12/17
Taylor Ernest William	Porter/Traffic/Cardiff		L/Cpl 7th Gloucester Regt	KIA 10/2/17	Amara War Cem
Taylor George Henry G.	Wagon Painter/L&C/Swindon	24	Pte 2nd Wilts Regt	KIA 9/4/17	Neuville-Vitasse Rd Cem
Taylor George Walter	Crane Lad/Goods/Brentford		Pte 2nd Middlesex Regt	KIA 27/10/17	Motor Car Corner Cem
Taylor J.	Creosoter/Engineer/Hayes				GWR Mag 12/18 & 2/19
Taylor Joseph Hugh	Premium Apprent/L&C/Swindon	21	Ft/Sub/Lt 'G' Sqdn RAF	KIA 17/4/18	East Mudros Mil Cem
Taylor Ratcliffe	Clerk/Goods/Halifax	19	Pte 1st Northumberland Fus	Dow 12/10/18	Abbeville Com Cem
Taylor Thomas	Labourer/L&C/Coleham		Pte 1st Shropshire L.I.	Dow 23/10/14	Ploegsteert Mem
Taylor William Henry	Ticket Collector/Traff/Malvern Link	24	Gnr 219th Bty RGA	KIA 5/11/17	Voormezeele No 1 & 2
Teague Edgar Vivers	Lad Clerk/Goods/Paddington	21	Sgt 12th Durham L.I.	Dow 27/10/18	Giavera Br Cem Italy
Terry W.T.	Goods/Shrewsbury				GWR Roll of Honour
Thatcher (aka Allen) W.F.	Wagon Riveter/L&C/Worcester	32	L/Cpl 4th Worcester Regt	KIA 6/8/15	Helles Mem
Thatcher Walter John	L&C/Swindon		Pte 6th Wilts Regt	KIA 23/3/18	Arras Mem
Theobald Charles Edward	Horsekeeper/Goods/Paddington	37	Pte 1st R West Surrey Regt	KIA 3/10/14	Vendresse Br Cem

Theobald Edward George	R/Labourer/Engineer/Newport	31	L/Sgt 6th SWB	KIA 10/7/16	Thiepval Mem
Theobald W. Henry/Harry	Packer/Engineer/Port Talbot	24	Pte 13th Gloucester Regt	Died 30/9/16	Couin Br Cem
Thomas A.C.	Signal/Newport				GWR Roll of Honour
Thomas A.E.	Porter/Traffic/Saltash				GWR Mag 12/18 & 1/19
Thomas Alfred John	Porter/Goods/Chester		Pte 55th Bn MGC (Infantry)	KIA 9/4/18	Loos Mem
Thomas B.	Porter/Goods/Newport Dock St				GWR Mag 7/17
Thomas Edwin Isaac	Time & Storekeeper/L&C/Llanelly	27	Cpl 1/5th Welsh Regt	KIA 3/11/17	Beersheba War Cem
Thomas E.T.	Invoice Typist/Goods/Bristol				GWR Mag 1&4/19
Thomas H.J.	Lad Porter/Traffic/Athelney				GWR Mag 8/16
Thomas J.	Engineer/Swansea				GWR Roll of Honour
Thomas James	Canal Lengthman/Clydach				GWR Mag 11/17 & 2/18
Thoams R.	Packer/Engineer/Kiidwelly				GWR Mag 12/19
Thomas T.	Clerk/Traffic/Pembrey				GWR Mag 3&12/18
Thomas T.J.	Caller-Off/Goods/Swansea				GWR Mag 9&12/18
Thomas W.	Office Porter/Goods/Hockley				GWR Mag 7&9/18
Thomas W.	Packer/Engineer/Kidwelly				GWR Mag 3&4/19
Thompson Arthur Charles	Porter/Goods/Paddington		L/Cpl 3rd London Regt	KIA 6/10/18	Maroc Br Cem
Thompson Benjamin H.	Off Porter/Goods/Charing Cross	20	Pte 2nd Hampshire Regt	Das 13/8/15	Helles Mem
Thompson Charles G.	Engine Cleaner/Loco/Chester	20	Pte 20th Manchester Regt	Dow 5/11/16	Boulogne East Cem
Thompson Edward	Labourer/L&C/Old Oak Common	29	Cpl 2nd Yorkshire Regt	KIA 22/10/14	Menin Gate Mem
Thompson George F.H.	Porter/Traffic/Adderley		Pte 14th Gloucester Regt	Died 28/6/18	Chauny Com Cem
Thompson John F.J.	Porter/Traffic/Salisbury	27	Pte 1st Northumberland Fus	Dow 24/9/15	Wandsworth Cem
Thompson Harold John	R/Labour/Engineer/Haverfordwest	21	Sto 1st Class HMS Bittern RN	SL 4/4/18	Plymouth Naval Mem
Thompson Herbert James	Labourer/L&C/Old Oak Common	28	Pte 9th Essex Regt	KIA 4/10/15	Loos Mem
Thomson H.	Surveyor/Engineer/Newport				GWR Mag 1/17
Thornbury Henry John	Machineman/L&C/Swindon	23	Pte 2nd Wilts Regt	KIA 21/3/18	Pozieres Mem
Thorne Albert Henry	Engine Cleaner/L&C/Barnstaple	19	Pte 1/6th Devonshire Regt	Dow 13/12/15	Kut War Cem
Thorne George	Restaurant Car Conductor/Padd		Rifm 3rd Rifle Brigade	KIA 9/8/17	Hooge Crater Cem
Thornton Edward Charles	Parcel Porter/Traffic/Trowbridge	30	CSM 1st Somerset L.I.	KIA 6/7/15	Alana Farm Cem
Thrupp W.	Bridge Labour/Engineer/Wolver'h	45	Pte 6th Worcester Regt	Died 30/1/19	Birmingham Cem
Thrush George	Frame-Builders Assist/Swindon		Pte 6th Wilts Regt	Dow 5/7/16	Heilly Station Cem
Tilley John Henry	Shunter/Goods/Withymoor	34	Pte 4th Worcester Regt	KIA 27/9/17	Artillery Wood Cem
Timmis Arthur	Porter/Goods/Kidderminster		Pte 1st Northumberland Fus	KIA 1/4/16	Menin Gate Mem
Timms Marcus John	Packer/Engineer/Bampton	21	L/Cpl 5th Ox & Bucks L.I.	KIA 27/4/16	Cabaret-Rouge Br Cem
Tindall George	Packer/Engineer/Panteg		Pte 1/2nd Monmouthshire Regt	KIA 30/1/17	A.I.F. Burial Flers
Tipton Bert	Clerk/Traffic/Wellington (Salop)	20	Pte 6th Shropshire L.I.	KIA 20/9/17	Tyne Cot Mem
Titchener Frank	Helper/L&C/Swindon		Sgt 1st Wilts Regt	Died 2/1/15	Valenciennes Com Cem
Titcombe O.H.	Stampers Assist/L&C/Swindon		Spr 33rd Base Park R.E.	Died 6/11/18	Mikra Br Cem
Titcombe Rupert Ernest	Machineman/R Shop/Swindon	23	L/Bom 14th Siege Bty RGA	KIA 23/12/17	Dunhallow A.D.S. Cem
Tompkins Arthur Vernon	Carman/Goods/Hockley	27	Pte 2nd Coldstream Guards	KIA 5/11/14	Sanctuary Wood Cem
Tompkins George James	Machineman/No 16 Shop/Swindon		Pte 1st Wilts Regt	KIA 13/10/14	Le Touret Mem
Toms Sydney Walter	Weigher/Goods/Swansea	23	Pte 13th Welsh Regt	Died 31/10/18	Etaples Mil Cem
Tonkin Charles	Clerk/Goods/Penzance	23	Sgt 1st DCLI	Dow 30/6/18	Aire Com Cem
Toop Donald Victor	Porter/Traffic/Lydney	19	Pte 1st Bn RMLI	Dow 29/9/18	Louverval Mil Cem
Topp Arthur Harold	Machineman/L&C/Swindon		L/Cpl 2nd Wilts Regt	KIA 9/4/17	Arras Mem
Tottle James	Foremans Clerk/L&C/Exeter	37	Pte RAMC	Died 28/7/18	Exeter St Thomas Cem
Tovey Frederick William	Lad Clerk/Goods/Paddington	18	Pte 7th R West Surrey Regt	Dow 3/5/17	Bucquoy Road Cem
Tovey Leslie Harold	Lad Clerk/Goods/Paddington	19	Pte 7th R Berks Regt	KIA 9/5/17	Doiran Mem
Townsend E.A.	Gaugeman/L&C/Swindon				GWR Mag 6/19
Townsend Ernest Arthur	Forgemans Help/Hammer Shop	27	Sgt 2nd Wilts Regt	KIA 12/3/15	Le Touret Mem
Townsend Reg George	Helper/L&C/Swindon	27	Pte 13th Welsh Regt	Dow 18/9/18	Thilloy Road Cem
Towns(h)end Ernest A.	Cartage Porter/Goods/Paddington	36	Pte 1/7th Middlesex Regt	Dow 31/7/18	South Ealing Cem
Tozer William Edwin P.	Carriage Cleaner/L&C/Plymouth	35	Pte 1/5th Devonshire Regt	KIA 10/4/18	Ramleh War Cem
Tracey Richard	Porter/Goods/Hockley	29	Pte 3rd Worcester Regt	KIA 7/11/14	Menin Gate Mem
Treacher Walter Richard	Instrument Maker/Signal/Reading	23	Pte 4th Seaforth Highlanders	KIA 9/5/15	Le Touret Mem
Treby James Edmund	L&C/Southall	25	Spr 145th ATC R.E.	KIA 9/4/18	Croix-du-Bac Br Cem
Trenmlett William Francis	Engine Cleaner/L&C/Newton Abbot	20	Pte 1/4th Devonshire Regt	KIA 3/2/17	Amara War Cem
Trenfield William Edwin	Wagon Repairer/L&C/Gloucester	23	Pte 1/5th Gloucester Regt	KIA 5/4/17	Villers-Faucon Com Cem
Trevellyan James	L/Packer/Engineer/Burlescombe	40	Spr 268th Rly Co R.E.	Dow 2/10/17	Dozingham Mil Cem

Name	Occupation/Department/Location	Age	Rank/Regiment	Death	Memorial/Cemetery
Trew Reginald Edwin	Wagon Repairers Assist/Panteg	23	L/Sgt 2nd Monmouthshire Regt	KIA 2/12/17	Cambrai Mem
Trigger Frederick	Lampman/Traffic/Newton Abbot	27	Pte RFA	Died 1/11/18	Kirkee Mem India
Trimby Archibald	Cleaner/Traffic/Slough	20	Spr 22nd Light Rly Co R.E.	Died 30/12/17	Upton-cum-Chalvey
Tripe Alfred King	Clerk/Estate/Plymouth	29	Lt RGA att Tank Corps	KIA 23/11/17	Cambrai Mem
Trollope Walter	Mechanics Labour/L&C/Trowbridge	32	Pte 1st Wilts Regt	Dow 5/7/16	Thiepval Mem
Trotman Richard Edward	Office Boy/Electrical/Paddington	19	Cpl 58th Div Signal Co R.E.	KIA 21/3/18	Pozieres Mem
Tucker Stanley	Labourer/Engineer/Dulverton		Pte 6th Leinster Regt	Dow 16/8/15	Alexandria War Cem
Tuffey Thomas	Riveter/L&C/Wormwood Scrubs	34	Spr 78th Field Co R.E.	Dow 31/12/17	Rocquigny Road Cem
Tullett George	Labourer/Engineer/Lostwithiel		Pte 1st DCLI	KIA 29/9/18	Fifteen Ravine Br Cem
Tupman Frederick	Stower/Goods/Birmingham	23	Pte 4th Worcester Regt	KIA 6/8/15	Helles Mem
Turner Albert	Striker/L&C/Wolverhampton	32	A/Cpl 3rd S Stafford Regt	Died 25/12/16	Wolverhampton Cem
Turner Albert Henry	Labourer/Engineer/Taunton		Pte 8th Somerset L.I.	KIA 28/4/17	Arras Mem
Turner Edward Walter	Labourer/L&C/Old Oak Common	27	Pte 1st Middlesex Regt	Dow 26/10/14	Ration Farm Mil Cem
Turner F.	Porter/Traffic/Durston				GWR Mag 1&5/18
Turner F.	Striker/Engineer/Worcester				GWR Mag 1/19
Turner G.	Traffic/St Fagans				GWR Roll of Honour
Turner H.	Porter/Traffic/Campden				GWR Mag 6/18
Turner W.J.	Traffic/Penygraig				GWR Roll of Honour
Turton Herbert Thomas	Helper/L&C/Swindon		Pte 1/4th Wilts Regt	Died 11/10/18	Ramleh War Cem
Turvey Alfred W. or H.	Tube Cleaner/L&C/Oxley	21	Gdsm 1st Grenadier Guards	KIA 17/10/15	Loos Mem
Twyford John Robert	Machinist/No 16 Shop/Swindon	22	Pte 5th Wilts Regt	Dow 12/8/15	Helles Mem
Tyler Albert Henry	Signalman/Traffic/Ogmore Vale	22	L/Cpl 4th SWB	Dow 13/8/15	Helles Mem
Tyler Clifford Frederick	Porter/Traffic/Bristol	19	Pte 2/4th Dorset Regt	Dow 11/6/18	Damascus War Cem
Underdown Bert	Carman/Goods/Bristol		Pte 2nd K Own Yorkshire L.I.	KIA 18/11/16	Mailly Wood Cem
Upton Walter Chase	Traffic/Shifnal	26	Cpl 2nd SWB	KIA 1/7/16	Y Ravine Cem
Upton William Ernest	Goods/Bristol	21	Dvr 2/3rd S Midland Field Co RE	Died 21/5/16	Bristol (Arnos Vale) Cem
Vanson Edgar	Porter/Traffic/St Germans	20	Pte 1/5th DCLI	KIA 19/11/16	Thiepval Mem
Vardy Harry	Parcel Porter/Traffic/Westbury		Pte 2/4th Wilts Regt	Died 27/7/17	Basra Mem
Vaughan G.	Packer/Engineer/Berrington				GWR Mag 10&12/18
Vaughan George Ernest	Packer/Engineer/Churchill		Pte 14th Worcester Regt	KIA 5/11/16	Thiepval Mem
Veal F.H.	Porter/Traffic/Smithfield	27			GWR Mag 2&3/15
Veal Reginald Frederick	Signal Porter/Goods/Bristol	19	Spr 1st S Midland Field Co RE	Died 22/5/15	Bristol (Arnos Vale) Cem
Veale F.W.	Office Porter/Traffic/Bristol				GWR Mag 11/19
Venton Stafford Hope	Painter/Eng/Kennet & Avon Canal	24	Pte 10th Lincolnshire Regt	KIA 23/11/17	St Martin Calvaire Cem
Vickery Ernest Alexander	Mileage Porter/Traffic/Radstock	23	Pte 6th R Inniskilling Fus	KIA 8/10/18	Prospect Hill Cem
Vickery John Francis	Carriage Frame Builder/21A Shop	22	L/Cpl 2nd Wilts Regt	KIA 26/9/15	Loos Mem
Vickery John T.S.	Porter/Goods/Bristol	24	Pte 1st Gloucester Regt	KIA 9/5/15	Le Touret Mem
Viner Frederick Reginald	L&C/Swindon	22	Spr 89th Field Co R.E.	KIA 9/8/15	Ramparts Cem Ypres
Vinson Sidney Edward	Porter/Traffic/Horrabridge		Gnr C Bty 122nd Bde RFA	KIA 6/11/18	Cross Roads Cem
Waite Enest Fred Walter	Engine Cleaner/Loco/Newton Ab't	20	Pte 12th Gloucester Regt	KIA 23/8/18	Vis-en-Artois Mem
Wakefield Tom	Carpenters Labour/L&C/Swindon	26	Pte 1st R Berks Regt	KIA 19/9/14	La Ferte-s-Jouarre Mem
Wakefield William Albert	Lampman/Traffic/Newport		Gnr V 39th Trench Mortar Bty	KIA 15/9/17	La Clytte Mil Cem
Waldron A.E.	Engine Cleaner/Loco/Bath				GWR Mag 4&7/19
Waldron Alfred Henry	L&C/Swindon	17	Pte 5th Wilts Regt	KIA 9/4/16	Amara War Cem
Waldron George	Lifters Mate/L&C/Newton Abbot		Pte 17th Lancashire Fus	KIA 21/11/17	Cement House Cem
Walker Charles W. B.	Restaurant Car Conductor/Padd	26	Pte 11th Middlesex Regt	Dow 14/4/17	Duisans Br Cem
Walker F.	Gen Labourer/Engineer/Bordesley				GWR Mag 1&7/18
Walker Frank	Clerk/Goods/Worcester				GWR Mag 5&7/17
Walker Frank Frederick	Audit Clerk/C.A.O./Paddington	19	Pte 2nd Middlesex Regt	KIA 18/8/18	Thelus Mil Cem
Walker George Edward	L&C/Swindon	34	L/Cpl 2nd Wilts Regt	KIA 9/4/17	Wancourt Br Cem
Walker Harry	Gas Engine Driver/L&C/Swindon	41	Sgt 4th Guards Machine Gun Regt	KIA 20/10/18	St Vaast Com Cem
Walker L.A.	Engineer/Paddington				GWR Roll of Honour
Wall George	Bricklayer/Engineer/Leominster	32	Pte 11th Border Regt	Died 28/2/17	Thiepval Mem
Wall Timothy Henry	L&C/Wolverhampton	34	L/Cpl 1st Coldstream Guards	KIA 25/1/15	Le Touret Mem
Wallis Richard Worth	Porter/Goods/Penzance	28	Seaman HMS Goliath RN	SL 13/5/15	Plymouth Naval Mem
Walter Ernest J.	Porter/Goods/Poplar	40	Gnr Z 34th Trench Mortar Bty	KIA 12/3/16	Brewery Orchard Cem
Walters Frank	Platform Attendant/Abercanaid	19	Pte 5th Shropshire L.I.	Dow 5/10/15	Ledbury Cem
Walton Harry	Apprent Boilermaker/L&C/Swindon	20	Pte 1st Wilts Regt	KIA 18/6/15	Menin Gate Mem
Ward C.J.	Clerk/CGMO/Paddington				GWR Mag 2/20

Ward George Harry	Clerk/Goods/Bretrell Lane	19	Pte MGC (Infantry)	KIA 18/9/18	Ephey Wood Farm Cem
Ward Robert Harry	Apprent/L&C/Old Oak Common	20	Pte 12th Royal Fus	KIA 15/3/16	Menin Gate Mem
Ware Sydney Stewart	Horsekeeper/Goods/Bristol	31	Pte 2nd SWB	Das 13/8/15	Helles Mem
Warner F.	L&C/Swindon				GWR Roll of Honour
Warner James William	Labourer/Engineer/Cirencester		Pte 13th Gloucester Regt	KIA 7/10/16	Blighty Valley Cem
Warren Frank	Porter/Goods/Menheniot	19	Pte 9th Devonshire Regt	KIA 25/9/15	Loos Mem
Warren Harold George	L&C/West London	28	Pte 8th K Own Yorkshire L.I.	KIA 1/7/16	Serre Road Cem 2
Warren Thomas William	Engine Cleaner/St Philips M. Bristol	22	Pte N Somerset Yeo	KIA 8/8/18	Hillside Cem Le Quesnel
Wason Cyril Ernest	Clerk/Goods/Cardiff		2/Lt 9th Royal Fus	KIA 30/11/17	Cambrai Mem
Wathen A.V.	Traffic/Winscombe				GWR Roll of Honour
Watkins Edgar T. or T.E.	Timekeeper/Engineer/Newport	29	A/Bom D Bty 120th Bde RFA	Dr 30/5/15	Pontypool Cem
Watkins W.H.	Engine Cleaner/Loco/Cardiff				GWR Mag 4/16
Watkiss Samuel	Checker/Goods/Shrewsbury		Rifm 2nd Rifle Bde	KIA 9/5/15	Ploegsteert Mem
Watson George	Clerk/Secretay's/Paddington	34	Pte 1/14th London Regt	KIA 1/11/14	Menin Gate Mem
Watson Tom	Carman/Goods/Hockley		L/Cpl 11th Hampshire Regt	KIA 17/8/17	Vlamertinghe N Mil Cem
Watson Walter Edward	Stampers Assist/L&C/Swindon		Pte 1st Wilts Regt	KIA 17/2/17	Ploegsteert Mem
Watts Charles	Bricklayer/Engineer/Worcester	49	Rifm 21st Rifle Bde	Das 30/12/17	Alexandria War Cem
Watts Isaac Charles	L&C/Swindon		Pte 2nd Wilts Regt	KIA 17/5/15	Le Touret Mem
Watts J.	Packer/Engineer/Marlborough				GWR Mag 7/16
Watts William	Labourer/L&C/Swindon		L/Cpl 5th Wilts Regt	KIA 10/8/15	Helles Mem
Watts William Henry	Policeman/Traffic/Cardiff	22	Cpl 4th Bn MGC (Infantry)	KIA 2/11/18	Preseau Com Cem
Weaver Henry John	Packer/Engineer/Yatton	28	Spr 268th Field Co R.E.	Died 19/6/17	Lijssenthoek Mil Cem
Weaver Leonard Henry	Parcel Clerk/Traffic/Cheltenham	22	Rifm 21st att 12th London Regt	KIA 20/7/16	Hebuterne Mil Cem
Weaver Victor Henry J.	Engine Cleaner/Loco/Gloucester	20	Pte 8th Gloucester Regt	KIA 30/7/16	Thiepval Mem
Weaver William George	Engine Cleaner/Loco/Gloucester	19	L/Cpl 2/5th Gloucester Regt	KIA 21/12/16	Thiepval Mem
Weaving Charles	L&C/Swindon	35	Pte 7th Wilts Regt	KIA 7/10/18	Templeux-le-Guerrard
Weaving Edwin	L/Packer/Engineer/Gloucester	35	Pte 8th Gloucester Regt	Died 13/11/16	Gloucester Old Cem
Webb Horace Bernard	Carriage Cleaner/L&C/Cheltenham	32	Pte Portsmouth Bn RMLI	Doi 27/6/15	Alexandria War Cem
Webb Oliver Albert	Porter/Traffic/Paddington		Pte 2nd Hampshire Regt	Dow 7/8/15	Cairo War Mem Cem
Webber Albert Henry	Machineman/L&C/Swindon	30	L/Cpl 2nd Gloucester Regt	KIA 1/9/18	Karasouli Mil Cem
Webber F.	Fitters Labourer/L&C/Port Talbot				GWR Mag 10/16
Webber Frank E.	Lad Porter/Traffic/Weymouth				GWR Mag 3&7/18
Webber George James R.	Fireman/Loco/Landore	21	Rifm 1st KRRC	KIA 14/11/16	Redan Ridge Cem 2
Webber W.	Packer/Engineer/Frome				GWR Mag 11&12/18
Webster Albert Ernest	Controller/Traffic/Birmingham	32	CSM 39th Bn MGC (Infantry)	Dow 21/9/18	La Kreule Mil Cem
Webster B.	Traffic/Old Hill				GWR Roll of Honour
Webster G.C.	Porter/Traffic/Codford				GWR Mag 2/19
Wedge George	Goods Porter/Traffic/Oakengates	24	Pte 7th Shropshire L.I.	KIA 13/5/17	Arras Mem
Weedon F.	Goods/Paddington				GWR Roll of Honour
Weeks Frederick	Porter/Goods/Swindon	29	Pte 1st Wilts Regt	KIA 19/10/14	Ration Farm Mil Cem
Weeks Herbert Stanley	Messenger/Goods/Bristol		Pte 8th Devonshire Regt	KIA 7/10/17	Tyne Cot Mem
Weinert Frederick Charles	Porter/Goods/West Ealing	23	Pte 1/5th Suffolk Regt	Dow 19/1/18	Port Said War Mem Cem
Welch C.W.	Goods/Southall				GWR Roll of Honour
Welc(s)h E.G.	Signalman/Traffic/Cookham				GWR Mag 3&7/18
Welch Henry James	Carman/Goods/Exeter	34	Sgt 9th W Yorkshire Regt	KIA 27/9/16	Thiepval Mem
Welch James	R/Labourer/Engineer/St Austell		Pte 1st DCLI	KIA 23/7/16	Thiepval Mem
Welch J.H.	Goods/Langley Green				GWR Roll of Honour
Wells A.J.	L&C/Swindon				GWR Roll of Honour
Wells Charles A.	Labourer/No 15 Shop/Swindon				GWR Mag 9&10/16
Wells Herbert George L.	Wood Wagon Builder/L&C/Swindon		Pte 9th N Staffordshire Regt	Dow 14/5/18	St Sever Cem
Wells Maurice G. Linham	Fireman/Loco/Old Oak Common	21	Pte 22nd Royal Fus	Dow 25/5/16	Barlin Com Cem
Welsh William	Loader/Goods/Gresham Street	35	L/Cpl 4th Middlesex Regt	KIA 29/9/15	Menin Gate Mem
West Edward Charles	R/Labourer/Engineer/Hereford	30	Pte 1st DCLI	KIA 30/4/15	First DCLI Cem (Bluff)
West Herbert	Slip Labourer/Engineer/Bath		Dvr 1st Field Sqdn R.E.	Dow 27/8/17	Mont Huon Mil Cem
Western Harry Charles	Engine Cleaner/Loco/Exeter	21	Pte 8th Devonshire Regt	KIA 2/4/17	Arras Mem
Westlake William J.	Labourer/L&C/Swindon		Gnr B Bty 76th Bde RFA	Dow 8/9/16	Heilly Station Cem
Weston Arthur	Labourer/L&C/Swindon	31	Sgt 6th Wilts Regt	KIA 12/6/17	Menin Gate Mem
Westwood W.A.	L&C/Wolverhampton				GWR Roll of Honour
Whale Arthur	L&C/Swindon		L/Cpl 1st Wilts Regt	KIA 16/6/15	Menin Gate Mem

Name	Role	Age	Unit	Death	Cemetery/Memorial
Whatley Frederick C.	Coach-Builder/L&C/Swindon	19	A/Mech Navigate & Bomb School	Died 12/10/18	Swindon Cem
Whatmore George	Carman/Goods/Hockley	30	Rifm 1st KRRC	KIA 27/10/14	Menin Gate Mem
Wheatley Roy Syd Page	Clerk/Goods/Liverpool	30	Pte 24th R Welsh Fus	Died 10/3/17	Cairo War Mem Cem
Wheeler Alfred Frank L.	Clerk/Goods/Paddington	20	Gnr 1/1st (Warwick) R.H.A.	Dow 4/3/17	Grove Town Cem
Wheeler Arthur	Engine Cleaner/Loco/Frome	21	Sto 1st Class HMS Warrior RN	SL 31/5/16	Plymouth Naval Mem
Wheeler Edward George	Labourer/Engineer/Hayes	22	Pte 32nd Royal Fus	Died 16/9/16	Corbie Com Cem
Whetham Charles(brother)	Wagon Painter/19E Shop/Swindon	23	Pte 2nd Wilts Regt	KIA 26/9/15	Loos Mem
Whetham George(brother)	Refreshment Room Page/Swindon	18	Pte 2nd Wilts Regt	Dow 22/11/15	Guards Cem Windy C.
Whetter(s) Joseph L.	Packer/Engineer/St Blazey	24	Pte 7th DCLI	KIA 2/4/18	Pozieres Mem
Whiddon William Alfred	Porter/Traffic/Tavistock	24	Pte 1/5th Devonshire Regt	KIA 30/9/18	Flesquieres Hill Br Cem
White C.	Wireman/Signal/Tyseley				GWR Mag 7&12/18 11/19
White Clarence C.W.	Porter/Goods/Oxford	30	Pte 2nd Ox & Bucks L.I.	KIA 14/9/14	La Ferte-s-Jouarre Mem
White E.F.G.	Brass Finisher/Signal/Reading	20	Aircraftman 20 Sqdn RAF	Died 10/7/19	Karachi 14-18 War Mem
White George	Shunter/Traffic/Exeter	31		Pneumonia	GWR Mag 11/14 & 3/15
White H.	Painter or Packer/Engineer/Reading				GWR Mag 11&12/18
White James	Packer/Engineer/Pontlliw		Pte 13th Middlesex Regt	KIA 14/3/16	Sanctuary Wood Cem
White Job William	Signal Porter/Traffic/Newport		Pte 1st Monmouthshire Regt	KIA 8/5/15	Menin Gate Mem
White Leonard George	Ticket Collector/Maiden Newton	21	Cpl N Somerset Yeo	Dow 16/6/15	Les Gonards Cem
White Richard Stephen	Clerk/Traffic/Ealing	21	Spr 64th Broad Gauge Co R.E.	Dow 28/5/18	Bac-du-Sud Br Cem
White W.	Fireman/Loco/Port Talbot				GWR Mag 1/17
White William Henry	Traffic/Shrewsbury	29	Pte 1st Somerset L.I.	Dow 21/6/18	Le Vertannoy Br Cem
Whitehouse Sid Charles	Messenger/Paddington Goods St		Rifm 1/9th London Regt	KIA 1/7/16	Thiepval Mem
Whiteley Leslie Albert	Plan Printer/Engineer/Paddington		L/Cpl 1/8th Middlesex Regt	KIA 16/8/17	Tyne Cot Mem
Whiteman Christopher	Bricklayer/L&C/Swindon	38	Spr 104th Field Co R.E.	KIA 26/6/17	Perth Cem (China Wall)
Whitfield Rich Houlbrook	Surveyor/Engineer/Neath	29	Lt 104th Field Co R.E.	KIA 12/5/16	Maple Leaf Cem
Whiting Albert John	Gas Fitter/Engineer/Gloucester		Pte 2/5th N Staffordshire Regt	Died 17/10/17	Boulogne East Cem
Whitman Edwin Riley	Dresser/Foundry/Swindon Works	18	Pte 1st Wilts Regt	KIA 6/7/16	Thiepval Mem
Whomack Samuel Charles	Bricklayer/Engineer/Wolverh'ton	36	Pte 1st S Staffordshire Regt	Dow 27/5/17	Etaples Mil Cem
Wicks James Harold	Gas Fitter/Eng/Reading or Padd'ton	31	Pnr ROD R.E.	Died 23/7/19	Wellington Cem
Wickson Charles R.	Shed Porter/Goods/Cardiff	26	Pte 3rd Worcester Regt	KIA 7/11/14	St Julien Dressing Station
Widdows Archibald	Clerk/Goods/Banbury		Lt 2nd DCLI att 8th Cheshire	Died 6/10/18	Karachi 14-18 War Mem
Wiggall Charles Henry	Ass. Examiner/L&C/Swindon	20	Pte 2nd Wilts Regt	KIA 28/9/15	Loos Mem
Wilby William Charles	Tableman/L&C/Goodwick	38	Pte 2nd Ox & Bucks L.I.	KIA 16/5/15	Le Touret Mem
Wilcock Henry Blamires	Clerk/Traffic/Paddington	20	Lt 3rd att 13th Essex Regt	KIA 13/11/16	Serre Road Cem 2
Wilcox Edgar James	Carman/Goods/Frome	31	Dvr 3rd Wessex Field Co R.E.	Died 27/7/16	Frome Churchyard
Wilcox Frederick Edward	Bricklayer/Engineer/Reading	28	Spr 204th Field Co R.E.	KIA 31/5/16	St Vaast Com Cem
Wil(l)cox George	R/Labourer/Engineer/Bristol	25	Pte 2nd R Warwick Regt	KIA 25/9/15	Loos Mem
Wild J.	Plasterer/Engineer/Wolverhampton				GWR Mag 11/17
Wilding Albert Victor	Clerk/Goods/Worcester	29	Pte 2nd Worcester Regt	KIA 25/9/17	Tyne Cot Mem
Wildman A.G.	Porter/Goods/Minories				GWR Mag 6&9/18
Wilkes W.H.	Platform Porter/Worcester Joint				GWR Mag 1&3/17
Wilkins Albert Edward	Labourer/L&C/Swindon		Gnr 104th Bty 216th Bde RFA	Died 1/6/18	Agra Cantonment Cem
Wilkins Charles	Masons Labourer/Newport	19	Pte 1st Welsh Regt	KIA 23/7/15	Lindenhoek Chalet Cem
Wilkins F.J.	Frame-Builders Assist/Swindon				GWR Mag 5/17
Wilkinson George Henry	Helper/L&C/Swindon	18	Pte 3rd Wilts Regt	Died 5/5/15	Swindon Cem
Wilkinson H.	Carman/Goods/Manchester				GWR Mag 1&2/19
Wilk(e)s Thomas William	Clerk/Goods/Paddington	25	Pte 1/13th London Regt	KIA 21/3/18	Arras Mem
Willcocks J.W.	R/Labourer/Eng/Newton Abbot		Spr 252nd Field Co R.E.	Dow 16/10/17	Godewaersvelde Br Cem
Willcox Sidney	Packer/Engineer/Somerton	26	Pte 7th Somerset L.I.	Dow 10/9/16	St Sever Cem
Williams Arthur John	Traffic/Ponthir	19	Pte 9th Cheshire Regt	KIA 6/6/18	Chambrecy Br Cem
Williams A.R.	Timekeeper/L&C/Stratford				GWR Roll of Honour
Williams Edward James	Smiths Apprent/L&C/Swindon	19	Pte 8th Gloucester Regt	KIA 25/3/17	Klein-Vierstraat Br Cem
Williams H.	Stower/Goods/Paddington				GWR Mag 10/17
Williams Harry	Labourer/L&C/Stafford Road				GWR Mag 1&7/17
Williams J.	R/Labour/Engineer/Stourbridge Jct				GWR Mag 3&6/19
Williams J.E.	Telegraphist/Traffic/Stapleton Rd				GWR Mag 3&4/19
Williams John Watham	Traffic/Neath	19	Pte 1st Welsh Guards	Dow 27/89/16	Grove Town Cem
Williams Kenneth George	Temp Employed	19	Lt 74th Co MGC (Infantry)	KIA 21/10/16	Thiepval Mem
Williams Robert	Carriage Cleaner/Old Oak Common	18			GWR Mag 9/15 & 2/16

Name	Role/Dept/Location	Age	Regiment/Unit	Death	Cemetery/Memorial
Williams R.M.	Steam Craneman/L&C/Bristol		Spr 94th Field Co R.E.	Died 24/11/18	Bristol (Greenbank) Cem
William W.A.	Fireman/Loco/Llanelly				GWR Mag 1/18
Williams William	Greaser/L&C/Gloucester	20	Pte 10th Worcester Regt	KIA 25/10/16	Thiepval Mem
Williams William George	Shunter/Traffic/Swansea Docks	32			GWR Mag 9/15
Williams Willie	Porter/Traffic/Bala	19	Pte 1/7th R Welsh Fus	Died 29/11/15	Lala Baba Cem Turkey
Willis H.	Clerk/Goods/Southall				GWR Mag 2&4/19
Willoughby William E.	Office Porter/Goods/Paddington	19	Pte 3rd London Regt	Died 9/8/16	Warlincourt Halte Br Cem
Wills A.G.	Lad Messenger/Goods/Cardiff				GWR Mag 1&3/17
Wills Henry George	Porter/Goods/Exeter	23	Pte 10th R West Kent Regt	KIA 31/7/17	Bedford House Cem
Willis William Henry	Labourer/L&C/Swindon	28	Pte 1st Gloucester Regt	Died 29/10/14	Menin Gate Mem
Willmott Charles Ernest	Lad Porter/Traffic/Fairford	18	Pte 7th Gloucester Regt	Died 23/10/15	Alexandria War Cem
Wilson Cyril Spencer	Ass Works Manager/C&W/Swindon	36	Major R.E.	Doi 27/10/18	Charlecombe Church
Wilson Henry David	Staff Clerk/L&C/Swindon	21	Pte 1/4th Wilts Regt	KIA 2/11/17	Gaza War Cem
Wilson Richard	Fireman/Loco/Southall	19	Pte 7th Seaforth Highlanders	Dow 23/10/15	Lijssenthoek Mil Cem
Wilson Walter	Packer/Engineer/Moreton-on-Lugg	23	Pte 1/1st Hereford Regt	KIA 9/1/17	Jerusalem Mem
Wilson William R. Henry	Dresser/L&C/Swindon		L/Sgt 1/4th Wilts Regt	Dow 11/5/18	Ramleh War Cem
Wilton J.	L/Packer/Engineer/Liskeard				GWR Mag 12/18 & 1/19
Wiltshire Charles Henry	Apprent/L&C/Swindon	21	A/Mech 1st Class RNAS	Died 16/10/18	Swindon Cem
Winchurst Bert	Labourer/V Shop/Swindon	19	Pte 2nd Wilts Regt	KIA 26/9/15	Loos Mem
Windridge Samuel Edward	L&C/Swindon	22	Pte 5th Wilts Regt	KIA 10/8/15	Helles Mem
Wingate Walter Leslie	Porter/Traffic/Reading	20	Pte 1st R Berks Regt	Dow 12/3/18	Rocquigny Road Cem
Wingrove Henry Francis	Restaurant Car Attend't/Paddington	23	Pte 1st Wilts Regt	KIA 15/1/15	La Laiterie Mil Cem
Winstone Alfred J. 'Jack'	Packer/Engineer/Stoke Gifford		Spr 262nd (GWR) Rly Co R.E.	Dow 6/9/17	Voormezeele 1 & 2
Winter Frederick George	Porter/Traffic/Uffington	24	Gnr D Bty 311th Bde RFA	KIA 4/4/18	Arras Mem
Winter John Charles	Toolman/Engineer/Taunton	18	Pte 33rd Training Reserve	Died 4/2/17	Oake Churchyard
Wintle George James	Clerk/Traffic/Severn & Wye Joint		Pte 8th Gloucester Regt	Died 2/2/17	Varennes Mil Cem
Wood E.J.	Porter/Goods/Smithfield				GWR Mag 3&7/18
Wood Owen Glen D.	Signal/Worcester	44	Pte 2/8th Worcester Regt	KIA 31/3/18	Pozieres Mem
Woodham James Herbert	Helper/L&C/Swindon	19	Pte 1/4th Wilts Regt	KIA 1/11/17	Gaza War Cem
Woodhams Fred George	Clerk/C.A.O./Paddington	22	Sgt 13th London Regt	KIA 16/8/17	Hooge Crater Cem
Woodhams Oswald C.	Improver/Traffic/Slough	25	Pte 2nd Grenadier Guards	KIA 21/10/18	St Vaast Com Cem
Woodley Sidney	Mileage Porter/Traffic/St Austell	19	Pte 59th Bn MGC (Infantry)	Dow 6/4/18	Mons (Bergen) Cem
Woodman Albert Fred J.	Apprent/L&C/Swindon	20	Pte 1/8th R Warwick Regt	KIA 1/7/16	Serre Road Cem 1
Woodman Edwin George	Traffic/Resolven	25	Pte 17th Welsh Regt	KIA 25/11/17	Cambrai Mem
Woodrow Reginald John	Porter/Traffic/Tavistock	24	Pte 1/5th Devonshire Regt	KIA 20/7/18	Marfaux Br Cem
Woods George Thomas	Carriage Fitter/L&C/Old O Common		Pte ASC	Died 27/10/16	Taplow Churchyard
Woodward Albert Sydney	Lad Porter/Fladbury Station	18	Pte 1st Worcester Regt	KIA 10/5/15	Ploegsteert Mem
Woodward E.	Porter/Traffic/Kings Sutton				GWR Mag 11&12/18
Woodward J.H.	Helper/L&C/Swindon				GWR Mag 3/18
Woodward Ray Henry	Sheet Repairer/Goods/Gloucester	22	Pte 2/5th Gloucester Regt	KIA 15/11/17	Browns Copse Cem
Woodward Reg William	Porter/Traffic/Tyseley		Pte 3rd Coldstream Guards	Died 13/4/18	Ploegsteert Mem
Woolaway Thomas Henry	Porter/Goods/Hereford		Pte 9th Lancashire Fus	Dow 26/4/17	Grevillers Br Cem
Woolford Henry	Issuer/Stores/Swindon		Pte 7th R Dublin Fus	KIA 7/8/15	Helles Mem
Woolfries Sam Charles	Coalman/L&C/Weymouth	34	Pte 1st Dorset Regt	Dow 15/10/14	Gorre Br & Indian Cem
Wollacott Charles E.	Carriage Cleaner/Weston-s-Mare	28	Pte 1/1st Northumbrian F/Amb	Died 27/5/18	Soissons Mem
Woolley Charles Henry	Fireman/Loco/Lydney	21	Pte 2nd Gloucester Regt	KIA 27/6/15	Ration Farm Mil Cem
Woolley Samuel	Engine Cleaner/L&C/Stourbridge	21	Pte 1/7th Worcester Regt	KIA 22/8/16	Thiepval Mem
Wootton Walter William	Labourer/Signal/Reading		Gnr 67th Siege Bty RGA	Dow 20/10/17	Lijssenthoek Mil Cem
Wordley Reginald Cecil	Porter/Traffic/Portland	21	Pte 1st Grenadier Guards	KIA 1/12/17	Cambrai Mem
Workman Arthur Bertram	Fitters Apprent/L&C/Swindon	28	Pte 1st Gloucester Regt	Died 4/12/14	Minchinhampton Church
Workman Frederick York	Clerk/Goods/Cheltenham	22	L/Cpl 2/5th Gloucester Regt	KIA 21/3/18	Pozieres Mem
Workman R.	Engineer/Gloucester				GWR Roll of Honour
Wordsell Charles L.V.	Clerk/Goods/Paddington	30	Pte 7th Yorkshire Regt	KIA 13/11/17	Poelcapelle Br Cem
Worsfold Frederick James	Fireman/Loco/Old Oak Common	20	Pte 1st Welsh Guards	KIA 27/9/15	Loos Mem
Worters Leonard George	Clerk/Traffic/Kensington	22	AS HMS Invincible RN	SL 31/5/16	Chatham Naval Mem
Worth Edwin	Vanguard/Goods/Paddington				GWR Mag 11/19
Wreford Victor Ernest	Coal Trimmer/Electrical/Park Royal	22	Rifm 2nd KRRC	Dow 23/7/16	Thiepval Mem
Wren Walter Alfred	Packer/Engineer/Bilston		Sgt 13th Gloucester Regt	Dow 31/7/17	Dozinghem Mil Cem
Wrigglesworth Theodore	Goods Guard/Traffic/Swansea	30	Pte 1st Devonshire Regt	KIA 18/11/14	Menin Gate Mem

Wright Frederick George	Lineman/Signal/High Wycombe	23	Pte 5th Ox & Bucks L.I.	KIA 22/6/15	Menin Gate Mem
Wright G.	Striker/Engineer/Carmarthen				GWR Mag 2&4/19
Wright George Henry	Shedman/L&C/Port Talbot	34	Pte 1st Gloucester Regt	Dow 24/11/14	Wimereux Com Cem
Wright George William	Office Porter/Goods/South Lambeth				GWR Mag 12/16 & 3/17
Wright W.J.	Porter/Traffic/Radstock				GWR Mag 5/17
Wroath Percy James	Fireman/Loco/Newton Abbot	28	L/Cpl 8th Devonshire Regt	KIA 25/9/15	Loos Mem
Wyatt Frederick	Packer/Engineer/Morriston	28	L/Cpl 4th Royal Fus	KIA 25/10/14	Canadian Cem 2
Wyatt J.H.	Painter/L&C/Swindon				GWR Mag 6/17
Wyatt Philip Charles	Packer/Engineer/Cardiff	22	Spr 262nd (GWR) Rly Co R.E.	Dow 31/10/17	Lijssenthoek Mil Cem
Wylde John	Plasterer/Engineer/Wolverhampton				GWR Mag 12/17
Wyman Sidney James	Porter/Traffic/Puxton	21	L/Cpl 10th Gloucester Regt	Dow 9/10/15	Chocques Mil Cem
Wynniatt Frank Charles	Packer/Engineer/Toddington	23	Pte 10th Gloucester Regt	KIA 25/9/15	Loos Mem
Wyre Albert	Packer/Engineer/Buildwas	28	Pte 7th R West Kent Regt	KIA 8/1/18	Artillery Wood Cem
Yabsley Albert Edward	Luggage Porter/Hotels/Paddington		Sgt 16th Middlesex Regt	Dow 4/12/16	Carnoy Mil Cem
Yardley F.	Fish Checker/Traffic/Milford Haven				GWR Mag 7/17
Yarranton Arthur	Bridge Labour/Engineer/Wolver'h	39	Pte 7th S Staffordshire Regt	KIA 21/11/17	Arras Mem
Yates A.E.	Clerk/Goods/Southall				GWR Mag 9/18
Yates Frank Albert	Painter/Engineer/Shrewsbury		Pte 3/4th W Surrey Regt	KIA 4/10/17	Tyne Cot Mem
Yeandle C.	Engineer/Watchet				GWR Mag 10/20
Yeatman John	Wireman/Signal/Worcester		Sgt 1st Gloucester Regt	KIA 22/8/16	Thiepval Mem
Yeo Thmas David	Chair Moulder/L&C/Swindon	20	Pte 5th Wilts Regt	Dow 1/5/16	Basra Mem
Yeomans Edward	Porter/Goods/Hockley	38	Pte 2nd Ox & Bucks L.I.	KIA 25/9/15	Loos Mem
Yeomans William Henry	Shunter/Traffic/Plymouth	29	Pte 1st Devonshire Regt	KIA 24/12/14	Menin Gate Mem
Young Arthur	Porter/Goods/Hockley	24	Pte 6th Wilts Regt	KIA 3/10/15	Loos Mem
Young Percival Howard	Clerk/Estates/Paddington	20	Pte 1/8th Middlesex Regt	KIA 11/9/16	Thiepval Mem
Young R.	Carman/Goods/Manchester				GWR Mag 2&4/17
Young Sidney	Clerk/Goods/Hockley	28	L/Cpl 15th R Warwick Regt	KIA 30/6/17	Orchard Dump Cem

INDEX

Visit our website and discover thousands of other History Press books.
www.thehistorypress.co.uk